PATERNOSTER BIBLICAL MONOGRAPHS

First-Century Guides to Life and Death

Epictetus, Philo and Peter

PATERNOSTER BIBLICAL MONOGRAPHS

First-Century Guides to Life and Death

Epictetus, Philo and Peter

David K. Burge

Copyright © David K. Burge 2017

First published 2017 by Paternoster

Paternoster is an imprint of Authentic Media
PO Box 6326, Bletchley, Milton Keynes, MK1 9GG

authenticmedia.co.uk
Authentic Media is a division of Koorong UK, a company limited by guarantee

The right of David K. Burge to be identified as the Editor of this Work
has been asserted by him in accordance with the Copyright, Designs
and Patents Act 1988.

All rights reserved. No part of this publication may be reproduced, stored in a retrieval system, or transmitted, in any form or by any means, electronic, mechanical, photocopying, recording or otherwise, without the prior permission of the publisher or a license permitting restricted copying. In the UK such licenses are issued by the Copyright Licensing Agency, Barnard's Inn, 86 Fetter Lane, London, EC4A 1EN.

British Library Cataloguing in Publication Data A catalogue record for this book is available from the British Library

ISBN 978–1–84227–974–8

Printed and bound by Lightning Source

PATERNOSTER BIBLICAL MONOGRAPHS

Series Preface

One of the major objectives of Paternoster is to serve biblical scholarship by providing a channel for the publication of theses and other monographs of high quality at affordable prices. Paternoster stands within the broad evangelical tradition of Christianity. Our authors would describe themselves as Christians who recognise the authority of the Bible, maintain the centrality of the gospel message and assent to the classical creedal statements of the Christian belief. There is diversity within this constituency; advances in scholarship are possible only if there is freedom for frank debate on controversial issues and for the publication of new and sometimes provocative proposals. What is offered in this series is the best of writing by committed Christians who are concerned to develop well-founded biblical scholarship in a spirit of loyalty to the historic faith.

Series editors

Robert P. Gordon, Regius Professor of Hebrew, University of Cambridge, UK

Tremper Longman III, Robert H. Gundry Professor and Chair of the Department of Biblical Studies, Westmont College, Santa Barbara, California, USA

Stanley E. Porter, President and Professor of New Testament, McMaster Divinity College, Hamilton, Ontario, Canada

Dedicated to Ashleigh

Acknowledgements

The impetus for this monograph came from Outer Mongolia. It was while lecturing at the Union Bible Theological Centre (UBTC) in Ulaanbaatar, Mongolia, that I was asked to consider doctoral study. I thank my team leaders in Ulaanbaatar, David and Wendy Hall, and the organisation with which we served, Pioneers of Australia, for supporting me to undertake this research.

On our return to Australia, the Department of Ancient History of Macquarie University, and within it the Society for the Study of Early Christianity, provided a stimulating community in which I could study. I would like to mention a number of scholars from Macquarie University who were particularly helpful.

First, I am deeply indebted to my research supervisor and 'Guide', Dr. Bruce Winter, who walked with me from the beginning of my research through to its completion. Always willing to go beyond the call of duty, Bruce regularly made the effort to connect with me even while we lived in different cities. His expertise in the intersection of the New Testament with the Graeco-Roman world has been invaluable, his enthusiasm contagious, and his way of living a model that has impacted me deeply. I also very much enjoyed the hospitality and friendship offered by Bruce and his wife Lyn.

Dr. Stephen Llewelyn and Dr. Chris Forbes also contributed significantly to this work. Dr. Llewelyn patiently read through early and later drafts of the entire work in some detail, and offered valuable comments, and Dr. Forbes' reading of the Epictetus chapters was beneficial.

Emeritus Professor Edwin Judge graciously made himself available on numerous occasions to discuss my progress, and to think through the overall direction and structure of the monograph. His willingness to read through and comment upon the early draft of the Peter chapters and advise me about the comparative chapter was deeply appreciated.

Dr. David Jackson, a scholar with close ties to Macquarie University, offered to read through the Peter section as it was nearing completion. Having completed a doctorate in the study of Jude, his comments on my argument for a sophistic imprint on 2 Peter were well-informed and much appreciated.

A number of other scholars and institutions have also benefited this work. It is a pleasure to recognise the early and ongoing assistance provided by Professor David Runia from the University of Melbourne. An internationally renowned Philonic scholar, Professor Runia graciously read the Philo section when it was little more than a long string of semi-organised notes. Through numerous interactions he assisted and guided me, and provided me with Philonic works that would otherwise have been difficult to access. His generosity in closely reading my Philo section again at a later stage was greatly appreciated, and led me towards a more nuanced appreciation of the complex figure of Philo. Any imperfections in the Philo section, however, remain mine.

Eminent NT scholar, and author of a benchmark commentary on 2 Peter, Professor Richard Bauckham made insightful suggestions for my approach to 2 Peter following a presentation of my work in Brisbane. Our discussion influenced my approach to the 2 Peter section.

Since completing my undergraduate studies, I have appreciated an ongoing relationship with the faculties of Sydney Missionary and Bible College (SMBC) and Christ College, Sydney. In particular, I'd like to thank the then Principals of the two colleges, Rev. David Cook and Rev. Dr. Ian Smith, both of whom have over a number of years offered wonderful advice and friendship. Special thanks also go to a friend and graduate of SMBC, Kylie Andrews, who added to her busy life the task of proof-reading the draft manuscript.

I am grateful to the team at Paternoster for working with me to produce this addition to their excellent series. In particular, the successive Commissioning Editors at Paternoster, Dr Michael Parsons followed by Reuben Sneller, have kindly guided the publishing process. Michael's willingness to apply his experience and skill to the final stages further improved this work.

My deepest gratitude, however, is reserved for Ashleigh, my best friend and wife. She has enthusiastically shifted continents and states with our four children in order that this study might be completed well. Her vitality, patience and encouragement made this work possible, and it is with pleasure that I dedicate it to her.

Ashleigh and I are indebted to the members of our families, who supported us as we have moved from country to country. I'd like to acknowledge in particular my parents John and Bronwyn Burge, and parents-in-law David and Maxine Cook, whose steadfast love continues to inspire us.

David K. Burge

Contents

Acknowledgements	vii
Abbreviations	xiii
Introduction	1
The Selection and Use of Three Guides	2
Epictetus	3
Philo	4
Peter	4
Critical Caveats	5
Critical Caveats in relation to Epictetus	7
Critical Caveats in relation to Philo	7
Critical Caveats in relation to the use of 2 Peter	8
Monograph Structure	9

PART I
EPICTETUS' GUIDE TO LIFE AND DEATH

Chapter 1 Epictetus in his First-Century Setting	**11**
Stoic Philosophy's Place in the First Century	11
The Nature of Stoic Philosophy in the First Century	14
The Public Perception of the Stoics	17
Epictetus the Slave and Student	22
Epictetus' Background	22
Musonius Rufus	25
Epictetus the Exiled Teacher	31
An Outsider's Perspective on Life and Rome	31
Epictetus' Style and Delivery	32
Epictetus' Perception of the σοφισταί	33
Chapter 2 Epictetus' Guide to θεός	**38**
θεός as the starting place for Philosophy	38
The Nature of θεός in Relation to Man	39
The Limitations of God	45
Chapter 3 Epictetus' Guide to Life	**47**
The Need for Philosophy	47
The Guide to Life in Theory	49
The Three τόποι of Training	49
ἀγαθὸς καὶ κακός	53
The Benefits of Living Well	54
Benefits for Individuals	54
Benefits for Society	56
The Guide to Life in Practice	57

The Starting Points	57
The Importance of Doing	58
The Devotion Required	60
Greatness comes from Oneself	64
Practical Exercises	66
The Benefits of Isolated Living	67
Perseverance and its Testimony	68

Chapter 4	**Epictetus' Guide to Death**	**70**
Death as a Return to the Elements		71
Death as a 'bugbear'		73
The Impact of Death upon Life		74

CONCLUSION	**76**

PART II
PHILO'S GUIDE TO LIFE AND DEATH

Chapter 5	**Philo in his First-Century Setting**	**78**
Introduction		78
Philo's *Sitz im Leben*		79
Philo the Alexandrian		81
Philo the Jew		83
Philo and the σοφισταί		84
Philo's Use of Source Material		91
The Authority of Scripture		92
The Authority of Other Sources		95
That the Best of Hellenism was already in Judaism		98
Summary		102

Chapter 6	**Philo's Guide to θεός**	**103**
The Nature of θεός		103
ἄνθρωπος in relation to θεός		106
θεός and ἀρετή		108

Chapter 7	**Philo's Guide to Life**	**114**
The Path to Philo's τέλος		114
A Lofty Standard		114
That Satisfactory Progress was Possible		118
A Hopeful Outlook Overall		121
Concluding Comments		124
Rewards and Punishments		126
The Rewards for Virtue		126
The Punishment for Vice		129
The Guide to Life in Practice		130
The Battle for Virtue		130

The Importance of ἄσκησις ('Practice')		132
Chapter 8 **Philo's Guide to Death**		**134**
Death and the Afterlife		134
Immortality through Progeny		134
Life after Death in Heaven or Tartarus		135
The Immortality of the Soul		136
The Relationship between Death and Life		138
A Messianic Age		140
Summary		141
Further Comments on the Relationship between Death and Life		142
CONCLUSION		**143**

PART III
PETER'S GUIDE TO LIFE AND DEATH

Chapter 9 **Peter in his First-Century Setting**		**145**
Simeon Peter, a Servant and Apostle of Jesus Christ		147
The Portrayal of Peter in the New Testament		147
The Portrayal of Peter in 2 Peter		151
The Recipients of the Letter		152
The Origins of Peter's Message		154
The Opponents in 2 Peter		158
Early Indications of a Sophistic Opposition		160
The Sophists' Approach to History and Knowledge		161
Resonance between the Opponents in 2 Peter and the 'Sophists' among the Ante-Nicene Fathers		165
Further Similarities between the Polemic of 2 Peter and 1 Corinthians		171
Conclusions		175
Chapter 10 **Peter's Guide to θεός**		**177**
The Person of θεός		177
The Work of θεός in 2 Peter		179
Humanity in Relation to God		180
Chapter 11 **Peter's Guide to Life**		**183**
Entry into Life		183
Continuing on the Path of Life		187
The Supplements of Faith		187
Summary		199
The Consequences of How One Lives: Two Ways to Live and Die		200
Conclusions		202

Chapter 12 Peter's Guide to Death	**204**
Peter's Own Death: The Putting off of the Body	204
The τέλος according to Peter	205
The τέλος for those without Faith	205
The τέλος for those with Faith	207
Summary	209
CONCLUSION	**211**

PART IV
RESONANCE AND DISSONANCE IN THE THREE GUIDES TO LIFE AND DEATH

Chapter 13 The Three Guides Compared	**213**
The Three Guides' *Sitz im Leben*	213
Three Different Responses to a Common Enemy	213
Three Responses to Internal Problems within their	
Communities	215
Three who called for Ethics that Exceeded Social Norms	216
An Emphasis on Ethical Implications	217
A Comparison of Three Guides to θεός	217
Three Descriptions of θεός as the Source of Knowledge	217
Three Formulations of the τέλος in Relation to θεός	219
Three Descriptions of θεός as Good and Powerful	219
A Comparison of Three Guides to Life	221
Three Descriptions of the ὁδός of Life	221
A Comparison of Three Guides to Death	225
Chapter 14 Conclusion	**228**
Three Guides facing Sophistic Opposition	228
Three Guides to θεός	229
Three Guides to Life	229
Three Guides to Death	231
Appendix: 'Sophistic' Opposition in Ante-Nicene Fathers	**233**
Bibliography	**246**
Indexes	**264**
Author	264
Person	267
Scripture	270
Subject	277

Abbreviations

Journals, Serials, Lexical Aids

ANRW	*Aufstieg und Niedergang der römischen Welt*
BAGD	*A Greek-English Lexicon of the New Testament and Other Early Christian Literature* (ed. Blass, Arndt, Gingrich and Danker)
BJS	*Brown Judaic Studies*
CTJ	*Calvin Theological Journal*
ErJb	*Eranos Jahrbuch*
EvQ	*Evangelical Quarterly*
Friberg	*Friberg Analytical Greek Lexicon*
Gingrich	*Greek NT Lexicon*
JBL	*Journal of Biblical Literature*
JETS	*Journal of Evangelical Theological Studies*
JSNT	*Journal for the Study of the New Testament*
JSNTSup	*Journal for the Study of the New Testament* Supplement Series
JTS	*Journal of Theological Studies*
LCL	*Loeb Classical Library*
LEH	*A Greek-English Lexicon of the Septuagint* (ed. Lust, Eynikel, Hauspie)
LN	*A Greek-English Lexicon of the New Testament Based on Semantic Domains* (ed. Louw and Nida)
LSJ	*A Greek-English Lexicon* (ed. Liddell, Scott and Jones)
New Docs	*New Documents Illustrating Early Christianity*
NovT	*Novum Testamentum*
NTS	*New Testament Studies*
OCD	*Oxford Classical Dictionary*
R-R	*Philo of Alexandria: an Annotated Bibliography 1937-1986* (ed. Roberto Radice and David T. Runia)
SBL	*Society of Biblical Literature*
SBLDS	*Society of Biblical Literature Dissertation Series*
SPh	*Studia Philonica*
SPhA	*The Studia Philonica Annual*
Thayer	*Thayer's Greek English Lexicon of the NT*
Tyn.B.	*Tyndale Bulletin*
YCS	*Yale Classical Studies*
ZNTW	*Zeitschrift für die neutestamentliche Wissenschaft*
ZPE	*Zeitschrift für Papyrologie und Epigraphik*

Works of Philo

Abr.	De Abrahamo
Aet.	De aeternitate mundi
Agr.	De agricultura
Anim.	De animalibus
Cher.	De Cherubim
Contempl.	De vita contemplativa
Conf.	De confusione linguarum
Congr.	De congressu eruditionis gratia
Decal.	De Decalogo
Det.	Quod deterius potiori insidiari soleat
Deus	Quod Deus sit immutabilis
Ebr.	De ebrietate
Flacc.	In Flaccum
Fug.	De fuga et inventione
Gig.	De gigantibus
Her.	Quis rerum divinarum heres sit
Hypoth.	Hypothetica
Ios.	De Iosepho
Leg. 1–3	Legum allegoriae I, II, III
Legat.	Legatio ad Gaium
Migr.	De migratione Abrahami
Mos. 1–2	De vita Moysis I, II
Mut.	De mutatione nominum
Opif.	De opificio mundi
Plant.	De plantatione
Post.	De posteritate Caini
Praem.	De praemiis et poenis, De exsecrationibus
Prob.	Quod omnis probus liber sit
Prov. 1–2	De Providentia I, II
QE 1–2	Quaestiones et solutiones in Exodum I, II
QG 1–4	Quaestiones et solutiones in Genesim I, II, III, IV
Sacr.	De sacrificiis Abelis et Caini
Sobr.	De sobrietate
Somn. 1–2	De somniis I, II
Spec. 1–4	De specialibus legibus I, II, III, IV
Virt.	De virtutibus

Works of Josephus

A.J.	Antiquitates Judaicae
C.Ap.	Contra Apionem
B.J.	Bellum Judaicum
Vita	Vita

Abbreviations

Works of other ancient writers

Athan. *Ar.*	Athanasius, *Orationes contra Arianos*
Athan. *Decr.*	Athanasius, *De decretis*
Athan. *Ep. Aeg. Lib.*	Athanasius, *Epistula encyclical ad episcopos Aegypti et Libyae*
Athan. *Apol. ad Const.*	Athanasius, *Apologia ad Constantium*
Athan. *Hist. Ar.*	Athanasius, *Historia Arianorum ad Manachos*
Cicero, *De Fin.*	Cicero, *De Finibus Bonorum et Malorum*
Cicero, *ND*	Cicero, *De Natura Deorum*
Clement, *Protr.*	Clement, *Protrepticus*
Clement, *Strom.*	Clement, *Stromata*
Cyprian, *Ep.*	Cyprian, *Epistles*
D. L.	Diogenes Laertius, *Lives of Eminent Philosophers*
Dio, *Or.*	Dio, *Orations*
Epictetus *Ench.*	Epictetus, *Encheiridion*
Epictetus, *Diss.*	Epictetus, *The Discourses,* as Reported by Arrian
Gregory, *Orat.*	Gregory Thaumaturgus, *Oratio Panegyrica*
Hes. *Op.*	Hesiodus Epicus, *Opera et Die*
Ignatius, *Ep.*	Ignatius, *Epistle to the Ephesians*
Irenaeus, *Adv. haer.*	Irenaeus, *Adversus haereses*
Minucius Felix, *Oct.*	Minucius Felix, *Octavius*
M. R.	Musonius Rufus, *Fragments* (ed. C. Lutz)
Origen, *C. Cels.*	Origen, *Contra Celsus*
Origen, *De princ.*	Origen, *De principiis*
Philostratus, *VA*	Philostratus, *Vita Apollonii*
Philostratus, *VS*	Philostratus, *Vitae sophistarum*
Pindarus, *N.*	Pindarus, *Nemean*
Plato, *Symp.*	Plato, *Symposium*
Posidonius *Fr.*	Posidonius, *Fragments* (ed. Edelstein and Kidd)
Sophocles, *Ph.*	Sophocles Tragicus, *Philoctetus*
Sapph.	Sappho, *Lyrica*
Seneca, *De Ben.*	Seneca, *De Beneficiis*
Seneca, *Ep.*	Seneca, *Epistulae Morales*
Simplicius.	*Commentary on the Enchiridion*
SVF	*Stoicorum Veterum Fragmenta* (ed. H. Von Arnim)
Tatian, *Orat.*	Tatian, *Oratio ad Graecos*
Tert., *Idol.*	Tertullian, *De idolatria*
Tert., *De anima*	Tertullian, *De anima*
Tert., *Apol.*	Tertullian, *Apologeticus pro Christianis*
Tert., *De carne Chr.*	Tertullian, *De carne Christi*

First-Century Guides to Life and Death

Introduction

Comparative studies are certainly not without ancient precedent. In around 45 BC, Cicero (106 – 43 BC) realised the benefits of a comparative discussion when the leading proponents of three dominant systems of thought were present at the house of his friend, representatives of the Epicurean, Stoic and Academic schools.[1] Cicero was very excited at the prospect of an open dialogue between the three, saying, 'I think I have come at the right moment, as you say. For here are you, three leaders of three schools of philosophy, met in congress' (I.7). His *De natura deorum* aimed to present a 'very searching and thorough discussion' investigating 'the topic of the immortal gods', with the implications also for life (I.6). The result was a lively and insightful discussion lasting a few days as each representative put forth their respective ideology, and had the opportunity to explore the points of resonance and dissonance between them.

The present book is a comparative study which also has a Stoic representative, and invites to the 'Ciceronian forum' a Hellenistic Jew as well as a Jewish Christian. Epictetus the Stoic (c. AD 50-60 – c. 135), Philo of Alexandria (BC 20-15 – AD 50) and the Apostle Peter (died c. 64 AD)[2] are prominent representatives of three traditions during the Julio-Claudian and Flavian periods. Each of them taught how to live in light of death, drawing from their differing philosophical or ideological perspectives. The aim is to better appreciate the resonance and dissonance between these three leading teachers. What were some of their points of agreement? And on these same points, to what extent might they have concurred?

Quite unexpectedly, in the process of comparing these Guides, an interesting similarity emerged between them. It became apparent that all three of the Guides were reacting to the same cultural and educational influence that was sweeping across the Roman Empire. They showcase for us three reactions to the same problem, a movement described by Philostratus in the third century AD as ἡ δευτέρη σοφιστική ('the Second Sophistic').[3] Since each Guide was

---

[1] The three participants included Gaius Cotta, an Academic trained in rhetoric and logic (I.15-16; II.1); Gaius Velleius, a member of the Senate and regarded by Epicureans as their chief adherent in Rome at the time (1.15, 58); and Quintus Lucilius Balbus, who was considered a leading exponent of Stoicism (I.15). Cicero, *De Natura Deorum*, trans. H. Rackham (Cambridge: Harvard University Press, 1933).

[2] For the discussion of the likely date of the composition of 2 Peter and his death, see chapter 9.

[3] Philostratus, *VS*, 481, 507. For the early usage of this phrase, see Tim Whitmarsh, *Greek Literature and the Roman Empire: The Politics of Imitation* (New York: OUP, 2001), 42-45. For recent works on the place of the movement within the Graeco-

motivated by, and responded in unique ways to the threat posed by this common enemy, it was possible to compare their responses.

Philo observed that the sophists were 'winning the admiration of city after city, and ... drawing well-nigh the whole world to honour them'.[4] G.W. Bowersock succinctly defines a sophist of this period as 'a virtuoso rhetor with a big public reputation'.[5] The sophists declaimed not only for legal or political reasons, but also to solicit the admiration and respect of their audience.

In recent decades, Bowersock has argued that the sophists were more influential than has been traditionally recognised, and that their re-emergence is visible in the first-century AD.[6] In the Foreword to Bruce Winter's *Philo and Paul among the Sophists*, Bowersock credits Winter for:

> documenting, for the first time, the sophistic movement of the mid-first century. Inspired by a remarkable papyrus from Oxyrhynchus and supported by rich documentation for Philo's Alexandria and Paul's Corinth, Winter has uncovered the foundations of the Second Sophistic.

With Bowersock, we acknowledge the significance of this further evidence of an influential first-century sophistic movement. This monograph builds upon Winter's research by revisiting the place of the sophists in the writings of Epictetus and Philo, and by considering the possibility of a sophistic imprint upon the opponents in the letter of 2 Peter.

The Selection and Use of Three Guides

A logical and useful comparison requires a degree of similarity, and in many respects our three Guides share much in common. They were elderly men who spoke at about the same time about the ὁδός ('path' or 'way') of life with a degree of retrospect.[7] Each of the Guides was a respected ambassador of his tradition and sought to establish reason, or truth, as the foundation for his goal of behavioural change. It will become apparent that each Guide ardently

---

Roman world, see S.C.R. Swain, *Hellenism and Empire: Language, Classicism, and Power in the Greek World, AD 50-250* (New York: OUP, 1996), Graham Anderson, *The Second Sophistic: A Cultural Phenomenon in the Roman Empire* (New York: Routledge, 1993), Tim Whitmarsh, *The Second Sophistic*, vol. 35 (Oxford: OUP, 2005).

[4] Philo, *Agr.* 143, cited in Bruce W. Winter, *Philo and Paul among the Sophists* (Grand Rapids: Eerdmans, 2002), 4.

[5] G.W. Bowersock, *Greek Sophists in the Roman Empire* (Oxford: Clarendon, 1969), 13. See, also, Whitmarsh, *The Second Sophistic*, 3, Winter, *Philo and Paul among the Sophists*, 4.

[6] See his early and influential work, Bowersock, *Greek Sophists in the Roman Empire*.

[7] This is explicitly so of Epictetus and Peter, but for Philo the period at which he wrote may have spanned decades. Certainly some of his treatises can be dated towards the end of his life (e.g. the writing of Flaccus can be dated by the persecution of 38 CE to which he responds).

Introduction

defended his respective view from an opposition bearing a sophistic imprint. Such similarities make them 'comparable'.[8]

On the other hand, the significant differences between the Guides offer a rich contrast of perspectives. Discovering parallels can be insightful, but misleading if the limits of such similarities are not given due cognizance. Furthermore, it is in the 'friction' between historical figures, rather than merely parallels between them, that 'matters of interest are to be found'.[9]

In terms of differences, the Guides come from vastly different worlds, not only in the geographical sense, but in terms of culture, social standing, educational background, and epistemology. Further differentiating them is the genre in which their teachings were recorded. Epictetus' *Discourses* were recorded by his student Arrian, who sought to convey 'word for word' the lively interactions between his teacher and students.[10] Philo wrote formal treatises for the learned, assuming in some of them that his predominately Jewish audience had a good knowledge of Greek and Jewish literature. And the extant letters of Peter, both of which may have been written by another hand (1 Pet. 5:12), could be described as both plain in style and yet quite complex, personal and yet intended for a wide audience.

Epictetus

Born to a slave woman, and for some years a slave himself, Epictetus was fortunate to learn the Stoicism of the Greeks under the greatest Stoic teacher of the age, the Roman equite Musonius Rufus. His privileged period of study was followed, however, by exile (with the other philosophers) from Rome under Domitian in AD 89 or 92. Epictetus later established a school in Nicopolis, a Roman Colony founded by Augustus after his victory at Actium. His experience of Rome, which included serving a cruel slave-master, followed by exile, influenced his estimation of Rome. He offers a particularly insightful critique of contemporary Roman culture.

Adding further value to his participation in our forum, Epictetus, unlike Seneca and Marcus Aurelius, attached great significance to the reasoning which stands behind his ethical exhortation.[11] He deliberately exposed the way in which his philosophy, and within it his view of θεός, underpinned his ethics. Such overt reasoning provides important material for comparison.

---

[8] We do not deny that other Guides could have been fruitfully added to our comparative study, or indeed that other Guides may have been well chosen instead of the three selected. But for the reasons offered above, and due to the constraints of monograph length, such choices were made.

[9] Bowersock, *Greek Sophists in the Roman Empire*, 89.

[10] See Arrian's Preface to Epictetus' *Discourses*, § 2.

[11] John M. Cooper, "The Relevance of Moral Theory to Moral Improvement in Epictetus," in *The Philosophy of Epictetus*, ed. Theodore Scaltsas and Andrew S. Mason (New York: OUP, 2007), 9.

Philo

Philo, likewise, received a Greek education, but in the intellectual city of Alexandria, the second Athens, which had been annexed under the Roman Empire following the same battle at Actium. Philo's Jewish identity, however, heavily influenced his perception of things Hellenistic. A Hellenised Jew, Philo straddled two worlds, and exegeted the Torah within a Greek philosophical framework. Because he believed that the Torah was God's gift to the nations, his expositions are not intended exclusively for Jews but had an apologetic for a wider audience. He skilfully filters narratives and ethics in the Torah through the grids of first-century Platonism and other apposite philosophical traditions.[12] Philo's critique of Hellenistic philosophy from a Jewish perspective makes him an important critic of his own day. Different parts of his large corpus explain his guide to the good life and the alternative, stated both implicitly and explicitly.

The timing of Philo's writing is another reason for his significance. This is not only because Philo's corpus is vast, and offers a significant window into this period of Jewish and Alexandrian history, but also because of the quality of information it contains – leading one commentator to make the bold, even if debatable, statement that they have 'more to tell us than the Dead Sea Scrolls'.[13] Like Epictetus, he provides a critique of Graeco-Roman culture, but from a very different perspective.

Peter

Peter the Galilean Jew (? – c. AD 64) approached his task as an (at least, allegedly) ἰδιώτης ('unlearned,' or 'uneducated,' Acts 4:13) fisherman.[14] Growing up in Galilee, however, did not mean that he was ignorant of Graeco-Roman culture.[15] Galilee was not a culturally sealed area – inroads of Hellenism had been made since 333 BC. Peter, too, is an insightful contemporary critic of his own time.

---

[12] Borgen elucidates well the significance of Moses and the Law for the nations in Peder Borgen, *Philo of Alexandria – an Exegete for His Time* (Leiden: Brill, 1997), esp. 43, 140-41, 215-16, 64-68. For the important observation that 'the oldest is the best' see R.J. Mortley, "The Past in Clement of Alexandria: A Study of an Attempt to Define Christianity in Socio-Cultural Terms," in *The Shaping of Christianity in the Second and Third Centuries: Jewish and Christian Self-Definition*, ed. E.P. Sanders (Philadelphia: Fortress, 1980), 193.

[13] Erwin R. Goodenough, *An Introduction to Philo Judaeus* (Oxford: Basil Blackwell, 1962), 2.

[14] See the helpful discussion of this topic in Sean Adams, "The Tradition of Peter's Literacy: Acts, 1 Peter, and Petrine Literature," in *Peter in Early Christianity*, edited by Helen K. Bond and Larry W. Hurtado (Grand Rapids: Eerdmans, 2015).

[15] See, for example, the work of Hengel (Hengel, 1989, 409; Hengel, 2010, 184). Though the term 'Hellenistic' is used in this monograph, it is not without cognizance of the difficulties of its use, which Hengel raises on pages 1-6.

Introduction

In 2 Peter 1, Peter provides a succinct explanation of how one can, under θεός, live a productive and ethical life. His letter provides a different perspective on the same topics addressed by Epictetus and Philo.[16] This elderly teacher's perspective of what the path entails in practice, as well as his graphic portrayal of the end of life's path, makes him a worthy participant in the forum.

Many have rightly observed that compared to other New Testament works, 2 Peter in particular has a disproportionately rich inclusion of Hellenistic vocabulary and concepts. And yet it has received arguably the least attention of all the New Testament texts.[17] The extent to which the Hellenistic language carries with it Hellenistic meaning is a matter that will also be clarified from our comparative approach.[18]

With respect to the identity of the false teachers in 2 Peter, recent commentaries concede that we have arrived at an impasse; there is no group known to us with which Peter's opponents can be identified.[19] In the process of this comparative study, however, we were able to identify the false teachers' characteristics as closely resembling those of a known first-century movement.

Critical Caveats

A potential pitfall one faces when doing comparative studies is to approach each figure with an agenda unduly influenced by one or more of the other characters. Aware that this danger exists, and conceding that it may be impossible to avoid absolutely, it is nevertheless the intention of this monograph to present each Guide in a way that each could have accepted as true to his own understanding.[20] This does not mean that we read their works

---

[16] Since the succinct summary of his position lies in 2 Peter 1, primary attention will be given to that chapter.

[17] Larry Helyer, *The Life and Witness of Peter* (Downers Grove: IVP, 2012), 13; John Snyder, "A 2 Peter Bibliography," *JETS* 22 (1979): 265.

[18] This is so in a way not dissimilar from Starr's comparative study of 2 Peter 1:4 which focuses on the phrase, 'sharers in the divine nature'. James M. Starr, "Sharers in Divine Nature: 2 Peter 1:4 in Its Hellenistic Context" (Almqvist & Wiksell, 2000). The work of J. Daryl Charles might also be mentioned in this regard: *Virtue Amidst Vice: The Catalog of Virtues in 2 Peter 1* (Sheffield: Sheffield Academic, 1997).

[19] T.R. Schreiner, *1, 2 Peter, Jude: An Exegetical and Theological Exposition of Holy Scripture* (Nashville: Broadman & Holman, 2003), 280; Simon S. Lee, *Jesus' Transfiguration and the Believers' Transformation: A Study of the Transfiguration and Its Development in Early Christian Writings* (Tübingen: Mohr Siebeck, 2009). Gene Green might also be placed in this group of scholars dissatisfied with previous attempts at identification. He suggests the pursuit is not over by pointing to other possibilities. Gene L. Green, *Jude and 2 Peter* (Grand Rapids: Baker Academic, 2008), 157-58.

[20] I am grateful to Emeritus Professor E.A. Judge for stressing the importance of this to me. For a discussion about the danger of importing Christian definitions into alternative ancient texts, in this case Philo's, see D.A. Carson, "Divine Sovereignty and Human Responsibility in Philo: Analysis and Method," *Novum Testamentum*

uncritically. Indeed, we will at times critique their views, and suggest that there are some troubling tensions and even inconsistencies. Seeking to reduce further the scope for misrepresenting our Guides, a significant number of apposite quotations were incorporated so that the texts speak for themselves and provide access to the writers' expression and literary context where deemed important.

In terms of the structure used for examining the three Guides, four headings emerged as a logical framework with which their views about life and death could be represented: (I) the historical setting in which the Guide lived; (II) his view of θεός, which underpins his ethics; (III) his teachings about life; and (IV) his views about death.

It emerged, however, that each author required a unique sub-structure within these four headings. The treatment of each Guide according to their emphases is visible in part in the Table of Contents.

Throughout this monograph, the terms 'Guide' (following Greek terms such as ὁδηγός and ἡγεμών) and 'path' (ὁδός) have been chosen because they occur in each author's works, and represent significant themes.[21] Since their working contexts varied, 'Guide' was deemed an inclusive and therefore preferable term. It loosely applies to all three figures in a way that alternative labels do not. 'Sage' or 'teacher' would be appropriate designations for Epictetus; 'scholar' or 'writer' might be apposite for Philo; and 'shepherd' or 'apostle' might suit Peter—but none of these more specific titles sit as comfortably as 'Guide' for all three authors.

Further, on the basis that the three figures are revealed in their writings, 'Guide' is used to refer to the person as well as his teachings, as in the sense of a Guide-book. Similarly, the phrase 'Guide to Life and Death' was chosen because it encapsulates the essential message of each person as expressed through his writings.

Lastly, the language of the three Guides, whether inclusive of both genders or not, has been echoed in this thesis. It is outside the boundaries of this thesis

---

23.2 (1981): 149-53. See, also, David T. Runia, "How to Read Philo," *Nederlands Theologisch Tijdschrift* 40 (1986).

[21] Epictetus urged his students to be a ὁδηγός ('guide') who, like Socrates, 'whenever he finds a person going astray, ἤγαγεν ἐπὶ τὴν ὁδὸν τὴν δέουσαν ('leads him back to the right path' *Diss.* II.12.3). Philo speaks of God as one's ἡγεμών ('guide,' *Det.* 29), and ποδηγέτης ('guiding one,' *Post.* 31). He is the 'Guide' who has made the ὁδός that leads to heaven (*Post.* 31). For Philo, a person, most often Moses, was said to hold this important role over others, whether well equipped for the role or not (*Leg.* 3.232; *Mig.* 23). In the NT, the triune God 'guides' (from ὁδηγέω) his people (Ps. 67:4; Rev. 7:17; Jn. 16:13). Humans could also be good or bad guides; as shown by John the Baptist (κατευθύνω, Lk. 1:76-79), and the Pharisees, who were likened to a blind guide (ὁδηγός τυφλός) leading the blind (Matt. 15:14; 23:16, 24). Further informing the Bible's depiction of God as the 'Guide' is another metaphor of ποιμήν ('shepherd'), which is used of God (Ps. 23), Jesus (1 Pet. 5:4; Jn. 10:11; Heb. 13:20; Rev. 7:17), Peter (Jn. 21:15-17), and the elders of the churches (1 Pet. 5:1-4).

Introduction

to make comment upon whether the exclusive language in each instance was for reasons greater than linguistic ones.[22]

Critical Caveats in relation to Epictetus

Epictetus is easy to misrepresent. First, the *Discourses* are not a systematic presentation of his views, but Arrian's collection of informal dialogues dealing with predominately practical concerns. That is not to say that this style was Epictetus' only approach to teaching; the *Discourses* refer to more theoretical sessions which were part of the students' training, but there are no extant records of these. The *Encheiridion*, or Handbook, is a more intentionally structured expression of Epictetus' thought, but again, it is brief and does not represent everything Epictetus taught. Thus, it might be said that although the *Discourses* are neither tightly organised nor comprehensive philosophical works, they are in some respects uniquely informative. The earthy style of the *Discourses* offers remarkably personal insights into the life of this Stoic teacher and his students.

Second, one must be careful in deciding which of the views contained in the *Discourses* Epictetus personally held. In his dialogical style, he freely switched between various characters. At times, he merely puts forth a common view for the didactic purpose of the discussion. At other times he started with a commonly accepted or 'known' premise, to which he may not have personally subscribed, in order to demonstrate a point. Irony and hyperbole were used so that students would grasp the main point, and so it is important with Epictetus that the thrust of his argument be observed rather than a literal interpretation of the illustrative details used to make his point. One can certainly use this material to extract insights into his views, but in order to represent Epictetus accurately it must be done with these caveats in mind.[23]

Critical Caveats in relation to Philo

Philo's corpus is one of the most extensive extant first-century Jewish sources. While it has been necessary to focus our attention on selected treatises, the aim has been to do so with cognizance that Philo addresses themes of relevance to this monograph in numerous other places throughout his writings. This attempt is evident in the footnotes, which are highly concentrated on our selected texts, yet include references to nearly all of the Philonic treatises.

---

[22] Many (though there were exceptions, including Musonius Rufus) saw philosophy as a profession for males, and so may often denote males exclusively when referring to 'a man' or 'men' even when speaking in an otherwise universal way. We acknowledge the unfortunate consequence of mirroring their language, viz. that the discussion within this thesis often has a male-orientation which clashes with modern practice.

[23] For a more detailed discussion, see A.A. Long's helpful chapter, 'Reading Epictetus' in A.A. Long, *Epictetus: A Stoic and Socratic Guide to Life* (Oxford: Clarendon, 2002), 128-41.

The works chosen for focused attention were those in which Philo speaks most directly about the matters under investigation in this monograph, particularly the matters of θεός, life and death. An obvious place to commence was the treatises commonly designated as the 'philosophical writings' because they speak very directly about what is quite a 'philosophical' subject. *De aeternitate mundi* (On the Eternity of the World), and *Quod omnis probus liber sit* (Every Good Man is Free) are two of the five philosophical writings. They have as their most substantial authority the Greek poets and philosophers, and as a result, resemble Greek philosophical writings.[24]

It would be restricting, however, to deal only with Philo's philosophical writings, since together they represent a small proportion of his corpus. The large sequence of treatises referred to as 'The Exposition of the Law' has also been given significant attention. The following exegetical treatises were selected because they too speak quite directly about topics germane to this thesis: *De Abrahamo* (On Abraham), *Quod deterius potiori insidiari soleat* (The Worse Attacks the Better), *De praemiis et poenis* (On Rewards and Punishments), *De virtutibus* (On the Virtues); *Quod Deus sit immutabilis* (On the Unchangableness of God), *De vita contemplativa* (On the Contemplative Life).

Lastly, *In Flaccum* (Flaccus) has been consulted for its helpful background information relating to the Jews' existence in Alexandria. As a historical-apologetic treatise, it anchors the monograph more closely to Philo's context.

Significant for this study, these three categories of Philo's treatises do not all operate on the same level. There are significant differences between them that should inform one's approach to their interpretation.[25]

Critical Caveats in relation to the use of 2 Peter

Compared to the extensive corpora of the other two Guides, the slender letter called 2 Peter offers little information about its historical setting.[26] This lack has led to considerable contention regarding the identity of the first- or second-century author. It is hoped that scholars from both sides of the authorship debate, however, may benefit from this study since, in the letter itself, a clear

---

[24] See, for example, his high estimation of the Pythagoreans (*Prob.* 2, 19), Sophocles (§ 19), 'the poet' (§ 22), and Antisthenes (§ 25).

[25] I thank David Runia for stressing this pertinent methodological precaution in personal correspondence.

[26] The genre of 2 Peter has been the subject of debate. The author refers to his writing as an ἐπιστολή ('letter'), a designation which is difficult to improve upon. 2 Peter will thus be treated as a genuine letter while discussing the 'Guide' for life it offers. For a helpful survey of contemporary discussion of 2 Peter's genre, see Green, *Jude and 2 Peter*, 162-70.

Introduction

connection is made between the letter and the fisherman-apostle (2 Pet. 1:1, 16-18).[27]

Second, for the purposes of reading 2 Peter within its Christian tradition, the NT and other Christian literature was consulted where relevant. Since the 'previous letter' (2 Peter 3:1) is usually understood to refer to the Book of 1 Peter, written by his amanuensis Silvanus (1 Pet. 5:12), 1 Peter has been given more attention than other NT books as a source of background information.

Monograph Structure

The symmetry of this study reflects the fact that each of the Guides shared a deep interest in θεός, life and death.

Part I is a study of Epictetus' Guide to Life and Death. Chapter 1 presents Epictetus in his first-century setting, describing: the nature and perception of the Stoics in this period; the background of Epictetus and how his teachings compare with those of his teacher, Musonius Rufus; and the effect that exile had on Epictetus' emphases and didactic style. Chapter 2 explores Epictetus' Guide to θεός, and discusses the ways in which his view of θεός is reflected in his ethics. Chapter 3 will present his Guide to Life, in theory and practice. Lastly, in Chapter 4, Epictetus' Guide to Death will be discussed, with comment made about the role that death plays in shaping his approach to life.

Part II follows a similar approach for Philo. Chapter 4 describes his first-century setting, and the city of Alexandria in which he lived. Because of the complexity of Philo's use of source material, attention had to be given to his methodology, in which he brought together two vastly different traditions of Platonic philosophy and Judaism. Chapters 5–8 will then be devoted to the resulting Guide to θεός, Life, and Death respectively.

In Part III we shift our attention to the letter of 2 Peter, with the major focus on 2 Peter 1, which contains a succinct presentation of how to live in light of death. The author's background and the context in which he wrote is the subject of Chapter 9. His view of θεός is explored in Chapter 10, which also describes the significant place given to his friend and κύριος, Jesus Christ. Tightly connected to this identification of θεός, he offers his Guide to Life (discussed in Chapter 11) and Death (Chapter 12).

Having benefited from an analysis of each Guide in their own right, Part IV brings the three together for comparative comment. The same three topics used to analyse each Guide (θεός, Life, and Death) provide a logical framework in which points of resonance and dissonance can be discussed.

---

[27] The historical reliability of the New Testament will be assumed, but cannot be defended here. So, too, the authorship debate surrounding 2 Peter lies outside of the purview of this monograph. For further comments about authorship, however, see Chapter 9. Other recent works on Peter and 2 Peter operate with the same assumption. See, for example, the approach of Larry R. Helyer, *The Life and Witness of Peter* (Downers Grove: IVP, 2012), 14-15.

First-Century Guides to Life and Death

The Conclusion aims to provide a succinct summary of things learned from the 'Ciceronian forum' of the three Guides. What did they emphasise for their audience to learn, and to what end? How was one to guard one's understanding from the attractive alternatives presented by false teachers? How should one conceive of the path of life and death? To what extent did their views converge?

PART I

EPICTETUS' GUIDE TO LIFE AND DEATH

CHAPTER 1

Epictetus in his First-Century Setting

In the time of Epictetus, cultured people of the Graeco-Roman world continued to be influenced by Stoicism. As well as being the

> dominant philosophical movement in the [first two centuries AD], Stoicism was also strongly embedded in Greco-Roman culture and, to some extent, in political life, and the ideal of living a properly Stoic life remained powerful.[1]

The approach of this monograph is to understand one Stoic from this period more deeply. What was this Stoic's view of θεός? How did Epictetus urge people to live? What followed death, and how should that affect the way one lived? In order to answer such questions it is important first to understand his *Sitz im Leben*, discussing: Stoic philosophy's place in the first century, Epictetus' background as a slave and philosophy student, Epictetus role as a teacher, and Epictetus' interaction with sophistic opposition.

Stoic Philosophy's Place in the First Century

The history of the Stoic school is generally divided into three broad phases. Early Stoicism was the period in which Zeno the founder (c. 334 – 262 BC), followed by Cleanthes (died 230 BC) and Chrysippus (perhaps the greatest Stoic, taught late second century BC), began a distinct school in Athens from Socratic foundations. Zeno's writings were 'canonised' and early debates among the Stoics (for example, between Cleanthes and his successor as *scholarch*, Chrysippus) centred on the interpretation of these writings.[2] Initially

---

[1] Christopher Gill, "The School in the Roman Imperial Period," in *The Cambridge Companion to the Stoics*, ed. Brad Inwood (New York: CUP, 2003), 33. For the influence of Stoicism on Roman Roman law, for example, see David Johnston, "The Jurists," in *The Cambridge History of Greek and Roman Political Thought*, ed. C.J. Rowe and Malcolm Schofield (Cambridge: CUP, 2000), 619-32.

[2] David Sedley, "The School, from Zeno to Arius Didymus," in *The Cambridge Companion to the Stoics*, ed. Brad Inwood (New York: CUP, 2003), 15-16.

called 'Zenonians', the group were later called 'Stoics' after the Στοά Ποικίλη ('Painted Stoa') where they would congregate.³ Middle Stoicism describes the period of Panaetius (*scolarch* 129-110) and Posidonius (who lived c. 135-51 BC).⁴ Roman Stoicism describes the Roman Imperial period, in which Seneca the Younger (c. 4 B.C – AD 65), Epictetus, and Marcus Aurelius were prominent figures.⁵ Throughout these phases, their allegiance to their forefathers (such as Socrates, Zeno, and to some extent Chrysippus), provided limits to the inevitable deviations of thought that come with time, the result being substantial continuity between early and later Roman Stoicism.⁶

A significant acknowledgement of the Stoics occurred in 155 BC, when Diogenes as the head of the Stoa, along with the heads of the Academy and the Peripatetics, were chosen to represent Athens to Rome. They were to plead for remission of a fine imposed on Athens for the sack of Oropos. The Stoics gave lectures in packed lecture halls, which ignited in Rome 'a fascination with philosophy which was to remain undiminished for the remainder of antiquity and to have special importance for the future fortunes of Stoicism.'⁷ Over the next two hundred years, with the decline of Athens as a centre for philosophy, Stoicism was somewhat decentralised and was made up of small, local philosophical schools proliferating in the Graeco-Roman world.⁸ In the late first-century BC, Strabo noted that

> the people at Tarsus have devoted themselves so eagerly, not only to philosophy, but also to the whole round of education in general, that they have surpassed Athens, Alexandria, or any other place that can be named where there have been schools and lecturers of philosophers.⁹

---

[3] Sedley, "The School, from Zeno to Arius Didymus," 10.
[4] Sedley, "The School, from Zeno to Arius Didymus," 20.
[5] Sedley, "The School, from Zeno to Arius Didymus," 33.
[6] For more detail regarding the development of Stoicism, see F.H. Sandbach, *The Stoics*, ed. M.I. Finley, *Ancient Culture and Society* (London: Chatto & Windus, 1975); A.A. Long, *From Epicurus to Epictetus: Studies in Hellenistic and Roman Philosophy* (Oxford: Clarendon, 2006); Marcia L. Colish, *The Stoic Tradition from Antiquity to the Early Middle Ages* (Leiden: Brill, 1985); Tad Brennan, *The Stoic Life: Emotions, Duties, and Fate* (New York: OUP, 2005).
[7] Sedley, "The School, from Zeno to Arius Didymus," 19-20.
[8] Sedley, "The School, from Zeno to Arius Didymus," 28.
[9] Strabo, *The Geography of Strabo*, XIV.5.13. In the first century AD, and in the centuries before and after, Stoicism was one of at least four prominent streams of philosophy included in a philosophical education. Cicero's *De natura deorum* is a first-century BC example of the way Stoicism occupied a place within philosophical discussion more broadly. Each philosopher had a reasonable knowledge of the alternative sects, and often studied under teachers of each. Cotta the Cynic had an intimate knowledge of Epicurean and Stoic foundations and beliefs. According to Philostratus, Apollonius of Tyana (mid-first century AD), in the town of Aegae, studied under various philosophers. 'There he had as his companions in philosophy followers of Plato and Chrysippus and peripatetic philosophers. And he diligently

Epictetus (c. 50 – 130 AD) taught in one such school. While in exile, he was free to teach philosophy, and recognised the privileged times in which he lived under the *pax Romana*. Caesar was deemed by all, according to Epictetus, to be 'Caesar, the lord of all' (ὁ πάντων κύριος Καῖσαρ), *Diss.* IV.1.12, or later, 'the common lord of all', IV.1.13.[10] While Epictetus points out the limitations of Caesar to safeguard people from all human suffering,[11] he does acknowledge the relative peace they enjoyed.

> Behold now, Caesar seems to provide us with 'profound peace' (εἰρήνην μεγάλην), there are no wars any longer, nor battles, no brigandage on a large scale, nor piracy, but at any hour we may travel by land, or sail from the rising of the sun to its setting.[12]

This εἰρήνη μεγάλη enabled wealthy Roman citizens to send their children to men such as Epictetus in Nicopolis for their education.[13] Other wealthy families would keep a philosopher, who was considered a 'doctor of the soul', or as Seneca referred to them, the *paedagogus* (usually a servant) of not only one's children, but the human race.[14] Certainly, by the latter half of the second century AD, the *pax Romana* was deteriorating with the end of the age of the Antonines. With the turmoil, civil war, and increasingly restrictive form of society came a sudden decline in the apparent influence of the Stoics.[15] Understanding the philosophical and religious milieu of the first-century is not straight-forward. It was a time of flux, with emerging and declining religious and philosophical movements. A.A. Long observes,

> The religious scene was notably fluid. Traditional cults of the Graeco-Roman pantheon, including worship of the emperor, continued; but those attracted to a

---

attended also to the discourses of Epicurus, for he did not despise these either, although it was to those of Pythagoras that he applied himself with unspeakable wisdom and ardour.' Even if this is not a historical reference, it at least indicates what Philostratus believed constituted a well-rounded education. Philostratus, *VA*, I.7.

[10] Henceforth, unless an alternative source is stated, all references are drawn from Epictetus' *Discourses,* using and adapting where appropriate the translations of W.A. Oldfather, *Epictetus: The Discourses as Reported by Arrian, the Manual, and Fragments* 2 volumes (Cambridge: Harvard University Press, 1925-28); Elizabeth Carter, *The Moral Discourses of Epictetus* (London: Dent, 1910); Thomas W. Higginson, "The Works of Epictetus. Consisting of His Discourses, in Four Books, the Enchiridion, and Fragments. A Translation from the Greek Based on That of Elizabeth Carter" (Boston: Little, Brown, and Co., 1865).

[11] This limitation is later contrasted with the far-greater peace that God and reason provide, III.13.13.

[12] *Diss.* III.13.9.

[13] See, for example, Stephen R. Llewelyn, "The Epitaph of a Student Who Died Away from Home," in *New Documents Illustrating Early Christianity*, ed. Stephen R. Llewelyn (Grand Rapids: Eerdmans, 1998), 8.117-21.

[14] Seneca, *Ep.* 89.13. Cited in Sandbach, *The Stoics*, 17.

[15] Sandbach, *The Stoics*, 17.

First-Century Guides to Life and Death

religion that promised salvation would turn to the worship of Isis and, with increasing momentum, Christianity.'[16]

Long's observation is an interesting one for our forum of first-century Guides. It raises the question: in a context of religious choice, what was Stoicism offering, and not offering, for living life and facing death?

The Nature of Stoic Philosophy in the First Century

By the time of Epictetus men had belonged to and developed the Stoic tradition for more than four hundred years. The founders of Stoicism, like most other philosophers from about 300 BC, 'belonged to schools that looked back to their founders as absolute authorities for the doctrines and methodologies they themselves espoused.'[17]

Regrettably, there are no extant complete writings from the first three hundred years. Early Stoics such as Zeno (335 – 263 BC), Cleanthes (330 – 230 BC) and Chrysippus (281 – 207 BC) are explicitly quoted by the later philosophers on a small number of occasions, but these are often very short and without context. Later Stoic proponents such as Diogenes Laertius (second-century AD) and the doxographer Arius Didymus (first-century BC) provide helpful biographical information, as does Cicero's translation of select Greek works into Latin and his own philosophical dialogues.[18] Further information can be gleaned from the Stoics' opponents such as Plutarch, Sextus Empiricus and Galen. They provide what appears a fair exposition of Stoic doctrine, written in the context of critiquing it.[19]

While some changes over the centuries were inevitable, as each philosopher approached his topic in his own way, the Stoics maintained a common interest in the ethical outworking of knowledge. The unity and diversity of Stoic thought can be seen by reading Seneca the Younger, Musonius Rufus (c. AD 30-100), Marcus Aurelius (emperor from 161-180), and Epictetus (c. AD 50-130), even though all of them learned their Stoicism in Rome.[20]

Sandbach exemplifies a common, though somewhat simplistic, view of Stoicism when he says they

> have a minimal interest in anything but ethics and see in Stoic philosophy an established system of beliefs that could guide, comfort, and support a man in the

---

[16] Long, *Epictetus: A Stoic and Socratic Guide to Life*, 16.
[17] Long, *Epictetus: A Stoic and Socratic Guide to Life*, 51.
[18] Cicero's *On Duties* was based on the Stoic Panaetius' thought (c. 185-110 BC), and *On the Nature of the Gods* made use of the Stoic Posidonius (c. 135–51 BC), but for the most part Cicero followed earlier, more orthodox, sources, as in *On Fate,* and the third book of *Goals of Life (De Finibus).*' Sandbach, *The Stoics*, 19.
[19] Sandbach, *The Stoics*, 18-19.
[20] Sandbach, *The Stoics*, 16-17, though Arrian, the student of Epictetus, could be considered an exception.

difficulties and dangers of life. They are preachers of a religion, not humble inquirers after truth.[21]

It is difficult to imagine this generalisation about mere ethics sitting well with Epictetus, who gave attention to logic and to the exposition of the fundamental teachings of Chrysippus (in *Diss.* I.4.6-9; I.17.13-18).[22] Even Epictetus' *Discourses*, which were the more practical discussions that took place after the technical lesson, do not easily accommodate themselves to this perception.[23]

Furthermore, it was the Stoic Diogenes Laertius who considered Cynicism as 'a short cut to virtue' (Diogenes Laertius, VIII.121) because it did not bother with the theoretical underpinnings considered vital by the Stoics.[24] For Epictetus, philosophy was an unfinished enquiry, not a sermon to be heard.

> And so are matters judged and weighed, if we have the standards ready with which to test them; and the task of philosophy is this – to examine and to establish the standards; and to go ahead and use them after they have become known is the task of the good philosopher.[25]

Sandbach's description of Stoicism may have been more true of Musonius Rufus' approach to philosophy than it was for Epictetus' approach, though this could only be hesitantly posited since such a small proportion of Musonius Rufus' teaching is extant.[26]

The traditional three-part division of Stoic education into fields of logic, physics and ethics appears to have been maintained. Physics and logic may have become less significant, but cannot be said to have been absent.[27]

It is probably true that first-century Stoic writings gave less attention to logic and metaphysics than earlier philosophers, and that ethics was a clear priority. But to claim with Sandbach that they were purely teachers of ethics is

---

[21] Sandbach, *The Stoics*, 17. Musonius' definition of philosophy: 'For manifestly the study of philosophy is nothing else than to search out by reason what is right and proper and by deeds to put it into practice.' *MR*, XIV.96.6-8.
[22] See also Gill, "The School in the Roman Imperial Period," 43-49.
[23] Pierre Hadot, *Philosophy as a Way of Life: Spiritual Exercises from Socrates to Foucault* (Oxford Blackwell, 1995), 191.
[24] Long, *Epictetus: A Stoic and Socratic Guide to Life*, 66.
[25] *Diss.* II.11.23.
[26] Dillon's work argues that Musonius Rufus' (49-58; 73-90) and Epictetus' (59-72) pedagogical model is worthy of imitation today. Far from being merely 'preachers,' both teachers used a multitude of methods, including ancient literature and Socratic-style discussion to guide the learning process. J.T. Dillon, *Musonius Rufus and Education in the Good Life* (Lanham: University Press of America, 2004).
[27] A further example of broader interest is Seneca's *Natural Questions*, in which questions of physics are explored; earthquakes, meteors and lightning are explained theologically. Gill, "The School in the Roman Imperial Period," 39. For the place of logic in Epictetus' curriculum see, also, A.A. Long, *Stoic Studies* (Cambridge: CUP, 1996), 104-106, Barnes, *Logic and the Imperial Stoa* (Leiden: Brill, 1997), ch. 3, and for Epictetus' teaching methods more broadly see, also, Hijmans, *Askesis: Notes on Epictetus' Educational System* (Assen: von Gorkam, 1959).

unsatisfactory. A better summary recognises the attention they also gave to non-ethical matters:

> At Epictetus' date, (and in fact, from long before) philosophy in general was taken to be a medicine for alleviating errors and passions that stem from purely reactive and conventional attitudes. To put it another way, the choice of Stoicism over another philosophy depended not on its promise to deliver an admirable and thoroughly satisfying life (that project would not distinguish it from rival schools) but on its detailed specification of that life and on the appeal of its claims about the nature of the world and human beings.[28]

The Stoics saw themselves as those seeking to think and behave in harmony with nature.[29] Cognitive and behavioural elements of Stoicism were derived with reference to God and nature – simply implications of the way things are.[30]

As such, the Stoic's and God's views aligned.[31] 'For the philosophers say, "We do not allow any but the educated to be free"; that is, God does not allow it.'[32] To hear and heed the philosopher's message was also, therefore, to act in accordance with nature, and pleasing to God. Stoic philosophy was about living as members of God, in the world God ordered, in the way God ordained.[33] For the Stoic, theology was part of the study of nature.[34] In *Encheiridion* 53, Epictetus recites Cleanthes' Hymn to Zeus:

> Lead thou me on, O Zeus, and Destiny,
> To that goal long ago to me assigned.
> I'll follow and not falter; if my will
> Prove weak and craven, still I'll follow on.[35]

Epictetus, among other first-century Stoics, perceived himself as being led by Zeus, to the end assigned by Zeus.

---

[28] Long, *Epictetus: A Stoic and Socratic Guide to Life*, 18.

[29] As is observable from Epictetus' repetition of the expressions συμφώνως τῇ φύσει and κατὰ φυσίν – living 'in harmony with nature' or 'according to nature'. For example, one needs 'education, so as to learn how, in conformity with nature, to adapt to specific instances our preconceived idea of what is rational and what is irrational', *Diss*. I.2.6; cf. II.23.42.

[30] Following Oldfather, Epictetus' θεός will usually be referred to in this monograph as 'God,' though 'god' may sometimes be preferable on the basis that Epictetus was not a monotheist. Since Epictetus and the other Guides held views of θεός that are not well represented by the English 'God', the Greek term is usually maintained in headings and comparative discussion.

[31] See Katerina Ierodiakonou, "The Philosopher as God's Messenger," in *The Philosophy of Epictetus*, ed. Theodore Scaltsas and Andrew S. Mason (New York: OUP, 2007), esp. 66-67.

[32] *Diss*. II.1.25; cf. II.7.3,11-14.

[33] See Chapter 2 for a treatment of Epictetus' view of θεός.

[34] Gill, "The School in the Roman Imperial Period," 38.

[35] This poem is ascribed to Cleanthes (Von Arnim, *SVF*, I. frag. 527). See the comment on *Diss*. II.23.42 in Oldfather, *Epictetus: The Discourses*.

The Public Perception of the Stoics

Epictetus offers fascinating insights into the public perception of the φιλόσοφοι. There was no consensus perception, neither among rulers nor among the οἱ πολλοί ('common people'). Sometimes they were honoured and admired and at other times exiled and scorned.

First, the positive perception of the philosophers will be discussed. The speech of some philosophers clearly impressed their audiences. Some people on hearing their speeches were inspired and would 'wish to be philosophers themselves.'[36] As can be gleaned from this quotation alone, Epictetus recognised that the desire to become a philosopher was often based on a very superficial appreciation of their profession. He felt it important to explain that in reality the philosophers' lives were difficult, and certainly not suited to everyone. It required dramatic changes, including external matters such as dress and drinking habits.[37] But the internal demands were even more rigorous. Their character and disposition needed radical transformation, affecting the way they interpreted and responded even inwardly to life.[38] Some people had a simplistic, even romanticised, view of the philosophers which lacked appreciation for its demands.

For Epictetus, to be called a philosopher was a high title.[39] At times the φιλόσοφοι were treated accordingly, with respect and honour, and Epictetus felt it necessary to prepare his students for this kind of attention. They should imitate Socrates, who, without need of public recognition would not even disclose to those wishing to be introduced to a philosopher that he himself was one.[40]

The *Discourses* give more attention to the negative perception of philosophers. This is not evidence that the negative perception was the dominant one *ipso facto*. It could simply be that the negative perception, even if very occasionally encountered, was the one that students needed more preparation to overcome. It was the negative perception that concerned Epictetus the most. Why was Epictetus so concerned? He shared the concern of his teacher, Musonius Rufus, who passionately conveyed the reason:

> it would be better if the majority of young men who say they are studying philosophy did not go near a philosopher, I mean those spoiled and effeminate fellows 'by whose presence the good name of philosophy is full of stains' (δι' οὓς προσιόντας ἀναπίμπλαται κηλίδων φιλοσοφία).[41]

---

[36] *Diss.* III.15.8. Musonius Rufus, also, notes that the philosophers' speech was considered impressive, though their praise was not to be sought. *MR*, XLIX.
[37] *Diss.* III.15.10.
[38] *Diss.* III.15.10.
[39] *Diss.* III.26.7.
[40] *Diss.* III.23.22.
[41] *MR*, XI.84.3-6.

Musonius Rufus' primary concern was not the injustice of negative sentiments towards the philosophers. More distressing was that the criticism was justified and that the problems were coming from within. What should have been 'the good name of philosophy' was κηλίδων ('stained') because not all students of philosophy sought to be ethically reformed by it. If Philostratus' account can be trusted, the experience of Apollonius of Tyana provides an insight into the distressing moral situation in Tarsus among the philosophers a century before Epictetus. When Apollonius

> reached his fourteenth year, his father brought him to Tarsus, to Euthydemus the teacher from Phoenicia. Now Euthydemus was a good rhetor, and began his education; but, though he was attached to his teacher, he found the atmosphere of the city harsh and strange and little conducive to the philosophic life, for nowhere are men more addicted than here to luxury: jesters and full of insolence are they all; and they attend more to their fine linen than the Athenians did to wisdom; and a stream called the Cydnus runs through their city, along the banks of which they sit like so many water-fowl. Hence the words which Apollonius addresses to them in his letter: 'Be done with getting drunk upon the water.' He therefore transferred his teacher, with his father's consent, to the town of Aegae, which was close by, where he found a peace congenial to one who would be a philosopher, and a more serious school of study.[42]

Young Apollonius is portrayed as seeking to avoid what was for Epictetus and Musonius Rufus, a distressing norm amongst philosophy students. On account of their behaviour, they blended in too much with those around them.[43]

Among those who professed to be philosophers were strong and weak adherents.[44] The effect of the latter was multiplied by a public that was always ready to seize upon incongruous living, seeing the immorality of one philosopher as a reason to condemn the entire profession.[45] Even the more impressive philosophers who would 'keep vigils, work hard, overcome certain desires, [and] abandon [their] own people' were often tarred with the same brush by members of all levels of society.[46] The lot of a philosopher was at times to 'be despised by a paltry slave, be laughed to scorn by those who meet you, in everything get the worst of it, in office, in honour, in court'.[47]

An insightful example of public scorn with its associated causes is in *Encheiridion* 22.[48]

---

[42] Philostratus, *Vita Apollonii*, I.7.
[43] Such a description resonates with other descriptions of the sophistic movement. The line between a sophist and a philosopher could be very unclear.
[44] *Diss.* IV.8.15.
[45] *Diss.* IV.8.13-14.
[46] *Diss.* III.15.11.
[47] *Diss.* III.15.11.
[48] Whether or not this was a literal recollection of the tormentors as opposed to a didactically motivated fabrication is unimportant for our purposes. We can assume that if Epictetus was simply expressing public opinion creatively rather than historically, he did so because he considered it a real sentiment.

> If you yearn for philosophy, prepare at once to be met with ridicule, to have many people jeer at you, and say, 'He has returned to us a philosopher all of a sudden, and Where do you suppose he got this high brow?' (πόθεν ἡμῖν αὕτη ἡ ὀφρύς;)

Both comments stem from what the people perceived as pride in the philosophy student. The man allegedly became a philosopher 'all of a sudden', and is mocked for his ὀφρῦς (lit. 'brow' or 'pride').[49] The questions suggest that the people think the fresh philosopher is not, in reality, as superior as he might think. It had not been long since he was a layman (usually ἰδιώτης) like them. The 'supercilious look', 'pride', or perhaps 'high brow',[50] suggests a perceived pretentious exterior overlaying an otherwise ordinary man. Both comments insinuate pretentiousness in the philosopher, and reveal the philosopher's struggle to be well received in his homeland.

The possibility that such accusations were too often warranted is reflected in the self-examining questions that follow:

> But do you not put on a high brow, and do you so hold fast to the things which to you seem best, as a man who has been assigned by God to this post; and remember that if you abide by the same principles, those who formerly used to laugh at you will later come to admire you, but if you are worsted by them, you will get the laugh on yourself twice.[51]

If the philosophers were guilty of appearing proud they deserved the criticism. However, if their lifestyle 'abides by the same principles',[52] viz. if they lived consistently with their teaching, they would be admired. Epictetus was optimistic that people could be persuaded to cease their scornful attitude. They were not averse to admiring a philosopher per se. Indeed they would respect him if, and only if, he proved genuine.

In the presence of a weak philosopher who was being mocked, Epictetus explicitly describes how 'the Romans' perceived philosophers.

> Hear how the Romans feel about philosophers, if you care to know. Italicus, who has a very great reputation among them as a philosopher, once, when I was present, got angry at his friends, as though he were suffering something intolerable, and said, 'I cannot bear it: you are the death of me! You will make me just like him,' and pointed at me![53]

It was a memorable occasion for all present. Italicus did not desire to live out the full demands of philosophy.[54] When pressed towards this end, he exposed

---

[49] Cf. *AP* 7.409 (Antip.), 9.43 (Parmen.), 10.122 (Lucill.). See LSJ.
[50] *Ench.* 22 using the translation of Oldfather, *Epictetus: The Discourses*.
[51] *Ench.* 22.
[52] *Ench.* 22.
[53] *Diss.* III.8.7.
[54] This suggestion follows the interpretation offered in Oldfather's footnote for *Diss.* III.8.7. Also significant is his suggestion that 'Roman popular feeling about philosophy is probably not greatly overdrawn in the well-known advice of Ennius (frag. sc. 376 Vahlen) to taste of philosophy, but not to gorge oneself upon it; and the

his weakness and Epictetus' strength. While acting appropriately might have been possible in this situation, Italicus did not desire such extreme application for himself.

The philosophers' day-to-day interaction with society was the public arena in which they had the opportunity to either reinforce or mitigate public scepticism.[55] Compromised behaviour at key moments by men with a philosophical veneer did the profession no favours.

The public scorn philosophers received was not, however, due solely to their behaviour. Part of it was intrinsic to their task, as bearers of a message that was unpalatable to common people. Unlike orators who would seek large audiences for themselves,[56] the philosophers saw their role to be more like that of a physician, and the lecture room like a hospital. It was not a place of praise and pleasure, but a place where an honest and cutting diagnosis of one's 'sickness' occurs.[57] Epictetus distinguishes between what the population want, and what they need. Regrettably, laymen (i.e. those who are untrained in philosophy) fail to realise what they need, and seek happiness in the wrong places.[58] Giving them what they want may make philosophers popular, but giving them what they need was the philosophers' task. This noble duty of truly healing the sick when all they seek is affirmation was practised by their esteemed predecessors Socrates, Zeno, and Cleanthes.[59]

History elucidates the aptness of Epictetus' illustration. Doctors (ἰατροί) in this period generally did not peddle their services to the people. On the contrary, individuals and even city rulers realised their need for ἰατροί, and sought 'to secure for their population the permanent residence of a competent physician.'[60] In return for their services, the ἰατροί might be voted some honour (a statue, gold crown, or inscribed decree recording their philanthropy) or privilege such as state-foreigner agreement (προξενία), the front seating at games, theatre and assemblies (προεδρία), as well as exemption from public liturgies and state service (ἀτέλεια).[61] Julius Caesar offered foreign ἰατροί Roman citizenship,[62] and Augustus provided them with permanent exemption from public taxes.[63] Further, both ἰατροί and φιλόσοφοι were honoured with the

---

jest of Plautus (*Captivi*, 284), apropos of a reckless romancer, that "he is not simply lying now, he is philosophizing".'

[55] *Diss.* III.8.7.
[56] *Diss.* III.23.24.
[57] *Diss.* III.23.27-30.
[58] *Diss.* III.23.35.
[59] *Diss.* III.23.32.
[60] J. Benedeum, ZPE 27 (1977) 265-76, has published five inscriptions which demonstrate their honoured place in Kos. G.H.R. Horsley, ed., *New Documents Illustrating Early Christianity* (Sydney: Macquarie University Ancient Documentary Research Centre, 1982), 2.12.
[61] LSJ.
[62] Suet. *Jul.* 42.
[63] *Diss.* III.23.24.

title of 'saviour' (σωτήρ, also translated as 'deliverer,' 'preserver') in the first century.[64] Other recipients of the title included wealthy benefactors, priests, Roman generals, other dignitaries, emperors and gods.[65] The ἰατροί did not characteristically seek the people; the people sought them.[66]

The mixed perception of the φιλόσοφοι is further nuanced by the fact that some parents discouraged their children from studying philosophy because it could oppose ambitions of political or material success.[67] Cicero's observation a century earlier was that the motive for piety in religion is so often material gain. 'The reason why men give to Jupiter the titles of Best and Greatest is not that they think that he makes us just, temperate or wise, but safe, secure, wealthy and opulent.'[68]

If such 'success' was their hope for their children, parents could do a lot better than Epictetus for a guide. We see this very problem addressed in the *Discourses*. Epictetus forbade the students the hope that philosophy was the path to honours of the elite class—'to sit where the senators do' and to 'have a good view at the amphitheatre'.[69] There was a regrettable disparity between what the parents' and students' motives were, and what their motives should have been.

Epictetus offered a model defence for students whose parents were angry because they had chosen to study Epictetus' brand of philosophy. He suggested the students say to their parents,

> Very well then, I do wrong and do not know what is proper and suitable for me to do. If this can neither be learned nor taught, why do you blame me? But if it can be taught, teach me; and if you cannot, allow me to learn from those who profess to know. For what do you suppose? That I voluntarily fall into evil and miss the good? Of course not. What, then, is the cause of my doing wrong? Ignorance. Don't you want me, then, to get rid of my ignorance?[70]

Those parents who undervalued philosophy needed to realise its fundamental importance for avoiding error and ignorance, and so to live well.

---

[63] *Diss.* III.23.27-30.
[63] *Diss.* III.23.32.
[63] *New Docs*, 2.12.
[63] LSJ.
[63] Suet. *Jul.* 42; *New Docs*, 2.12-13.
[64] Epicureus, *P. Herc.* 346.4b.7.
[65] See the inscription which refers to a public official's work as being 'for the salvation of the people' (ἐπὶ σωτηρίαι τοῦ δήμου). J.R. Harrison, 'Saviour of the People' in *New Docs*, 9.4.
[66] Cf. Philostratus, *VA*, I. 7.
[67] *Diss.* I.26.5.
[68] Cicero, *ND*, III.87.
[69] *Diss.* I.25.26-27.
[70] *Diss.* I.26.5-7.

A further criticism of philosophers in the first century can be seen in writings from Alexandria. Dio of Prusa (c. AD 40 – 110), who was later given the name Dio Chrysostom, 'golden tongue', for his ability as an orator, studied under Musonius Rufus in the 60s.[71] He considered that philosophers had great potential as agents of reform in the city of Alexandria. The vices of the city could be overcome by *paideia*, the precipitate of virtue, and the responsibility for this reform rested with the 'so-called philosophers' (Dio Chrysostom, *Or.* 13.11; 34.3).[72] He bemoaned that some philosophers 'do not appear in public at all' because they have lost hope in effecting change among people. They have 'quit the field and are silent' (*Or.* 32.19). 'In my opening remarks also I laid blame for this [disorder] upon the philosophers who will not appear before the people or even deign to converse with you' (§20).[73]

Dio, the ambassador for the emperor, and perhaps others with him, recognised the potential of philosophers to affect a more virtuous society. Yet they were deemed impotent because they avoided engagement.

There was another category of philosophers who were deemed ineffective in Alexandrian society. They should have been 'saviours and guardians', but were instead too much ὥσπερ οἱ σωφισταί ('like the sophists').[74] They had become too preoccupied with such distractions as wealth and political power to be of any use to society. As is discernable from his Doctor metaphor, Epictetus would have shared such criticisms, thinking it inappropriate for philosophers to mimic the sophists, who gave public declamations and sought to fill lecture halls through invitation. Instead, the substance rather than performance of philosophy benefits society, and draw to itself those whom it would benefit.[75]

Epictetus the Slave and Student

Epictetus' Background

Epictetus (c. AD 50 – 130) spoke much less about himself, for the purposes of self-promotion, than did the Stoic Marcus Aurelius (AD 121 – 180). In the self-effacing tradition of Socrates, Epictetus preferred to be considered a παιδευτής (trainer of the young).[76]

This is not to say that he did not reveal a lot about himself. Perhaps by nature of the informal genre of the classroom setting in which Arrian took his notes, Epictetus' *Discourses* captures much of Epictetus' self-disclosure; he shares his own convictions, his likes and dislikes, and most strikingly, his internal struggles and sense of inadequacy.

---

[71] Gill, "The School in the Roman Imperial Period," 53.
[72] *Or.* 13.11; 34.3; J.L. Moles, "The Career and Conversion of Dio Chrysostom," *Journal of Roman Studies* 68 (1978): 91.
[73] Cited in Winter, *Philo and Paul among the Sophists*, 45.
[74] The phrase of Musonius Rufus warning against idle living in *MR*, XI.82.10-11.
[75] *Diss.* III.23.27.
[76] *Diss.* II.19.29. Long, *Epictetus: A Stoic and Socratic Guide to Life*, 123.

Some of the external circumstances that Epictetus divulges include his time as the slave of Epaphroditus, a freedman and Nero's secretary. Though there is some doubt concerning the story of Celsus (*Contra Celsum,* 7.53),[77] it was probably true that Epaphroditus twisted Epictetus' leg until it broke, causing a lameness that remained until his death.[78] Epictetus' gentle warning that his leg was near breaking point, and then his legendary calmness at the time it broke, suggests that he was practising Stoicism while still a slave.[79] As a freedman, he continued to live with few possessions and, according to Simplicius, in old age he adopted a child who would have been abandoned.[80]

His life as a slave almost certainly contributed to his trademark emphasis of 'freedom' as a philosopher. When Epictetus calls a freedman 'You slave,' his words were 'charged with a resonance that goes well beyond either this convention or the Stoic paradox that only the wise man is free' – he knew the indignity of slavery from personal experience.[81] He taught, 'Freedom is the highest good', and thus offered a radical alternative definition to Roman ideas of slavery and freedom.[82] In philosophical terms, most Romans were enslaved people. Since *paideia* made one free, Epictetus' loyalty lay with reason and God much more than with any Roman authority. He sided with philosophers over society, by supporting the maxim that 'education should not be restricted for the free, but that the free are the educated'.[83] For Epictetus true freedom, through reason, was available to all.

An individual's nobility was not determined according to Roman cultural norms. Instead, it had everything to do with the way one applied λόγος ('reason') to life. This is not to say that he exalted the commoner and despised those of the upper echelons. Sadly, neither group lived according to reason. Theirs was a senseless way to live, and the life to which failed students of philosophy would return.

---

[77] Suidas casts doubt on Celsus' account (Celsus, "Contra Celsum." 7.53), though as Oldfather points out Suidas, in the context of his writing may have been motivated to discredit this impressive act. Oldfather, *Epictetus: The Discourses*, 1.ix. See, also, Iason Xenakis, *Epictetus: Philosopher-Therapist* (The Hague: Martinus Nijhoff, 1969), 1-2.

[78] Epictetus refers to himself as a lame old man in I.16.20.

[79] This supposition accords with the dating of Epictetus' training proposed by Xenakis. He suggests that Epictetus was still a slave while taking lessons from Musonius Rufus (around AD 65), and probably was still under his tutelage during the burning of the capital in 69. Xenakis, *Epictetus: Philosopher-Therapist*, 2.

[80] Simplicius, "Commentary on the Enchiridion", 46. Epictetus' affection for children and knowledge of their ways can be sensed at a couple of places in the *Discourses*, though this was by no means excessive (III.9.22, 19.4-6, 24.53, IV.7.22-24,32). Xenakis, *Epictetus: Philosopher-Therapist*, 13.

[81] Long, *Epictetus: A Stoic and Socratic Guide to Life*, 11.

[82] *Diss.* IV.1.52.

[83] *Diss.* II.1.25.

For if you are not accomplishing anything, it was no use for you to have come [to Epictetus' school] in the first place. Go back and tend to your affairs at home. For if your volition cannot be brought into conformity with nature, no doubt your paltry piece of land can be made to conform with it. You will increase the amount of your small change; you will care for your father in his old age, you will walk up and down in the market, you will hold office; a poor wretch yourself, you will do wretchedly whatever comes next.[84]

There was little value in doing what most people did, including deeds that some considered virtuous, such as the humane treatment of one's elderly father (according to such virtues as φιλαδελφία and φιλανθρωπία).[85] Epictetus never fitted comfortably into any Roman mould. Despite his dramatic increase in social influence, his philosophical disdain for secular pursuits only reinforced his cynicism for Rome with its institutions and offices.[86]

Musonius Rufus may well have had students like Epictetus in mind when he taught that those with difficult backgrounds had an advantage over wealthy students when it came to studying philosophy.[87] His reasoning was that those who were not so committed to indulgent living were in a better position to objectively consider and choose an alternative path of life; they were more pliable. It follows then, that Musonius probably considered Epictetus' experience as a slave to be more an asset than a liability. Epictetus made good use of the opportunity given to him by Musonius Rufus. With his rise to prominence, his background ceased to disadvantage him socially. He was visited and esteemed by the noble, and engaged with all echelons of society.[88]

In order to better understand Epictetus, it is beneficial to discuss further his teacher, Musonius Rufus.

---

[84] *Diss.* III.5.3-4.

[85] φιλαδελφία expressed the love for one's kin, while φιλανθρωπία more commonly associated with love for humanity in general. Plutarch expresses something of the relationship between love for family and for humanity in Plutarch, "De Fraterno Amore" 479D: 'For most friendships are in reality shadows and imitations and images of that first friendship which Nature implanted in children toward parents and in brothers toward brothers'; cf. 478E-F; 482E-F; Hierocles, *On Duties*, 4.27.20; 4 Macc. 13:23, 26; 14:1; Philo, *Legat.* 87; Josephus, *A.J.* 4.2.4 §26. See examples in LSJ, BDAG, 1055-56, and further discussion comparing the two virtues in Green, *Jude and 2 Peter*, 195.

[86] *Diss.* III.5.2-3.

[87] *MR*, I.34.5-15.

[88] See Hock's social analysis of Epictetus for insights into audience and influence. Some of Epictetus' visitors had direct relationships with Caesar; the Roman who visits with his son (*Diss.* II.14.18); the *praefectus annonae* (I.10.5), the *procurator* of Epirus (III.4.2,4), the *corrector* of the free cities of Greece (III.7.29-30), and possibly the *patronus* from Cnossus (cf. III.9.18). Ronald F. Hock, ""By the Gods, It's My One Desire to See an Actual Stoic": Epictetus' Relation with Students and Visitors in His Personal Network," *Semeia* 56 (1991): 126-31.

Musonius Rufus

Important details of Gaius Musonius Rufus' life can be gathered from ancient sources.[89] The son of Capito, Musonius was born sometime before AD 30 in the town of Volsinii. His influence peaked under Nero, who banished him in 65 to the barren island of Gyara. It was probably during the reign of Galba, following Nero's death, that Musonius Rufus returned to Rome where he was a teacher of philosophy. In AD 69 he was part of an embassy sent by Vitellius to Vespasian's approaching General to seek peace, and later was victorious in a significant legal prosecution against P. Egnatius Celer. Under Vespasian, Musonius was at first exempted from the general expulsion of all philosophers, but later exiled a second time and probably spent time in Syria and Greece, before being allowed to return by Titus. He had probably died by AD 101 or 102, since Pliny speaks of him as though he was no longer living.[90]

As for Musonius' impact, his students included Euphrates of Tyre, Timocrates of Heracleia, Athenodotus, and Dio of Prusa. The most recognised of his followers, however, and the one who most closely continued the 'spirit and intent' of his master's life and teaching, was Epictetus.[91]

Musonius was remembered for living a life that accorded impressively with his teaching. He and Socrates were deemed the two saints of the pagan world.[92] The extant teachings were produced by his pupil Lucius, who probably studied under Musonius during his first exile. He edited his notes a number of years after Musonius' death, and after AD 105.[93]

Discussion of Musonius Rufus' life and teaching is best done with considerable restraint. Since Lucius' record of Musonius' teachings involved the editing of (perhaps shorthand) notes taken years earlier,[94] it might be expected that some of the passion and colour of Musonius' language was diluted. The courageous, colourful and charismatic Musonius Rufus attested to by others is only dimly visible from Lucius' writings. Lutz concludes: 'As a result, we get the impression of Musonius as a man who was good, to be sure,

---

[89] See C. Lutz, "Musonius Rufus: The Roman Socrates," *Yale Classical Studies* 10 (1947): 14-20.

[90] Pliny, "Epistulae." III.

[91] Lutz, "Musonius Rufus: The Roman Socrates," 19-20. Musonius Rufus is esteemed not only in the works of Epictetus, but, also, Dio (XXX.1.122), Himerius (*Or.* XXIII.21), Julian (*Ep. ad Theodorum*, Rh. Mus. 42,24); as well as Roman authors such as Pliny (*Ep.* III.11), Tacitus (*Ann.* XV.71), Fronto (*Ep. ad Verum*, I.1), and Christians including Justin (*Apol.* II.8) and Origenes (*C. Cels.* III.66), where he is respectfully named alongside Heracles, Odysseus and Socrates. See A.C. Van Geytenbeek, *Musonius Rufus and Greek Diatribe* (Assen: Royal VanGorcum, 1962), 14-15.

[92] Lutz, "Musonius Rufus: The Roman Socrates," 3.

[93] *MR*, IX.49.10. Van Geytenbeek, *Musonius Rufus and Greek Diatribe*, 8-10.

[94] *MR*, VIII.32.5.

but mild and tolerant, and, in contrast with his pupil Epictetus, quite lacking in spirit.'[95] The limitations of primary sources must be considered when comparisons are made between the two Stoics.

A further feature of Lucius' record is that he did not intend to construct a systematic and comprehensive recollection of Musonius' teaching, even if such a work was possible. Instead, what remains are somewhat disjointed and informal discussions addressing questions raised by his students, which may have constituted only an element of Musonius' overall didactic approach.[96]

Despite the limited perspective available to us, a clear resonance between Musonius' and Epictetus' philosophy is still perceptible. Direct quotations in Epictetus' *Discourses* recalling the words of his former teacher reveal the impression Musonius left on him. There are divergences, however, or at least different emphases between the two.

First, some similarities will be mentioned. About the vanity of teaching for display, Epictetus quotes the words and sentiments of Musonius. Like Epictetus, Musonius clearly had little time for praising fellow men, which he equates to the deception of calling sick people well:

> Rufus used to say, 'If you have nothing better to do than to praise me, then I am speaking to no purpose.' Wherefore he spoke in such a way that each of us as we sat there fancied someone had gone to Rufus and told him of our faults; so effective was his grasp of what men actually do, so vividly did he set before each man's eyes his particular weaknesses.[97]

Musonius diagnosed the general human condition: 'so effective was his grasp of what men actually do.' He brought conviction about his students' shortcomings: 'so vividly did he set before each man's eyes his particular vices'.[98] Like his teacher, Epictetus knew that at the core of the philosopher's message was the news that all was not well with the hearers. This sober view of self was not common to all in the first century. Seeking the praise of an audience was common practice, but was not to be so for philosophers.[99]

Like Epictetus, Musonius had a direct style of confronting error in his students. Epictetus recalls when as a student he underestimated the seriousness

---

[95] Lutz, "Musonius Rufus: The Roman Socrates," 12.
[96] See *MR*, XVIIIA.113.7-8, where the editor recalls Rufus' teaching about food: 'Once, putting aside other themes such as he habitually discussed, he spoke somewhat as follows.' One may wonder what he habitually discussed? That the extant material does not reflect his overall approach is explicit. What remains, however was the 'noteworthy' divergence. Concluding this section, the editor concedes, 'The words spoken on that occasion concerning food and nourishment seemed to us more unusual than the customary discourses day by day', XVIIIA.115.30-31. For a more comprehensive discussion, see Lutz, "Musonius Rufus: The Roman Socrates," 24-25.
[97] *Diss.* III.23.29.
[98] *Diss.* III.23,29.
[99] *Diss.* III.23.23-24.

of error, 'If then, I err in these matters, I have not murdered my own father, have I?' Musonius' rebuke is sharp: 'Slave, pray where was there in this case a father for you to murder? What, then, have you done, you ask? You have committed what was the only possible error in the matter.'[100]

Again, when Epictetus did not discover an omission in a certain syllogism he said to Musonius: 'Well, it is not as bad as if I had burned down the Capitol.' Musonius retorts: 'Slave, (or, perhaps, 'Captive,' ἀνδράποδον), the omission here *is* the Capitol.'[101]

Neither Epictetus' nor Musonius Rufus' logic is always convincing,[102] but on the whole, a comparison of the two philosophers reveals Musonius to have been more measured in his demands, and his teaching techniques were probably deemed more palatable. In the difficult areas Musonius was gentler than Epictetus. Epictetus applied principles to their limits, thus denouncing behaviour that Musonius considered natural and good. Such differences may be explained in part by their vastly different backgrounds: Musonius, the son of a Roman from the *ordo equester*, and Epictetus, the *libertinus*. One shows measure and respectability; the other uses hyperbole and abruptness to make a point.

One example of their different approaches can be seen in the area of self-interest. Epictetus used the strongest of terms, and repeated the point that, ἐμοὶ παρ' ἐμὲ φίλτερος [sic] οὐδείς ('No one is dearer to me than myself').[103] By contrast, Musonius was more nuanced and respectable, explaining the inadequacy of absolute self-centredness:

> If you say that each one should look out for his own interests alone, you represent man as no different from a wolf or any other of the wildest beasts which are born to live by violence and plunder, sparing nothing from which they may gain some advantage, having no part in a life in common with others, no part in cooperation with others, no share in any notion of justice. [It must be acknowledged that] man's nature most closely resembles the bee which cannot live alone (for it dies when left alone) ... and in addition you recognize that for man, evil consists in injustice and cruelty and indifference to a neighbour's trouble, while virtue is

---

[100] *Diss.* I.7.31.

[101] *Diss.* I.7.30-33. The sense of this interchange is that Musonius Rufus was rebuking Epictetus' indolence towards perfecting reason. Epictetus' view that a small oversight was inconsequential grated against Musonius, who insisted that failing to observe one omission represents *absolute* failure in the whole exercise, which was testing their ability to detect any such errors.

[102] One example of unconvincing logic in Rufus' comes in *MR*, XVIIIB.118.6-9, where he states, '[T]he throat was designed to be a passage for food, not an organ of pleasure.' Therefore, food is not meant to be enjoyed. Since food clearly is enjoyed by people, that taste is not recognised by the throat is a poor argument. He himself admits it is the hardest of all [pleasures] to combat, *MR*, XVIIIB.116.22-25.

[103] *Diss.* III.4.10.

brotherly love and goodness and justice and beneficence and concern for the welfare of one's neighbour.[104]

The normality of loving emotions and attachment in human relationships, which Epictetus technically proscribed, Musonius endorsed as natural and good:

> For what man is so longed for when absent as a husband by his wife, or a wife by her husband? Whose presence would do more to lighten grief or increase joy or remedy misfortune?[105]

A virtuous mother loves her children deeply; she 'would love her children more than life itself'.[106] Like a hen protects her chicks, mothers are expected to be courageous in defence of their young.[107] This is a sentiment that would not be echoed by Epictetus without great caution. In Musonius' concession for human love, though it may have been an illustration more than an imperative, he does not condemn this desire for human companionship. Among the things deemed by Epictetus to be merely external to one's volition and thus ἀδιάφορα ('matters of indifference') were one's spouse, children and brothers, but according to Musonius, such people had a role to play for enhancing one's life.[108]

The above concessions of Musonius might be held as 'natural' by many, yet could not be conceded by Epictetus who stressed the benefits of being independent from any such externality, whether it be family or human affairs more generally.

Musonius' more moderate application of Stoic principles may explain his opinion that a philosopher would make the best king or ruler.[109] Certainly, a 'Musonian king' (closer to the mould of Stoic Emperor Marcus Aurelius, also of the equestrian order) is less difficult to imagine than a hard-line 'Epictetan king', the latter being committed to a level of detachment from circumstances that would make a position of authority difficult, if not impossible. The freedman, now in exile, took to its limit the well-known principle, *nil admirari*.[110]

---

[104] *MR*, XIV.92.20-33; cf. XIX.122.28-32; IV.48.7-8.

[105] *MR*, XIV.94.5-8.

[106] *MR*, III.40.31-32.

[107] *MR*, IV.44.28-30.

[108] *MR*, XV.100.12-16 cf. Epictetus, *Diss.* III.40.31-32; IV.44.28-30; XIX.122.28-32. Other distinctives of Musonius Rufus among extant Stoic literature is his overt respect for the capacity of women to reason and to study philosophy, and his affirmation that husband and wife have an equal obligation to remain faithful in marriage, *MR*, XV.100.12-16; IV.44.16-18; XII.86-88

[109] *MR*, VIII.66.2-11.

[110] Horace, *Epistulae* 1.6.1. A connection rightly made in Oldfather, *Epictetus: The Discourses*, 1.122.

The extreme detachment required by Epictetus is well illustrated by the exhortation, μὴ θαύμαζε ('stop admiring') your clothes, and you are not angry at the man who steals them; stop admiring your wife's beauty, and you are not angry at her adulterer.'[111] For the sake of self-preservation, even admiration for one's wife was off limits. It was a hard and yet vital requirement of Epictetus' philosophy, that the invincible man is one for whom 'nothing that is outside the sphere of his volition can dismay.'[112] Gill rightly observes,

> One can also see Epictetus as the exponent of a particularly 'tough' version of Stoicism, which de-emphasizes the role of selecting 'preferable' advantages in ethical life and which favours the austere Cynic ideal rather than the practice of virtue within more conventional life-styles.[113]

To modern and ancient readers alike, including perhaps even Musonius Rufus, the level of detachment required by Epictetus might be deemed a divergence from nature, and certainly one the ἄσκησις ('application', 'practice') of which he and his followers found difficult. To Epictetus' credit, however, his tougher ethical requirements are consistent with his theory, for if externalities truly are of no consequence, then they must be treated so—one should not admire one's wife, nor resent her adulterer. Musonius Rufus, on the other hand, softened the ethical requirements to permit such 'natural' feelings of joy, grief, love for children and wife. To the extent that he did this, however, he might have been deemed by Epictetus as being inconsistent with strict Stoic principles, even if it did make Stoicism more workable.

Yet Epictetus does himself occasionally soften the demands of philosophy in terms of its otherwise strict principles of detachment. Though 'no one is dearer to me than myself', there may be times, he explained, when it 'becomes necessary for me to risk my life for my friend, and if it becomes my duty – even to die for him'.[114]

Compared to the observations above, which raise a question of Epictetus' internal consistency,[115] Long provides what might be considered a more accommodating interpretation of Epictetus. Denying that Epictetus lacked social concern, Long attempts to reconcile the detachment ideal with family and civic life by stating that it is not merely attachment to family that Epictetus forbids, but '*passionate* attachments' that are of concern.[116] Further,

> the context in which we are expected to deploy these powers is precisely our families and a fully engaged social and civic life. There is no hint of ascetic withdrawal from the world in Epictetus' discourses, no suggestion that, in order to

---

[111] *Diss.* 1.18.11.
[112] *Diss* 1.18.21.
[113] Gill, "The School in the Roman Imperial Period," 52.
[114] *Diss.* II.7.3.
[115] A similar criticism of inconsistency is expressed in the Introduction of the translation by Carter, *The Moral Discourses of Epictetus*, xviii-xix.
[116] Long, *Epictetus: A Stoic and Socratic Guide to Life*, 256 (italics his).

safeguard our tranquillity, we should disengage from the ordinary business of life or erect boundaries between ourselves and other people.[117]

Long's opinion might be summarised this way: Epictetus did not prescribe detachment, he proscribed *passionate* attachments. There is therefore a large grey area and cause for tension as one, for example, seeks to fulfil the role of a husband while avoiding deep attachment on the other. He loves his wife to a safe extent.

If, as Long asserts, there is in Epictetus an overall warmth of human relationships, and even joy, it is far less transparent than in Musonius Rufus, perhaps because of a different didactic purpose.[118] The reader is forced one of two ways when reading Epictetus: the indications he gives of a deep concern for people are either a compromise of his detachment principles, or the detachment principles need to be interpreted quite liberally in light of his permission of some attachment. The latter option, taken by Long, allows him to view Epictetus' teaching and practice to be coherent.[119]

Certainly, the matter is complicated by Epictetus' use of hyperbole and irony. Long charged Hock with overlooking these features of Epictetus' style when Hock, in my opinion correctly, observed that Epictetus experienced significant frustration.[120] But the extent to which Long must soften either the theory or the exhortatory material may be the extent to which he over-rides one set of data to accommodate the other. It will be suggested, however, that there is a discrepancy between Epictetus' theory and practice. In order to live according to nature, Epictetus sometimes softened or gently compromised his theory in the context of discussing the practical outworking.

The implications of these differences between Musonius and Epictetus are significant. For both philosophers, philosophy was not only to be known, but lived. Τέλειος ('perfection')[121] of reason and of life, even if considered unachievable, made a good goal. Musonius' version of Stoicism, however, might be deemed more achievable than that of Epictetus; Musonius demanded slightly less. This conclusion should inform Lutz's assertion that Musonius

---

[117] Long, *Epictetus: A Stoic and Socratic Guide to Life*, 256. The underlying premises in this quotation are questionable. The context of Epictetus' philosophical school may not have been as natural and as integrated with the real world as Long asserts. Many of the young students, having travelled from their homeland, were probably not currently responsible for a wife or family, nor fully engaged in social and civic life. And Epictetus does in fact advise a level of physical distance from one's homeland while studying, as well as the maintenance of emotional boundaries between oneself and those who are troubled around him.

[118] See Long's chapter, 'Stoic eudaimonism' in Long, *Stoic Studies*, 179-201.

[119] Long, *Stoic Studies*, 198-99; cf. Long, *Epictetus: A Stoic and Socratic Guide to Life*, 256.

[120] Long was referring to Hock's article: Ronald F. Hock, "By the Gods," 121-42. Long, *Epictetus: A Stoic and Socratic Guide to Life*, 65; cf. 198-200.

[121] See *Ench.* 50; *Diss.* II.23.40.

Rufus' 'high idealism, combined with the noble humanitarianism of his teachings, represents the greatest height Stoicism ever reached.'[122] Musonius allowed humanitarianism at the expense of strict consistency.[123]

Epictetus the Exiled Teacher

An Outsider's Perspective on Life and Rome

The geographical setting of Epictetus' *Discourses* in Nicopolis had a definite bearing on Epictetus' work.[124] First, Nicopolis was considered by Epictetus to be a much easier place to practise philosophy than Rome. The riches of Nicopolis were insignificant compared to the social and material allurements of Rome. Fewer distractions made it easier to control external impressions.[125] Second, Nicopolis permitted more freedom of speech than Rome. Musonius mentioned the liberty that exiles had to speak freely without fear of punishment, though courageous men should speak freely wherever they dwell.[126]

Like Musonius, but unlike Seneca the Younger, Epictetus had the freedom that came with distance from Rome.[127] Rome may have brought greater public recognition for Epictetus, but this was more a threat to his integrity as a philosopher than something he desired. Peddling philosophy for praise or income was a contradiction of the message itself, and was the practice of one ignorant of the treasure that is philosophy.[128]

---

[122] Lutz, "Musonius Rufus: The Roman Socrates," 30.

[123] In her footnote on this text, Lutz points to the similarities with early Christian writings, and the 'Scriptural ring' of Musonius Rufus' work. She points specifically to four similarities with texts in the book of Matthew, one with Colossians, and one with Acts. Without allowing this statement to steal attention from our focus on Epictetus in this chapter, her observation invites further comparative work between the two traditions.

[124] Nicopolis, the 'city of victory,' was built by Caesar Augustus to commemorate his important naval victory over Anthony in 31 BC. By the time of Epictetus, Nicopolis had become a significant city for its position between Italy and Greece. The Apostle Paul wintered there (Titus 3:12), and Strabo described Nicopolis as 'populous, with numbers increasing daily', to perhaps 300,000. It was well fortified, and had its own stadium, odeum, theatre, and mint.

[125] *Diss.* I.26.9-11.

[126] 'For it is not as exiles that men fear to say what they think, but as men afraid lest from speaking pain or death or punishment or some such other thing shall befall them ... For to many, nay to most, even though dwelling safely in their native city, fear of what seem to them dire consequences of free speech is present. However, the courageous man, in exile no less than at home, is dauntless in the face of all such fears; for that reason also he has the courage to say what he thinks equally at home or in exile.' *MR*, IX.74.1-4.

[127] *MR*, IX.74.13-14.

[128] *Diss.* III.23.19-21.

Epictetus' Style and Delivery

Epictetus' ejection from Rome also helps to explain his teaching style and delivery. In a classroom far removed from Rome, Arrian revealed that his teacher's style was earthy, abrupt, and brutally honest. He spoke with urgency about the folly of following the default Roman guide for life. His mockery of those who pursued public office would have been an outrageous though refreshing perspective for the wealthy Roman youth.

But Epictetus was engaging not only because of his radical political views. His lectures on a diverse array of topics reveal a stimulating and most entertaining communicator. He engaged students' emotions as well as their minds, and refers to their laughter during one of his stories.[129] The colour in his lectures did not obscure his passion, but powerfully conveyed it.

He spoke with imperatives, short expositions, anecdotes, examples, and quotations, and positioned himself 'within the three pedagogical traditions simultaneously – Stoic (doctrinal), Cynic (reproving/*protreptic*), and Socratic (combining *protreptic* and *elenctic*).'[130] He engaged his students by raising and then answering his own questions, shattering their complacency and forcing them to interrogate themselves.[131]

The rhetorician Fronto described Chrysippus' style in words that befit Epictetus:

> Wake up and hear what Chrysippus himself aims at. Is he content to give information, expound the facts, make definitions and lay everything out? No. He expanded on everything as far as possible, exaggerates, anticipates objections, repeats himself, defers matters, retraces his path, gives descriptions, makes divisions, introduces characters and puts what he has to say in other people's mouths.[132]

Or as Xanakis notes,

> He would shock his students somewhat in order to motivate and instil interest in learning new things. He would expose one exaggeration by another, thinking perhaps of Aristotle's point made in reference to ethical education that the way to straighten a crooked stick is to bend it in the opposite direction (*Nic. Eth.* 1109b5; cf. Diogenes, *D.L.* 6.35).[133]

This may account for some of Epictetus' most extreme teachings. Certainly, his language is too colourful to be read in a monotone fashion, too nuanced to always be taken literally. The reader must, as much as possible, read within the contours of the text, understanding the spirit in which his words were recorded.

---

[129] I.26.11.
[130] Long, *Epictetus: A Stoic and Socratic Guide to Life*, 64.
[131] Long, *Epictetus: A Stoic and Socratic Guide to Life*, 64.
[132] *On Eloquence* 2.17. This connection was made by Robert F. Dobbin, *Epictetus Discourses* Book I (Oxford: Clarendon, 1998), xviii.
[133] Xenakis, *Epictetus: Philosopher-Therapist*, 6-7; citing, Théodore Colardeau, *Étude Sur Épictète* (Paris: Fontemoing, 1903), 187.

Epictetus understood that learning was not the sole responsibility of the student, but one which belonged also to the teacher. Xenakis oversimplifies this, however, saying: 'His purpose is not domination but teaching. If he fails to reach his pupil or the layman, he feels that *he* is to blame'.[134] There are clearly occasions when he lays the blame on the recalcitrant student for his failure to be transformed. Xenakis' similar observation that Epictetus 'certainly does not belittle his audience'[135] is also difficult to maintain. At times he clearly does belittle his audience.[136]

In summary, what might be said about Epictetus' version of Stoic philosophy? As a freedman Epictetus emphasised freedom more than other Stoics. He reiterated and developed his predecessor's emphasis on the doing of philosophy, seeking not the appearance of wisdom, nor the reputation of being wise, but the appropriation of wisdom in daily living. His version of Stoicism was austere, and its application particularly difficult. Lastly, Epictetus' experience of exile gave him the sharpened conviction that Rome could stand opposed to truth and reason. An important implication of this was that the hopes and goals of his students insofar as they were tied to those of Rome were unsatisfactory; they needed to be guided on the true path of life.

Epictetus' Perception of the Sophists (σοφισταί)

About the battle being fought between the rhetors and sophists on the one hand, who were accused of focusing on ἐπίδειξις ('display'), and the philosophers on the other, who dressed humbly and identified themselves more as enquirers of truth, Bowersock states,

> Of a genuine rivalry between philosophers and rhetors there can be no doubt ... for philosophy and rhetoric constituted the two principal parts of higher education. Their practitioners competed for the allegiance of the young. Because of the nature of their work rhetors were, of course, more eloquent in denouncing philosophers than were philosophers in denouncing rhetors.[137]

The fascination with rhetoric was an unfortunate reality to be faced by philosophers like Epictetus, and explains why the rhetoricians and σοφισταί ('sophists') occupy a significant place in the *Discourses*.[138] Knowing when Epictetus is referring to the sophists is somewhat complicated because the 'σοφισ-' word group, including such terms as σόφισμα ('captious argument,' 'fallacy,' or 'sophism') or the adjective σοφιστικός ('sophistic') were used more broadly than for things pertaining to the sophistic movement per se. And

---

[134] Xenakis, *Epictetus: Philosopher-Therapist*, 7 (italics his).
[135] Xenakis, *Epictetus: Philosopher-Therapist*, 7.
[136] See, for example, his treatment of the visitor from Rome, *Diss.* II.14.19-21, or the Corinthian whom Epictetus insinuates is ugly, III.1.41.
[137] Bowersock, *Greek Sophists in the Roman Empire*, 11.
[138] This is the case despite Epictetus identifying these well-known opponents explicitly only twice (II.20.23; and III.2.11).

the term σοφιστής ('sophist') could itself refer not only to a professional sophist, or one who was wise or a master of one's craft, but more negatively and broadly, to a quibbler or cheat.[139] Verbal forms of the σοφισ- stem were also used by Epictetus, who asked, 'how then will you know if I 'play tricks' (or perhaps 'defraud' – σοφίσωμαι) you?'[140] In this instance he clearly is not referring to the work of sophists, but to sophistic deception.

During the imperial period, the term σοφιστής still bore a pejorative force, 'particularly among partisans of philosophy who wished to distance themselves from accusations of flash triviality.'[141] Loosely speaking, σοφιστής could refer to anyone with the ability to mislead people with sophisticated yet unsustainable arguments. When Epictetus engaged in a dispute with an Epicurean, for example, the Epicurean points out that many are misled by false philosophy: 'the piety and sanctity which the multitude talk about is a lie told by imposters and sophists (ἀλαζόνων ἀνθρώπων καὶ σοφιστῶν), or, I swear, by legislators to frighten and restrain evildoers'.[142] Unlike the legislators, who at least had good intent, the term 'sophists' was used because the σοφισταί were regarded by other branches of philosophy as incessant liars, and completely unreliable sources of knowledge. To be called a sophist, or to be accused of sophistry, was usually an insult.[143]

It is clear from the *Discourses* that Epictetus looked disparagingly at a rival group who held the traits of the Second Sophistic movement, even if he did not use that label in each case. His scorn for the sophists was inherited from such figures as Diogenes the Cynic (mid 4th century BC), who intentionally revealed the weakness of a sophist's (perhaps Demosthenes') character.[144] After Diogenes pointed his middle finger rudely at a sophist, the sophist revealed what kind of a man he was by becoming 'furious with rage' at what was to a philosopher a harmless gesture.[145] Epictetus' point was that one discloses who one is by how one responds to circumstances. The sophist, perhaps chosen as the stereotypical failure in terms of substance, would always fail in practice. The philosophers were to be distinguished from them.

---

[139] LSJ.

[140] *Diss.* II.25.2.

[141] Whitmarsh, *The Second Sophistic*; cf. G.R. Stanton, "Sophists and Philosophers: Problems of Classification," *AJP* 94 (1973): 351-58, P.A. Brunt, "The Bubble of the Second Sophistic," *BCIS* 39 (1994): 41-42; 48-50.

[142] *Diss.* II.20.23.

[143] There are exceptions where, if a philosopher was particularly able as an orator, he could be complimented with the term σοφιστής. The question over which was the more prestigious term depended on what one most valued. For Epictetus, the superior title was without question φιλόσοφος. The abovementioned works of Bowersock, Whitmarsh *et al.* have helpfully nuanced what were previously simplistic stereotypes.

[144] According to Diogenes Laertius, 6, 34.

[145] *Diss.* III.2.11.

In *Philo and Paul among the Sophists,* Bruce Winter devotes a chapter to 'Epictetus and the Corinthian Student of the Sophists'. He argues that

> Epictetus clearly engages in an anti-sophistic polemic which attacks this form of hollow oratory. He appears to be intent on steering philosophers away from it, for his questions suggest that he strongly opposes the inroads made by declamation into his profession.[146]

The first polemical discourse against the sophists, Περὶ καλλωπισμοῦ (*Of Personal Adornment*), records the reception Epictetus gave a visitor from Corinth.[147] This νεανίσκος ῥητορικός ('young student of rhetoric') certainly fitted the key criteria of a sophist's profile, taking not only his rhetorical ability, but also his appearance very seriously.[148] He is introduced as having an elaborate hairstyle, and 'highly embellished' attire, and a smooth (hairless) body.[149] This young rhetor came to Epictetus to improve the impression he could make on people rather than seeking what was truly beautiful – living as a man in harmony with nature and with reason:

> Epictetus – What then, makes a man beautiful? Is it not the presence of a man's excellence? Very well, then, young man, do you too, if you wish to be beautiful, labour to achieve this, the excellence that characterises a man.
> Student – And what is that?
> Epictetus – Observe who they are whom you yourself praise, when you praise people dispassionately; is it the just, or the unjust?
> Student – The just.
> Epictetus – Is it the temperate, or the dissolute?
> Student – The temperate.
> Epictetus – And is it the self-controlled, or the uncontrolled?
> Student – The self-controlled.
> Epictetus – In making yourself that kind of person, therefore, rest assured that you will be making yourself beautiful; but so long as you neglect all this, you must remain ugly, no matter if you employ every artifice to make yourself beautiful.[150]

The reforms demanded by Epictetus were confronting, and his charge of ugliness was a most devastating blow. Epictetus sought to re-direct this young student onto a far superior path.

The second polemic is *Discourse* III.23: Πρὸς τοὺς ἀναγινώσκοντας καὶ διαλεγομένους ἐπιδεικτικῶς (*To those who read and discuss for the purpose of display*). Epictetus criticised the sophists' emphasis on ἐπίδειξις ('display' or 'declamation') at the expense of substance (§38), and of seeking the applause

---

[146] Winter, *Philo and Paul among the Sophists*, 121.
[147] *Diss.* III.1.
[148] Cf. See, for example, the description of the Sophists, Hadrian and Aristides of Pergamon, in Philostratus, *VS*, 586-88.
[149] *Diss.* III.1. Philostratus makes much of the elaborate presentation and appearance of the sophists in his *Vita sophistarum* ('Lives of the Sophists'), though written primarily about Sophists from the second century AD.
[150] *Diss.* III.1.6-9.

of large audiences instead of teaching how to live (§17-19).[151] He asked the sophist what good will come from listening to the sophist's lecture, to which the frustrated man said,

> Sophist: 'But praise me.'
> Epictetus: What do you mean by 'praise'?
> Sophist: 'Cry out to me, "Bravo!" or 'Marvellous!'

Epictetus was reacting to this spreading movement which was capturing the hearts of youth. The sophists' rhetorical ability and lifestyle were widely admired, and teachers of this alternative path were in high demand.[152]

In Book I.7, Epictetus shows his disdain for the hypothetical and untested arguments of the sophists. One must not only seek to live by the truth, but to first test and identify genuine knowledge from the counterfeit.[153] The sophists are implicated when he stresses the importance of the testing faculty of philosophers:

> Is it not, then necessary that a man should also acquire this power [of discernment], if he is to acquit himself intelligently in argument, and is himself not only to prove each point when he tries to prove it, but also to follow the argument of those who are conducting a proof, and is not to be misled by men who quibble as though they were proving something? There has consequently arisen among us, and shown itself to be necessary, a science which deals with inferential arguments and with logical figures and trains men therein.'[154]

The philosopher was to be equipped to follow and expose 'deceit and sophistic fallacies'[155] by a group which he says had 'consequently arisen among us'.[156] The opponents were skilful in their deceptions, a fact which demanded that philosophers avoid indolence in their own training. Epictetus' attitude towards the sophists lacked the usual pity he had for those who lacked reason; he held them in contempt for their folly.[157]

Despite disrespect for the sophists' methods, Epictetus nonetheless considered it important to study them. Whether it came from the lips of sophists or from others who promoted error, a 'sophistic argument' (σοφιστικος λόγος) and 'sophism' (σόφισμα) was a serious threat requiring a diligent response:[158]

> To meet 'sophistic arguments' (σοφιστικοὶ λόγοι) we must have the processes of 'logic' (λογικός) and the 'exercise' (γυμνάσιον) and the 'familiarity' (τριβή) with

---

[151] Winter, *Philo and Paul among the Sophists*, 118-22.
[152] See Winter, *Philo and Paul among the Sophists*, 19-23.
[153] *Diss.* I.7.5-8.
[154] *Diss.* I.7.11-12.
[155] *Diss.* I.7.27.
[156] *Diss.* I.7.12.
[157] As he does, also, the Academics and Epicureans.
[158] Epictetus refers, for example, again negatively, to what he claims are the sophisms of Pyrrho and the Academy (I.27.2). The antonyms of σόφισμα would be φιλοσόφημα or ἐπιχείρημα ('true logical argument').

these; against the plausibilities of things we must have our preconceptions clear, polished like weapons, and ready at hand.[159]

As discussed earlier, part of Epictetus' own education under Musonius Rufus included what seemed (at the time) to him to be a pedantic and inconsequential exercise of perfecting syllogisms, following an argument, demonstration, or sophism.[160] Keenly aware of sophistic opposition, Epictetus ensured that his own students were similarly trained in sophistic argumentation.[161] In this way they would be secure, 'studying so as to avoid being shaken by sophisms'.[162] Learning to hold one's ground, to avoid being defeated or 'shaken' by the sophistic arguments was important, not as an end in itself so much as a safeguard on the path of life.

In summary, the *Discourses* indicate that the σοφισταί were an influential force in the world of Epictetus, and threatened to destabilise the ill-equipped philosopher. Philosophy students were to be trained in sophistic argumentation in order to detect and expose sophisms, and replace them with proper logic. The quality of a man, particularly when facing painful trials or death, must always be more highly esteemed than mere appearance and rhetorical ability. Persuasive argumentation was important to learn, but was certainly no substitute for true reason, nor was oratory a satisfactory alternative path of life.

---

[159] *Diss.* I.27.6.
[160] μὴ παρακολουθεῖν λόγῳ μηδ' ἀποδείξει μηδὲ σοφίσματι (*Diss.* I.7.33).
[161] *Diss.* III.8.1.
[162] *Diss.* III.26.16.

CHAPTER 2

Epictetus' Guide to θεός

θεός as the starting place for Philosophy

One century before Epictetus, in his *De natura deorum* (c. 45 BC), Cicero exposed the controversy among Romans regarding the question of who or what θεός, or any divine being, was. There was no consensus over the existence of θεός, let alone over the finer points of theology:

> [M]ost thinkers have affirmed that the gods exist, and this is the most probable view and the one to which we are all led by nature's guidance; but Protagoras declared himself uncertain, and Diagoras of Melos and Theodorus of Cyrene held that there were no gods at all ... Many views are put forward about the outward form of the gods, their dwelling-places and abodes, and mode of life, and these topics are debated with the widest variety of opinion among philosophers ... And until this issue [about God's activity in the world] is decided, mankind must continue to labour under the profoundest uncertainty, and to be in ignorance about matters of the highest moment.[1]

In Cicero's forum, the Stoic representative Balbus, claimed to have 'not a shifting and unsettled conception of the immortal gods ... but a firm and definite one'.[2] Balbus asserted that there was a standard sequence to present the nature of the gods.[3] 'First they prove that the gods exist; next they explain their nature; then they show that the world is governed by them; and lastly, that they care for the fortunes of mankind.'[4]

How did Epictetus' presentation of θεός compare with the traditional sequence?[5] This is a question of both style and content. To study Epictetus' style, his *Discourses* are more revealing than his *Encheiridion* because they attempted to record his lectures 'word for word'. In terms of content, however, it could be argued that *The Encheiridion* is the preferable source, since it was Arrian's attempt to represent a summary of Epictetus' content in a systematic

---

[1] Cicero, *ND*, I.2
[2] Cicero, *ND*, II.2.
[3] See also Bruce W. Winter, "On Introducing Gods to Athens: An Alternative Reading of Acts 17.18-20," *TynB* 47 (1996).
[4] Cicero, *ND*, II.3.
[5] For a helpful introduction and historical survey of scholars' approach to this question see Keimpe Algra, "Epictetus and Stoic Theology," in *The Philosophy of Epictetus*, ed. Theodore Scaltsas and Andrew S. Mason (New York: OUP, 2007), esp. 34-35.

way. Thus, the overall presentation of θεός, which may not have followed the Stoic norm in any one lecture, might follow it when systematised. Both sources, therefore, have something to contribute to this investigation.

First, it can be affirmed that Epictetus was aware of this traditional introductory formula for the presentation of θεός.

> Now the philosophers say that the first thing we must learn is this: That there is a God (ὅτι ἔστι θεός), and that He provides for the universe, and that it is impossible for a man to conceal from Him, not merely his actions, but even his purposes and his thoughts. Next we must learn what the gods are like.[6]

He explicitly refers to what 'the philosophers say', suggesting awareness of a tradition. Just as a tradesman or helmsman becomes so through study of his craft,[7] so too a philosopher has a course of learning set out for him. When he does introduce the formula mentioned in the earlier quotation, 'the first thing we must learn is this: ὅτι ἔστι θεός ('That there is a God'),' he does not dwell long on this premise, or even on the subject of θεός, before moving on to his immediate concern of illuminating a man's pride.[8]

When Epictetus did refer to this introductory formula, it was in shorthand form, providing a summary of what was already a summary. Instead of treating theology in a dedicated way, it typically serves his ethical concerns. Epictetus' two most significant discourses about θεός serve the more pressing concerns of living in awareness of providence (in *Diss.* I.16) and of our failure to live according to reason (in II.16).

θεός has a significant, though instrumental place in Epictetus' didactic and ethical purposes. Perhaps this should not be surprising given the more casual setting of the *Discourses*. What is more telling in this matter, however, given the stated centrality of theology for philosophy, is the absence of any presentation of God in the more systematised presentation in the *Encheiridion*.

The Nature of θεός in Relation to Man

Ζεύς, or θεός, often referred to in the singular, was a deity with impressive power. Unlike other gods who were liable to be fooled and limited in knowledge, the θεός of Epictetus was powerful to provide for, and intimately know, the universe he made.[9] Epictetus very freely spoke of the divine being in the plural, even in the same sentence as his use of a singular figure.[10] Thus, he could be referred to as τὸν Δία καὶ τοὺς θεοὺς τοὺς ἄλλους ('Zeus and the rest of the gods').[11]

---

[6] *Diss.* II.14.11-12.
[7] *Diss.* II.14.9-10.
[8] *Diss.* II.14. 14ff.
[9] *Diss.* II.14.11.
[10] Cf. D. L. VII, 119.
[11] *Diss.* I.27.13. Oldfather's translation 'Zeus and the rest of the gods' is probably legitimate in light of Epictetus' theology.

Next we must learn what the gods are like; for whatever their character is discovered to be, the man who is going to please and obey them must endeavour as best he can to resemble them.[12]

Indeed the imitation of θεός, or of the θεοί, was at the heart of the philosopher's task:

> If the deity is faithful, [the student of philosophy] also must be faithful; if free, he also must be free; if beneficent, he also must be beneficent; if high minded, and so forth; therefore, in everything he says and does, he must act as an imitator of God.[13]

Philosophers were to imitate God for three reasons. First, because of the nature of God, and the inherent goodness of what he did.[14] If a certain trait was observed in God, it could be labelled 'virtue' *ipso facto*.[15]

Second, because of the nature of man. Each person was a 'kinsman of the gods'.[16] Coming from God, man was a being of primary importance, a fragment of God, one who had within him a part of God.[17] Since θεὸν περιφέρεις ('you bear God') about with you, you could defile him with impure thoughts and filthy actions.[18] Conversely, what is good for the 'Father' and 'Source' was good, natural and pleasing to him when displayed in the lives of his offspring.[19]

Third, as Long observes, the Stoic outlook is 'an invitation to become completely assimilated to divine rationality; to become a god instead of a man, and to have communion with Zeus as his purpose'.[20]

> Because God's nature is perfect rationality, and this condition is at least theoretically available to human beings, it was Stoic doctrine that while God or Zeus was incomparably more powerful than any person could be, he was not necessarily superior in virtue and happiness to what a human being might in principle achieve. Epictetus never quite endorses this thought (which was worse than heresy to Christianity), but the assimilation to the divine that he advocates (II.14.13) gives persons a potential status that virtually eliminates the qualitative

---

[12] *Diss.* II.14, 12.
[13] *Diss.* II.14, 13.
[14] E.g. *Diss.* II.8.13.
[15] While it is true that Zeus bestows praiseworthy benefits on humanity, he is doing these things for his own sake, I.19.12. For unless he 'proves himself useful to the common interest', his wish to win such appellations as 'Rain-bringer' and 'Father of men and of gods', cannot be achieved. Like other divine traits, the self-interest of Zeus may and should be imitated. It should 'no longer be regarded as unsocial for a man to do everything for his own sake' (*Diss.* I.19.14), since the appropriation of a man's own needs is an action for the common interest. In this way, Epictetus defends the need for man to have an interest in his own affairs which takes precedence over his concern for others.
[16] *Diss.* I.9.25.
[17] *Diss.* II.8.11.
[18] *Diss.* II.8.13.
[19] *Diss.* II.8.9-23.
[20] *Diss.* II.19.27. Long, *Epictetus: A Stoic and Socratic Guide to Life*, 146.

difference between the ideal human and the divine. Far from being tainted by sin at birth, human beings are innately equipped by God to perfect themselves by their own efforts. There is no need, then, for a divine act of grace or redemption or sacrifice.[21]

In Epictetus' view, it was a common tragedy that so few people realised the theological significance of virtuous living. Most live out of harmony with such a reality.[22] Epictetus accuses his students of this flaw, though with all mankind implicated, when he says,

> But when God Himself is present within you, seeing and hearing everything, are you not ashamed to be thinking and doing such things as these, O insensible of your own nature, and object of God's wrath! (θεοχόλωτος).[23]

This statement was a strong invective against widespread human insolence. Those who lived with complacency towards virtue, whether through ignorance or choice, were culpable objects of divine wrath.[24]

This regrettable insensibility of man was virtually universal, since reason is derived from observations available to all.[25] In his section, Περὶ προνοίας ('Of Providence'),[26] the appreciation for θεός is the starting place of philosophy.[27] Θεός was knowable not only to the most intelligent, but to all through the testimony of the created order. Epictetus argues that 'one single gift of nature would suffice to make a man who is reverent and faithful perceive the providence of God'.[28] To deny the existence of 'Zeus and the gods' is nothing less than a demonstration of human 'stupidity and shamelessness'.[29] In agreement, Cicero's Balbus the Stoic asserts, 'For the habit of arguing in support of atheism, whether it be done from conviction or in pretence, is a wicked and an impious practice.'[30]

Indeed it was natural and right after observing such phenomena as the self-sufficiency of the animal world, or the way men can be distinguished from

---

[21] Long, *Epictetus*, p. 146.
[22] *Diss.* II.8.12-14.
[23] *Diss.* II.8.14.
[24] This divine wrath is likely the natural consequences of living in discord with reason, suffered in *this life,* as opposed to any sense of eschatological judgement.
[25] According to Cicero, the gods Stoicism acknowledged were not always a neutral force over all nations, but often had nationalistic interests, reflected in their usefulness in battle; 'while in all other respects we are only the equals or even the inferiors of others, yet in the sense of religion, that is, in reverence for the gods, we are far superior'. Auspices and omens were considered important for serious matters such as battle. Cicero, *ND*, II.8-9.
[26] *Diss.* I.6.
[27] cf. *Diss.* I.3.1.
[28] *Diss.* I.16.7-8.
[29] *Diss.* I.16.8.
[30] Cicero, *ND*, II.168.

women, to praise with hearts and minds the One who established these things.[31] The works of providence of God are praiseworthy, and his benefits should be rehearsed. He has furnished humanity with bodies that function impressively, grow without their effort, and continue breathing even while asleep. However, the greatest reason of all to praise him is 'the faculty to comprehend these things and to follow the path of reason'.[32]

God is often referred to in exalted terms, not only for his majestic power, but his benevolence in nature and in personal relationship with humankind. His essence is defined as being 'intelligence, knowledge, right reason' (νοῦς· ἐπιστήμη· λόγος ὀρθός).[33] θεός is helpful (ὠφέλιμος) and is 'our guide' (ὁδηγός, *Diss.* II.7.11) whose plans are best for us even when they include hardship.[34] He is trustworthy[35] and gives us promptings, directions and commands.[36] Epictetus speaks of the extent to which θεός can be trusted with one's life when asking, 'Is anything else best for you than what pleases God?' The character of God was thus beyond question, and the view of his providence, though mocked by Epicureans, was an essential safety-net of knowledge for a life that was otherwise uncertain. For the Stoics his providence was 'most conducive to the interests of virtue, and lays the foundation of all true piety'.[37]

Some of the other titles for God include 'Saviour', 'Rain-bringer', and 'Fruit-giver'.[38] He is the common father of all,[39] the 'Father of men and of gods',[40] 'a good king and in truth a father'.[41] Sometimes, he is referred to simply as ἄλλος 'another',[42] indicative of the assumed position that God held in the students' view of the world.

While language was powerfully used to admonish his students to praise God, it was inadequate in its capacity to praise τό θεῖον ('the deity') to the extent he deserved. Aside from this being an ἔργον ('duty') that one δεῖ ('must') do, it was ultimately one's λόγος ('reason') and good sense which compelled this appropriate response. His students at least (in both 1.6 and 1.16, and probably all of humanity by implication), were blinded to this duty. As an alternative to praise, they found faults in others, complain against and even blame God.[43]

---

[31] *Diss.* I.16. 9-14.
[32] *Diss.* 1.16, 15-19.
[33] *Diss.* II.8.2.
[34] *Diss.* II.7.14; 1.9.24.
[35] *Diss.* I.25.6.
[36] *Diss.* I.25.3-6.
[37] Carter, *The Moral Discourses of Epictetus*, xiii.
[38] *Diss.* I.22.16; I.19.12.
[39] *Diss.* III.22.82.
[40] *Diss.* I.19.12.
[41] *Diss.* 1.7.40.
[42] *Diss.* 1.25.13; 1.30.1.
[43] *Diss.* 1.6, 38, 42 and 43.

They were exhorted to see afresh his benefits and so render lifelong praise to him.[44] He was worthy of public and private praise, when at work and at home, indeed on every occasion to be sung the 'greatest and most divine hymn'.[45] This was not dependent upon one's circumstances nor upon what kind of creature one happens to be; it was fitting for all, and all the more for rational beings.

It would be far too simplistic, however, to conclude with what has so far been a theistic portrayal of God which resonates closely with the Jewish or Christian God. We have already mentioned the seamless switch to the plural θεοί from θεός, but the differences run much deeper.[46]

The complexity of early and middle Stoic theology is elucidated in Cicero's *De natura deorum*. Like Epictetus, Balbus the Stoic blends ideas of plurality with those of 'a single divine and all-pervading spirit'.[47] This picture is further complicated by his words, 'nothing is superior to the world. From this it will be argued that the world is god. Zeno also argued thus.'[48]

And not only was the world considered god, but Balbus stretched further to say that the elements of reason were also deified by their ancestors. It was the practice of our ancestors to deify

> *Mens, Fides, Virtus, Concordia* ('Mind, Faith, Virtue and Concord'), and to set up temples to them at the public charge; and how can we consistently deny that they exist with the gods, when we worship their majestic and holy images?[49]

Cotta, the Cynic in this discussion, revealed that not all were willing to accept Stoic ideas about θεός. Fanciful explanations of θεός would not be accepted, even when delivered with rhetorical skill and vigour.[50] He esteemed reasonable argumentation much more than speculative notions.

The limits of Stoic theology are certainly difficult to define. At times, Epictetus' views were intensely theistic, and at other times pantheistic, though to attach these late systematic theological labels is not the best way forward for understanding his thought.[51]

---

[44] *Diss.* I.16, 15-21.
[45] *Diss.* I.17.18
[46] Algra sees in Epictetus a 'strikingly theistic conception of God, that is a conception of god as a person, who sees us, who speaks to us, who helps us, and to whom prayers can be meaningfully addressed'. Algra, "Epictetus and Stoic Theology," 33.
[47] *Diss.* II.19.
[48] *Diss.* II.21.
[49] Cicero, *ND*, II.79.
[50] Cicero, *ND*, II.
[51] Following Zeno, Cleanthes, Chrysippus, and Posidonius declared 'the substance of God to be the whole world and the heavens'. Diogenes Laertius, 'Zeno', *Lives of Eminent Philosophers* VII.14, Cicero, *ND*, I.39. Cited by Winter, 'Public and Private: Early Christians and Religious Pluralism,' *One God, One Lord: Christianity in a World of Religious Pluralism* (Grand Rapids: Baker, 1992), 119.

It is somewhat comforting for modern readers to realise that the struggle to comprehend Epictetus', and indeed Stoic theology, is not a new phenomenon caused only by their temporal and epistemological distance. The Epicurean philosopher of *De natura deorum*, Gaius Velleius, persuasively demonstrates the confused picture of God and the gods that Stoicism had produced.[52] In his mind, the blame for any confusion to comprehend Stoic theology lay with the Stoics, not the interpreter. He concludes his survey of the great Stoic thinkers Zeno, Aristo, Cleanthes, Persaeus, Chrysippus, and Diogenes of Babylon, with the stinging words, 'I have given a rough account of what are more like dreams of madmen than the considered opinions of philosophers.' The theology of the Stoics and other philosophers is 'intolerably inconsistent',[53] a muddle of 'a great many confused notions',[54] 'inherently false and mutually destructive'.[55]

These were particularly serious allegations because they ridiculed that which the Stoics prided themselves on, namely, that Stoic philosophy was absolutely rational, and built upon ὀρθὸς λόγος ('right reason').[56]

Perhaps Epictetus' inheritance of a tradition in apparent disarray was a further reason for his trademark emphasis on the more fruitful matter of ethics, and 'practical' rather than 'pure' theology. Since we have no systematic ontological or theological treatise, we are left only with his frequent and seemingly casual use of various historical perspectives. When these references are systematised, however, it appears that Velleius' charge against the earlier Stoics could also be applied to Epictetus, that under scrutiny his theology is also an inherited hotchpotch of ideas difficult to reconcile. Velleius' invective expresses the fanciful nature of Stoic theology:

> why, he [the Stoic Balbus] thinks that even our dreams are sent to us by Jupiter – though dreams themselves are not so unsubstantial as a Stoic disquisition on the nature of the gods.[57]

A.A. Long is certainly less critical of Stoic theology than the Stoics' contemporaries were. He seems to incorporate the various doctrines into a very broad theological framework without Cicero's interest in scrutinising their consistency. If the Stoics were unconcerned about coherence, Long's presentation, which smooths over the discrepancies, might be an appropriate representation. Balbus' concern, however, that doctrine should be reasonable, and Epictetus' similar devotion to the reasoning faculty (ἡ δύναμις ἡ λογική),[58]

---

[52] Cicero, *ND*, I.36-41.
[53] Cicero, *ND*, I.35.
[54] Cicero, *ND*, I.33.
[55] By 'mutually destructive' Cicero meant mutually exclusive arguments simultaneously propounded as true, Cicero, *ND*, I.30.
[56] e.g. *Diss.* II.8.12.
[57] The Cynic Cotta, likewise expresses confusion, 'I do not understand the divine existence; ... but the Stoics do not in the least explain it.' Cicero, *ND*, III.15.
[58] *Diss.* I.1.4

suggest that such charges as 'intolerable inconsistency' may be, or perhaps must be, on the agenda of commentators. Perhaps Long is more accommodating of their doctrines than is reasonable.

This is not to say the Long does not recognise the troubled history which preceded first-century Stoic theology. On the contrary, he mentions three sound reasons why Epictetus was reticent about matters of 'esoteric physics and pantheism'. First, after much disagreement between Stoics over cosmology, the doubts were unlikely to be overcome by any attempt he might have made. Second, philosophical scepticism was on the rise. He taught the general principles, but did not want to over-extend the claims with complex and unprovable arguments. He preferred the stronger and more central arguments. Third, Epictetus was largely influenced by Socrates, and thus followed the 'Socratic precedent for ignoring questions about the ultimate composition of matter'.[59]

Both the ancient (of Cicero) and contemporary (of Long) perspectives benefit our understanding of Stoic theology. The ancient critics sought to demonstrate the incoherence of Stoic theology. Long provides a helpful explanation of the doctrines without the same explicit motivation of finding the flaws of Stoic theology in order to promote his own, as the defeated Epicurean did. Long helps us to see from the Stoic's perspective how their theology worked; Cicero offers us an outsider's perspective, to see how it did not work. Both of these perspectives, if held in isolation from each other, are inadequate.

The Limitations of God

Around the time of Epictetus, the commercial world considered 'natural disasters' as being within the control of God – they described them as 'acts of Zeus' (Διὸς βίας)[60] or 'an act of θεός' (θεοῦ βίας).[61] Numerous extant shipping agreements, such as leases and delivery arrangements, were conditional upon favourable weather. In one early example, dated during the Augustan period, the lessee had to return the ship in the condition in which it was taken,

> except for wear and tear, unless some act of God (πλὴν ἐὰν μή τι βίαιον ἐκ θεοῦ) occur by storm or the boat suffer fire from land or be stripped bare by enemies or pirates, which also [the lessee] will prove'.[62]

Epictetus' philosophy prevented him from attributing control over such disasters to God. Weaved throughout his portrayal of an exalted God are also striking revelations of divine weakness. While God might be aware of every

---

[59] Long, *Epictetus: A Stoic and Socratic Guide to Life*, 151-52.
[60] *P. Laur.* I 6 *ll. 7-11* (AD 97/8 – 116/7). Cited in *New Docs* 6 (1992), 84.
[61] *New Docs* 6, 84, citing *P. Oxy. inv.* 21 3B25G (AD 176).
[62] *New Docs* 6, 82-83 citing *P. Köln* III.147 (Opladen, 1980), 101-107. This papyrus is dated in the Augustan period, and mentions the ship's location in Alexandria. Ed.pr. – B. Kramer, M. Erler, D. Hagedorn and R. Hübner.

thought and action of man, he is not all-powerful to prevent the operation of evil in the world. This inability was explained by Epictetus in the context of people blaming God for the adverse circumstances in which they lived. Instead of blaming him, they were to realise that he had endowed them with the resources to overcome, putting the 'whole matter under [their] control without reserving even for Himself any power to prevent or hinder'.[63]

Had the gods been able to entrust man with control over what is ἐκτός ('external') to his reason, they would have done so; but they were quite unable.[64] Indeed if Zeus could have made the body and one's estate 'free and unhampered' he should have done so.[65] As a consolation, in order that his own son (referring to humanity) should not become a slave,[66] he was able to give mankind a portion of himself (i.e. λόγος), thereby enabling the use of reason to navigate a free and unhampered course through life.[67] The possession of this is cause for unceasing contentment.[68]

But again, Cotta the sceptic was not at all satisfied with these very arguments a hundred years earlier. He believed that 'the prosperity and good fortune of the wicked, as Diogenes used to say, disprove the might and power of the gods entirely'.[69] Likewise, on the co-existence of a good God and human suffering, Cotta held that the gods ought to be criticised: 'either providence does not know its own powers, or it does not regard human affairs, or it lacks power of judgment to discern what is best'.[70]

Such lively historical debate may be one reason why Epictetus, compelled to wed theology with ethics, was wary of teaching in detail about such matters. Many Stoics had been down this road, and did not always fare well. Epictetus did not offer complex argumentation, but he did hold the same views as his Stoic predecessors and presented them confidently. His students may have been less qualified and motivated to challenge him than Cotta was to challenge Balbus.

---

[63] *Diss.* I.6.40.
[64] *Diss.* I.1.8, 11.
[65] *Diss.* I.1.10.
[66] *Diss.* I.19.9.
[67] *Diss.* I.1.12.
[68] *Diss.* I.1.13.
[69] Cicero, *ND*, III.88.
[70] Cicero, *ND*, III.92.

CHAPTER 3

Epictetus' Guide to Life

The Need for Philosophy

It has been observed that for the Stoics, philosophy was needed because of the nature of God and the gods, and in particular, the belief that God was unable to give man control over his environment. Yet humanity did have the power to live well in all physical circumstances through their God-given capacity for λόγος ('reason'), regardless of the physical circumstances they found themselves in. In Epictetus' view, philosophy addressed this most pressing need. It asked the questions,

> πῶς ἂν ἑποίμην ἐγὼ ἐν παντὶ τοῖς θεοῖς καὶ πῶς ἂν εὐαρεστοίην τῇ θείᾳ διοικήσει καὶ πῶς ἂν γενοίμην ἐλεύθερος;
>
> How may I follow the gods in everything, and how may I be acceptable to the divine administration, and how may I become free?[1]

Essential for philosophy was the proposition that the matters of utmost consequence were not ἀτέκμαρτα εἶναι καὶ ἀνεύρετα ('undeterminable and undiscoverable').[2] Despite the confusion caused by countless human attempts to discover what is right and true, there was a μέτρον ('standard' or 'measure').[3] And once found, one would 'henceforth use it unswervingly, not so much as stretching out our finger without it'.[4]

Discovering this standard, a term related to right λόγος ('reason') and λογικός ('logic'), was the first step for a person to understand all other matters.[5] It is the measure by which all other matters must be considered. What is required is 'the thorough knowledge and intellectual mastery of our standard of judgement for all other things, whereby they come to be known thoroughly'.[6]

---

[1] *Diss.* I.12.8.
[2] *Diss.* II.11.16.
[3] *Diss.* II.11.16
[4] *Diss.* II.11.17.
[5] Words that denote 'reason': intelligence, deliberation, thought, wisdom. (Lat. *Mentem consilium cogitationem prudentiam, ubi invenimus, unde sustulimus.*) Cicero, *ND*, II.18.
[6] *Diss.* I.17.8.

Reason and logic are therefore ἀναγκαῖα ('indispensable'); there is nothing superior to it.[7]

The centrality of reason can be further seen as Epictetus summarises the purpose of philosophy:

> What, then, is the subject matter for the philosopher? It is not to wear a rough cloak, is it? 'No, but reason' (οὐ· ἀλλὰ ὁ λόγος). What is the end for the philosopher? It is not to wear a rough cloak, is it? 'No, but to keep his reason right' (οὐ· ἀλλὰ τὸ ὀρθὸν ἔχειν τὸν λόγον). What is the nature of his principles? ... to understand the elements of reason, what the nature of each [element of reason] is, and how [the elements of reason] are fitted to one another, and all the consequences of these facts.[8]

Prepared for life with tested and approved reason, a philosopher was prepared 'to meet the things that come upon [him]'.[9] Aware that 'external' matters were outside the realm of man to control, the Stoic emphasis is almost entirely 'internal'. That is, you are to be master only of what is always ἐφ᾽ ὑμῖν (that which is truly 'up to you' and thus always 'under your control').[10] A person should keep their γνώμη ('will,' 'view,' or 'judgement') in harmony with what takes place.[11]

The ability to reason means that 'as to the λόγος you are not inferior to the gods, nor less than they; for the greatness of the reason is not determined by length nor by height, but by the decisions of its will'.[12] The value of reason could hardly be spoken of more highly. The fact that one's greatness is determined by one's use of this knowledge explains Epictetus' emphasis that one goes beyond the mere attainment or ἐπίδειξις ('display') of knowledge, but that one rightly uses it. Epictetus' message is largely ethical, but his ethics are the corollary of the way things are, which incorporates theology. Thus it can be said that philosophy begins with God, and its τέλος ('end' or 'goal') is to follow him, to resemble and even become equal with θεός.[13] And in light of the theological and ontological connections we have just observed, to 'follow θεος'

---

[7] Diss. I.17.2.
[8] Diss. IV.8.11-12.
[9] Diss. III.10.6.
[10] E.g. 'the gods have put ἐφ᾽ ὑμῖν ('under our control') only the most excellent faculty of all and that which dominates the rest, namely, the power to make correct use of external impressions, but all the others they have not put under our control (οὐκ ἐφ᾽ ὑμῖν). That which is ἐφ᾽ ὑμῖν is our ἡγεμονικόν – translated as *principatum autem* in Latin, or 'ruling principle' into English (Oldfather). According to Cicero, the ruling principle is that which lets every natural object know how to exist as part of a complex and composite environment. i.e. intelligence in man, something resembling intelligence in animals, and a principle in plants believed to be located in the roots. Everything possesses sensation and reason, II.29 Cicero, *ND*, II.30.
[11] Diss. I.12.17.
[12] Diss. I.12.26.
[13] Diss. I.30.5.

means to embody and resemble reason: τέλος δὲ τί; τὸ σοὶ ἀκολουθεῖν (What is the goal? To follow you').[14]

In summary, then, we see that the τέλος of right living is 'to follow God' (θεῷ ἀκολουθεῖν), a statement virtually synonymous with 'to follow reason' (λόγῳ ἀκολουθεῖν). This accords with what Plutarch observes was a widely known fact: 'But you have often heard that to follow God and to obey reason are the same thing' (σὺ δὲ πολλάκις ἀκηκοὼς ὅτι ταὐτόν ἐστι τὸ ἕπεσθαι θεῷ καὶ πείθεσθαι λόγῳ).[15]

The Guide to Life in Theory

Having considered Epictetus' assertion that wisdom and reason are discoverable, and that these gifts from the gods lead to freedom and contentment in a difficult world, the question of how this freedom and contentment is attained will be discussed. To achieve this, an appreciation for the theoretical undergirding of Epictetus' philosophy is required.

The Three τόποι of Training

There were three core τόποι ('topics') of training for Epictetus' students.

> There are three fields of study in which the man who is going to be 'good and excellent' (καλὸς καὶ ἀγαθός) must first have been trained. The first has to do with 'desires and aversions' (ὀρέξεις καὶ ἐκκλίσεις), that he may never fall into what he avoids; the second with cases of 'choice and refusal' (ὁρμὰς καὶ ἀφορμάς), and, in general, with duty, that he may act in an orderly fashion, upon good reasons, and not carelessly; the third with the avoidance of error and rashness in judgement, and, in general, about 'cases of assent' (συγκαταθέσεις).[16]

These three topics, seemingly unique to Epictetus, were not systematically explained in the four extant *Discourses* nor in the *Encheiridion*. Epictetus presupposed his audience's knowledge of these latent undergirding principles.[17]

First, desire and aversion. While introducing a Roman citizen and layman to philosophy, Epictetus explained this first essential principle:[18]

> [W]e consider the work of a philosopher to be something like this: He should bring his own will into harmony with what happens, so that neither anything that happens against our will, nor anything that fails to happen fails to happen when we wish it to happen. The result of this for those who have so ordered the work of philosophy is that in desire they are not disappointed, and in aversion they do not fall into what they would avoid; that each person passes his life to himself, free from pain, fear, and perturbation, at the same time maintaining with his associates

---

[14] *Diss.* I.30.5.
[15] Plutarch, *On Listening to Lectures*, 1.
[16] *Diss.* III.2.1-2; cf. I.4.11.
[17] E.g. *Diss.* II.17.15ff.; 14.7; IV.10.13; I.4.11ff.
[18] Abstaining from desire is the recommended focus for new students (*Diss.* III.9.22; 3.12.8; 3.13.21).

both the natural and the acquired relationships, those namely of son, father, brother, citizen, wife, neighbour, fellow-traveller, ruler, and subject.[19]

Some of Epictetus' key concepts are introduced in this section. Firstly, a philosopher brings his own will into σύναρμος ('harmony') with God's will, which is always discernable by the events taking place; to accept these events is wisdom. Realising he has no real control over external circumstances, the wise man ceases trying to control them. He lets go.

This letting go must be understood in positive and negative terms. That is, one must not desire what may not take place, nor should one have an aversion to what takes place. Put simply, one accepts both 'what will be will be' and 'what will not be, will not be'.

Despite the efforts of exponents of Stoic philosophy throughout the first century, the above outlook on life was not at all commonplace. Epictetus cited Cleanthes to explain that philosophers often speak what is contrary to popular opinion: ὅτι παράδοξα μὲν ἴσως φασὶν οἱ φιλόσοφοι· οὐ μὴν παράλογα ('Possibly the philosophers say what is contrary to opinion, but not what is contrary to reason').[20] Most people believed that happiness and freedom came from getting what they desired. But Epictetus contended that 'freedom is not acquired by satisfying yourself with what you desire, ἀλλὰ ἀνασκευῇ τῆς ἐπιθυμίας ('but by destroying your desire').[21] By following this principle, a man could be safe and free from external circumstances. His will, passions and emotions were detached from vulnerable things. Externalities were of no consequence.

In an imaginary scenario, God examines a student's grasp of desires and aversions. Four questions with answers are provided:

> He then who is above asks of you, 'In your school, what did you call exile and imprisonment and bonds and death and disrepute?'
> 'I called them "things indifferent."' (ἐγὼ ἀδιάφορα).
> 'Tell me, then, what things are "things indifferent"' (ἀδιάφορα)?
> 'Those that are independent of the volition' (τὰ ἀπροαίρετα).
> 'Tell me also what follows.'
> 'Things independent of the volition are nothing to me' (ἀπροαίρετα οὐδὲν πρὸς ἐμέ).
> 'Tell me also what you thought were "the good things."'
> 'A proper moral purpose and a proper use of external impressions' (προαίρεσις οἵα δεῖ καὶ χρῆσις φαντασιῶν)
> And what was the "end"? 'To follow You (τὸ σοὶ ἀκολουθεῖν).'[22]

Unlike other Stoics, Epictetus made the idea of 'volition' (or 'moral purpose' προαίρεσις) central to his whole philosophy in a way that resembled Aristotle's

---

[19] *Diss.* II.14.7-8.
[20] *Diss.* IV.1.173.
[21] *Diss.* IV.1.173.
[22] *Diss.* I.30.2-5.

thought.[23] One's attention was to be given to one's volition, and not to any external matter. Such thinking might have consoled Epictetus, and others like him, who had been ejected from Rome after experiencing slavery. For Epictetus, reason was in a sense the 'saviour' because it freed people from life's troubles and pain.

In *De natura deorum*, the Cynic Cotta was unconvinced about the alleged goodness of reason and its capacity to help. Reason was not enough, he argued, since man with right reason could still do pernicious acts. Cotta considered reason to be something of a curse since it was used to intensify harm more than it was used for good. He argued that more essential than reason was 'virtuous reason':

> all have cause to know that just as right actions may be guided by reason, so also may wrong ones (*ut quem ad modum ratione recte fiat sic ratione peccetur*) and that whereas few men do the former, and on rare occasions, so very many do the latter, and frequently; so that it would have been better if the immortal gods had not bestowed upon us any reasoning faculty at all than that they should have bestowed it with such mischievous results.[24]

It would have been better if

> reason (*rationem*), being as it is disastrous to many and wholesome to but few, had never been given to the human race at all, than it should have been given in such bounteous abundance. If therefore the divine intelligence and will displayed care for men's welfare because it bestowed upon them reason, it cared for the welfare of those only to whom it gave virtuous reason (*bona ratione*), whom we see to be very few, if not entirely non-existent. We cannot, however, suppose that the immortal gods have cared for only a few; it follows therefore that they have cared for none.[25]

For,

> The divine bestowal of reason upon man was not in itself an act of beneficence like the bequest of an estate; for what other gift could the gods have given to men in preference if their intention had been to do them harm? And from what seeds could injustice, intemperance and cowardice spring, if these vices had not a basis in reason?[26]

Perhaps the argument is one of semantics, exacerbated by the Latin translation of Greek ideas. Cicero translates the idea of λόγος with the word *ratio*, which he defines by saying, *celerem cogitationis, acumen, sollertiam quam rationem vocamus* ('nimbleness and penetration and cleverness of thought, which we term "reason"').[27] It is a narrow definition, however, without any moral or

---

[23] Richard Sorabji, "Epictetus on *Proairesis* and Self," in *The Philosophy of Epictetus*, ed. Theodore Scaltsas and Andrew S. Mason (New York: OUP, 2007), 87.
[24] Cicero, *ND*, III.69.
[25] Cicero, *ND*, III.69-70.
[26] Cicero, *ND*, III.71.
[27] Cicero, *ND*, III.69.

divine connotations. When Epictetus speaks of λόγος it is pregnant with ethical significance, including that to which *ratio* refers, but much more. Its goodness is somewhat intrinsic to its sense of a fixed law or formula, closely associated with Fate or Providence. And more than merely ordained by God, the Stoics believed that λόγος *is* God. This broader definition of λόγος renders Cicero's attack on the Stoics' λόγος, along with the accusations targeted at their θεός, baseless.

At the end of the quotation to the Roman laymen referred to earlier, however, is a difficult tension. For while one's internal world, or volition, was everything, one was also responsible to hold his position in society, namely 'son, father, brother, citizen, wife, neighbour, fellow-traveller, ruler, and subject'. Such duties may have been difficult to fulfil without compromising first principles.[28]

Having considered 'desire and aversion', the two less critical topics will be mentioned only briefly.

The second topic was ὁρμὴ καὶ ἀφορμή ('choice and refusal').[29] Once desires and aversions had been moulded according to wisdom, one needed to be motivated to live accordingly. 'Choice and refusal' is the process by which we determine 'what we each should do as an individual in our own unique set of circumstances to successfully fulfil the role of a rational, sociable being who is striving for excellence'.[30] The consequences of such wise living are then beyond one's control or concern.

The third topic was συγκατάθεσις ('case of assent'), whereby infallibility was sought as one gave assent to the various impressions that one experienced.[31] It sought to eradicate all error in judgement, and to achieve 'complete consistency within one's belief system and between beliefs and action'.[32]

Gill provides a useful summary of the three τόποι. Epictetus calls a person to:

---

[28] Some philosophers were clearly active in serving the state. E.g. in the inscription, *I.Eph.* III.616 (dated after AD 212), M. Aurelius Daphnus honours a man named Appius Alexandrus who was both imperial procurator and a φιλόσοφος. Daphnus refers to this philosopher as τὸν ἐν πᾶσιν τῆς πατρίδος καὶ ἑαυτοῦ εὐεργέτην ('the benefactor in all things of his state and of himself'), §12-13, cited in *New Docs* 4 (1987), 71. For an introduction to the mutual benefits of benefactor-patron relationships, see, also, Bruce W. Winter, *Seek the Welfare of the City* (Grand Rapids: Eerdmans, 1994).

[29] Or 'impulses to act and not to act'. Keith Seddon, *Epictetus' Handbook and the Tablet of Cebes: Guides to Stoic Living* (London: Routledge, 2005), 17.

[30] Seddon, *Epictetus' Handbook*, 16.

[31] Gill, "The School in the Roman Imperial Period," 42.

[32] Brad Inwood, *Ethics and Human Action in Early Stoicism* (Oxford: OUP, 1985), 116-19.

(1) re-examine the overall goals of his desires; (2) adjust his moral impulse to action and his view of his social commitments in the light of thought about goals; and (3) aim at complete consistency in belief, attitude, and state of mind.[33]

ἀγαθὸς καὶ κακός

In order to understand Epictetus in any depth, one must adopt his re-definition of ἀγαθός ('good') and κακός ('evil, bad'). The emphasis he gave to re-defining this expression indicates that it was clearly counter-cultural.[34] He set forth the radical principle: ὅτι ἔξω τῆς προαιρέσεως οὐδέν ἐστιν οὔτε ἀγαθὸν οὔτε κακὸν ('Outside the volition there is nothing either good or bad').[35] No event in life should be reckoned ἀγαθός or κακός.

Epictetus found it liberating to know that it was not circumstances that disturb men, but their judgements about them. For example, death in itself was nothing dreadful, or else Socrates too would have thought so, but the judgement that death was dreadful was the true tragedy.[36]

Outside Epictetus' definition of κακός were events considered by society as evil or bad, such as natural disasters, death, and torture. Excluded from ἀγαθός were those things normally considered good, such as promotions, marriage, children, honour and wealth. If they were external, they were of no significance.

Fundamental is the 'proven' statement that 'the nature of the good as well as of the evil lies in a use of the impressions of the senses'.[37] It was the human response to an event, his judgement or interpretation of it, that was either ἀγαθός or κακός. At stake for the Stoics is the all-important corollary: ἀγαθός and κακός remain within the control of man.

Epictetus gave concrete examples of what was for many a new way to think. When news of terrible hardship was brought to a philosopher, none of it was deemed κακός: 'So-and-so's son is dead', 'His father has disinherited So-and-so', and 'Caesar has condemned him.' Epictetus' standard answer to these scenarios is, ἀπροαίρετον, οὐ κακόν ('That lies outside the sphere of the volition, it is not an evil').[38]

What was good or evil was the man's response to the difficulties. It is the man's grief, not circumstances, that are judged with the words, προαιρετικόν, κακόν ('That lies within the sphere of volition, it is an evil').[39] When he bore with it 'manfully', the judgement is, προαιρετικόν, ἀγαθόν ('That lies within the sphere of the moral purpose, it is a good'). News about his son's death, the

---

[33] Gill, "The School in the Roman Imperial Period," 43.
[34] Epictetus often refers to the normality of senseless behaviour by the οἱ πολλοί, as in *Diss.* I.19.7.
[35] *Diss.* III.10.18.
[36] *Ench.* 5; cf. *Diss.* II.1.13.
[37] *Diss.* II.1.4.
[38] *Diss.* III.8.2-3.
[39] *Diss.* III.8.3.

loss of a ship, and castigation, are all met with indifference. The real news of import to the listener is the victim's response to these events, the effect on his volition: εἰ γὰρ ἐν κακῇ προαιρέσει τὸ κακόν ('For the evil lies in an evil exercise of the volition').[40]

Zeus had taken from such events 'the quality of being evil, because you are permitted to suffer these things and still to be happy'.[41] For the great and terrible things have their origin in the impression of one's senses, over which each person is master.[42]

The inability to live in harmony with nature was the unfortunate fate of the masses.[43] Thus, when men hurt each other, the victim should not respond with rage, anger, reviling behaviour, blame, hate or offence. Rather, the offender should be pitied.[44] 'As we pity the blind and the lame, why do we not pity those who have been made blind and lame in their governing faculties?'[45] For they are deceived, and are victims of their own waywardness in the greatest matters.[46]

The Benefits of Living Well

Benefits for Individuals

The dominant benefits of philosophy were oriented towards a free and virtuous life for individuals. Ethical outcomes include not going astray, knowing one's duty, finding the good and avoiding the evil,[47] enduring anger, grief, joy, and other emotions.[48]

> And what greater good than this are you looking for? (Καὶ τί ζητεῖς τούτου μεῖζον;) Instead of shameless, you will be self-respecting (ἐξ ἀναισχύντου αἰδήμων ἔσῃ); instead of unfaithful, faithful (ἐξ ἀπίστου πιστός); instead of dissolute, self-controlled (ἐξ ἀκολάστου σώφρων). If you are looking for anything else greater than these things, go ahead and do what you are doing; not even a god can any longer save you (οὐδὲ θεῶν σέ τις ἔτι σῶσαι δύναται).[49]

Three vices are listed with their corresponding ἀρεταί ('virtues'). Vice consists in being ἀναισχύντος ('shameless'), ἄπιστος ('unfaithful'), and ἀκολασία ('dissolute, intemperate'). The virtuous have αἰδήμων ('self-respect'), πιστός ('faithfulness'), and σωφροσύνη ('self-control').

---

[40] *Diss.* II.1.6.
[41] *Diss.* III.8.6.
[42] *Diss.* I.28.11.
[43] *Diss.* I.19.7.
[44] *Diss.* I.28.9.
[45] *Diss.* I.28.9.
[46] *Diss.* I.28.8-9.
[47] *Diss.* I.26.
[48] Epictetus, *Fragments*, 20.
[49] *Diss.* IV.9.17-18; IV.10.22.

By focusing on this life, Epictetus echoes the tradition handed down by the Stoics and by Musonius Rufus.[50] The benefits were for this life only. 'For surely there is no other end in becoming good than to become happy and to live happily for the remainder of our lives.'[51] And elsewhere, 'Now in very truth philosophy is training in nobility of character and nothing else.'[52]

One end of philosophy was to lead a good life; it was 'the way by which a person becomes good'.[53] Musonius Rufus considered a good man to be equivalent to a philosopher, and a philosopher to be a good man.[54]

Some of the key terms used when describing the benefits are εὐδαιμονία, εὔροια and ἐλεύθερος. Two of these terms, as well as εὐστάθης,[55] are used when he asks (according to Oldfather's translation):

> And for what purpose do you devote to scholarship? Slave, is it not that you may be happy? (οὐκ ἵνα εὐροῇς;) Is it not that you may be secure? (οὐκ ἵνα εὐσταθῆς) 'Is it not that you may conform to nature and live your life in that way?' (οὐκ ἵνα κατὰ φύσιν ἔχῃς καὶ διεξάγῃς;)[56]

Long provides a more nuanced definition of εὐδαιμονία than is conveyed by the common rendering, 'happiness' (which is often used for want of a more satisfactory English equivalent), by defining it as

> a condition in which a person of excellent character is living optimally well, flourishing, doing admirably, and steadily enjoying the best mindset that is available to human beings.[57]

Εὔροια is defined by Liddell and Scott as 'a good flow, free passage', and beyond the literal sense related to the flow of water, it expressed 'prosperity.'[58] It was understood as a life which was flowing well.[59]

---

[50] *MR*, VIII.60.10-15; VIII.62.10-30.
[51] *MR*, VII.58.13-15. It is both understanding and self-mastery that are the means to this end. Lutz, 28.
[52] *MR*, IV.48.25-26.
[53] *MR*, IV.46.10-12; cf. III.40.4-7.
[54] *MR*, 64.35-VIII.66.1.
[55] The term means 'well-based' or 'well-built', as in Homer, Il.18.374; Od.20.258, 23.178 as cited in LSJ. One related benefit of philosophy is what Epictetus calls an ἀήττητος ('invincible') life. In the significant battles of life, one always had the ability to win. Battles which he was unable to win were insignificant because of their external nature. So long as one chose to make his own will his only battle, he would be invincible and live victoriously (III.6.5-7). καὶ γὰρ οὐκ ἀγωνίζεται. ὅπου μὴ κρείσσων ἐστιν ('For he enters no contest where he is not superior'). Accordingly, Epictetus could say, 'No door is locked in my face, but rather in the face of those who would force themselves in' (*Diss.* IV.7.21).
[56] *Diss.* III.10.10.
[57] Long, *Epictetus*, p. 193.
[58] LSJ.
[59] Polyb. 2.44, 2; cf. D. L. 7.88. Cited in LSJ.

Epictetus defined ἐλεύθερος as nothing but τὸ ἐξεῖναι ὡς βουλόμεθα διεξάγειν ('the right to live as we wish').[60] As one lived for the volition, and not for what was vulnerable, one could live without hindrance. The emphasis Epictetus gave to ἐλεύθερος is indicative of its significance in his Guide to Life.

By promising εὐδαιμονία, εὔροια and ἐλεύθερος, Epictetus, like Musonius Rufus, promised the kind of happiness that many sought. Both philosophers saw no greater pursuits than these.[61]

Benefits for Society

On a social level, Stoicism also promised significant benefits. While in discussion with an Epicurean, who was also Imperial Bailiff,[62] Epictetus asserted the value of Stoicism for society and for men of responsibility. The thought of a purely Epicurean state horrified him for its lack of structure and virtue. The Stoic virtues in contrast make for a state that works because it governs men as λογικῶν ('rational beings'). He listed some of the resulting social values imparted to the people:

> the duties of citizenship, marriage, begetting children, reverence to God, care of parents, in a word, desire, avoidance, choice, refusal, the proper performance of each one of these acts, and that is, in accordance with our nature.[63]

By educating society, Stoicism promised to bring out the best in people.[64] But Stoicism was not without its critics on the basis of its social implications.

---

[60] *Diss.* II.1.23.

[61] *Diss.* IV.9.17-18; IV.10.22.

[62] More literally, the διορθωτὴς ('Corrector') τῶν ἐλευθέρων πόλεων ('of the Free Cities'). In his footnote on this text in III.7, Oldfather defines the διορθωτὴς as 'an extraordinary official, of senatorial rank, appointed by the Emperor, and charged with carrying out administrative reforms in matters which lay outside the general competence of the ordinary civil authorities'.

[63] *Diss.* III.7.26-27.

[64] Musonius Rufus believed *paideia* to be the cure-all of wrong-doing – 'the majority of wrongs are done to men through ignorance and misunderstanding, from which man will cease as soon as he has been taught', X.78.29-30. This agrees with Cora Lutz's evaluation that Musonius Rufus was genuinely concerned for the city: 'He is one of the first to advocate contributing to the common good by devoting one's resources to charity. These are details in the larger plan which Musonius keeps ever before his hearers, namely to prepare a social order wherein men may find a "benevolent and civilised way of life". Resting upon the integrity of the individual, the high moral and spiritual qualities of husband and wife in marriage, the deep loyalty of the family, the will to cooperate with one's neighbour, and a concern for the welfare of one's city, Musonius' goal is to make men honorable and responsible citizens of the city of God.' Lutz, "Musonius Rufus: The Roman Socrates," 30.

Epictetus' Guide to Life

Epictetus raised the question, 'Is it possible for one man to make the mistake and yet another suffer the harm?' The short and immediate answer is 'No.'[65]

While one can comprehend the meaning of Epictetus on this, that externalities are not evil, it does not sit well with other values he holds for philosophers or for society. His ideals for society are not that all are unconcerned with the lot of their neighbour, but that there is a sense of love and service. But does a society work if it does not treat malevolent acts as evil?

Cotta, while handling a different matter, expressed his awareness of this issue in Cicero's *De Natura Deorum* (III.69). He compares the philosophers' view that folly is the greatest evil, with the 'evil' done by tyrannical rulers. They can and did wield terrible harm during their reigns that Cotta considered regrettable. To deny the evil of harmful acts may have therefore been a difficult argument for Epictetus to maintain among contemporaries.

It would be right to consider Epictetus a less ardent advocate than Musonius Rufus for social matters, such as family and social welfare, but it has been observed that Epictetus did touch upon these matters.

The Guide to Life in Practice

Having considered the theoretical framework and benefits of Epictetus' philosophy, his practical advice will now be discussed. What would his Guide to Life look like in the sphere of day-to-day living?

The Starting Points

The best way to enter Epictetus' classroom was with the willingness to learn. Epictetus raises the matter: 'What is the first business of one who practices philosophy? To get rid of thinking that one knows, for it is impossible to get a man to begin to learn that which he thinks he knows.'[66]

Regrettably, some students came to philosophers without any interest in receiving advice. When advice was given by a well-meaning teacher, they showed indignation and resentment. Such a person was unlikely to fare well through life. Epictetus concludes:

> It is this conceit of fancying that we know something useful, that, as I have said, we ought to cast aside before we come to philosophy, as we do in the case of geometry and music. Otherwise, we shall never even come near to making progress.[67]

The absence of conceit was necessary for both intellectual and behavioural progress. In the intellectual sphere, philosophy used words familiar to all people, including the newest of students, but often with a completely different meaning. As was observed, words such as ἀγαθός and κακός were to be

---

[65] *Diss.* II.13.18.
[66] *Diss.* II.17.1-2 cf. Plutarch, *On Listening to Lectures*, 4.
[67] *Diss.* II.17.39-40; cf. 1-3.

understood through a new lens. A willingness to learn would allow students to redress their faulty understanding even in the most elementary matters of life – to re-learn concepts they thought they understood as infants.

One man 'advanced in years' and who had served three military campaigns found it difficult to concede ignorance. According to Epictetus, he knew

> neither what God is, nor what man is, nor what good, nor what evil is – if I [Epictetus] say that you are ignorant of these other matters you may possibly endure that; but if I say that you do not understand your own self, how can you possibly bear with me, and endure and abide my questioning? You cannot do so at all, but immediately you go away offended.[68]

The best learners were those who knew they needed to learn everything again.

For behavioural change, admitting one's ignorance allowed one to abandon previous habits, and entrust oneself to a new way of living. While lamenting the conceit of his students, Epictetus describes what such intellectual humility would look like in a student. He would be prepared to 'let everything else go' for the sake of living as a man completely free of hindrance and fear, one who considers God his friend.[69] He would want to re-learn his duty towards his gods, his parents, brothers, country and strangers. It was this kind of man's destiny 'to adorn philosophy'.[70]

Students were to allow themselves to 'be accounted a no-body and a know-nothing'.[71] In reality, however, many students came to philosophers not as humble enquirers, but with abstract questions aimed at impressing others, and with no interest in ethical change.[72] Many came to admire the style of writing, or the pleasures of listening to the classic literature. Epictetus condemns such sophistic enquiry with the words, 'Go hang yourself, pitiful wretch, with only such an aim as this!'[73]

The Importance of Doing

It has been mentioned that Epictetus emphasised the ἄσκησις ('application') of philosophy, and that the quality of a student's education should be measured in large part by his behaviour. Instead of boasting of one's grasp of philosophic concepts, one should boast as follows:

---

[68] *Diss.* II.14.19-21.
[69] *Diss.* II.17.29.
[70] *Diss.* II.17.30.
[71] δὲ μηδεὶς εἶναι καὶ εἰδέναι μηδέν, *Diss.* II.1.36.
[72] *Diss.* II.17.34.
[73] *Diss.* II.17.34. This citation refers to the debate surrounding a stock sophism, to which Chrysippus gave much attention (*Diog. Laer.* VII. 196): 'If a person says, "I am lying," does he lie or tell the truth? If he is lying, he is telling the truth; if he is telling the truth, he is lying.' Cf. Von Arnim, *Stoicorum Veterum Fragmenta*, II.92, frag. 280ff. Cited by Oldfather, in footnote for *Diss.* II.17.34.

'See how in my desire I do not fail to get what I wish. See how in my aversions I do not fall into things that I would avoid. Bring on death and you shall know; bring on hardships, bring on imprisonment, bring on disrepute, bring on condemnation.' This is the proper display (ἐπίδειξις) of a young man come from school.[74]

At a time when Stoicism had become a highly scholastic system,[75] Epictetus longed to see fundamental change in students' attitude to life and death. Sadly, the opposite was the norm; even the seasoned philosophers including Epictetus were found wanting:

> This is why the philosophers admonish us not to be satisfied with merely learning, but to add thereto practice also, and then training. For in the course of years we have acquired the habit of doing the opposite of what we learn.[76]

In addition to rhetorical competence, Epictetus' students were urged to practise 'how to die, how to be enchained, how to be racked, how to be exiled'. 'If you didn't learn these things so as to be able to manifest them in action, what did you learn them for?'[77]

In a world impressed by external matters such as wealth, power or prestige, the true measure of a man was in the way he lives, with αἰδώς ('reverence'), πίστις ('faith'), and δικαιοσύνη ('justice'). 'Prove yourself superior in these points, in order to be κρείττων ('superior') as a person'.[78] A general appreciation for such attributes was common, but doing them made a person superior.

The importance of putting what you know into practice was expressed in various ways. In his rebuke of the student of a Corinthian rhetor, mentioned earlier, Epictetus expresses the above 'superiority' through the language of 'beauty'.[79] 'What, then, makes a man καλὸς ('beautiful')? Is it not the presence

---

[74] *Diss.* II.1.35.
[75] Long, *Epictetus: A Stoic and Socratic Guide to Life*, 90.
[76] *Diss.* II.9.13-14.
[77] *Diss.* I.29.35. Musonius Rufus deals explicitly with this issue of the relationship between theory and practice. Which is more important? Action is superior to knowledge, but they are both required. Theory gives man the ability to speak about virtuous living, and to know what is right, but practice is nevertheless more important. Using the analogy of a doctor, it is not the doctor's knowledge which saves a patient, but the application which is critical (though one could argue for the pre-eminence of right theory from the same analogy) *MR*, V.50.3-10. 'Finally whatever precepts enjoined upon him he is persuaded are true, these must follow out in his daily life. For only in this way will philosophy be of profit to anyone, if to sound teaching he adds conduct in harmony with it.' *Diss,* I.36.8-12.
[78] *Diss.* III.14.13-14.
[79] The Apostle Paul also interacted with those in Corinth concerned for bodily presence and strength of speech. 'For they say [about Paul], "His letters are weighty (βαρύς) and strong (ἰσχυρός), but his bodily presence is weak (ἡ δὲ παρουσία τοῦ σώματος ἀσθενὴς), and his speech of no account (καὶ ὁ λόγος ἐξουθενημένος)"' (2 Cor. 10:10).

of a man's ἀρετή ('virtue')?' Being just, temperate, and self-controlled are examples of virtuous behaviour,[80] as are acts of self-respect, dignity and gentleness.[81] By paying attention to the virtues rather than to outward adornment, 'you will be making yourself beautiful; but so long as you neglect all this, you must needs be ugly, no matter if you employ every artifice to make yourself look beautiful.'[82]

Some of the 'ugly' ways of unreasoning beasts were also evident among people. We act like beasts when we 'act for the sake of the belly, or for our sex-organs, or at random, or in a filthy fashion, or without due consideration'.[83] 'When we act pugnaciously, and injuriously, and angrily, and rudely', we are not fulfilling the profession of a rational man.[84] Epictetus lists other vices: the one given to unnatural lust, adultery, anger, and fear.[85] The focus of Epictetus' disdain for the vices in this instance is not their offensiveness to God so much as their destructiveness for the one who performs them. For example, the adulterer ἀπολλύει τὸν αἰδήμονα· τὸν ἐγκρατῆ τὸν κόσμιον· τὸν πολίτην· τὸν γείτονα ('loses the man of self-respect that was, the man of self-control, the gentleman, the citizen, the neighbour').[86] And, οὐδεὶς δίχα ἀπωλείας καὶ ζημίας κακός ἐστιν ('no one is evil without loss and punishment'), §19. Again, Epictetus' philosophy delivered one not from eschatological judgement, but from folly and hindrance in this life.

To summarise, doing good and helping others should be natural outcomes of studying philosophy. The impressive display of one's ability to memorise and interpret philosophic phrases is an unworthy ambition for a philosopher.

> Ought they not be, when they return home [from their philosophical training], forbearing, ready to help one another, tranquil, with a mind at peace, possessed of some such provision for the journey of life, that, starting out with it, they will be able to bear well whatever happens, and to derive honour from it?[87]

The Devotion Required

The path of life that Epictetus set forth is one of travail. The same effort that is commonly given to things which are of no real consequence should be applied instead in accordance with true reason. 'Yes, but this requires much preparation, and much hard work, and learning many things,' complained the student.[88] Epictetus' reply is that no great art comes without commensurate

---

[80] *Diss.* III.1.6-9.
[81] *Diss.* III.1.15.
[82] *Diss.* III.1.6-9. Man was endowed with the virtues at birth: reverent, faithful, high-minded, undismayed, unimpassioned, unperturbed, *Diss.* II.8.23.
[83] *Diss.* II.9.4.
[84] *Diss.* II.9.5.
[85] *Diss.* II.10.17-19.
[86] *Diss.* II.10.18.
[87] *Diss.* III.21.9.
[88] *Diss.* I.20.13.

effort. And if one rightly appraised philosophy for what it is, zeal would follow. For one naturally pays close attention to that which one values.[89]

A mistake in virtue can have devastating consequences, not only as the direct result of the foolish behaviour, but because it can lead one to grow accustomed to carelessness.[90] This in turn can make it too difficult for self-restoration as the desire for improvement wanes. One's moral purpose, or volition, must be carefully guarded and monitored.[91]

Vices to be cleared from one's mind include: grief, fear, desire, envy, joy at others' ills, greed, effeminacy and incontinency.[92] The method of purging these things is at times couched in theocentric terms: 'These things you cannot cast out in any other way than by looking to God alone, being specially devoted to Him only, and consecrated to His commands.'[93]

Besides God, Socrates provided further reason to be devoted to progress or moral improvement. While most join the daily pursuit of 'improving his own farm, and another his own horse, so [Epictetus] rejoice[s] day by day in following the course of [his] own improvement'.[94] The progress he was referring to was in daily practices such as not blaming others, and always wearing the same expression on his face. 'Who, then, among you make this purpose [of Socrates] the purpose of his own life?'[95] At the end of this section, Epictetus compares devotion to philosophy with being in love with a pretty woman; one would happily endure hardship and discomfort for her sake.[96]

In Book IV, Epictetus spoke similarly about making progress—leaving bad habits behind, developing in noble behaviour, and living in accordance with volition. He says,

> Rejoice in what you have and be satisfied with what the moment brings. If you see any of the things that you have learned and studied thoroughly coming to fruition for you in action, εὐφραίνου ἐπ' αὐτοῖς ('rejoice in these things'). If you have put away or reduced a malignant disposition, and reviling, or impertinence, or foul language, or recklessness, or negligence; if you are not moved by the things that once moved you, or at least not to the same degree, then you can keep the festival day after day; today because you behaved well in this action, to-morrow because you behaved well in another. 'How much greater cause for a sacrifice offering than a consulship or a governorship!' (πόσῳ μείζων αἰτία θυσίας ἢ ὑπατεία ἢ ἐπαρχία)[97]

---

[89] *Diss.* I.20.10-11.
[90] *Diss.* IV.12.1-2.
[91] *Diss.* IV.12.5-6.
[92] *Diss.* II.16.45.
[93] *Diss.* II.16.46.
[94] *Diss.* III.5.14.
[95] *Diss.* III.5.18.
[96] *Diss.* III.5.19.
[97] *Diss.* IV.4.46-48.

Remarkably, Epictetus shows disdain for the highly sought-after consulship and governorship, positions representing the pinnacle of Roman ambitions. He considers them nothing compared to that which is available to all: a more virtuous life.

It is in this area of devotion to progress, however, that a logical difficulty emerges. With such joy over progress comes an apparent vulnerability in Epictetus' philosophy that he never addresses in detail. If one's contentment can be attached to progress, leading to celebration and joy, then does not this emotional attachment to progress have a flip-side during times of failure that should rightly cause lamentation and grief? If progress is the quest of one's life, and a reason to celebrate, does it not also have the potential to cause lamentation? Am I a slave to my ability, or perhaps more fundamentally, to my will to perform?

The philosophy of Epictetus relies on the individual student willing to make progress. It is vanity to merely know philosophy and not live it out; the philosophy is as strong or as weak as the individual's resolve and performance.

On the basis of their atypically impressive adherence to philosophic principles, the great sages were more free than others. Diogenes, and Socrates to a greater degree, were two such men. Epictetus refers to them often, as he does in this example from *Encheiridion* 51: 'This is the way Socrates became what he was, by paying attention to nothing but his reason in everything that he encountered.' He set the standard for living in accordance with his philosophy. This is evident in another text, where the metaphor of the Olympic games conveys the need for urgent and consistent striving.

> Make up your mind, therefore, before it is too late, that the fitting thing for you to do is to live as a mature man who is making progress, and let everything which seems to you to be best be for you a law that must not be transgressed. And if you meet anything that is laborious, or sweet, or held in high repute, or in no repute, remember that *now* is the contest, and here before you are the Olympic games, and that it is impossible to delay any longer, and that it depends on a single day and a single action, whether progress is lost or saved. This is the way Socrates became what he was, by paying attention to nothing but his reason in everything that he encountered. And even if you are not yet a Socrates, still you ought to live as one who wishes to be a Socrates (σὺ δὲ εἰ καὶ μήπω εἶ Σωκράτης· ὡς Σωκράτης γε εἶναι βουλόμενος ὀφείλεις βιοῦν).[98]

There are a number of noteworthy points in this paragraph that can be mentioned by way of conclusion.

First, unlike some teachers of philosophy, Epictetus taught not as one merely interested, or even fascinated, by his subject. He taught as one completely devoted to philosophy's pre-eminence over his professional and personal life. He was a teacher captivated by his subject, and insisted that his students be the same. The pretentiousness of the sophists, doing well in theoretical

---

[98] *Ench.* 51.2-3.

examinations, or taking any opportunity to display knowledge, was lamentable. A life transformed, and the tenacious pursuit of further transformation, was everything.

Second, the weight of the philosophers' task in the last sentence of this quotation was enormous. 'And even if you are not yet a Socrates, still you ought to live as one who wishes to be a Socrates.'[99] The mandate places a heavy burden on those students who took it seriously. Put more bluntly, Epictetus is, in effect, saying, 'Desire to be that which you are not!' For all his care to prescribe detachment from everything outside one's own control this appears to be an Achilles heel that frustrates his philosophy. It is unlikely, perhaps impossible, to attain the standard set by Socrates.

Epictetus expresses this frustration. In a chapter lamenting his own and his students' inability to live as they ought, Epictetus includes himself when he admits that 'we' do not live

> in sympathy with our own reason (ἀσυμπαθεῖς πρὸς τὸν λόγον), far from applying the principles which we profess (μακρὰν ἀπὸ τοῦ χρῆσθαι τούτοις ἃ λέγομεν), yet priding ourselves upon them as being men who know them. So, although we are unable even to fulfil the profession of man, we take on the additional profession of the philosopher – (οὕτως οὐδὲ τὴν τοῦ ἀνθρώπου ἐπαγγελίαν πληρῶσαι δυνάμενοι προσλαμβάνομεν τὴν τοῦ φιλοσόφου·) so huge a burden (τηλικοῦτο φορτίον)! It is as though a man who was unable to raise ten pounds wanted to lift the stone of Aias (οἷον εἴ τις δέκα λίτρας ἆραι μὴ δυνάμενος τὸν τοῦ Αἴαντος λίθον βαστάζειν ἤθελεν).[100]

It is a lucid explanation of the problem: the philosophers failed to apply the principles they profess. Though they have reduced their responsibility and concerns to be merely their volition, they failed in this pursuit. Not only should they be stripped of the title of φιλόσοφος, but they even fail the title of ἄνθρωπος. They were attempting a task far too great for them.

Further, Epictetus lamented the lack of practicing Stoics:

> But as for a Stoic, show me one if you can! Where, or how? No, but you can show me thousands who recite the petty arguments of the Stoics. Yes, but do these same men recite the petty arguments of the Epicureans any less well? Do they not handle with the same precision the petty arguments of the Peripatetics also? Who, then, is a Stoic? As we call a statue 'Pheidian' that has been fashioned according to the art of Pheidias, in that sense show me a man fashioned according to the judgements which he utters. Show me a man who though sick is happy, though in danger is happy, though dying is happy, though condemned to exile is happy, though in disrepute is happy. Show him! By the gods, it is my one desire is to see a Stoic! But you cannot show me a man completely so fashioned; then show me at least one who is becoming so fashioned, one who has begun to tend in that direction; do me this favour; do not begrudge an old man the sight of that

---

[99] *Ench.*51.3.
[100] *Diss.* II.9.22.

spectacle which to this very day I have never seen...Show him to me! But you cannot.[101]

Adherence to Epictetus' teaching about freedom and living in accordance with one's knowledge, carried with it the unending duty to make progress. While freed-man Epictetus would perhaps shudder at the terms 'captivity', or even 'enslavement', to describe the level of commitment to this cause, in practical terms it may have been not far from that. Even if the ancients were not normally as introspective as Epictetus, on a purely theoretical basis it is difficult to see how one whose contentment was to be based solely upon perfection, whether it be of volition or of progress, would not be frustrated that this pursuit was elusive.

The question of whether the Stoic path was achievable or not is not simply a modern concern. In his *De natura deorum*, Cicero noted the absence of anybody who fitted the profile of a Stoic sage. He too identified what he considered a profound problem:

> [I]f wisdom on the other hand is attained by nobody, we, for whose welfare you say that the gods have cared most fully, are really in the depth of misfortune. For just as it makes no difference whether no one is in good health or no one can be in good health, so I do not understand what difference it makes whether no one is wise or no one can be wise.[102]

Cicero was questioning the value of this path to wisdom since nobody followed it. He did not need to prove that it was theoretically unachievable to make his point, 'for it makes no difference whether no one is wise or no one can be wise'.

Greatness comes from Oneself

Epictetus laboured the point that the philosopher needs none other than himself to be free and at peace. There is no reason to imitate commoners (οἱ πολλοί) who appeal to others to have their perceived needs met. He illustrates this point:

> For, in fact, it is foolish and superfluous to try to obtain from another that which one can get from oneself. Since, therefore, I am able to get greatness of soul and nobility of character from myself, am I to get a farm, and money, or some office, from you? Far from it! I will not be so unaware of what I myself possess.[103]

The end goal, greatness of soul and nobility of character, is theoretically within reach of all, because it is a God-given feature of rational humanity.[104]

---

[101] *Diss.* II.19.21-27.
[102] Cicero, *ND*, III.79.
[103] *Diss.* I.9.31-32.
[104] Cicero shared the view that virtue comes from within when saying, 'but virtue no one ever imputed to a god's bounty. And doubtless with good reason; for our virtue is a just ground for others' praise and a right reason for our own pride, and this would not

Freedom was to be found within, and insulated from that which lies without. The secret of contentment, or allowing one to sail smoothly through the rough seas of life, was to limit concerns to that which is impervious to external threat: namely, one's *response* to these impressions. Indeed, to concern yourself with things for which you are not responsible was 'to make trouble for yourself'.[105] Should you be interested in the wellbeing of your parents, your brothers, property, death or life? No, this would be to your own detriment. The gods have declared that you are ἀνυπεύθυνος ('not accountable') for the welfare of others.[106] To 'draw upon yourself that for which you are not responsible' is foolish.[107] In the teaching of Epictetus, it is impossible to maintain inner harmony and have a genuine concern for others at the same time. Empathy is the enemy of detachment.

As Epictetus said, 'I have learned to see that everything which happens, if it be outside the realm of my volition, οὐδέν ἐστι πρὸς ἐμέ ('is nothing to me').[108] This includes not only Epictetus' possessions, but also those around him. 'Take my paltry body, take my property, take my reputation, take those who are about me'.[109] It may be that Epictetus was driven to this perspective not only by his Stoic predecessors, but by his experience of slavery and exile. Strictly speaking, despite mention of fulfilling civic duties, when pressed on this matter, Epictetus' philosophy leaves little room to care for others. If threatened that his family will be taken away he must happily conclude, 'And what do I care for them?'[110]

As was introduced earlier, even the virtues and vices have one's own good as the primary motivation. Vices are to be avoided not because they hurt others, but because they are self-destructive.[111] So too the acts of virtue and reason bring freedom for the virtuous, with little attention given to the beneficiaries of such acts.

A lack of interest in the circumstances of others is also due largely to his perception of ἀγαθός and κακός. Their hardships are not bad or evil in the true sense. In a section entitled, 'That we ought not to allow any news to disturb us', Epictetus asks, 'What have you to do with another man's evil? Your own evil is to make a bad defence.'[112] While the common response of people may be to have concern for those experiencing hardship, Epictetus taught that there are at least two good reasons why one should not have such concern.

---

be so if the gift of virtue came to us from a god and not from ourselves.' *ND*, III.86-87.

[105] *Diss.* I.13.35.
[106] *Diss.* I.13.33.
[107] *Diss.* I.13.35.
[108] *Diss.* I.29.24.
[109] *Diss.* I.29.10.
[110] *Diss.* I.29.8.
[111] E.g. *Diss.* II.10.14-21.
[112] *Diss.* III.18.7-8.

First-Century Guides to Life and Death

Across a number of publications, A.A. Long succeeds in demonstrating the presence of such traits as emotion and compassion in Epictetus and the Stoics.[113] We recognise with him, that Epictetus and the Stoics are not as 'stone-hearted' as they may have been historically understood. On a few occasions, such as when discussing καθῆκον 'duty', Epictetus said,

> for I ought not to be unfeeling like a statue, but should maintain my relations, both natural and acquired, as a religious man, as a son, a brother, a father, a citizen.[114]

But in making corrections, over-corrections are easily made. Epictetus' writings, taken as a whole, make the case for care and compassion a difficult one to maintain. Tenets of human warmth are evident in Epictetus, but are overwhelmed by the coolness of self-concern.

Practical Exercises

Epictetus took the eradication of wrong deeds seriously. The first step was to take full responsibility for the wrong, seeing the root cause not as a circumstance, but of a wrong judgement or incorrect use of one's volition. He taught, 'whenever we do anything wrongly, from this day forth we shall ascribe to this action no other cause than the decision of our will which led us to do it'.[115] The second step was to obliterate this cause of wrong behaviour in the future, 'endeavour to destroy and excise that cause more earnestly than we try to destroy and excise from the body its tumours and abscesses'.[116] One's actions are a result of one's decisions, whether good or bad.[117] The examination of these decisions of the will, and further conforming them to reason, was an ongoing work.[118]

One who liked to give concrete application to his principles, Epictetus vividly portrayed the process by which sense impressions lead to desires which compromise the training of the volition, and how one was to wage war against them: 'when your imagination bites you (for this is something you cannot control), fight against it with your reason, beat it down, do not allow it to grow strong, or to take the next step and draw all the pictures it wants, in the way it wants to do'.[119] Certain thoughts must be intentionally guarded against, so that we restrict the supply lines of the desires which enslave. 'If you have these

---

[113] Some of his important works include Long, *Stoic Studies*; *Epictetus: A Stoic and Socratic Guide to Life*, and *From Epicurus to Epictetus: Studies in Hellenistic and Roman Philosophy*.

[114] *Diss.* III.2.4. See, also, I.11 discussing the nobility of caring for children, family affection, love, etc.

[115] *Diss.* I.11.35.

[116] *Diss.* I.11.36-37.

[117] *Diss.* I.11.37-38.

[118] *Diss.* 1.11.40; cf. III.24.103.

[119] *Diss.* III.24.108.

thoughts always at hand and go over them again and again in your own mind, and keep them in readiness, you will never need a person to console you, or strengthen you.'[120]

Another exercise for progress was to live beneath one's comfort level.[121] To voluntarily live with the restrictions of an invalid, eating little food, and drinking only water would help control desire. Such ascetic practices were an empty expression of human vanity when done to impress others,[122] but powerful for developing strength to live according to the volition.[123]

The Benefits of Isolated Living

A helpful step for becoming distinct from society and its desires was to avoid over-exposure to them. 'It is impossible for the man who brushes up against the person who is covered with soot to keep from getting soot on himself.'[124] For two diametrically opposed systems of thinking were bound to impact one another and in time, one or both would conform to be like the other. Until the young student could be confident that he would be the changer and not the changed, he should be very cautious about social engagement with the uneducated.[125]

The stakes were high, and wisdom was a vulnerable possession for young students who were not yet thoroughly convinced of the philosophy they professed. The ideas learnt in the classroom were waxen, and their time of intercourse with society comparable to periods in the sun where they would quickly melt away.[126] They understood and even propagated the principles of philosophy, but their personal conviction about them was transparently weak. In public debates, their knowledge was by far superior, but their presentation lame.

> Why then are they stronger than you are? Because their rotten talk is based on convictions, but your fine talk comes merely from your lips; that's why what you say is languid and dead, and why a man may well feel nausea when he hears your exhortations and your miserable 'virtue,' which you babble to and fro.[127]

People would be persuaded by those with the most conviction, which tended to be the philosophers' opponents.[128] Epictetus was concerned for his students, and familiar with their weakness. The confidence of his students in the classroom was no guarantee of protection when they came face to face with an

---

[120] *Diss.* III.24.115-116.
[121] *Diss.* III.13.20-21.
[122] *Diss.* III.14.4-6.
[123] *Diss.* III.13.21.
[124] *Diss.* III.16.3.
[125] *Diss.* III.16.3.
[126] *Diss.* III.16.10.
[127] *Diss.* III.16.8.
[128] For 'everywhere judgement is strong, judgement is invincible', *Diss.* III.16.

opponent. In public, the propositions stated confidently in the classroom, sounded more like a whimper, or else trite religiosity, lacking the personal attachment that might have made it otherwise convincing. The result is a defeated student, or a compromised one. This regrettable state of affairs seems not so much a hypothetical occurrence, but one which Epictetus had experienced. Speaking somewhat like a parent, he knows the vulnerability of his young, and seeks their protection.

When students frequently went to and fro between school and their homeland, their resolve for the new way of life was weakened. 'It is for this reason that philosophers advise us to leave even our own countries, because old habits distract us and do not allow a beginning to be made of another custom.'[129] Students who were still vulnerable should 'flee from [their] former habits, and φεύγετε τοὺς ἰδιώτας ('flee from the laymen'), if [they] would begin to be somebody some time'.[130]

This endorsement of isolation in the formative stages of transformation does not mean Epictetus disdained the world. In dialogue with one unable to tolerate the public, Epictetus exhorts φιλανθρωπία ('benevolence, love of humanity'). The untrained masses were not a threat to one who rightly used desire and aversion, choice and refusal.

> But if you happen on a crowd, call it one of the public games, a grand assembly, a festival. Try to share in the festival with the rest of the world. For what sight is more pleasant to a lover of mankind (τῳ φιλανθρώπῳ) than a great number of men?[131]

Such passages warn against a simplistic perception of Epictetus as one who lacked any affection for his fellow man. His theoretical lack of concern for another's problems in other sections of his writings, and his wariness about the world's influence on young philosophers, must be tempered by this concern that his students have benevolence. The other extreme should also be avoided whereby the φιλανθρωπία mentioned in this text is interpreted as more than a general appreciation and fondness of fellow man.[132] In this context, Epictetus is not speaking of a love that empathises and participates in the sufferings of others; he is merely pointing out the perversion it is for people to be averse to people.

Perseverance and its Testimony

Perseverance under trial was another important trait for the philosopher. Suffering was not to be despised, but was to inspire gratitude. Such trials as poverty, imprisonment, demotion and sickness were never to be attributed to

---

[129] *Diss.* III.16.11.
[130] *Diss.* III.16.16.
[131] *Diss.* IV.4.27.
[132] *LSJ* defines the term as meaning 'humanity', 'benevolence', 'kind-heartedness', 'humane feeling', or, in a weaker sense, 'kindliness', 'courtesy'.

God's hate or even neglect, but intentional elements of a man's training process, by which God makes use of him 'as a witness to the rest of men'.[133] The nature of the witness is not specified here, but is probably referring to the demonstration that he is able to live contentedly, even under hardship, on account of his reason.

As a philosopher, you could be enchained, racked, and exiled, while living according to the προαίρεσις ('volition') with confidence, and

> with trust in Him who has called you to face them and deemed you worthy of this position, in which having once been placed you shall exhibit what can be achieved by a rational governing principle when arrayed against the forces that lie outside the province of the volition.[134]

The philosopher thus becomes a living exhibition of the principles in practice, even to death. This is one purpose greater than himself, for which the philosopher lives. He is a μάρτυς ('witness') ὑπὸ τοῦ θεοῦ κεκλημένος ('summoned by God'). For 'God says, "Go and bear witness for me; for you are worthy to be produced by me as a witness"'.[135] His important task was to bear witness to the value of philosophy.[136]

So too the quality of the messenger's witness was significant. Such a κλῆσις ('summons') was an honour, but it could be disgraced by an incongruous life.[137]

To summarise, Epictetus' Guide to Life provided a fulsome picture of what was involved in living as a Stoic. Those who admitted their ignorance would willingly receive instruction in the most fundamental concepts of life. The philosopher was to learn afresh how to discern good from evil, and live accordingly. To the theoretical framework were added concrete methods of application. This urgent task of self-reform required daily attention and became one's sole responsibility. Epictetus presented practical methods of achieving progress, one of which was isolation during the formative stage of a philosopher's training. The hindrances of the body and physical hardship were not to be escaped on a whim since the philosopher had a duty to remain as a witness at the post God had given.

For Epictetus, this path of life held great promise for the select group of philosophers who had the opportunity to follow it. In the process of describing his path of life in theoretical and practical terms, however, this chapter identified some significant inconsistencies and tensions which were also exposed by Epictetus' contemporaries.

---

[133] *Diss.* III.24.113-14.
[134] *Diss.* II.1.38-39.
[135] *Diss.* I.29.46.
[136] *Diss.* I.29.47.
[137] *Diss.* I.29.49.

CHAPTER 4

Epictetus' Guide to Death

Death was an extremely important doctrine for Epictetus, because it represented the most difficult event for philosophy to overcome. According to Epictetus, most people feared more than anything else the threat of death or death itself.[1] It followed that if students were ready for death, they would be ready for everything else. Overcoming the fear of death was necessary for achieving true 'freedom' and 'contentment', since freedom could not co-exist with 'fear, instability, and perturbation'.[2] For this reason the *Discourses* refer regularly to death and to that which follows it.

Epictetus conceded that the fear of death was normal among men: 'where death, or exile, or hardship, or ignominy faces us, there we show the spirit of running away, there we show violent agitation'.[3]

In his honesty, he included himself in the multitude who respond senselessly to death by seeking self-preservation. Socrates faced his death courageously, but Epictetus admitted his failure to emulate Socrates' fortitude:

> But if it had been you or I, we should forthwith have fallen into the philosophic vein, and said, 'One ought to repay evil-doers in kind,' and added, 'If I save my life I shall be useful to many persons, but if I die I shall be useful to no one'; yes, indeed, and if we had had to crawl out through a hole to escape, we should have done so!

According to Epictetus, Socrates benefited more people through his confident approach to death than he could have by merely living longer. Indeed, the death of Socrates was deemed more useful to the world than all he did and said while alive.[4]

Already, three important observations have emerged. First, death in itself was not to be feared. Second, and following from the first, though death was not to be feared, this truth was difficult to apply. It defied the common inclination of man to preserve his life. Third, while death itself was of no great significance, dying for the right cause may be more significant even than one's

---

[1] *Diss.* I.1.25.
[2] *Diss.* II.1.13.
[3] Musonius Rufus said, '[D]eath is a debt which every man owes. Yet it is certain that that which renders life most miserable for the aged is this very thing, the fear of death.' *MR*, XVII.110.1-4.
[4] *Diss.* IV.1.170.

life. The philosopher was in training for dying, and for giving up 'everything that [was] not [his] own'.⁵

Death as a Return to the Elements

At death, a person returns to the four basic elements: 'What there was of fire in you shall pass into fire, what there was of earth into earth, what there was of spirit into spirit, what there was of water into water'.⁶ And 'the σῶμα ('body') must be separated from the πνεῦμα ('spirit-element') just as it existed apart from it before'.⁷ The 'dust to dust' concept held by some religions in relation to the body, was equally applicable to the spirit for Epictetus. It returns to be that which it was, and apparently nothing more. Both elements of a person re-join their respective impersonal elements, and lose any form of consciousness.

Despite this common end for both body and spirit, Epictetus treated the body as lower than the spirit. Oldfather is probably helpful in reflecting this contempt for the body by rendering the Greek σωμάτιον as 'paltry body'.⁸ Epictetus' indifference, especially to the σῶμα, applies equally to a living body and a corpse.

> Why say 'die'? Make no tragic parade of the matter, but speak of it as it is: 'It is now time for the material of which you are constituted to be restored to those elements from which it came (ἐξ ὧν συνῆλθεν· εἰς ἐκεῖνα πάλιν ἀποκαταστῆναι).'⁹

A rational attitude to death negated emotions and 'tragic parades'. Epictetus noted with admiration the way Socrates 'calls death soft names, and jests at it'.¹⁰ He chose to die rather than to compromise his principles.¹¹ Death could bring with it a sense of gladness for those who had adopted the purpose of Socrates as their own. Such people 'would have been glad even to be ill, to go hungry, and to die'.¹²

An interesting description of death occurs in Chapter 8 of Book III. God usually provides all one needs, yet there comes a time when

> He does not provide the necessities for existence, He sounds the recall; He has thrown open the door and says to you, 'Go.' Where? To nothing you need fear, but back to that from which you came, to what is friendly and akin to you, to the physical elements.¹³

---

⁵ *Diss.* IV.1.172-173.
⁶ *Diss.* III.8.15.
⁷ τὸ σωμάτιον δεῖ χωρισθῆναι τοῦ πνευματίου, *Diss.* II.1.17.
⁸ e.g. 'to the paltry body of Socrates' (σωματίῳ τῷ Σωκράτους), *Diss.* I.29.16.
⁹ *Diss.* IV.7.15.
¹⁰ *Diss.* IV.1.166.
¹¹ *Diss.* IV.1.169.
¹² *Diss.* III.5.18.
¹³ Oldfather attributes this particular saying to Anaxagoras, Aristippus, Diogenes, and others. *Diss.* III.8.13-14; cf. I.9.12-13.

Sometimes, Epictetus' view of death is not so straight-forward. It is complicated by references to a descent, with or without reference to Hades as the destination.

> Have they not also much the same descent thereto, and the same world below? (οὐχὶ καὶ ἡ αὐτή που κάθοδος; τὰ κάτω τὰ αὐτά;) Are you not willing, then, to look with courage sufficient to face every necessity and want, at that place to which the wealthiest needs must go, and those who have held the highest offices, and very kings and tyrants? Only you will descend hungry.[14]

Elsewhere he says, 'What concern is it to you by what road you descend to the House of Hades? They are all equal.'[15] Such references to Hades seem to be made in an unguarded manner while making a different point, and Hades may have been used as a metaphor for death, rather than intended to expose his belief about it. For at other places he denied the existence of Hades: 'There is no Hades, nor Acheron, nor Cocytus, nor Pyriphlegethon, but everything is filled with gods and divine powers.'[16]

The confusion may also be explained by the conflicting views among his respected sources. Cleanthes taught that souls lasted until the cyclical conflagration of the world. Chrysippus taught that only the good will live until the conflagration. Seneca appears to waver between an immortal soul and a soul that perished with the body.[17] None of them, however, seems to believe in post-mortem rewards or punishments.

Despite vague allusions to a descent, or Hades, or even banquets with the gods,[18] in the end there was no life after death. Life would end at death. This is certainly the most dominant perspective throughout Epictetus' writings, and it aligns itself with the more general Stoic perception of the human being as an ensouled, mortal and rational being.[19] There was an interdependence of the soul and body: the soul requiring the body for growth and consciousness, and the body requiring the soul for its humanity.[20]

---

[14] *Diss.* III.26.5 πεινάω can refer to hunger, but also more broadly of unmet desires.
[15] *Diss.* II.6.18.
[16] *Diss.* III.13.15.
[17] Carter, *The Moral Discourses of Epictetus* (London: J.M. Dent & Sons, 1910), xiv.
[18] Great promise is held out to those who can perceive the things of life with indifference. Such people will then some day 'be worthy of the banquets of the gods'. To those who do not pursue the world's offerings, but despise them, 'then you will not only share the banquet of the gods, but share also their rule. For it was by so doing that Diogenes and Heracleitus, and men like them, were deservedly divine and deservedly so called' (*Ench.* 15).
[19] See, for example, the extended treatment given in A.A. Long, "Soul and Body in Stoicism," *The Center for Hermeneutical Studies* 36 (1980): 3.
[20] Long, "Soul and Body in Stoicism," 16.

Epictetus does, however, revert to treating the body as the mere container of the 'divine' soul or ego.[21] In order to negate the fear of death, Epictetus separates 'you' from 'your body'; the murderer does 'not murder *you* but your trivial body'.[22]

On four occasions Epictetus quotes from Plato, *Apology* 30C-D, to make this point. ἐμὲ δὲ Ἄνυτος καὶ Μέλιτος ἀποκτεῖναι μὲν δύνανται, βλάψαι δὲ οὔ ('Anytus and Meletus can kill me, but they can't hurt me').[23] While conceptually plausible, it would be a mistake to take such verses as a reference to an immortal soul. In context, Epictetus is emphasising the imperviousness of one's volition (προαίρεσις), even to the point of death.

Perhaps what has emerged most 'clearly' from this survey of death so far is that it was formulated in an unclear way. As with his perplexing theology, what was conveyed most lucidly from his view of death were the ethical implications.

Death as a 'bugbear'

In Epictetus' opinion 'Not death is dreadful, but a shameful death.' One's dignity and handling of oneself were paramount, and the way one was treated was of no consequence even to death. 'Our θάρσος ('confidence') ought, therefore, to be turned toward death, and our caution toward the *fear* of death.'[24] He laments that this is not a reality for most people, including himself: 'we do just the opposite – in the face of death we turn to flight…But Socrates did well to call all such things μορμολύκεια ('bugbears').'

A μορμολυκεῖον was a mask used in drama, which was apparently feared by children.[25] 'What is death? μορμολυκεῖον. Turn it about and learn what it is; see, it does not bite.'[26] Like a mask, death is in substance nothing to be feared.[27] Terror was a childish response.

His justification for this was, again, that death was simply the return of man from whence he came, and part of the universe moving on.[28] For τὸ σωμάτιον δεῖ χωρισθῆναι τοῦ πνευματίου ('the body must be separated from the spirit'), either now or later, just as it existed apart from it before'.[29] Appearing to

---

[21] Long, "Soul and Body in Stoicism," 16, citing Adolf Bonhöffer, *Epictet Und Die Stoa* (Stuttgart: Enke, 1890), 29-30, John M. Rist, *Stoic Philosophy* (Cambridge: CUP, 1969), 256ff.
[22] σε οὐ· ἀλλὰ τὸ σωμάτιον (*Diss.* III.13.17).
[23] *Ench.* 53.4. Cf. *Diss.* I.29.18; II.2.15; III.23.21.
[24] *Diss.* II.1.14.
[25] *Diss.* II.1.15.
[26] *Diss.* II.1.17.
[27] The English word 'bugbear' has come to mean 'a cause of excessive fear or anxiety'. *Concise Oxford Dictionary*.
[28] Oldfather comments briefly at this point on the Stoic idea of 'cyclical regeneration', whereby all things repeat themselves in cycles. *Diss.* II.1.18.
[29] *Diss.* II.1.17.

assume his audience's acceptance of this notion of separation of body from spirit, he suggests their grieving is due more to the timing of the separation, than the separation itself. It must happen, so why worry about when?

A helpful summary of these matters can be found in the conversation between θεός and the student of philosophy. When God asks, 'In your school what did you call exile and imprisonment and bonds and death and disrepute?' The answer of the student is, 'I called them τὰ ἀδιάφορα ('things indifferent').[30] Death was external to the volition, and so in theory was of no concern to the free man. In his discussion, however, Epictetus admits that this theory is difficult to live out.

The impact of death upon life

The nexus between life and death is nowhere more powerfully conveyed by Epictetus than it is in Book III, chapter 5. At his death, Epictetus accounts for his life. It is a hypothetical setting, and uses hyperbole, but this takes nothing away from the ethical intent. It crystallises much of Epictetus' teaching and exposes the way his view of death affected what he valued in life.

Many things come to light. The importance of living well is most obvious, but also significant is the way he perceived his own moral potential. His mention of 'other men' suggests he considered it important to compare well with others. His death defined the purpose of his life. In life, he wanted to be occupied with the worthy pursuit of his own προαίρεσις ('volition'), even at the moment when death overtakes him (III.5.7). If such a time of reckoning existed, and it did not, he would have lived in a way that would enable him to convince θεός of his moral strengths:

> As for me, I would fain that death overtook me occupied with nothing but my own volition, trying to make it tranquil, unhampered, unconstrained, free. This is what I wish to be engaged in when death finds me, so that I may be able to say to God, 'Have I in any respect transgressed your commands? Have I in any respect misused the resources which you gave me, or used my senses to no purpose, or my preconceptions? Have I ever found fault with you? Have I blamed your governance at all? I fell sick, when it was your will; so did other men, but I willingly. I became poor, it being your will, but with joy. I have held no office, because you did not will it, and I never set my heart upon office. Have you ever seen me for that reason greatly dejected? Have I not ever come before you with a radiant countenance, ready for any injunctions or orders you might give? And now it is your will that I leave this festival; I go, I am full of gratitude to you that you have deemed me worthy to take part in this festival with you, and to see your works, and to understand your governance.' May this be my thought, this my reading, when death comes upon me.[31]

---

[30] *Diss.* I.30.2-3.
[31] *Diss.* III.5.8-11; cf. IV.10.14-17.

When his life had been lived, his one desire is that he could say that it was *well-lived*. Before θεός, who sees all, and who knows even our thoughts, Epictetus' life pursuit was to make the above boasts an accurate description of his life. His impressive record of virtue would leave God no accusation or charge against him.

The last sentence of the quotation demonstrates the centrality of this pursuit in his life. Not only is it to be his dying thought (a place often reserved for life's most critical concerns), but making such statements at death an accurate description, was the purpose of his *life*.[32]

In summary, death's perspective is informative. It provides the conceptual vantage point from which one's life comes into perspective. The questions and priorities one should have in life are clear in light of death. What is truly important? What is good and evil? How well or how poorly am I performing in the Olympic competition? How well am I imitating θεός and giving thanks to him in all situations?

No less significant, death's perspective also bears a motivational force for life. Since Epictetus appears not to believe in life after death, nor in a moment of divine reckoning like the hypothetical one made above, the implications are primarily ethical, and are probably absent of eschatological intent. Even if there is some possibility that such a moment may follow death, however, the ethical force of the narrative is undiminished: how you live, matters.

The ethical implications of this passage are similar to those derived from a theistic conception of God: live well because θεός is watching and evaluating your life even as you live it.

> When you come into the presence of some prominent man, remember that Another looks from above on what is taking place, and that you must please him rather than this man.[33]

What is true in life is crystallised by the perspective of death.

A further corollary of Epictetus' view of death is that it raises the stakes on the question of achievability. Is this death-enlightened pursuit of progress, or perhaps even perfection, one that brings freedom or bondage? What can be said is that it is a relentless pursuit. What one might extrapolate is that with failure comes frustration, and even despair depending upon how literally one takes his desire for a blameless record at death. The attainment of his life and death pursuit may be as vulnerable as he is.

---

[32] The living application of one's death is clear in the text that proceeds the quotation (e.g. *Diss.* IV.10.18). Epictetus brought the discussion back from death to how one lives.

[33] *Diss.* I.30.1.

CONCLUSION

Anthony Long contends that Epictetus was satisfied with Stoicism.

> Having encountered Stoicism through Musonius, studying and testing it in his own life, noticing its practice by others, and teaching it, he clearly found this philosophy not only theoretically sound but also validated by his own experience. He saw no reason to experiment with other options.[34]

There are certainly passages that support this characteristically positive estimation by Long. The problem is that there are some passages that challenge it. Epictetus, through his unique self-disclosure, exposes his struggles, unfulfilled desires, and even the impossible nature of his task. This emerges not only implicitly, but explicitly, and not once, but on many occasions. This makes Long's assertion questionable when he says, 'he clearly found this philosophy not only theoretically sound but also validated by his own experience'. We do not deny however, that Epictetus learned to live with such tensions and difficulties, and maintained an important place for progress and not only perfection.

But Epictetus' personal struggles aside, one might suggest, as his contemporaries did, that there are fundamental theoretical problems with Stoicism according to Epictetus. Indeed in all forms of philosophy the sage was elusive; there were none like Plato, none who were philosophers in the purest sense, none who walked satisfactorily on this path of life.[35] Our view of Epictetus fits better with Hadot's more nuanced view:

> Both the grandeur and the paradox of ancient philosophy are that it was, at one and the same time, conscious of the fact that wisdom is inaccessible, and convinced of the need of pursuing spiritual progress.[36]

Epictetus was keenly aware that his task was greater than him and his students:

> So, although we are unable even to fulfil the profession of man, we take on the additional profession of the philosopher – so huge a burden (τηλικοῦτο φορτίον)! It is as though a man who was unable to raise ten pounds wanted to lift the stone of Aias.[37]

---

[34] A.A. Long, *Epictetus*, 17.
[35] Hadot, *Philosophy as a Way of Life*, 261.
[36] Hadot, *Philosophy as a Way of Life*, 265. A more ancient source for the same point is Quintilian, who said, 'We must ... strive after that which is highest, as many of the ancients did. Even though they believed that no sage had ever yet been found, they nevertheless continued to teach the precepts of wisdom.' Quintilian, *Institiutio Oratorica*, Preface of Book 1.
[37] *Diss.* II.9.22.

For Epictetus, if any blame was to be laid it should not be at the feet of philosophy, nor with θεός, but with man. Epictetus would argue that Stoic philosophy is satisfactory because, to the extent that one learns and applies it, one would experience freedom, happiness, and a life which follows θεός.

PART II

PHILO'S GUIDE TO LIFE AND DEATH

CHAPTER 5

Philo in his First-Century Setting

Introduction

It was but fifteen years prior to Philo Judeaus' birth (c. 20-15 BC) that the Ptolemaic dynasty ended, and Alexandria, the second Athens, was taken. The securing of Jewish rights for the Jews in Alexandria bolstered Philo's confidence to not only defend but promote the ancient tradition of Moses.[1] He believed that the Septuagint, and the path of life it contained, should be recognised by all to be God's gift to the nations. Important for this agenda was the commonly held view that the more ancient sources were purer bearers of truth. Moses had, before others, reached 'the very summit of philosophy'.[2] He was 'the Father of Greek philosophy'.[3] If people listened to Plato, they should also listen to Moses, and learn what he had to teach all nations about the path of life.

Like Part I, which discussed Epictetus' Guide to Life and Death, Part II also comprises four chapters which deal with the same topics in relation to Philo: I) the *Sitz im Leben* in which Philo operated;[4] II) Philo's views pertaining to θεός; III) Philo's Guide to Life; and IV) Philo's Guide to Death.

---

[1] See P. London, 90, 10; cf. Josephus, *Ant.* 14.113-17.
[2] David T. Runia, "Philo's *De Aeternitate Mundi*: The Problem of Its Interpretation," *Vigiliae Christianae* 35.2 (June, 1981): 2.
[3] David Winston, "Sage and Super-Sage in Philo of Alexandria," in *Pomegranates and Golden Bells : Studies in Biblical, Jewish and near Eastern Ritual, Law, and Literature in Honor of Jacob Milgrom*, ed. David P. Wright, et al. (Winona Lake: Eisenbrauns, 1995), 824. He cites *Leg.* 1.108; *QG* 3.5; 4.152, 167; *Her.* 214; *Prob.* 57; *Aet.* 18-19; *Spec.* 4.60-61.
[4] On the basis that this work is not focused primarily on the methodology and background of each author, and because excellent work has been done in recent decades on understanding Philo in his context, the orientation to Philo offered in this section has been kept relatively brief. A few works which represent significant development in Philonic scholarship in recent decades include Valentin

Philo's *Sitz im Leben*

The battle that would bring about Alexandria's demise was already mentioned for its significance in the introduction to Epictetus. The battle at Actium, in which the Roman Antony and Egyptian Cleopatra were defeated by Octavian in 31 BC, was commemorated with the founding of Epictetus' city of residence, Nicopolis, 'the city of victory'. But it was also a significant battle for the life of Philo. Following the defeat of the Ptolemaic dynasty, Egypt became a Roman province in 30 BC and Alexandria, the Ptolemaic capital and the city in which Philo was born and later worked, became a provincial city in the Roman Empire.

One could expect enormous upheaval in such a period of transition for Egypt, but Roman rule was introduced relatively smoothly over the decaying nation and capital. Some of the existing Jewish leaders and commanders simply transferred their allegiance from the Ptolemaic kings to Rome. Philo's younger brother, Tiberius Julius Alexander Major (c. 15-10 BC – AD 69), a wealthy Jew with the office of Alabarch, is one such example.[5] The fate of the Jews within what was a Hellenistic city was in new hands.

Between 30 BC and AD 117 the three significant uprisings and revolts are indicative of the underlying tensions during this period. Philo's Jewish compatriots had to live with what was 'an ancient and innate hostility' of both the Egyptians and Greeks against them.[6] Sometimes the tensions erupted into widespread racial cruelty and persecution. In AD 38 when Gaius was emperor and Flaccus was governor, there was a cruel pogrom against the Jews. Then, in AD 41, there was an armed uprising at the death of Gaius. Again in AD 66, after Nero cancelled the rights of the Jewish community, there was another conflict which was crushed by the Roman prefect, Tiberius Julius Alexander. His participation is interesting not only because he was an apostate Jew involved in the destruction of Jerusalem, but also because he was Philo's nephew.[7] His involvement reflects the complexity of the times in which Philo and the Jews lived.

Following this revolt, the impact of the Jewish war in Palestine caused tensions in Egypt in AD 66 and 70-73. Much later, in AD 115-117, there was a suicidal Messianic revolution of Jews in Cyrene and Egypt. Such tensions illustrate Claudius' earlier observation: the Jews lived 'in a city not their own'.[8]

Nikiprowetzky, *Le Commentaire De L'écriture Chez Philon D'alexandrie*, Alghj 11 (Leiden: 1977), vol. 1; David Winston, *Philo of Alexandria: The Contemplative Life, the Giants, and Selections*, ed. Richard J. Payne (Ramsey: Paulist, 1981); J.M. Dillon, *The Middle Platonists: A Study of Platonism 80 B.C. To A.D. 220* (London: Duckworth, 1977), 139-83; David T. Runia, *Philo of Alexandria and the Timaeus of Plato* (Leiden: Brill, 1986); Borgen, *Philo of Alexandria – an Exegete for His Time*.

[5] Borgen, *Philo of Alexandria – an Exegete for His Time*, 36.
[6] Borgen, *Philo of Alexandria – an Exegete for His Time*, 178.
[7] Borgen, *Philo of Alexandria – an Exegete for His Time*, 36.
[8] Cited in Borgen, *Philo of Alexandria – an Exegete for His Time*, 42.

They were not considered Egyptians by the Egyptians; the Greeks placed them in the broad 'barbarian' category, and the Romans' treatment of them was mixed.[9]

How did Philo perceive Roman rule?[10] It depended to a large extent on the ruler. He sharply criticised Gaius, but was positive towards Augustus and in a guarded way, towards Tiberius.[11] His writings have been described as 'the first detailed expression of a sustained pro-Roman attitude on the part of a Jewish intellectual'.[12] His positive estimation of Roman influence was based partly on its size, stability, moral and cultural superiority,[13] as well as their recognition of the Jews' right to live in accordance with the Law of Moses and worship of the One God.[14]

Despite the tensions, Alexandria was an important centre for Judaism in terms of its cultural and social riches (boasting Jewish literature, high ranking Jewish military officers, traders, and artisans),[15] but also in terms of its population and numerous synagogues.[16] Philo may have exaggerated when he estimated the Jewish population in Egypt was more than a million (*Flacc.* 43), which was more than Judea.[17] Regardless of the precise number, the Jews constituted a significant minority in both city and rural areas of Egypt,[18] and provided Philo with his social and political context.[19] Indeed, this Alexandrian setting provides an important hermeneutical insight into what and why Philo

---

[9] Borgen, *Philo of Alexandria – an Exegete for His Time*, 141.

[10] For a detailed treatment of this question, see Maren Niehoff, *Philo on Jewish Identity and Culture* (Tübingen: Mohr Siebeck, 2001).

[11] Niehoff, *Philo on Jewish Identity and Culture*, 119-22.

[12] Niehoff, *Philo on Jewish Identity and Culture*, 112.

[13] Niehoff, *Philo on Jewish Identity and Culture*, 112-14; *Leg.* 8, 10, 147.

[14] Borgen, *Philo of Alexandria – an Exegete for His Time*, 42.

[15] *Flacc.* 57; Ellen Birnbaum, "Portrayals of the Wise and Virtuous in Alexandrian Jewish Works: Jews Perceptions of Themselves and Others," in *Ancient Alexandria between Egypt and Greece*, ed. W.V. Harris and G. Ruffini, *Columbia Studies in the Classical Tradition* (Leiden: Brill, 2004), 126. For helpful surveys of the Jews' place in Egypt, see V. Tcherikover, "Prolegomena," in *Corpus Papyrorum Judaicarum*, ed. V. Tcherikover and A. Fuks (Cambridge: Harvard University Press, 1957), 175-83; John M.G. Barclay, *Jews in the Mediterranean Diaspora: From Alexander to Trajan (323 BCE - 117 CE)* (Edinburgh: T&T Clark, 1996); J.M. Modrzejewski, *The Jews of Egypt: From Ramses II to Emperor Hadrian* (Princeton, 1997).

[16] *P. Lond.* 1910; Cf. Ronald Williamson, *Jews in the Hellenistic World: Philo*, ed. P.R. Ackroyd, A.R.C. Leaney and J.W. Packer (Cambridge: CUP, 1989), 7; Borgen, *Philo of Alexandria – an Exegete for His Time*, 17.

[17] Williamson, *Jews in the Hellenistic World: Philo*, 7. Goodenough offers a less committed estimate of 'hundreds of thousands'. Goodenough, *An Introduction to Philo Judaeus*, 2.

[18] Birnbaum, "Portrayals of the Wise and Virtuous in Alexandrian Jewish Works: Jews Perceptions of Themselves and Others," 125.

[19] David M. Hay, "Philo's View of Himself as an Exegete," in *The Studia Philonica Annual: Studies in Hellenistic Judaism*, ed. David T. Runia (Atlanta: Scholars, 1991), 51.

Philo the Alexandrian

Philo lived in Alexandria during an illustrious period, and there had been a shift from Athens to Alexandria in terms of producing new movements and religions. Alexandria boasted the greatest library of the ancient world and the most advanced science.[20] Towards the end of Philo's life (AD 40),[21] Alexandria 'dominated the cultural and philosophical life of the Roman Empire'.[22]

It has been suggested that in the period in which Philo lived, Alexandria *was* Hellenism, and that the Jews of Alexandria were the most thoroughly Hellenised in the Diaspora.[23] Philo's writings certainly demonstrate the powerful influence of Greek literature. He cites fifty-four classical authors,[24] including poets, philosophers, and historians, and refers often to aspects of Greek culture such as athletic contests, banquets, and theatre performances.[25] He personally benefited from, and refers often to the ἐγκύκλιος ('encyclical') education as well as other sciences and philosophies studied by the Greeks.[26]

Philo respected Alexandria as a city which had not only surpassed Athens for its intellectual culture, but had also become second only to Rome in political significance.[27] Yet his affection for Alexandria was not without a keen awareness of its problems. It was within this impressive city that Philo observed almost unspeakable crimes against fellow humans.[28]

The everyday moral deficiencies of society also disturbed him. People indulged their senses through the vain pursuits of pleasure and excess, and revellers gathered

> by night and in darkness, drink-besotted, ignorant and skilful only for mischief to inflict dishonour, insult and grievous outrage on the objects of their assault. And if no one plays the umpire and comes forward to intervene and separate them they

---

[20] Goodenough, *An Introduction to Philo Judaeus*, 1.
[21] Philo calls himself an 'old man' while describing events of AD 40. Goodenough, *An Introduction to Philo Judaeus*, 2.
[22] Goodenough, *An Introduction to Philo Judaeus*, 1.
[23] Williamson, *Jews in the Hellenistic World: Philo*, 7.
[24] Samuel Sandmel, *Philo of Alexandria: An Introduction* (Oxford: OUP, 1979), 15.
[25] Goodenough, *An Introduction to Philo Judaeus*, 7.
[26] *QG* 3:19; Cf. *Ebr.* 1:33-51; *Sob* 1:9; *Mig* 1:72; *Her.* 274; *Congr.* 1:9-19; *Fug.* 1:183, 213; *Mut* 1:229; *Somn* 1:240; *Mos* 1:23; *Spec* 1:336; *Prob* 1:160; *Legat* 1:166-8; *QG* 3:23-35. For Philo, an encyclical education was a Greek education in the liberal arts, and included the study of grammar, rhetoric, geometry, arithmetic, music and astronomy. For an extended treatment see Alan Mendelson, *Secular Education in Philo of Alexandria* (Cincinnati: Union College Press, 1982).
[27] Williamson, *Jews in the Hellenistic World: Philo*, 7.
[28] See the extended record in *Flacc.* 43-132.

carry on the bout with increased licence to the finish, ready both to kill and to be killed.[29]

For others, the problem was not senselessness through intoxication, but their appetite for extravagance, beauty, and for that which was scarce. Philo provided colourful glimpses into Alexandrian life. He describes an opulent dinner scene, which followed the

> method of banqueting now prevalent everywhere through hankering for the Italian expense and luxury emulated by Greek and non-Greeks who make their arrangements ostentation rather than festivity...[30]

> Then while some tables are taken out emptied by the gluttony of the company who gorge themselves like gulls, so veraciously that they nibble even at the bones, other tables have their dishes mangled and torn and left half eaten. And when they are quite exhausted, their bellies crammed up to the gullets, but their lust (ἐπιθυμία) still ravenous, impotent for eating [they turn to the drink].[31]

In Philo's opinion, the Greek literature he esteemed was partly to blame for the lax ethical values of first-century society. Illuminating a tension between Judaism and Hellenism, Philo mentions 'two celebrated and highly notable examples' of the banquets held in Greece.[32] These events, one of which Socrates attended, 'serve to posterity as models of the happily conducted banquet'.[33] Philo disapproved of its pleasures, which included food, wine, merry-making, and advocated homosexuality.[34] To reject the values of this banquet was to reject 'conventional opinions and the commonly handed down report declaring them to have gone off with the most eminent success'.[35]

Generally speaking, however, Philo held considerable respect for philosophers and philosophy. The Jews in Alexandria, with significant social opposition and theological divergence from the Greek polytheists and Egyptians, saw in the philosophers a respected element of Hellenism with

---

[29] *Contempl.* 42-43; cf. 46-47.
[30] *Contempl.* 48-49; cf. 50-59.
[31] *Contempl.* 55.
[32] *Contempl.* 57. Philo's literary agenda should be remembered when drawing from such social descriptions. In this section of *De vita contemplativa*, he is not setting out to provide a description of what was common, but what were the problematic elements of society. Philo flags the prominence of such classic vices (κακίαι) as folly (ἀφροσύνη), intemperance (ἀκολασία), cowardice (δειλία), and injustice (ἀδικια).[32] The place of this passage in *De vita contemplativa* is to provide a contrasting foil with which he can present a better alternative: the darker the problem, the more necessary his solution. To treat such reports as objective descriptions of everyday life would be to over-extend their literary function. So, too, it should be remembered that Philo belonged to, and may more often describe, the habits of wealthy Alexandrians. Nevertheless, there seems no reason to doubt that his descriptions of these situations, for whatever literary reason, still took place as described.
[33] *Contempl.* 57.
[34] *Contempl.* 57-62.
[35] *Contempl.* 64.

which they could claim a much-needed degree of solidarity.[36] The Jews, educated in the Scriptures, also learned Homer, Hesiod, and the philosophers, most of whom had a higher view of God than the idol-worshiping Greeks.[37] 'Not idols did these philosophers worship, but one God, invisible, immaterial, good, and just.'[38] And Aristotle 'endeavoured to prove by arguments that there cannot be more than one god'.[39] It was probably true that some Jews besides Philo also tried to show that their God, and not one of the gods of popular religion, was the God of philosophers.[40]

Philo the Jew

Having observed the Greek and Alexandrian influences on Philo, it must be remembered that Philo was still very much a Ἰουδαῖος ('Jew' or 'Judean'),[41] in his views as well as by birth. At least once he travelled to Jerusalem where he prayed and sacrificed at the temple. He represented Jewish interests in the Roman world, being entrusted to lead a delegation to the contemptuous Caligula on behalf of the persecuted Jews. The mission was a complete failure, though this was probably more on account of Caligula's contempt and mockery than any inadequacy of Philo.[42]

Besides being their defender, Philo also saw himself as a proponent of the Jewish Law to the world. In *Philo of Alexandria – An Exegete for His Time*, Borgen highlights Philo's agenda to demonstrate that the Septuagint was God's 'gift to the nations', and that the Law resonated at many points with the Hellenistic philosophical traditions.[43] With a foot in each world, he endeavoured to elucidate the congruence between the two. Mortley, however, highlighted an important principle in the process of synthesising ideas from two traditions that may have been under-appreciated by Borgen: that the older takes

---

[36] See the study by Sarah J.K. Pearce, *The Land of the Body: Studies in Philo's Representation of Egypt* (Tübingen: Mohr Siebeck, 2007).
[37] Harry Austryn Wolfson, *Philo: Foundations of Religious Philosophy in Judaism, Christianity, and Islam*, 2 volumes (Cambridge: Harvard University Press, 1968), 17-18.
[38] Cited in Wolfson, *Philo: Foundations of Religious Philosophy*, 18.
[39] *Phys.* VIII.6.259a, 8ff. Cited in Wolfson, *Philo: Foundations of Religious Philosophy*, 18.
[40] Wolfson, *Philo: Foundations of Religious Philosophy*, 19.
[41] It is difficult to define in detailed terms what a first-century Ἰουδαῖος was. For simplicity we have rendered Ἰουδαῖος as 'Jew.' The term is problematic, however, because of geographical and cultural differences among those referred to as Ἰουδαῖοι in the first century AD.
[42] Tcherikover, "Prolegomena," 69.
[43] *Mos.* 2.41. Borgen, *Philo of Alexandria – an Exegete for His Time*, 140-43. For a focused study on Philo's view of the superiority of Jewish worship, and that Philo's Judaism was, in a sense, 'the ultimate Hellenistic cult', see Jutta Leonhardt-Balzer, *Jewish Worship in Philo of Alexandria* (Tübingen: Mohr Siebeck, 2001), 293-95.

precedence over the newer.⁴⁴ The oldest was the truest, and therefore Moses was a more fundamental source of truth even than Plato. Using an allegorical method of interpretation, which was commonly used among Jewish and Hellenistic scholars alike, Philo sought to persuade Jew and Greek to give due reverence to Moses' writings. This idea may have caught on in some circles beyond the Jews. Numenius, the neopythagorean made the remarkable claim that Plato was nothing but a Μωυσῆς ἀττικίζων ('Moses who spoke in Attic').⁴⁵

That later Greeks were aware of Philo's writings raises the question: who were the initial recipients? The answer is unclear, and continues to be debated. Sterling asserts, on admittedly thin evidence, that the most probable setting was a private school owned by the wealthy Philo.⁴⁶ He suggests that classes were held in a private residence or other building purchased for that purpose.⁴⁷ They were 'a sophisticated group who knew the biblical text exceptionally well and were capable of appreciating extended philosophical expositions of it'.⁴⁸

Any attempt to describe the audience requires some conjecture, and the possibilities are broadly ranging. David Hay, for example, suggests a largely Jewish readership that had knowledge of the Scriptures, of allegorical exegesis, and who knew of Philo and tended to side with him on the matters he raised.⁴⁹ Yet this detail is followed by a concession for broader possibilities when he acknowledges that Philo's intended audience may not have been limited to Alexandria, nor limited even to his own time.⁵⁰ One such broader possibility, which is yet to be discounted, is Runia's view that Philo's writings are *'scriptural commentaries in the technical sense of the term*, reflecting exegesis in the synagogue and based on the question and answer method used there'.⁵¹

Philo and the σοφισταί

In Part I of his *Philo and Paul among the Sophists,* Bruce Winter devoted five chapters to the description of first-century Alexandrian sophists. The evidence Philo's corpus provides about the Second Sophistic movement had not been

---

⁴⁴ Mortley, "The Past in Clement of Alexandria: A Study of an Attempt to Define Christianity in Socio-Cultural Terms," 193.

⁴⁵ Fr. 8, 30; cited in David T. Runia, *Philo in Early Christian Literature: A Survey*, ed. Aschkenasy *et al.* (Assen: Van Gorcum, 1993), 3.8. Cf. Clement of Alexandria, *Str.* 1.150.

⁴⁶ For comments regarding Philo's wealthy family, see, also, Goodenough, *An Introduction to Philo Judaeus*, 2-3.

⁴⁷ Gregory E. Sterling, "'The School of Sacred Laws': The Social Setting of Philo's Treatises," *Vigiliae Christianae* 53 (1999), 163.

⁴⁸ Sterling, "'The School of Sacred Laws'" 159. The extent to which the scriptures had been canonized by this time is also not transparent from Philo's writings.

⁴⁹ Hay, "Philo's View of Himself as an Exegete," 51-52.

⁵⁰ Hay, "Philo's View of Himself as an Exegete," 52.

⁵¹ Runia, *Philo of Alexandria and the Timaeus of Plato*, 19. Italics his.

previously examined.[52] From the writings of Philo, Dio of Prusa (c. AD 40-112), and a student engaged in the study of rhetoric (in *P.Oxy.* 2190),[53] Winter described the sophists' expensive and prominent schools, the emphases of their curriculum, the large number of students, as well as some detail into the personal life of a sophist student.[54]

Building on this research, further reflection will be given to Philo's perception of the Alexandrian sophists by looking again at a polemical treatise against them: *Quod deterius potiori insidiari soleat* ('That the Worse is Accustomed to be Always Plotting Against the Better').[55]

A couple of caveats are required before proceeding. First, Philo could use the word σοφιστής to refer literally to a sophist, who belonged to the Sophistic movement.[56] At other times, however, as was the case with Epictetus and various Greek and Roman authors, the term σοφιστής could be used, often pejoratively, to describe those who were not sophists *per se*, but who were deemed to be acting like them. Due consideration needs to be given to this distinction.

Second, in order to draw attention to the significant role the sophists and sophistry play throughout Philo's corpus, and to avoid dependence on *Quod deterius potiori insidiari soleat*, reference will be made to other Philonic treatises which describe the sophists (in both the literal and broad sense of the word σοφισταί). Due consideration has been given to context of each of these references to the σοφισταί.

The question being addressed by *Quod deterius potiori insidiari soleat* is, 'wherein lies the good?' And it was Philo's contention that the ἀγαθός ('good') was to be sought in things of the soul and not in external things.[57] Following his introduction to the problem of sophistry in the first paragraph of the treatise, Philo repeatedly engages with sophistry and the present-day sophists throughout the discourse.

---

[52] Winter, *Philo and Paul among the Sophists*, 59.
[53] For the text and comment on this papyrus, see C.H. Roberts, "The Greek Papyri," in *The Legacy of Egypt*, ed. J.R. Harris (Oxford: Clarendon, 1971), 145-47; J. Rea, "A Student's Letter to His Father: *P.Oxy.* XVIII 2190 Revised," *ZPE* 99 (1993).
[54] Winter, *Philo and Paul among the Sophists*, 87-89.
[55] References made to this treatise will be made in the text. But in order to draw attention to the significant role the sophists and sophistry play throughout Philo's corpus, and to avoid dependence on this treatise alone to elucidate the sophistic opposition in Philo, references will be given to other Philonic treatises in the footnotes which express similar sentiments.
[56] In referring to the 'Second Sophistic' it is not implied that the sophists had an identifiable agenda. As Goldhill rightly cautions, 'the criteria for inclusion are difficult to pin down'. Simon Goldhill, ed., *Being Greek under Rome: Cultural Identity, the Second Sophistic and the Development of Empire* (Cambridge: CUP, 2001), 14.
[57] E.g. *Det.* 1, 7, 9, 35, 158.

The stage was set with Cain's deception of Abel (*Det.* 1). Cain invited him to a field of 'rivalry and contention' so that Cain might 'convince him by force, using plausible and probable sophisms' (§1). Abel became victim to Cain's sophistry in a way that Jacob did *not* when he fled from Laban (§ 4-5). Jacob was not only wise like Abel, but was discerning as to the nature of sophistry and battled against ignorance (§10, cf. *Agr.* 16). Confusion brought by the sophists in this matter of what was truly good had great potential to detract one from the way (ὁδός, § 10).

Following Abel, Jacob and other wise men since Abel understood that the good consists only of things related to the soul, and that such knowledge leads to a virtuous life.[58] Cain, Laban,[59] and the (ancient) 'sophists' were charmed by the outward senses towards external things. Worse still, they deliberately sought to persuade others to live similarly. In this way, it can be said that 'the worse (person and philosophy) was accustomed to be always plotting against the better'. It was so in Cain's day, in Jacob's day, and also, much to Philo's dismay, in his own day.

There were two parties: 'the lovers of virtue' on the one hand and the sophists, or 'lovers of pleasure', on the other. 'Cain' was the way Philo referred in shorthand to Cain's typological descendants—those who follow sophistic deceptiveness and 'self-loving' ways.[60]

Within this treatise, Philo offered three extended dialogues which acquaint readers with the sophists of his time. In the first (§ 33ff.), Philo presented the essence of the sophists' position on the good. Their beliefs, expressed with characteristic rhetorical skill, emerged as they began what was both a defence of their practices as well as an offence against the so-called 'lovers of virtue'. Rhetorical questions were used to great effect: 'Is not the body the house of the soul?' From this premise, which contravened the more traditional conception of the body as the 'prison-house' of the soul, the sophists continued their persuasive discourse, arguing that pleasure, enjoyments, and delights were entirely appropriate for the house of the soul. It is a masterfully constructed justification for a view contrary to Philo's, and worth quoting in full.

> Is not the body the house of the soul? Should we not take care of the house so that it may not become ruinous? Are not the eyes and the ears, and all the other outward senses, guards, as it were, and friends of the soul? Ought we not, then, honour men's friends and allies equally with themselves? And has nature made pleasures and enjoyments, and all the delights which are spread over the whole of life for the dead, or for those who have never even had any existence at all, and not rather for those who are alive? And ought we not procure for ourselves riches,

---

[58] Cf. *Mut.* 225.
[59] Cf. *Legat.* 3.16.
[60] Conversely, Abel represents those who are 'God-loving' (*Legat.* 3.32) and 'lovers of virtue' (3.33).

and glory, and honours, and authority, and all other things of that sort, which are the only means of living not only safely, but happily?[61]

For the multitude who sought to fulfil their desires according to external impressions (§173-4), the sophists provided a reasoned basis for self-indulgent living.[62] But their homily was not complete until it mockingly pitted the attractiveness of body-honouring living against the pitiable 'lovers of virtue'.

> And our opponents, the 'lovers of virtue' are a witness (μάρτυς) of what we are saying—they are inglorious, easily to be despised, lowly, in need, more dishonourable than subjects or even than slaves, sordid, pale, cadaverous-looking, bearing want and hunger in their countenances, full of diseases, men who would be glad to die.[63]

It was a pitiable outcome that the 'lovers of virtue' failed to share in the prosperity of those who held the sophists' view:

> But those who take care of themselves are men of reputation, rich, leaders, men in the enjoyment of praise and honour; moreover, they are healthy, stout, and vigorous; living delicately, nursed in luxury, strangers to labour, living in the constant company of pleasure, and using all their outward senses to bring delights to the soul, which is capable of receiving them all.[64]

The opponents were identified as the σοφισταί in *Det.* 38-39, and again as the debate continues in §78-79. Though the label of σοφιστής was not repeated for each reference to them, they were identified with reference to their forefather Cain (in the first and last verse, and scattered throughout the treatise).[65]

Philo exhorted his audience about how they ought respond (§35-42) to the sophists:

> In this manner, then, it is useful to oppose those who are ostentatious about doctrines. For if we have been well exercised in various types of discourses, we shall no longer stumble through inexperience and want of acquaintance with the manoeuvres of sophists. But rising up and making a firm and resolute stand against them, we shall with ease escape from their artificial entanglements. But they, when their tricks have once been found out, will appear to be exhibiting the conduct of sparrers rather than of regular combatants. For they too, in their own opinion, get great credit by their style of beating the air; but when they come to a real contest they meet with no moderate disgrace.[66]

The sophists entangled their audience, but their arguments were without substance. They were a threat not far removed from Philo's audience, particularly endangering those who were bold or foolhardy enough to engage with them εἰς σοφιστικὸν ἀγῶνα ('in a sophistic contest'):

---

[61] *Det.* 33.
[62] Cf. *Opif.* 45; *Legat.* 74.
[63] *Det.* 34.
[64] *Det.* 34; cf. *Agr.* 143; *Mig.* 76
[65] *Det.* 1:1, 32, 47, 50, 61, 68, 74, 78, 96, 103, 119, 140-41, 163, 165-168, 177-78.
[66] *Det.* 41.

And if anyone is adorned as to his soul with all imaginable virtues, and yet has paid no attention to the art of speaking and arguing, if he only preserves silence he will obtain safety, a prize won without danger.[67] But if he comes forth like Abel into a sophistic contest, he will be thrown down before he has obtained a firm footing.[68]

Unlike the philosophers, who were generally regarded as being earnest in their pursuit of truth,[69] the sophists were intentionally false and thus a chief accusation against them was not merely error, but deceit.[70] Those whom the sophists defeated, or worse persuaded, lost their footing. The sophists were opposed to the truth,[71] which they twisted to persuade their audience to believe that which they knew was fallacy.[72] The effect was that they were not only overcome by their adversaries,[73] but were said to 'die to the life of knowledge':

> And this ought to happen to those who allow themselves to be deceived by the sophists; for when they are not able to find a solution for their sophisms, believing their fallacies as if they were true statements, they die as to the life of knowledge.[74]

The sophists angered Philo for numerous reasons. They hindered earnest seekers from finding the truth, and caused those who were travelling with piety on the 'royal' (βασιλικός) or 'middle' (μέσος) path, to stumble.[75] And besides the content of their teaching, it was the facetious manner with which they taught alternative views, delighting in being contentious, and mocking views held dear by their opponents.[76]

In *Quis rerum divinarum heres sit* 246, Philo lists some of the favourite matters about which sophists and philosophers were 'bitterly divided',[77] such as the creation or otherwise of the universe, the destruction of the universe, as well as matters relating to the providence of the Creator. The philosophers

---

[67] Cf. *Agr.* 164; *Conf.* 39.
[68] *Det.* 42; cf. 35, 39; *Agr.* 162.
[69] *Cong.* 79.
[70] *Gig.* 159; *Mut.* 240; *Mig.* 83.
[71] *Agr.* 159.
[72] *Agr.* 164.
[73] *Agr.* 159, 163, 168.
[74] *Agr.* 164.
[75] *Agr.* 177; *Post.* 101.
[76] *Fug.* 209 – 'And by his saying, "His hand shall be against every man, and every man's hand against him," he means to describe the design and plan of life of a sophist, who professes an over-curious scepticism, and who rejoices in disputatious arguments (χαίροντος ἐριστικοῖς).'
[77] Runia, "Philo's "De Aeternitate Mundi": The Problem of Its Interpretation," 132. Cf. *Aet.* 132. It seems that both the sophists and philosophers are being described in this passage. Throughout the treatise, Philo speaks positively of natural philosophy (*Her.* 98, 152) and negatively of sophistry (*Her.* 85, 304). He may not be describing sophists immediately here, but his point was to show that the true seekers of wisdom (philosophers) resembled the sophists in their discordant views on this topic.

resembled the sophists in the sense that they held no unified position about such matters, and debated about them not only with others but among themselves.

Although Cain was the chief representative of the 'sophists' in *Quod deterius potiori insidiari soleat*, it was not without mention of Balaam, who was in other treatises, the quintessential 'sophist'.[78]

> For neither was the sophist, Balaam, who was an empty multitude of contrary and contending doctrines, when he was desirous to imprecate curses upon and to injure the good man, able to do so; since God turned his curses into a blessing, in order to correct the unjust man of wickedness and to display his own love of virtue.[79]

A further very serious problem with the sophists was that while they were somewhat pretentiously orthodox in the Greek philosophical sense by their promotion of the classical virtues, they disclosed their true nature by living according to the virtues' antonyms.[80]

Lastly, the sophists' teachings were judged internally inconsistent, and at other times built upon myths.[81] Their rhetorical skills could not be denied; they were 'learned as far as words go' but lacked real knowledge.[82] They practised 'sophistry rather than wisdom, and juggling tricks in preference to the truth'.[83]

---

[78] *Mut.* 202-3; *Conf.* 165.

[79] *Det.* 71.

[80] *Det.* 72 says, 'But it is the nature of sophists to have for enemies the faculties which are in them, while their language is at variance with their thoughts and their thoughts with their language, and while neither is in the least degree consistent with the other. At all events, they wear out our ears [cf. *Leg.* 3.232; *Agr.* 136], arguing that justice is a great bond of society, that temperance is a profitable thing, that continence is a virtuous thing, that piety is a most useful thing, and, of each other virtue, that it is a most wholesome and saving quality. And, on the other hand, that injustice is a quality with which we ought to have no truce, that intemperance is a diseased habit, that impiety is scandalous, and so going through every kind of wickedness, that each sort is most pernicious.' cf. *Det.* 73: 'And, nevertheless, they never cease showing by their conduct that their real opinion is the reverse of their language. But, when they extol prudence (φρόνησις) and temperance (σωφροσύνη) and justice (δικαιοσύνη) and piety (εὐσέβεια), they then show that they are, above all measure, senseless (ἀφραίνω), and intemperate (ἀκολασταίνω), and unjust (ἀδικέω), and impious (ἀσεβέω); in short, that they are throwing into confusion and overturning all divine and human regulations and principles. (cf. *Post.* 86). Note also the similar sentiments expressed in *Det.* 101-103, where Philo is again referring to the sophists. That he has the sophists in mind is evident from his reference to their own argument which justifies cormorant-like excess (101, 103), they have the faculty of eloquence (102), and his mention of the proto-sophist, Cain (103). For comment on these texts see, also, Winter, *Philo and Paul among the Sophists*, 156; D. Zeyl, "Socratic Virtue and Happiness," *Archiv für Geschichte der Philosophie* 64 (1982); C.J. Rowe, *Plato* (Brighton: Harvester, 1984).

[81] *Praem.* 8.

[82] *Det.* 43-44.

[83] *Praem.* 8.

For of what use is it to say what is excellent, but to think and to do what is most shameful? This is the way of the sophists. For those who make long speeches about prudence and perseverance, annoy the ears even of those who are very fond of hearing good conversation; and yet, in their designs and in the actions of their lives they are found to err.[84]

Sophistic reason, though appearing to promote virtue, was actually the 'enemy of virtue'.[85] As a result, even while they were alive in the body, all good things were dead in their souls – none of the sophists were really alive.[86] According to Philo, they thought and practised shameful things,[87] and claimed to benefit their soul by prioritising external pleasures. The reality was, however, that such a φαῦλος ('worthless man') harmed not only his soul but also the house of the soul, which he pampered and indulged. Such a man awaited God's judgement.[88]

Philo stressed that sophistry was not only powerless to help one escape the passions, it actually worsened one's condition. It promised freedom but failed to deliver it, as experience had shown:

> they are found to be sophists rather than philosophers: of these men the language indeed is praiseworthy but the life is blameable; for they are powerful at speaking, but are powerless (ἀδύνατος) to do what is best.[89]

And again,

> Therefore a vast number of those who are called sophists, being admired in their respective cities, and having attracted almost all the world to look upon them with honour, on account of the accuracy of their definitions and their excessive cleverness in inventions, have grown old while vehemently bound by the passions, and have passed their whole life in them, in no respect differing from private individuals who are of no account and are held in no consideration. For which reason the lawgiver very admirably compares those of the sophists who live in this manner to the race of swine (σῦς), who live a life in no respect pure or brilliant, but foul and muddy (βορβορώδης), and who are devoted to the basest habits.[90]

The sophists had no excuse for living in like manner to swine because their promotion of the virtues proved they knew much better. Nevertheless, they undervalued wisdom, seeking 'only a discovery of plausible arguments and not...a certain belief in well-assured knowledge of facts'.[91] The sophists' path was also regrettable because although they

> have received that greatest of all the blessings bestowed upon man by nature, namely speech, they have abused and corrupted it, employing it ungratefully and

---

[84] *Post.* 86.
[85] *Somn.* 2.281.
[86] *Det.* 74.
[87] τὰ δ' αἴσχιστα καὶ φρονοῦντες καὶ ἐπιτηδεύοντες ἀεἰαιεί ἁλίσκεσθε, *Det.* 74.
[88] *Mut.* 203.
[89] *Cong.* 57.
[90] *Agr.* 143-4.
[91] *Mig.* 171.

treacherously, to the injury of her who has bestowed it. Such are flatterers, impostors, devisers of plausible sophistries, men who rather cultivate the skill to delude and to cheat, and who have no concern to speak truly, and these men study indistinctness. Now indistinctness is equivalent to deep darkness in discourse.[92]

Rightly appreciated, truth which leads to virtue had a beauty and harmony, even if communicated plainly.[93] Philo compared this natural beauty of truth with the admittedly beautiful rhetoric of the sophists:

> And in the account of the creative power of God you will find no cunningly devised fable,[94] but only unalloyed laws of truth firmly established.[95]

To summarise this discussion of the σοφισταί, with particular reference to *Quod deterius potiori insidiari soleat,* Philo provided vivid descriptions of the sophists' contemptible methods and morality in the process of establishing his point that the good lies in the things of the soul and not in external things.

The sophists, in both present and past (stereotyped) forms, provided Philo with an apt contrastive foil. Their reputation among philosophers for indefensible arguments and for lifestyles which violated the very virtues they promoted, made them a most obvious opponent for this particular topic.

The sophists posed a real threat to the pious. It was important for Philo that representatives of his own community be equipped to defeat them in the context of debate, and so prevent the more vulnerable among them from being deceived.[96]

Philo's Use of Source Material

Philo was deeply interested in the concept of truth.[97] In a small section of his *De aeternitate mundi,* as one example, he mentioned a multitude of terms

---

[92] *Her.* 302.
[93] Cf. *Cher.* 9-10; *Sob.* 1.9; *Mig.* 85; *Spec.* 3.77; *Congr.* 18; *Det.* 111. Agricultural and medical analogies are used to convey the same sentiments, urging that we give pre-eminence to the soul, and to virtuous living. See, for example, *Mut.* 224; *Agr.* 14-15.
[94] Cf. *Agr.* 164.
[95] *Det.* 125; cf. *Opif.* 157: 'And these things are not mere fabulous inventions, in which the race of poets and sophists delights, but are rather types shadowing forth some allegorical truth'; *Mig.* 72: 'Others, again, have been exceedingly skilful in explaining their ideas, but very bad hands at forming intentions, as, for instance, those who are called sophists, for the mind of these sophists is destitute of all harmony and of all real learning; but their speeches, which are uttered by the organs of their voice, are full of music and beauty.'
[96] *Cong.* 18; *Aet.* 132; *Mig.* 82; *Her.* 125, 304. 'But if once, all unreal plausibilities are convicted and refuted by true proofs, and if their offenses are shown to be full and running over, then we shall flee away without ever turning back, and as it were slipping our cables we shall set sail from the region of falsehoods and sophistries, hastening to cast anchor in the safe harbours and havens of truth' *Her.* 305.
[97] Forms of ἀλήθεια appear over 400 times throughout the Philonic corpus, yet his level of interest in the concept of truth extends beyond his use of this single noun.

related to truth: 'examine the argument', 'evident', 'demonstration', 'proofs', 'inventor of fables', 'their falsehoods', 'fiction of fable', and 'truth—that most valuable possession'.[98] He believed that 'truth is beyond all things beautiful, as falsehood on the contrary is enormously ugly'.[99]

As previously mentioned, an important aspect of his approach to source material was a priority for those which were older. This priority is often implicit, as it is in his *De aeternitate mundi* ('Eternity of the World'), where Philo began with the philosophers, then to Hesiod (who is above even Socrates, *Aet.* 18), and concluded with Moses, who was the purest source because he preceded them all.

> Chaos in Aristotle's opinion is a space because a body must have something there already to hold it, but some of the Stoics suppose that it is water and that the name is derived from its diffusion. But whichever of these is right Hesiod very clearly states the view that the world is created, and long before Hesiod Moses the lawgiver of the Jews said in the Holy Books that it was created and imperishable.[100]

This quotation also serves as an illustration of Philo's fascinating assimilation of Scriptural and philosophical ideas. He knows truth comes from God in the Torah, but it was also found in the poets and philosophers. As Dio of Prusa said, 'if one hears words of wisdom, we must believe that they too were sent by god.'[101] His attitude to these two major sources of authority will now be discussed.

The Authority of Scripture

What did Philo perceive 'Scripture' to be? The first five books of the Old Testament, referred to in this monograph as the Law, Torah or Pentateuch, were esteemed more than any other source for their truth, reason, and wisdom. 'The Laws of Moses are "stamped with the seals of nature itself".'[102]

To Philo, the Jewish legal code coincided with universal cosmic principles. There was no sense therefore, that the Law was threatened or nullified by the philosophical principles derived later.[103] There was an exciting congruence between the two traditions. Therefore, one can learn principles by training under the Law or indeed through a good (Greek) education.[104] Philo was trained in both the Law and in philosophy, and considered both beneficial.[105]

---

[98] *Aet.*. 56-58.
[99] *Aet.*. 76.
[100] *Aet.* 19.
[101] Dio, *Or.* 12.
[102] *Mos.* 2:14.
[103] Borgen, *Philo of Alexandria – an Exegete for His Time*, 147.
[104] 'δι' ἀγωγῆς νομίμου ἢ καὶ παιδεύσεως ὀρθῆς' (*Det.* 16). The ἢ καὶ construction is captured well by 'or indeed' in this concluding sentence. It is not a conjunction which is necessarily between two mutually exclusive alternatives (either law or education), but is also used as a conjunction between two similar or related terms

And [Moses'] exordium, as I have already said, is most admirable; embracing the creation of the world, under the idea that the law corresponds to the world and the world to the law, and that a man who is obedient to the law, being, by so doing, a citizen of the world, arranges his actions with reference to the intention of nature, in harmony with which the whole universal world is regulated.[106]

By Philo's time, there was some recognition of a completed and authoritative canon of Jewish Scripture, though the word 'canon' understates the level of fluidity that still existed in the minds of some Jews.[107] Philo refers to 'laws and oracles pronounced through the prophets and hymns' which may, as Birnbaum argues, refer to the 'tripartite division of the Hebrew Bible into Torah, Prophets, and Writings'.[108] Clearly then he was aware of other books, but he treats them as less significant for his purposes.[109] The statistics of Philo's usage illustrate the priority given the Pentateuch. Of the 1161 quotations of the Hebrew Bible in Philo, only 41 refer to texts outside the Pentateuch.[110] Quotations from the Psalms make up 20 of these 41 occasions, which means the remaining 33 books of the Old Testament receive the attention of only 21 direct quotations.[111] The term 'Scripture' in Philonic studies should, therefore, be informed by this Pentateuchal priority.

If *The Letter of Aristeas* offers a true account, the translation of the Hebrew Torah into Greek began during the reign of Ptolemy II Philadelphus (284-246 BC) and was completed towards the mid-second century BC.[112] In any case, the

---

(law or also/even an education). See, for example, the range of use in 2 Cor. 1:13; Rom. 2:15; 1 Cor. 16:6.

[105] We will consider this in more detail, however in *Praem.* 11, Philo asserts that the virtues excite an interest in philosophy, which then further enlighten the virtuous, the result of which is greater happiness.

[106] Opif. 3.

[107] Jesus, for example, referred to πάντα τὰ γεγραμμένα ἐν τῷ νόμῳ Μωσέως καὶ προφήταις καὶ ψαλμοῖς ('all the things written in the Law of Moses, the Prophets, and the Psalms'), Lk. 24:44; and Luke refers to these as the αἱ γραφαὶ ('the Scriptures'), v. 45.

[108] Ellen Birnbaum, "Philo on the Greeks: A Jewish Perspective on Culture and Society in First-Century Alexandria," in *The Studia Philonica Annual*, ed. David T. Runia and Gregory E. Sterling (Providence: Brown Judaic Studies, 2001), 116.

[109] Birnbaum, "Philo on the Greeks: A Jewish Perspective on Culture and Society in First-Century Alexandria," 115.

[110] David T. Runia, "Philo's Reading of the Psalms," in *In the Spirit of Faith: Studies in Philo and Early Christianity in Honor of David Hay*, ed. D.T. Runia and G.E. Sterling (Providence: Brown Judaic Studies, 2001), 114, citing H. Burkhardt, *Die Inspiration Heiliger Schriften Bei Philo Von Alexandrien* (Basel: Giessen, 1988), 134.

[111] As Runia states, '"Scripture" is effectively restricted to the books of Moses, i.e. the Pentateuch. The remaining books of the Septuagint are attributed to 'disciples of Moses', and possess only derivative authority.' Runia, *Philo in Early Christian Literature: A Survey*, 38.

[112] Borgen, *Philo of Alexandria – an Exegete for His Time*, 38. For the Ptolemaic rulers and administrators, it enabled them to understand the customs and convictions of the

translation of Israel's history was immensely valuable to Philo, who sought to show the significance of these Scriptures for the Jews and Greeks of his own day. He drew a contemporary message from the ancient text through allegorical readings of its stories, and spiritualised the details of genealogies, names and numbers.[113]

As a Jew, Philo had a clear allegiance to the Scriptures of his people, who perceived them to contain words from God himself.[114] He expressed delight in the law, and considered, for example, that the law of jubilee 'exceeded every philanthropy' (πᾶσαν ὑπερβάλλει φιλανθρωπίαν).[115] Much more than a dry legal code, many feasted abundantly 'and revelled in its most lovely ordinances' (ἐντρυφησάντων ἡδίστοις ἅμα καὶ καλλίστοις δόγμασιν).[116]

Philo's view of Scripture as God's 'revelation' shaped his methodology. Since Scripture bore a message of great importance, his greatest contribution would come by discerning and conveying it, rather than creating his own message. A growing consensus has developed in recent years among Philonic scholars that Philo was, above all other designations, an exegete, who sought to explain the truths contained in Scripture. Concluding his survey of recent scholarship in this matter, David Runia writes,

> The most important result of the above survey is the complete agreement on the fact that Philo must be regarded first and foremost as exegete of Mosaic scripture. The primary focus of his activity is on explaining the scriptural text, and above all on penetrating to its hidden deeper meaning. Philo has apologetic aims, arguably also philosophical aims, but these are primarily effectuated by means of his

---

Jews living among them. This need was likely the motivation for commissioning the translation (according to Aristeas). For the Jewish people, it gave all of them access to the laws and customs which they were permitted to observe. For Philo, the significance of having the Law in the language of the world is difficult to overstate. He saw little reason to seek the meaning of the Hebrew text, instead commenting on nuances of Greek phrases which indicate that he considered the LXX was verbally inspired and correct. An exception to this however, is his interest in the Hebrew translation of names. See Goodenough, *An Introduction to Philo Judaeus*, 9. It was a 'universal and eschatologically significant work: these texts contained God's cosmic and universal Laws, to be revealed to all nations, so that in the end all nations should make them their own and become proselytes'. Cf. Mos. 2.44; Borgen, *Philo of Alexandria – an Exegete for His Time*, 143. Since that time, on the Island of Pharos, where the translation took place, was an annual festival which included Jews and Greeks. Philo understood this mutual appreciation for the event 'as a sign of the coming universal recognition of the Laws of Moses. The fact that Gentiles attended this celebration may suggest that among Philo's readers were such Gentiles who saw the Laws of Moses as significant for them.' Borgen, *Philo of Alexandria – an Exegete for His Time*, 24.

[113] Runia, *Philo in Early Christian Literature: A Survey*, 38-39.
[114] *Det.* 126; *Praem.* 53.
[115] *Virt.* 99.
[116] *Virt.* 99.

exegetical activity. It is easy to take this insight for granted, but we should bear in mind that it is in fact still quite new.[117]

It was as an exegete, belonging to a wider community of exegetes, that Philo worked as a philosopher and exposed these 'hidden deeper' meanings of Scripture.[118]

The Authority of Other Sources

It may be impossible to trace the development of Philo's view that the Laws of Moses and philosophy were to a significant degree complementary. Besides the theological resemblances, political reasons have been mentioned for emphasising similarities with Hellenistic thought. At some stage in his life, however, Philo came to the significant realisation that the Greek system had problems that the Jews could help solve. One such problem, conceded by Plato and Aristotle, was that the perfect state was unattainable. Why? The inevitable imperfections in the law and in the Greek legal system would mean an imperfect society.[119] Greek law may have been imperfect, but Moses' Law was not.

Further, the Torah not only set ethical standards, it also implanted the virtue that was essential for meeting them.[120] This 'Greek' problem of imperfect law was only one of a number of areas in which the Torah could contribute to human understanding and progress. While we will argue that Philo's loyalty to biblical principles outweighed his loyalty to any other source, there was certainly a perceived mutual benefit to be gained by inviting the two great traditions to be in dialogue. Before considering in more detail the other sources Philo respected, brief mention will be made of those he rejected.

Philo's acceptance of many philosophical principles certainly did not mean that he took on all Hellenistic ethical standards as his own. Jewish moral laws grated against customs acceptable to some Greeks, such as marriage of close

---

[117] David T. Runia, "Further Observations on the Structure of Philo's Allegorical Treatises," *Vigiliae Christianae* 41.2 (June, 1987): 112. See, also, Runia, "Philo's "De Aeternitate Mundi": The Problem of Its Interpretation," 166-67.

[118] Hay, "Philo's View of Himself as an Exegete," 46 (citing *Spec.* 3.1-6). Cf. Borgen, *Philo of Alexandria – an Exegete for His Time*, 24. Another designation for Philo which encourages wider comparisons of Philo's work with Palestinian Jewish scholars of his time is that of a midrashist. Runia defines 'midrash' as 'a type of literature, oral or written, which stands in direct relationship to a fixed, canonical text, considered to be the authoritative and the revealed word of God by the midrashist and his audience, and in which this canonical text is explicitly cited or clearly alluded to'. Runia, "Further Observations," 117. With this definition, we can legitimately regard Philo as a Hellenizing midrashist. See also Goodenough, *An Introduction to Philo Judaeus*, 27.

[119] Wolfson, *Philo: Foundations of Religious Philosophy*, 2.202.

[120] Wolfson, *Philo: Foundations of Religious Philosophy*, 2.202.

relatives, homosexuality, pederasty, bestiality, and murder through exposure of infants.[121]

Religious and cultic laws between the traditions were likewise in conflict. Unlike other religions within the Hellenised world, many Jews in Philo's time were basically aniconic as a consequence of the Second Commandment (Exod. 20:4; Deut. 5:8). They were forbidden to make images of God,[122] and the Jerusalem temple contained no representation of him.[123] Even artistic depictions of humans or animals were less prevalent among Jews in Philo's time. The Hellenistic and Egyptian religions were by contrast full of various cultic images, and perhaps especially so in such a 'deeply religious and cultural centre' as Alexandria.[124]

The Jewish disdain for pagan practices was reciprocated by some Greeks, who considered Jewish theology to be 'primitive and barbarous'.[125] These conflicting beliefs and practices led Philo to use the categories of virtue and vice to refer to the Jewish and pagan practices respectively;[126] paganism and vice were often mentioned in close proximity as a word pair.[127]

More dominant in Philo's writings however, was his respect for alternative sources of knowledge, and for philosophy in particular. This respect was sometimes, though perhaps only rarely, reciprocated by the Greeks. Josephus refers proudly to a book of Clearchus of Soli, written by a student of Aristotle, in which Aristotle was impressed by a certain Jew. Aristotle saw him as belonging to a 'race of philosophers', and one who 'communicated to us more information than he received from us'.[128]

The same Jews who condemned Greek popular religion and mythology, considered Greek philosophers to be their spiritual kindred.[129] There were some Greek figures whom Philo esteemed almost as highly as Moses: there was 'admirable truth' in the work of Homer,[130] and 'the great Plato'[131] 'would never have spoken falsely'.[132] The poets, likewise, were authoritative guides towards virtue:

> And if we are justified in listening to the poets, and why should we not, since they are our educators through all of our life (παιδευταὶ γὰρ οὗτοί γε τοῦ σύμπαντος

---

[121] Borgen, *Philo of Alexandria – an Exegete for His Time*, 214.

[122] *Spec.* 2.224, *Legat.* 290-92.

[123] *Legat.* 310, 317-31. For further discussion, see Karl Gustav Sandelin, "Philo's Ambivalence Towards Statues," in *SPHA* (2001), 122.

[124] Sandelin, "Philo's Ambivalence Towards Statues," 123.

[125] Roberto Radice, "Observations on the Theory of the Ideas as the Thoughts of God in Philo of Alexandria," in *The Studia Philonica Annual: Studies in Hellenistic Judaism*, ed. David T. Runia (Atlanta, Georgia: Scholars, 1991), 132.

[126] Borgen, *Philo of Alexandria - an Exegete for His Time*, 214.

[127] See also Pearce, *The Land of the Body: Studies in Philo's Representation of Egypt*.

[128] Josephus, *Apion* 1.181.

[129] Wolfson, *Philo: Foundations of Religious Philosophy*, 1.20.

[130] *Aet.* 132.

[131] *Aet.* 52.

[132] *Aet.* 16. His attitude towards Aristotle is less perspicuous in § 10.

Philo in his First-Century Setting

βίου), and as parents in private life teach wisdom to their children, so do they in public life to their cities.[133]

Despite Philo's esteem for philosophy as a source of wisdom and truth, it was usually treated as a subordinate source. Wolfson argues that

> to these Alexandrian Jewish writers, while philosophy in its teachings about God and about the duties of men was reminiscent of the teachings of Scripture, it never really reached the full truth of Scripture. It only groped after it, and occasionally approached it in a vague way. The full truth in all its splendour is to be found only in Scripture, which was revealed to men directly by God; philosophy is only the product of the human mind, and hence subject to error.[134]

We concur with parts of this generalisation about the Alexandrian Jews as being applicable to Philo, so long as exceptions are acknowledged. Philo's *Quod omnis probus liber sit* is an example of a work, however, that does not easily submit to this description. Philosophy was treated as truth, not as merely groping after truth, nor approaching it in a vague way. Philo presents philosophically-derived arguments with a conviction comparable to that of his exegetical works.

We suggested that Philo's approach to the Bible followed, to some degree, his exegetical Jewish community. But what can be said about his philosophy? Was he original, or merely a well-educated eclectic?

Clearly, Philo was indebted deeply to the philosophy of Plato. Speaking of Philo in *De viris illustribus* 11, Jerome says that there was a proverb about Philo in circulation among the Greeks: ἢ Πλάτων φιλωνίζει ἢ Φίλων πλατωνίζει ('either Plato Philonises or Philo Platonises') on account of their similar doctrines and style.

More developed is Winston's identification of a later stream of Platonic philosophy that closely resembles Philo's Platonism, which had significant Stoic influences. It is probably right to see that Philo was not necessarily drawing purely from Plato's works, nor was he an eclectic.[135] Rather, he inherited an eclectic, though still broadly Platonic, philosophical worldview from more intermediate sources.[136] It is incorrect, therefore, to attribute to Philo

---

[133] *Prob.* 143.

[134] Wolfson, *Philo: Foundations of Religious Philosophy*, 1.20. Cf. Runia, "Philo's "De Aeternitate Mundi": The Problem of Its Interpretation," 167.

[135] See John M. Dillon, *The Middle Platonists : A Study of Platonism, 80 B.C. to A.D. 220* (London: Duckworth, 1977), 143.

[136] Winston argues, 'To label Philo as an eclectic because of his amalgamation isn't quite accurate. Two generations before (c. 90 B.C.E), Antiochus of Ascalon had propounded, in Athens, a revived dogmatic Platonism, incorporating a good deal of Stoic doctrine and terminology, on the argument that Zeno and his successors were in fact the truest successors of the Old Academy, rather than the Skeptic Arcesilaus and his followers, Antiochus' own immediate predecessors. Peripatetic elements, especially in logic and ethics, had already penetrated the Academy in the first generations after Philo's death, and Antiochus does not reject these...This

a new form of Platonism because his views can be located within the spectrum of contemporary Platonism. This is not to say that Philo did not add his own emphases and perspective to that which he inherited.[137] It should also be recognised that others too were producing Greek readings of Moses, discussing Homer's use of Moses, and doing so through the allegorical method.[138] So we see that even Philo's attempt at conjoining these traditions was not new. Unlike any known predecessor, however, Philo produced a sustained, extensive, and relatively cohesive corpus conjoining the Platonic and Jewish world views. Though it is now well recognised that Philo inherited much, it is still fair to view his corpus as a thoughtful and significant work.[139]

That the Best of Hellenism was already in Judaism

We have observed that Philo perceived himself to be an exegete, primarily of the Pentateuch, and as one who interpreted them through a Greek philosophical lens. Indeed, the best of Hellenism was already present in Judaism.[140] Most studies of Philo, including the present one, find it necessary to discuss Philo's methodology because it affects the way one interprets him. Of particular interest for this monograph in relation to Philo's methodology, are the philosophical treatises. The reason is that in these treatises Philo's attention was further from any particular part of the Pentateuch, and as a result he had to work harder to maintain his proposition that philosophy was the handmaiden of Scripture. That is, this genre made it more difficult to work according to his usual *modus operandi*, which was exegesis of Scripture. Though Philo did not consider that there was a clash between the two genres, in his philosophical treatises the harmony appears more strained.

As a starting point, we noted that the Greek poets, though not part of Israel, contributed to the broader goal of revealing 'that most sacred possession, "truth"'.[141] Since truth was the common goal of Jew and Greek alike, Philo saw no need to divorce Scriptural revelation from natural philosophy.[142]

---

combination of Stoicizing Platonism with a Pythagorean-influenced view of the transcendence of God, and of the significance of Number, together with a more austere ethics than that of Antiochus (who was inclined to peripatetic broad-mindedness about bodily and worldly goods) is the Platonism which Philo inherited.' Winston, *Philo of Alexandria*, xiii.

[137] Winston, *Philo of Alexandria*, xiii.
[138] Winston, *Philo of Alexandria*, 4.
[139] Winston, *Philo of Alexandria*, 6.
[140] As shown by Runia, *Philo of Alexandria and the Timaeus of Plato*, 528. For a more lengthy comparison of Philo and the Middle Platonists, see III.3.3-5 (pages 480-519) of the same work.
[141] *Prob.* 158.
[142] In *Prob.* 62 the phrase 'living in accordance with the law' is followed in parallel by, 'the right reason of nature' (reflecting the philosophical tradition): 'in former times there were some persons who surpassed all their contemporaries in virtue, ἡγεμόνι μόνῳ θεῷ χρώμενοι ('taking God alone for their sole guide'), and living καὶ κατὰ

By showing that the end (τέλος) of the two traditions was essentially the same, Philo could say that both traditions were essentially pointing in the same direction. Not only was the end aligning, but all the material leading to the end had this goal in common. As we might expect, the philosophical τέλος of Philo, to live in conformity to Law, or nature, resonates more closely with the more 'philosophical' genre of Old Testament wisdom literature than it does the Torah.[143] The τέλη prescribed by the wisdom literature of the Old Testament, including Job, Ecclesiastes, and Proverbs in particular, are in some respects quite similar to the philosophical works of Philo. For example, Philo teaches that

> we must nurse and cherish [souls] carefully, prescribing for them at first tender food instead of milk, namely, instruction in the encyclical sciences, and after that stronger food, such as is prepared by philosophy, by which they will be strengthened so as to become manly, and in good condition, and conducted on to a favourable end, not more that recommended by you than enjoined by the oracle, "To live in conformity to nature" (τὸ ἀκολούθως τῇ φύσει ζῆν).[144]

Drawing lessons from nature, Proverbs says, 'go to the ant, you sluggard; consider its ways and be wise' (Prov. 6:6). The proverbs were written

> for attaining wisdom and discipline; for understanding words of insight; for acquiring a disciplined and prudent life, doing what is right and just and fair; for giving prudence to the simple, knowledge and discretion to the young – let the wise listen and add to their learning, and let the discerning get guidance.[145]

Wisdom in the Jewish Scriptures sought to understand the way creation operates, with its Creator at the centre (Prov. 1:7). Israel's sages explored seasons, human relationships (6:34-35), animals (6:6), and the way one should live in light of all of these realities: 'to walk in the way of understanding' (9:6). Exploration was undertaken upon the theological foundations laid by Moses.[146]

νόμον, τὸν ὀρθὸν φύσεως λόγον ('according to the law, the right reason of nature').' Living according to law and according to right reason are closely related, and perhaps a hendiadys.

[143] Philo cites the wisdom literature only occasionally: the Book of Proverbs in *Ebr.* 1.84; *Congr.* 1.177; and the Book of Job in *Mut.* 1.48. He refers to some of the Psalms (e.g. Pss. 1, 49, 73), often referred to as 'wisdom psalms', for their emphasis on this theme.

[144] *Prob.* 160.

[145] Prov. 1:2-5 (NIV).

[146] The sages of Israel were exploring their world, but within the framework of perceiving God, creation and themselves as set forth in their covenantal history with *YHWH*. The wisdom literature reflects the reflections of not just people, but the people of Yahweh. For useful discussion about the place of Wisdom Literature within the Old Testament overall, see W. Brueggemann, " A Convergence in Recent Old Testament Theologies," *JSOT* 18 (1980), 18; John Goldingay, "The 'Salvation History' Perspective and the 'Wisdom' Perspective within the Context of Biblical Theology," *EvQ* 51 (1979); R.L. Schultz, "Unity or Diversity in Wisdom Theology? A Canonical and Covenantal Perspective," *Tyndale Bulletin* 48.2 (1997); C.

In this pursuit of natural science, the sages of different wisdom traditions could discover truths valuable also to the Jews. Philo taught about the 'foreign' sages who had lived in Persia, India, Palestine and Syria. Israel did not hold the monopoly on the search for wisdom, nor on those who attain it.[147] And the Stoic father, Zeno, was praised by Philo because he was, 'as much as anyone else, being under the influence of virtue'.[148]

Generally speaking, Philo considered the sages of various 'wisdom' or philosophical traditions to be legitimate and in harmony with each other. This was because, as Winston says,

> Philo's whole position is based on the premise that Greek philosophy is a development from the God-given teaching of Moses, and thus that it is quite proper for him to claim it back, as it were, accepting it as the best mode of expressing to a 'modern' audience (one influenced by Greek modes of thought) the substance of Moses' message.[149]

It is a remarkable presupposition, but explains in part Philo's disinterest, or perhaps blindness, to the enormous divide that exists between the Jewish and philosophical ideologies. He simply did not expect a troubling dichotomy to exist, and after constructing a complex and vast synthesis of two traditions, he seems quite satisfied with the resulting product. His expectation for harmony is explicable in light of his view that

> the unerring law is right reason; not an ordinance made by this or that mortal, a corruptible and perishable law, a lifeless law written on lifeless parchment or engraved on lifeless columns; but one imperishable, and stamped by immortal nature on the immortal mind.[150]

The Torah was the most important manifestation of ὀρθὸς λόγος ('right reason').

Such observations serve as a precaution about the metaphors used to describe Philo's approach. Terms such as 'blend' or 'synthesis' are inadequate if used to describe Philo's perception of his task; he did not see his task as forcing, nor even creating a synthesis. His task was to reveal and explain it to others. And he did not see his task as borrowing philosophical language to serve exegesis.[151] Rather, he 'recovered' what had been missed by Jew and Greek alike: that philosophy had sprung from Jewish tradition, and represented

---

Westermann, *Roots of Wisdom* (Louisville: WJKP, 1995); L. Wilson, "The Place of Wisdom in Old Testament Theology" *RTR* 49 (1990); W. Zimmerli, "The Place and Limit of Wisdom in the Framework of the Old Testament Theology," *Scottish Journal of Theology* 17 (1964).

[147] *Prob.* 73.
[148] *Prob.* 53.
[149] Winston, *Philo of Alexandria*, xiii.
[150] *Prob.* 46-47.
[151] Winston, *Philo of Alexandria*, xiii.

Philo in his First-Century Setting

the same tradition dressed in more contemporary garb. Moses had, before the Greeks, reached 'the very summit of philosophy'.[152]

Philo conceded that on some matters philosophers erred, and so the development offered by later Greek philosophy had to be recalibrated against the earlier Laws of Moses. For Philo, such departures from the truth further justified returning to earlier sources when differences emerged. It also explains why he could, without concern that he was stepping into 'pagan' territory, confidently engage in philosophical discourse.

A deeper appreciation for Philo's presupposition of continuity between the two great traditions has been an important development in recent Philonic studies. It corrects earlier scholarship which, to take Wolfson as one example, believed that it was Philo's intent 'to present Judaism as a philosophy, but philosophy had to yield to Judaism on every point on which the two met in real conflict'.[153]

There are times when Philo, so enamoured by the adornment of the philosophers' dress, expressed approval for philosophical doctrines that were foreign to the Hebrew Scriptures. Such wanderings are most obvious in his philosophical treatises, which at times contradict and at other times were simply not in the Torah.[154]

Because of the disparity between the various first-century philosophies, we might expect that Philo was of a mixed opinion about them, and he was. He sometimes distanced himself from the Stoics,[155] in part because of the diverse opinions they held even among themselves. He was aware of their beliefs about the nature of the world, and aptly compared their views with those of Democritus and Epicurus.[156] But their views were deemed intolerably disparate; Chrysippus and the Stoics on one point are confused and wrong, and 'have wandered so far from true doctrine' and advocate 'inconsistent principles'.[157] He reserved his most damning evaluation, however, for the sophists, because they deceived with intent.[158]

At times, philosophy was plainly wrong, as was their practice of πολύθεος ('polytheism'). Philo rejected such Greek philosophical views, sometimes

---

[152] Runia, "Philo's 'De Aeternitate Mundi': The Problem of Its Interpretation," 2.

[153] Wolfson, *Philo: Foundations of Religious Philosophy*, 1.86. This is unhelpful for at least two reasons. First, Philo saw no reason for attempting to 'present Judaism as philosophy' at all, since for Philo true philosophy was Judaism in contemporary dress. Second, sometimes Judaism did at times yield to philosophy.

[154] Mendelson provides examples of when Philo 'goes further than Scripture' (93-94), or contradicts its ethical teachings with his 'extreme views' (103) which are 'in a sense so foreign to the Spirit of the Bible' (98), in Alan Mendelson, *Philo's Jewish Identity* (Atlanta: Scholars, 1988).

[155] *Aet.* 94.

[156] *Aet.* 8.

[157] *Aet.* 4-5; 47-50.

[158] *Aet.* 132.

because they were contrary to λόγος (by which he often meant 'Scripture'),[159] at other times because it was contrary to ὀρθὸς λόγος (by which he meant 'right reason' in the philosophical sense).[160]

Summary

This investigation into Philo's use of sources has yielded some observations that are necessary for understanding Philo's view of God, life and death. Philo the Jew had a deep loyalty to the Scriptures; Philo the Alexandrian was deeply influenced by Greek philosophy and culture; and Philo the scholar perceived a synergy to exist between the two.

In accordance with this observation, there was no internal battle within Philo whereby each tradition was vying for dominance. On the contrary, Philo's satisfaction is demonstrated by his vigorous promotion of this divine union of traditions. It was a positive development from the joining of two great traditions more than it was a distortion of either. Philo's Hellenistic Judaism made a contribution that neither Hellenism nor Judaism offered independently—the synthesis was greater than its parts.

In the end, his loyalty was neither to what might be loosely described as 'Mosaic' Judaism nor 'Platonic' Hellenism exclusively.[161] The two belonged felicitously together.[162] On the basis of its earlier origins, however, the Law was treated as the purer source and given priority over Greek φιλοσοφία.

---

[159] Yonge may be justified in translated Philo's various references to the ὁ ἱερὸς λόγος (e.g. *Leg.* 3.36; *Post.* 153) or θεῖος λόγος (e.g. *Leg.* 3.8) as 'Scripture', though its connection with both philosophical and Jewish worlds is lost in the translation.

[160] E.g. *Opif.* 143.

[161] These adjectives were chosen as the best of problematic alternatives. It could be well argued, for example, that there was no such thing as 'orthodox' Judaism or 'classical' Hellenism in Philo's day.

[162] Cf. David Runia's understanding of Philo's use of the two traditions to be something like an ellipse, wherein even when Philo's views seem far away from Hellenism, some degree of connection with Judaism remains, and vice versa. David T. Runia, "The Theme of Flight and Exile in the Allegorical Thought-World of Philo of Alexandria," in *The Studia Philonica Annual*, ed. David T. Runia and Gregory E. Sterling (Atlanta: SBL, 2009), 24; cf. SPhA 5(1993): 130.

CHAPTER 6

Philo's Guide to θεός

The Nature of θεός

In order to understand Philo, one must recognise the foundational nature of his theology.[1] He sought to think God's thoughts after him:

> Therefore, O my mind, if you in this manner investigate the holy thoughts of God with which man is inspired by divine agency and the laws of such men as love God, you will not be compelled to admit anything lowly, anything unworthy, of their greatness.[2]

As could be expected from the previous chapter, Philo's portrayal of God was derived primarily from his key source, the Torah. Whatever else Philo says about God, it is important to remember that his God was the God of Abraham and the patriarchs, who identified himself to Abraham with the words, 'I am your God' (ἐγώ εἰμι ὁ θεός σου, Gen. 17:1). In the LXX, God was referred to as κύριος ὁ θεός ('the Lord God'), τὸ θεῖον ('the Deity')[3] and the πατήρ ('Father').[4] His holy name, the τετραγράμματον, *YHWH*, was only to be pronounced by the high priest in the temple.[5] He was an omniscient being, knowing 'not only all that is present, and all that is past, but all that is to come',[6] and knowing it perfectly.[7]

Philo's God was the ποιητής ('Creator'),[8] and so also 'the Ruler of all things'.[9] Nature testifies to God's existence: 'That you are and you subsist; of this the world has been my teacher and guide.'[10] God is not the cause of

---

[1] Runia, *Philo of Alexandria and the Timaeus of Plato*, 433.
[2] *Det.* 13.
[3] *Det.* 57; cf. Exod. 31:3; 35:31.
[4] *Praem.* 166; *Mos.* 2.288.
[5] *Mos.* II, 23; *Decal.* 19.
[6] *Det.* 57.
[7] *Contempl.* 5.
[8] *Det.* 86; *Opif.* 7.
[9] *Praem.* 166. The doctrine of creation is usually very significant for the theology of philosophers: 'A philosopher's theory of creation invariably reveals the fundamental presupposition of his thought and is inextricably intertwined with his doctrine of God.' Winston, *Philo of Alexandria*, 7; for his chapter on 'Philo's Theory of Creation', see 7-20.
[10] *Spec.* I.8.41.

'disorder, and irregularity, and destruction, but of order, and beautiful regularity, and life, and of every good thing'.[11]

He is the 'merciful saviour'[12] and described as being 'good',[13] merciful, gentle, compassionate, and 'one who would always rather have mercy than punishment'.[14] His riches are eternal, and he willingly shares them with his creation.[15] There is nothing blameworthy in him, meaning that he does not err as humans do.[16] He is the 'guide of wisdom'[17] and the 'author of virtuous laughter and joy'.[18] God is benevolent and self-sufficient,[19] not in need of supply or improvement from the service of his people.[20] One's service of God was therefore not to supply his needs, but done simply because it was intrinsically good to do so, not for his ability to bless, but in order to know and enjoy him. His servants would 'benefit themselves greatly by determining to become friends with God'.[21]

God's attributes are knowable from τοῦ θεοῦ πολυώνυμον ὄνομα ('the multiform name of God'), which employs negative Greek philosophical terms.[22] God is:

unborn (ἀγένητος), unbribable (ἀδέκαστος), incomprehensible (ἀκατάληπτος), unnamable (ἀκατονόμαστος), invisible (ἀόρατος), uncircumscribable (ἀπερίγραφος), ineffable (ἄρρητος), and incomparable (ἀσύγκριτος).[23]

Departing from Greek ideas, however, Philo denied the existence of other gods.[24] Through the Jewish laws and customs the Jews had

---

[11] *Aet.* 106.
[12] *Praem.* 163.
[13] *Det.* 93.
[14] Praem. 166.
[15] See M. Wolter, "Der Reichtum Gottes.," *Jahrbuch für biblische Theologie* 21 (2006): 145-60.
[16] *Praem.* 55.
[17] *Det.* 30.
[18] *Det.* 124.
[19] *Det.* 55; *Virt.* 8-9.
[20] *Det.* 56.
[21] *Det.* 56.
[22] *Decal.* 94. For a helpful discussion about the concurrence between God as both ὁ ὤν and τὸ ὄν, see Runia, *Philo of Alexandria and the Timaeus of Plato*, 436-38. For the interplay between the personal God of Scripture and the abstract God of philosophy, see Goodenough, *An Introduction to Philo Judaeus*, 86-87; Nikiprowetzky, *Le Commentaire De L'écriture Chez Philon D'alexandrie*, 128-30; Sandmel, *Philo of Alexandria: An Introduction*, 89-94. Cited in Runia, *Philo of Alexandria and the Timaeus of Plato*, 436.
[23] Wolfson, *Philo: Foundations of Religious Philosophy*, 2.127.
[24] On this point, Goodenough seems to make a significant error, by claiming not only that Philo does acknowledge the existence of lesser gods, but that this was normative of Judaism. He claims that Philo 'shows us Judaism in its most essential position, not denying the existence of lesser gods, but denying that they should be worshipped'. Goodenough, *An Introduction to Philo Judaeus*, 83. If Goodenough means the

rejected all errors about gods who have been created themselves; for there is no created being who is truly God, but such a one is so only in appearance and opinion, being destitute of that most indispensable quality in God, namely, eternity.[25]

Other so-called gods were the μυθικὰ πλάσματα ('mythical inventions') of humans and no substitute for τοῦ ἑνὸς καὶ ὄντως ὄντος θεοῦ ('the one true and living God'), who could be known with certainty and clarity of truth.[26] Other philosophies, insofar as they advocated mere gods rather than God, were inadequate. Indeed, the worship of creation reflects ἀμαθία ('ignorance').[27]

Philo's theology was generally well anchored to a Jewish framework comprising some non-negotiables. Such a framework provided Philo and the Alexandrian Jews with an important sense of a boundary in their syncretistic world. On the basis of *Opif.* 172, Mendelson suggests Philo's stance entailed the following propositions: God is and is from eternity; he that really IS [sic] is One; he has made the world; he has made it one world, unique as he himself is unique; and lastly, he ever exercises forethought for his creation.[28] Philo remained quite fixed, therefore, to a few core Jewish beliefs, with monotheism perhaps being at the top of the list.[29]

Besides other matters, the miraculous workings of Israel's God were sometimes at odds with Greek conceptions, as Wolfson observed, 'There is no room for miracles in the philosophy of Plato.'[30] Plato's god is distant, a creator who is not involved in individuals' lives.[31] Philo's rejection of some Graeco-Roman theological conceptions led to his refusal to worship the Emperor Caligula as having the nature of a god.[32]

Judaism of Philo's day acknowledged the real existence of other gods, it is a matter for further investigation, though it does defy other clear statements which deny the presence of other gods. By saying 'Judaism in its most essential position' believed such, he is suggesting the acknowledgment (not worship) of lesser gods is normative for Jews. He may or may not have confused mention of 'gods' in the Old Testament to be equivalent to an acknowledgement of their existence. Certainly the Old Testament does discuss the phenomenon of other gods without commenting on their existence. The first commandment is one example, 'You shall have no other gods before me' (Exod. 20:3). This is not, however, an acknowledgement that 'gods' or 'idols' are anything more than human invention. The passages that do make comment on their existence deny them to be anything more than man-made concepts or images, so-called 'gods' (e.g. Isa. 44:6-20; or implicit in referring to God as 'the living God,' as in Deut. 5:26; cf. the Apostle Paul's interpretation in 1 Cor. 8:4-5).

[25] *Virt.* 65; cf. *Virt.* 42.
[26] *Virt.* 102.
[27] *Contempl.* 4-10; *Virt.* 220-221.
[28] Mendelson, *Philo's Jewish Identity*, 29-30.
[29] *Virt.* 219 indicates that for Philo, while there were other conceptions of gods, there indeed is only one God. Philo advocates both monolatry and monotheism.
[30] Wolfson, *Philo: Foundations of Religious Philosophy*, 1.429.
[31] Wolfson, *Philo: Foundations of Religious Philosophy*, 1.434.
[32] *Legat.* 367.

For Philo, it was God, not Fate, who would judge wrongdoing. This did not create a conflict with his bountiful and merciful nature, for he was compassionate even in punishment.[33] Philo struggles to present a cogent theodicy, arguing that God 'is the cause of good things only; and of nothing at all that is bad'.[34] He 'cannot be the cause of evil in the universe'[35] though at other times Philo seems less certain about this.[36]

ἄνθρωπος in relation to Θεός

Philo's portrayal of ἄνθρωπος ('man,' 'person,' or 'humanity') was again a blend of Jewish and Greek ideas. As in both traditions, Philo drew a distinction between humans and other elements of creation. The world (as well as the sun, moon, stars, planets and whole heaven)[37] was perfect and eternal; humans were corruptible and perishable.[38] A human was 'a compound animal, made up of both a mortal and immortal nature'.[39]

To be called ἄνθρωπος was, according to Philo, 'the most proper, and appropriate, and felicitous name' and related to human potential for a 'regulated and rational mind'.[40] Man is, 'according to his body, a terrestrial animal, made up of the four elements which make up the universe – earth, water, air and fire'.[41] But a body also requires a soul to live,[42] and a soul requires reason.[43]

The following quotation presents a useful window into Philo's dualistic view of man.

> The truth is that every one of us according to the nearest estimation of numbers, is two persons, the animal and the man...To the one portion is assigned the vivifying faculty according to which we live; and to the other, the reasoning faculty in accordance with which we are capable of reasoning...Therefore, the faculty which is common to us with the irrational animals, has blood for its essence. And it, having flowed from the rational fountain, is spirit, not air in motion, but rather a certain representation and character of the divine faculty which Moses calls by its proper name an image, showing by his language that God is the archetypal pattern

---

[33] *Virt.* 41.
[34] *Conf.* 180. For fuller discussion, see David T. Runia, "Theodicy in Philo of Alexandria," in *Theodicy in the World of the Bible*, ed. Antti Laato and Johannes C. de Moor (Leiden: Brill, 2003), esp. 599-604.
[35] See Williamson, *Jews in the Hellenistic World: Philo*, 45. and his wider discussion, 45-48.
[36] Williamson, *Jews in the Hellenistic World: Philo*, 46.
[37] *Contempl.* 4-5.
[38] *Praem.* 1.
[39] *Praem.* 13.
[40] *Det.* 22.
[41] *Det.* 151.
[42] *Det.* 142; cf. 159; *Aet.* 124; *Opif.* 117.
[43] *Det.* 142.

Philo's Guide to θεός

of rational nature, and that man is the imitation of him, and the image formed after his model.[44]

Further differentiating humans from animals, as Philo demonstrated from the Psalms, is their capacity to have relationship with God.[45] The soul is vital for conversing with, and crying to, the living God, sometimes voluntarily and at other times involuntarily.[46] Correct λόγος ('reason'), a highly significant theme in Philo, makes one similar to the Father.

> And all those who, through the improvement of their reason, are adorned in the similitude of the Father, in consequence of education, unlearn all subserviency to the irrational impulses of the soul, selecting the plain as a suitable place.[47]

Philo was probably using hyperbole when taking this idea of similarity a step further when he said, 'the man who is wholly possessed with the love of God and who serves the living God alone, is no longer man, but actually God'.[48] Such an idea aligned with philosophical ideas, but was irreconcilable with ancient Jewish conceptions. Reflecting this elsewhere, Philo maintained the importance of God's distinctness, as in *Virt.* 64: 'The most important of all professions, the worship of the one true and living God, who is Creator and the Father of the universe'.[49]

Besides the more positive aspects of man's ability to relate with God, Philo portrayed a darker picture of the world tarnished by the κακός of mankind.[50]

> Cities are full, and all the earth from one side to the other, is full of these evils (μεσταὶ μὲν αἱ πόλεις, μεστὴ δὲ ἀπὸ περάτων ἐπὶ πέρατα πᾶσα ἡ γῆ τῶν κακῶν τούτων), in consequence of which, continual and unceasing and terrible wars are set on foot among men, even in times of peace, both publicly and privately.[51]

But evils were ever-present, 'constantly budding forth, and inflict an incurable disease on all who are once infected by them'.[52] The cause of evil was not God, but 'our' own hands.[53]

---

[44] *Det.* 82-83.
[45] Runia, "Philo's Reading of the Psalms," 114, 18.
[46] *Det.*, 92. It may be useful at this point to note Philo's separation of women from his general portrayal of man or mankind. Philo's view of women is not as complementary, perhaps reflecting popular opinion rather than biblical ideas. 'The female is "incomplete" or "imperfect" (τὸ γὰρ θῆλυ ἀτελές), and is identified throughout Philo with weakness, incompleteness, and on occasions, to represent sin. See Goodenough, *An Introduction to Philo Judaeus*, 127. So, too, θήλεα δὲ φύσει τὰ πάθη ('the passions are female by nature'), and to be abandoned (from ἔκλειψις), *Det.* 28.
[47] *Det.* 5.
[48] *Prob.* 43.
[49] *Virt.* 64.
[50] κακός is the translation in the Septuagint for the word רע, and appears also from Homer down to refer to bad or evil (Thayer's *Greek Lexicon*).
[51] *Det.* 174.
[52] *Det.* 174, 178.

Ὁ ἱερὸς νόμος ('The holy Law") was connected with the worship of God – if one departed from these, vice would follow:

> just as, on the contrary, one may see that those who forsake the holy laws of God are intemperate, shameless, unjust, disreputable, weak-minded, quarrelsome, companions of falsehood and perjury, willing to sell their liberty for luxurious eating, for strong wine, for sweetmeats, and for beauty, for pleasures of the belly and of the parts below the belly; the miserable end of all which enjoyment is ruin to both body and soul.[54]

The τέλος for those who forsake God and his laws entails the heaviest (or perhaps 'miserable' or 'grievous', βαρύς) punishments.[55] It was not merely the soul that suffered while the body was indulging in pleasure: σῶμα τέ καὶ ψυχή ('the body and soul') would experience this miserable end.[56]

θεός and ἀρετή

Within his discussion of the τέλος of philosophy, Philo incorporates and closely connects ideas of θεός and ἀρετή. Though ἀρετή occurs 955 times in Philo's corpus, the importance of the virtuous life cannot be limited to a study of this one word. Weaved throughout his corpus are other terms which represent ideal behaviour, such as that which is καλοκἀγαθία ('excellent'),[57] ἀγαθός ('good'),[58] εὐγένεια ('noble')[59] and even ἀστεῖος ('beautiful' in the moral sense). For Philo, virtuous living was more important than the semantic domain of any one word used to describe it.[60] Life in accordance with virtue was an essential facet of his τέλος.

> But in all the subjects which I have here mentioned, there are admonitions and lessons engraved lastingly in many passages of the law, persuading the obedient with great gentleness, and the disobedient with some severity, to despise all the things which affect the body and all external circumstances (καταφρονεῖν τῶν περὶ σῶμα καὶ ἐκτός) holding the life of virtue to be the one sole end (ἓν μὲν τέλος ἡγουμένους τὸ κατ' ἀρετὴν βιοῦν), and pursuing after everything else that is conducive to this end (ζηλοῦντας δὲ καὶ τἆλλα ὅσα ἀγωγὰ πρὸς τοῦτο).[61]

At the same time, God was the 'Lover of virtue',[62] and was virtuous in essence. He provided man with laws that demonstrate virtue, and modelled virtue to

---

[53] *Det.* 122.
[54] *Virt.* 182.
[55] *LSJ*.
[56] *Virt.* 182.
[57] *Prob.* 41; cf. 62, 71, 75, 91; *Virt.* 117.
[58] *Praem.* 126.
[59] e.g. *Virt.* 195.
[60] There may also be stylistic reasons why ἀρετή is used in combination with closely related terms.
[61] *Virt.* 15; translation of Yonge.
[62] *Opif.* 81.

us.⁶³ Furthermore, τὸ κατ' ἀρετὴν βιοῦν ('to live in accordance with virtue') was in no way different from πρὸς ἀλήθειαν βίος ('a life in accordance with truth').⁶⁴

Philo highlighted the importance of a life that responded appropriately to God. As recipients of God's provision, which included the wealth of nature,⁶⁵ there was nothing more useful or respectable than 'to believe in God and throughout one's life to be continually rejoicing and beholding the living God'.⁶⁶ He concludes: τῷ γὰρ ὄντι μόνος ἐλεύθερος ὁ μόνῳ θεῷ χρώμενος ἡγεμόνι ('For the man alone is free who has God for his guide').⁶⁷

Such a life entailed displaying the virtues, which were immortal, and a stamp of God upon all men.⁶⁸ For, 'the mind of the good man is the guardian and steward of the doctrines of virtue'.⁶⁹ It was also said that 'the good man is the guardian of the words and of the covenant of God'.⁷⁰ In this way, ἀρετή and the λόγοι τοῦ θεοῦ are closely related.⁷¹

It was observed earlier that man was born with ἀδελφὸν κακόν ('kindred evil' [trans. Yonge] or lit. 'an evil brother') from which he must flee during adulthood. 'We,' according to Philo, 'live on the borders between virtue and vice', and the study of virtue leads to our flying to it, leaving our kindred evil behind. Philo seemed optimistic about the permanence of our resolve once we flee.⁷²

So man has a pernicious kindred evil which seeks to ensnare him, but a remedy comprised of the right mix of ἀγαθῆς μὲν φύσεως ἀγαθῆς δὲ καὶ παιδεύσεως ('both good natural disposition and a good education'), as well as training in ἀρετή.⁷³ The benefits included acquisition of health and power, 'which are followed by a good complexion, owing to modesty, and also good health and beauty'.⁷⁴

> Wickedness is established in the souls of foolish men; the remedy for which, as one seeks for remedies for a 'severe disease' (νόσος βαρύς), is found to be the just man, who is in possession of the panacea (πανάκεια), justice.⁷⁵

---

⁶³ *Det.* 160; *Virt.* 51.
⁶⁴ *Virt.* 17.
⁶⁵ *Virt.* 5-6.
⁶⁶ *Praem.* 27.
⁶⁷ *Prob.* 20: In this way he becomes the viceroy to the great king, 'the moral lieutenant of an immortal sovereign'.
⁶⁸ *Det.* 77.
⁶⁹ *Det.* 66.
⁷⁰ *Det.* 68.
⁷¹ *Virt.* 15.
⁷² *Praem.* 62.
⁷³ *Praem*, 64.
⁷⁴ *Praem.* 64.
⁷⁵ *Det.* 123.

With proper development, the wise man's mind could be described as 'the palace of God' who is the Holy One of holies.[76] Worship of God and virtuous living are thus inextricably linked.[77] For 'as in the sun shadow follows the body, so also a participation in all other virtues must inevitably follow the giving due honour to the living God'.[78] For

> those who come over to this worship become at once prudent, and temperate, and modest, and gentle, and merciful, and humane, and venerable, and just, and magnanimous, and lovers of truth, and superior to all considerations of money or pleasure.[79]

Though Philo could speak of virtues in relation to 'the Holy One of holies', he was also certainly aware of Plato's four classical virtues: φρόνησις ('wisdom'), σωφροσύνη ('self-control'), ἀνδρεία ('courage') and δικαιοσύνη ('justice').[80] These were like the four rivers which flowed out of the μέγιστος ποταμός ('greatest river'), or generic virtue (Yonge's translation of ἡ γενική ἐστιν ἀρετή), which Philo also called ἀγαθότης ('goodness').[81]

Philo adds virtues to those which were common. His emphasis on the virtue of ἀγάπη ('love') and εὐσέβεια ('piety'),[82] the highest ἀρεταί, distinguished him from Hellenistic emphases,[83] as did his esteem for εὐχή ('prayer') and πίστις ('trust').[84] About trust Philo says,

> trust in God (ἡ πρὸς θεὸν πίστις), then, is the one sure and infallible good, consolation of life, fulfilment of bright hopes, dearth of ills, harvest of goods, inacquaintance with misery, acquaintance with piety (εὐσέβεια), heritage of happiness, all-round betterment of the soul which is firmly stayed on him who is the cause of all things and can do all things yet only wills the best.[85]

Μετάνοια ('repentance'), if not a virtue in itself, was the return to virtue.[86] Certainly repentance could be seen in Jewish and Greek literature, but not as a

---

[76] *Praem.* 123.
[77] *Virt.* 34.
[78] *Virt.* 181.
[79] *Virt.* 182.
[80] E.g. *Leg. all.* 1.63 and *Spec.* 4:133-38. For further discussion of this, see Borgen, *Philo of Alexandria – an Exegete for His Time*, 74; Runia, *Philo in Early Christian Literature: A Survey*, 41; Wolfson, *Philo: Foundations of Religious Philosophy*, 2.200-37; Naomi Cohen, *Philo Judaeus: His Universe and Discourse*, ed. M. Augustin and M. Mach (Frankfurt am Main: Peter Lang, 1995), 86-89.
[81] *Leg.* 1.63-64; see Winston, *Philo of Alexandria*, 226.
[82] For a more thorough treatment of Philo's use of ευσέβεια, see Gregory E. Sterling, "'The Queen of Virtues': Piety in Philo of Alexandria," in *SPhA*, ed. David T. Runia and Gregory E. Sterling (2006).
[83] Runia, *Philo in Early Christian Literature: A Survey*, 41.
[84] Williamson, *Jews in the Hellenistic World: Philo*, 209.
[85] *Abr.* 268.
[86] *Leg.* 2.78.

virtue.⁸⁷ And holiness was added because Philo regarded the worship of God as being basic to virtuous life.⁸⁸ The 'chief of the virtues' according to *De virtutibus* 95 are piety and φιλανθρωπία ('benevolence, humanity'), the latter of which was at this time becoming more prominent in Hellenistic ethical writings.⁸⁹

A compilation of Philo's virtues would be extensive. One part of his *De virtutibus* places nine of them closely together: φρόνιμος ('prudent', 'wise', or 'sensible'); ἀγχίνοος ('ready of wit', 'sagacious', or 'shrewd');⁹⁰ σώφρων ('temperate', 'sensible', or 'discreet'); ἐγκρατεῖς ('self-controlled');⁹¹ ἀνδρεῖος ('courageous', 'virtuous', or 'brave');⁹² δίκαιος ('just', 'righteous', or 'civilised'); ἀγαθός ('good', 'admirable');⁹³ ἀτυφία ('freedom from arrogance', or 'unpretentious');⁹⁴ and φιλανθρωπία.⁹⁵

By emphasising virtue, Philo was in theory (and perhaps only in theory) redefining the class structures that existed in Alexandrian society. Ideally, the term 'noble' should not refer to those privileged by ancestry or social status, but to the possessors of virtue. Virtue was the πατρίς ('homeland') of the noble, and fools had been driven from it.⁹⁶ He offered a two-fold division of humankind: the ἀγαθός, or σπουδαῖος ('good')⁹⁷ who could anticipate an ἆθλον

---

⁸⁷ See, for example, Aristotle, *Eth. Nic.* III.1.1110b; and the Stoics' view in *SVF* 3.548. Cited in Borgen, *Philo of Alexandria – an Exegete for His Time*, 74.
⁸⁸ Borgen, *Philo of Alexandria – an Exegete for His Time*, 75.
⁸⁹ David Winston, "Philo's Ethical Theory," *ANRW* II.21.1 (1984): 394.
⁹⁰ LSJ.
⁹¹ Winter observes that Philo endorsed self-control as the foundation of life, upon which one can build other virtues, pursuing 'the summit of virtue' which 'procured for them God's friendship', *Contempl.* 34, 72, 90. Winter, *Philo and Paul among the Sophists*, 104-105.
⁹² LEH.
⁹³ *Virt.* 167.
⁹⁴ *Virt.* 178. For other virtue lists, see *Praem.* 15, 100, 116, 160, 161. The vast number of virtues was made explicit in *De Sacrificiis Abelis et Caini*, 20-27, where Philo was speaking of the battle between two 'women' vying for dominance over the human soul: lady ἡδονή and lady ἀρετή. Describing lady virtue, he concludes, 'One day would fail me if I were to enumerate all the names of the particular virtues', §27 Such comments suggest that none of Philo's many virtue lists were intended to be exhaustive.
⁹⁵ *Virt.* 99.
⁹⁶ *Virt.* 190. The σπουδαῖος ('earnest') in this pursuit of goodness or virtue, whether an individual or a multitude of people, would be κεφαλὴν μὲν τοῦ ἀνθρωπείου γένους ('head of the human race'), by which Philo meant a superior part of humanity (*Praem.* 125).
⁹⁷ Philo used these terms interchangeably, referring to those who are zealous or earnest.

('prize of contest') and the πονηρός ('wicked'), or φαῦλος ('bad' or 'worthless' man)[98] who could anticipate ἐπιτίμιον ('punishment').[99]

Οἱ ἄνθρωποι οἱ ἀγαθόι 'fulfil the laws by their actions' and are rewarded 'by the grace of the bounteous and beneficent God, who rewards all that is good for the sake of its similarity to himself'.[100] Virtue was the best wealth, a wealth that could be shared with heaven and even with God.[101] Though it did lead to rewards, which will be discussed later, it was clearly worth pursuing for its own sake.[102]

Such terms as ἀρετή or καλοκἀγαθία highlight the important ethical dimension of Philo's τέλος. But were there other more fundamental τέλη than obtaining ἀρετή?

Certainly virtue was a key component of the goal or end, but it would be inadequate to conclude there. For although a life in accordance with virtue was an end, virtue was actually the means to another more final aspect of the end of εὐδαιμονία (a difficult term to translate, but something like 'well-being').[103] A number of texts point this way.[104] Philosophy trained the Essenes, for instance, towards the attainment of virtue, which led them towards a τέλειος ('perfect' or 'complete') life.[105]

> But everyone being subdued by the virtue of these men, looked up to them as free by nature, and not subject to the frown of any human being, and have celebrated their manner of messing together, and their fellowship with one another beyond all description in respect of its mutual good faith, which is proof of a life which is perfect and very prosperous (ἢ βίου τελείου καὶ σφόδρα εὐδαίμονός).[106]

But was there a more important goal even than εὐδαιμονία? Certainly, a life of virtue, and experiencing well-being were significant parts of the goal, but to conclude, a more fundamental and theocentric τέλος must be recognised. As in

---

[98] E.g. *Virt.* 9, 90. Philo used the adjective κακός ('evil') with man very rarely (e.g. in *Decal.* 91). Much more often, κακός is used to describe actions or thoughts of man, or that which is in a person's soul (*Deus.* 138).

[99] *Praem.* 2-3.

[100] *Praem.* 126.

[101] *Virt.* 85.

[102] *Leg.* 3.167-168.

[103] Εὐδαιμονία is often translated 'happiness,' and usually with the admission that there is no better alternative. The close association of 'happiness' with one's emotions in the English language, however, means that it fails to convey its important broader dimensions. For this reason, better alternatives might be 'completeness,' 'prosperity,' or other terms which capture 'the good life'. Williams defends his translation of 'well-being' in B. Williams, *Ethics and Limits of Philosophy* (London, 1985). For a focused study on Philo's use of this term, see David T. Runia, "Eudaimonism in Hellenistic-Jewish Literature," in *Shem in the Tents of Japhet: Essays on the Encounter of Judaism and Hellenism*, ed. James L. Kugel, *Supplements to the Journal for the Study of Judaism* (Leiden: Brill, 2002), 39-44, 52-57, 136.

[104] E.g., *Virt.* 178; *Det.* 60, 136-37.

[105] *Prob.* 88, 91.

[106] *Prob.* 91.

Philo's Guide to θεός

Platonic thought, so with Philo, to be virtuous was to resemble God, and to be his συγγένεια ('kinsman').[107] Such a goal involved, to the extent it could be attained, obeying the Law, knowing God, and walking with him. This divine end, and in particular the path of life which leads there is the subject of the following chapter.[108]

---

[107] *Virt.* 218.

[108] Runia, *Philo in Early Christian Literature: A Survey*, 39. Cf. *Virt.* 218, in which Abraham craved for kinship with God and strove by every means to live in familiarity with him. This goal harmonizes more broadly with our discussion of the nature of ἄνθρωπος. See, also, Runia's treatment of this topic in David T. Runia, "The Reward for Goodness: Philo, De Vita Contemplativa 90," in *Wisdom and Logos: Studies in Jewish Thought in Honor or David Winston* ed. David T. Runia and Gregory E. Sterling (Atlanta, 1997).

CHAPTER 7

Philo's Guide to Life

As Cicero taught, it was one thing to know the path to life and quite another to attain it.[1] The conclusion to the previous chapter intimated a gap between ideal and actual behaviour with the phrase, 'to the extent it could be attained'. If fellowship with God and well-being relied on living in a satisfactory way, how could one be sure of attaining it? How achievable did Philo perceive his path to be?

The path to Philo's τέλος

A Lofty Standard

Philo expressed a lofty ideal of virtuous living in a multitude of ways. At times, he wrote in triumphal and florid tones about walking in virtue.

> For as when the sun arises, the darkness disappears and all places are filled with light, so in the same manner when God, that sun appreciable only by the intellect, arises and illuminates the soul, the whole darkness of vices and passions is dissipated, and the pure and lovely appearance of bright and radiant virtue is displayed to the world.[2]

This text does stipulate a process, but hardly offers practical advice. Similar are the exalted portrayals of Abraham and the patriarchs as examples of virtue. On account of his virtue, Abraham reached the goal of life; he was a συγγένεια ('kinsman'), γνωριμός (an 'acquainted one', 'familiar one', 'friend') of God.[3] And Noah became perfect, showing that he acquired not one virtue but all.[4]

The patriarchs' capacity for virtue, however, could not be taken as normative. Friends of Abraham were πάντα μεγαλεῖον τῆς φύσεως αὐτοῦ καταπληττόμενοι τελειοτέραστέλεος οὔσης ἢ κατὰ ἄνθρωπον ('awe-struck at the all-embracing greatness of his nature and its more than human perfection').[5] Joshua too had ἀρετὴ τέλειος ('perfect virtue'), and Moses was full of the virtues that stemmed from love,[6] his uniqueness being due to a special work of the θείου πνεύματος ('divine Spirit'):

---

[1] Cicero, *ND*, III.79.
[2] *Virt.* 164.
[3] *Virt.* 218.
[4] *Abr.* 34; Williamson, *Jews in the Hellenistic World: Philo*, 202.
[5] *Virt.* 217.
[6] *Virt.* 55, 60.

for he did not use the same conversation as ordinary men, but, like one inspired, spoke in general in more dignified language. Whenever, therefore, he was possessed by the Holy Spirit he at once changed everything for the better, his eyes and his complexion, and his size and his appearance while standing, and his motions, and his voice; the Holy Spirit, which, being breathed into him from above, took up its lodging in his soul, clothing his body with extraordinary beauty, and investing his words with persuasiveness at the same time that it endowed his hearers with understanding.[7]

The attribute of 'perfection' is given to few in the Hebrew Bible, and there is certainly no embellishment to match that of Philo's descriptions.[8] The ideal of perfectly virtuous people was much more common in the Hellenistic world. The benefactor and Sophist Herodes Atticus of Athens (ca. AD 101-177) was described on the base of a statue found in Corinth dedicated to his wife, as ἔξοχος ἄλλων· παντοίης ἀρετῆς εἰς ἄκρον εἰκόμενος ('pre-eminent above others, who had attained the peak of every kind of virtue').

Perhaps typical of most ethical exhortation, the standard seems impossibly high, and spells out an ideal without concern for the difficulty involved in attaining it:

> But you ought to be pre-eminent in temperance and the practice of all virtues; being reckoned in the most admirable of all classifications and enrolled in obedience to a most excellent captain, the right reason of nature, by all which considerations you ought to be rendered humane, avoiding receiving in your mind anything which is wrong.[9]

The virtuous man does not do evil even in his dreams, let alone his waking hours.[10] Unlike ordinary men, the 'seven senses are unpolluted and pure in the soul of the wise man'.[11] And the Therapeutae community, through meditation on Scripture, increased in knowledge and piety:

> Therefore they always retain an imperishable recollection of God, so that not even in their dreams is any other object ever presented to their eyes except the beauty of the divine virtues and of the divine powers.[12]

---

[7] *Virt.* 217.
[8] Enoch 'was well-pleasing to God' (from εὐαρεστέω in LXX, Gen. 5:22, 24) and Job was, according to the LXX, ἀληθινός ἄμεμπτος δίκαιος θεοσεβής ἀπεχόμενος ἀπό παντὸς πονηροῦ πράγματος 'true, blameless, righteous and godly, abstaining from everything evil' (Job 1:1). This is more embellished than the Hebrew text, though still short of Philo's attributions to many characters. Most of the other 'greats' of the Old Testament err in otherwise upright lives. David is perhaps the clearest example of this, but in the Law, the weaknesses of Abraham, Isaac, Jacob, and Moses form an important part of their character and the overall plot.
[9] *Virt.* 127.
[10] *Prob.* 61.
[11] *Det.* 169.
[12] *Contempl.* 26.

But is one doing Philo a disservice by taking these standards of perfection too literally? Philo's use of the Therapeutae Community was, after all, to present the ideal rather than what was normal or even expected.

This caution granted, there remains in Philo a standard of behaviour that was to be respected and imitated. Perfection was not demanded only in this treatise, but throughout his corpus while addressing various topics. Perfect freedom, for example, was contingent upon perfect actions: 'But the good man always acts sensibly' and 'the wise man only desires such things as proceed from virtue, in which it is impossible for him to be disappointed'.[13]

In theory, for Philo as it was for the Stoics, the object of one's desire was to be only his προαίρεσις, which was always under his control and therefore guaranteed his freedom.[14] Philo likewise argued that man should pursue one thing only, not perfecting his προαίρεσις, but acting in accordance with ἀρετή. There are actions that proceed ἀπ' ἀρετῆς, those which proceed from ἀπὸ κακίας, and those which are τὰ ἀδιάφορα ('matters of indifference').[15] The wise man desired only 'the things which proceed from virtue'.[16]

Philo's categories of voluntary and involuntary actions only heightened the demands, since, in Philo as in Plato, one could err voluntarily and involuntarily. But virtuous acts were only ever done deliberately; one could not effortlessly live in virtue as one could in vice.[17]

Would the attainment of more knowledge guarantee sufficient virtue? Unfortunately, it would not. Knowledge helped its possessor make good decisions, but it also made him more accountable for doing wrong.[18]

According to Philo, perfection of virtue may be, strictly speaking, impossible. We concur with Winston, who said that for Philo

> the complete possession of virtue is impossible for man as we know him (*Mut.* 50; cf. 225; *Mos.* 2.147; Seneca, *Ep.* 75.13-15; *Ira* 2.10.6)... It is a mark of great ignorance to believe that the human soul can contain the unwavering, absolutely steadfast excellencies of God...happy is he to whom it is granted to incline towards the better and more godlike part through most of his life, for to do so throughout the whole of his life is impossible' (*Mut.* 181-5).

Elsewhere [Philo] insists that all perfection, joy, and gladness belong to God alone (*Her.* 121; *Cher.* 86) ... 'or possibly to a divine man' [Moses].[19]

---

[13] *Prob.* 60.
[14] *Prob.* 60.
[15] *Prob.* 60.
[16] *Prob.* 63.
[17] Wolfson, *Philo: Foundations of Religious Philosophy*, 1.441. For extended discussion, see 434-41.
[18] Wolfson, *Philo: Foundations of Religious Philosophy*, 1.437.
[19] David Winston, "Philo of Alexandria on the Rational and Irrational Emotions," in *Passions and Moral Progress in Greco-Roman Thought*, ed. John T. Fitzgerald (London: Routledge, 2008), 202-203.

Winston's observation highlights a point that has been emerging from this study of Philo, namely, that his sage (who adheres to his path) seems as elusive as the sage of other Hellenistic philosophers.[20] Philo's sage was virtually a 'mirror image of the Stoic sage and echoes many of the paradoxes attached to the figure' in Stoic tradition.[21] His sage is as rare as the Stoic counterpart, and for the same reasons.[22]

Philo did not leave the problem completely unresolved, however. God's help extended not only to willing subjects, but strikingly, also to those who were unwilling. Those who are greedy and ungrateful to God, and

> who have not laboured in the cause of virtue of their own free will, [God] reproves and chastises against their will by his sacred laws, which the virtuous man obeys voluntarily, and the wicked man unwillingly.[23]

The Law was given to curb the extent of wickedness, and promoted such virtues as humanity and justice. But it also sought to engage the minds and hearts of man towards God. 'Obedience' to the first-fruits requirement, for instance, fostered within people a concern for others, and sought to keep them from 'treating all things as gain'.[24] The ceremonies, holy days, and other rituals including the singing of hymns, nurtured their wills and hearts for the path of virtuous living.[25] Besides the written Law, God also provided visible imperatives through those whose lives exhort virtue: 'and what is it that we ought to look upon as unwritten laws, except the lives of those persons who have imitated virtue?'[26]

Philo imagined the way one who embodied perfect nobility might see the world. He would be in a unique and holy position to rebuke the behaviour of others:

> But you have pursued an opposite line of conduct, thinking hateful such actions as are dear to me, and loving such deeds as are hateful to me; for in my eyes modesty (αἰδώς), and truth (ἀλήθεια), and moderation of the passions (μετριοπάθεια), and simplicity (ἀτυφία), and innocence (ἀκακία), are honourable (τίμιος), but in your opinion they are dishonorable (ἄτιμος); and to me all shameless behaviour is hateful, and all falsehood, and all immoderate indulgence of the passions, and all

---

[20] Winston, "Philo of Alexandria on the Rational and Irrational Emotions," 202. He cites Leg. 1.1.2; Ebr. 26; Migr. 51, 59, 63, 123; Mut. 34-56, 213; Spec. 2.47; Virt. 10; Abr. 19; Prob. 63, 72; Agr. 180; Cicero, Off. 3.16-17; Seneca, Constant. 7; Ira 2.10.6; Ep. 42.1.

[21] John T. Fitzgerald, ed., *Passions and Moral Progress in Greco-Roman Thought* (London: Routledge, 2008), 202. See, also, Winston, "Sage and Super-Sage in Philo of Alexandria."

[22] Fitzgerald, ed., *Passions and Moral Progress in Greco-Roman Thought*, 202.

[23] *Virt.* 94.

[24] *Virt.* 95. For an extended treatment of this topic, see Leonhardt-Balzer, *Jewish Worship in Philo of Alexandria*.

[25] *Virt.* 95.

[26] *Virt.* 194.

pride, and all wickedness. But you look upon these things as near and dear to you.[27]

Though the scene was imaginary, the standards conveyed were not. One should critique oneself from the perspective of perfect virtue. The result for those who fall short was to be treated as the enemy of nobility, and one who has 'kindled the fuel of enmity into a flame' so as to be frowned upon, with an implied divine displeasure and τιμωρία ('punishment') attached.[28]

In summary, we have noted the high standard of living prescribed by Philo. The virtuous life, as established and modelled by God, was followed by Israel's forefathers and codified in the Torah. The nobility of the Jews of Philo's time were not to be perceived on the basis of their physical ancestry, but their lives, which, under the lens of perfect virtue, were to reflect a moral likeness.[29]

That satisfactory progress was possible

Some of Philo's contemporaries were concerned with the question of whether or not the standards he set were achievable. Philo himself felt it necessary to address this issue of achievability, and sought to prove that perfect virtue was attainable.

In *Quod deterius potiori insidiari soleat*, Philo acknowledged the concerns of some that the prescribed life of virtue could not be demonstrated by any living examples. Although Philo's sage seems somewhat elusive, in the context of this polemic against his critics, he asserted that his path was indeed achievable. He did so by first showing disdain for those with this concern, since it was those 'who are not versed in the arts, who have little understanding of logical deduction, but who make general statements based on appearances' who are accustomed to this question.[30] Nevertheless he answers their question, 'who have there been in the past, and who are there living now of the kind that you imagine?'

> An excellent answer is that in the past there have been those who surpassed their contemporaries in virtue, who took God for their sole guide and living according to a law of nature's right reason, not only free themselves, but communicating to their neighbours the spirit of freedom: also in our own time there are still men formed as it were in the likeness of the original sages.[31]

The beginning of his answer contains a helpful concession that should inform the way one interprets Philo's conception of the good life. That is, despite expressing virtue in hyperbolic terms elsewhere, in this description he refers simply to 'those who surpassed their contemporaries in virtue' and who, perhaps generally speaking, 'took God for their sole guide' and 'lived

---

[27] *Virt.* 195-197.
[28] *Virt.* 197, 200.
[29] *Virt.* 196-198.
[30] *Prob.* 63.
[31] The group of contemporaries he is referring to is the Essene sect.

according to a law of nature's right reason'.³² To simply surpass one's contemporaries was a softer expression of the ideal, but it required an impressive and rare degree of virtue nonetheless. To conclude that they were merely better-than-average people from this text, however, would be to flatten the exalted descriptions elsewhere. But to address this very direct challenge, Philo resists using the usual superlative language about perfect virtue in favour of a more measured explanation.

He conceded that 'the number of such men is small, for virtue is not widespread among mortal kind'.³³ One should not be surprised by this, since whatever is exceedingly beautiful is rare, and because virtuous people are reclusive. They avoid the 'great crowd of the more thoughtless and keep themselves at leisure for the contemplation of the things of nature'.³⁴ The 'wise and just and virtuous' are small in number,³⁵ but Philo was adamant that though their numbers are 'scanty, they are not absolutely non-existent'.³⁶

To gather sufficient evidence for the possibility of truly virtuous people Philo was forced to resort to what was ancient 'history', referring to the legendary 'seven wise men' of Greece. Sadly, more recent examples of virtuous Greeks since the time of the Seven had not been recorded due to the neglect of their contemporaries.³⁷ Some examples could, however, be cited from other nations, but aside from his detailed account of the Essenes of the Jews, he had only a vague knowledge of these distant groups. He referred to the 'Barbarian' sages: the Magi of the Persians, the Gymnosophists of India, people of high moral excellence in Syria and Palestine.³⁸ Some of Philo's other examples were those who did a single virtuous act, which may at best demonstrate that people wholeheartedly pursued something for a time, but it does not demonstrate people lived continually according to his prescribed path. Overall, Philo's use of ancient and foreign examples are a sketchy attempt to bolster his claim that his path of life was actually achievable.

It may have been due to this awkward absence of living sages that Philo, in *De praemiis et poenis*, made a significant concession.

> And very admirable is this fullness and completeness, not of months or years, but of days, so that no day whatever in the life of a virtuous man ever leaves an empty and open door for the entrance of sins, but is filled in all its parts and all its intervals with absolute virtue and excellence. For virtue and goodness (ἀρετὴ καὶ

---

[32] For a Jewish example of this sense of uprightness, see Ps. 22. David, who could be considered a righteous man in general terms, was clearly unrighteous in the detail, as he himself concedes in his prayer of confession in Ps. 51. Repentance and the sacrificial system were factors in enabling self-confessed sinners to declare themselves righteous.
[33] *Virt.* 11.
[34] *Prob.* 63.
[35] φρονίμων δὲ καὶ δικαίων καὶ ἀστείων ὀλίγος ἀριθμός, *Prob.* 72.
[36] *Prob.* 72 cf. *Mut.* 35-37.
[37] *Prob.* 73.
[38] *Prob.* 74-75.

ὁ καλός) are judged not by quantity but by quality (κρίνεται γὰρ οὐ ποσότητι ἀλλὰ ποιότητι). Therefore, I look upon it that the wise man's single day successfully spent (from κατορθόω) is of equal value to an entire life time.[39]

This concession may be the difference between hope and despair of ever attaining perfect virtue, but the good 'life' presented here was far less impressive than normal. It was by no means a conspicuous concession in Philo's overall corpus, and was absent from the treatise which raised and dealt with the problem of achievability. Generally speaking, Philo does not depict the standard to be anything less than the consistently and absolutely virtuous life. Indeed it was his normal assumption that the path of life was attainable, and that the Law provided the way to it.[40]

Another solution offered by Philo was that the problem lay with people who desired and pursued the wrong things, not that the attainment of virtue was too difficult.[41] Citing Deuteronomy 30:10, Philo argued that the obedience that God demanded was within reach. It was not far off, and did not involve a long pilgrimage or any humanly impossible task. Rather virtuous living was comprised of humanly possible behaviour, compartmentalised into three realms: our mouth, our heart, and our hands (στόματι καὶ καρδίᾳ καὶ χερσί), which represent our 'speech, thought, and actions' (λόγῳ καὶ διανοίᾳ καὶ πράξεσιν).[42]

In theory, the potential for virtuous behaviour always existed because one was never forced to do wrong. In practice, however, the notable absence of any such sages remained an issue for the critics to whom Philo refers, as it was for Cicero the previous century.

For Philo, as it was for many philosophers, the notion of προκοπή ('progress') was key for evaluating one's performance. Philo conceived of a 'middle' or 'intermediate' group called the ὁ μέσος, who, unable to live perfectly, instead dwell somewhere between good and evil.[43] They could be taught and benefit from God's law.[44]

While discussing progress in Epictetus, it was observed that the only impervious possession for him, and thus the focal point of his attention, was his own volition (προαίρεσις). Philo adopted the Stoic idea of a single untouchable pursuit, but declared it to be living in accordance with virtue (ἀρετή).

---

[39] *Praem.* 112.

[40] E.g. *Prob.* 68; where Philo cites Deut. 14; cf. *Virt.* 183.

[41] *Prob.* 71. Yet some crimes and some evil doers are beyond forgiveness and correction. The 'bad' and those 'separated' from virtue can be restored, but not the 'entirely bad' nor those 'divorced' from virtue. Their sickness is beyond healing. *Det.* 144, 149-50.

[42] *Praem.* 80. See, also, *Virt.* 183.

[43] *Leg.* 1.93, 95. In *Agr.* 120-1, Philo also refers to the practicers or athletes (οἱ ἀθληταί) when using an Olympic metaphor to say that it is not only first and second placed should be honored, but also those who perform to receive a 'moderate prize'.

[44] *Leg.* 1.93, 95. See further discussion in Williamson, *Jews*, 206-207.

Philo's Guide to Life

Since then it is only in the virtues of the soul (ἐν τοῖς τῆς ψυχῆς μόνοις ἀγαθοῖς) that genuine and unadulterated joy is found, and since every wise man rejoices, he rejoices in himself (ἐν ἑαυτῷ), and not in the things about him (οὐκ ἐν τοῖς περὶ αὐτόν); for the things that are in himself are the virtues of the mind (διανοίας εἰσὶν ἀρεταί) on which it is worthy for a man to exalt in; but the circumstances which surround him are either a good condition of body or an abundance of external wealth, which are not proper objects for a man to pride himself on.[45]

As with the Stoics, much was at stake with this single pursuit, as it could guarantee or deny freedom from pain and perturbation.

From that soul therefore, in which justice has brought forth a male offspring, that is to say just thoughts, it has also at the same time 'removed all painful things' (τὰ λυπηρὰ πάντα ἐξῴκισται).[46]

A Hopeful Outlook Overall

Despite the critics' concerns, Philo maintains a generally hopeful outlook for those who follow his exhortation towards virtue. Why was this so? It may be that in the Alexandrian context where similarly demanding paths were being promoted by the Stoics and other philosophers, Philo thought little about the achievability 'problem' that his critics raised. To some degree he was unperturbed to promote a path that so few had walked.[47]

It would be too simplistic to say that Philo did not recognise that this was a problem for some on the basis that he felt it necessary to address it. Besides the concessions discussed above, which reduced what constituted perfection, perhaps the most significant reason for hope was God's involvement in the outcome. It is at this point that Philo departed significantly from Greek philosophy.

Repentance and a keen appreciation for human imperfection were oft-repeated principles in the Pentateuch as well as the Jewish Scriptures.[48] The whole sacrificial system bore testimony to this, as did such passages as Leviticus 26:40-42, which anticipated sin and repentance:

And they shall confess their sins, and the sins of their fathers; that they have transgressed and neglected me, and that they have walked contrary to me, and I walked contrary to them; and I will destroy them in the land of their enemies: then shall their uncircumcised heart be ashamed, and then shall they acquiesce in the punishment of their sins. And I will remember the covenant of Jacob, and the covenant of Isaac, and the covenant of Abraham will I remember.[49]

---

[45] *Det.* 137.
[46] *Det.* 121.
[47] If Philo was an elitist like many others of his class in ancient society, then the scarcity of adherents may have added to, not detracted from, the value of his path. On the other hand, Philo seemed to envision a large scale acceptance of it.
[48] Wolfson, *Philo: Foundations of Religious Philosophy*, 2.255-56.
[49] English translation of LXX.

Philo referred often to Leviticus, and learned from Leviticus 10:16, for example, that

> To never sin is the peculiar attribute of God; and to repent is the part of a wise man. But this is very difficult and very hard to attain to.
> τὸ μὲν μηδὲν ἁμαρτεῖν ἴδιον θεοῦ, τὸ δὲ μετανοεῖν σοφοῦ· παγχάλεπον δὲ καὶ δυσεύρετον τοῦτό γε.[50]

God could bridge the gap between imperfect effort and his own perfection. Philo's importation of non-Hellenistic 'virtues' such as faith and repentance may be telling in this regard. Faith in Israel's history involved the conviction that God would deliver his people in accordance with his character and promises. So too, the theme of repentance and the sacrificial system in the Law assumes moral imperfection requiring God's mercy.[51]

In his section, Περὶ μετανοίας, Philo focused on the important place of repentance, 'For absolute sinlessness belongs to God alone, or possibly to a divine man' (τὸ μὲν γὰρ μηδὲν συνόλως ἁμαρτεῖν ἴδιον θεοῦ, τάχα δὲ καὶ θείου ἀνδρός). [52]

> For how can it be anything but a most intolerable evil, for a creature which is inconstant and easily moved in every direction, to lay down any positive decision and determination about itself, attributing to itself the virtues of the Creator?[53]

It is at this point that one might ask more penetrating questions about God's involvement in one's progress towards virtue. Philo also suggested that χάρις ('grace') shown by God was the basis for the imperfect to have hope.[54] But was

---

[50] *Fug.* 157.
[51] Forgiveness following repentance is a key concept in the Law and sacrificial system. An ancient Jewish reflection of this effect of the Law can be seen in such Psalms as 51 and 119.
[52] *Virt.* 177. The λόγος of Philo was also called the 'Son of God' (*Conf.* 146), and the 'divine man' was a figure whose qualities in some respects approached the divine man and λόγος of NT writers. But 'there is nothing in that Philonic conception that is precisely the same as the Christian concept of the Incarnation with a particularly human life (Jesus of Nazareth), of the Person within a Triune Deity designated the Son or Logos'. Williamson, *Jews in the Hellenistic World: Philo*, 2.117-18; cf. 25-26, Winston, "Sage and Super-Sage in Philo of Alexandria," 824. For further discussion of the 'divine man', and the extent to which logos was personified in people, see H. Leisegang, "Der Gottmensch Als Archetypus," *ErJb 18 [Aus der Welt der Urbilder: Sonderband für C. G. Jung zum fünfundsiebzigsten Geburtstag, 26. Juli 1950]* (1950). Cited in *R-R*, 88.
[53] *Praem.* 148.
[54] Forms of χάρις occur 345 times in Philo. For passages relating to God's participation in our path to virtue, some with mention of χάρις, see *Leg.* 3.78; *Virt.* 161-74; *Leg.* 3.136; *Cher.* 50; *Somn.* 1.173; 2.25, 266-7; *Post.* 30-1; *Leg.* 2.86; 3.219; *Her.* 272-3. See also Borgen, *Philo of Alexandria – an Exegete for His Time*, 255; Winston, "Philo of Alexandria on the Rational and Irrational Emotions," 212-13; Wolfson, *Philo: Foundations of Religious Philosophy*, 1.448-51.

this grace simply God's response to the good intentions of good people? Or did God's grace precede this, and actually cause their good intentions?

Sometimes it is difficult to ascertain whether God's grace precedes human virtue or whether it simply accompanies and rewards it. Taken in isolation from its context, the following passage seems to place the onus on God for the human escape from vice to virtue:

> This is the mind which a little while ago was enslaved to many pleasures and many desires, and to innumerable necessities arising from weaknesses and desires; but has been redeemed into freedom by God, who broke the miseries of its slavery. This is the mind which has received a favour not to be suppressed in silence, but rather to be proclaimed abroad and announced in every quarter, because of the mightiness of its defender, by which it was not thrust down to the tail, but was raised upwards to the head.[55]

God is certainly the active agent in these verses. The enslaved one was redeemed by God, the mind was the recipient of favour, and the benevolence of God is inferred by the need to proclaim him abroad as the 'mighty defender'.

Taken in its context, however, we are prevented from concluding that God's grace initiated and caused the transformation. The text continues by saying that the punishment was deserved by the evildoer, and the rewards come upon

> good men, men who fulfil the laws by their deeds, which blessings will be accomplished by the gift of the bounteous God, who glorifies and rewards moral excellence because of its likeness to itself.[56]

Usually, there is a cooperative effort between humans who struggle for virtue, and God who helps those who seek it.

> For when God is favourable everything is made easy. And he is favourable to those who display modesty and due reverence, and who seek to pass over from intemperance to temperance, and who reproach themselves for all the blameable actions of their life, and for all the base images which they have stamped upon their polluted souls, and who aim at a tranquil state of the passions, and who keep constantly in view, as the proper object of their pursuit, a calmness and serenity of life.[57]

Even references to God as 'merciful Saviour' describe his mercy as being in response to the initiative of repentant people. When they have changed, then they will obtain God's εὐμένεια ('goodwill,' 'favour,' or 'grace'). Concerted effort would put one in good stead to receive God's favour.

Philo's description of the *Therapeutae* community accords with this observation. In *De vita contemplativa* 90, the initiative of mankind to 'procure

---

[55] *Praem.* 124.
[56] *Praem.* 126.
[57] *Praem.* 116.

them his love' is clear. It was 'because of their virtue' that God loves and rewards them.[58]

But perhaps the most explicit text on the question of whether grace was earned, is *De virtutibus* 184-85, where Philo exhorts correct speech, thoughts, and actions.[59] When these three are in harmony, the result was εὐδαιμονία. Such a man 'will be well-pleasing to God, thus becoming at once God-loving and God-beloved'.[60] There was a 'reciprocation of choice' (τῆς αἱρέσεως ἡ ἀντίδοσις) taking place, in which a person chose to serve God, and God immediately took the supplant to himself'. This text brings clarity to a point made often, though less explicitly, in many other texts. Man's choice of God was the trigger for God's choice of him.

Concluding Comments

De Abr. 4-6 provides us with a succinct summary of some of the thoughts above, and reiterates some of the tensions involved in what it means to be virtuous, and to fulfil all that was expected. On the one hand, people are to praise, and to imitate, the earliest characters of the Bible. They

> lived irreproachably and admirably, and their virtues are durably and permanently recorded as on pillars in the sacred scriptures, not merely with the object of praising the men themselves, but also for the sake of exhorting those who read their history, and of leading them on to emulate their conduct.[61]

They taught that

> it is not very difficult or laborious for those who wish to live according to the laws established in these books, since the earliest men easily and spontaneously obeyed the unwritten principle of legislation before any one of the particular laws were written down at all.[62]

Israel's founding fathers 'never of deliberate purpose did anything open to reproach'.[63] On the other hand, Philo did not attribute absolute ethical perfection to them either, saying 'and for their accidental errors, they propitiated God, and appeased him by prayers and supplications'.[64] Imperfection of behaviour, at least in the sphere of what was unintentional, was

---

[58] C.f. *Virt.* 79. God's graces are 'not dispensed to all men, however, but only to such as are suppliants for them; and suppliants are those persons who love virtue and piety, and it is lawful for them to drink up those most sacred springs, inasmuch as they are continually thirsting for wisdom'.

[59] *Praem.* 80. See also *Virt.* 183.

[60] *Virt.* 183.

[61] *Abr.* 4.

[62] *Abr.* 5.

[63] *Abr.* 6. In this matter of describing the wise, good, pious, or godly, we must realise that for much of the treatise the writer is speaking on a theoretical level. It is an ideal humanity who follows the guide, not a known group in a way perhaps not dissimilar from 'the wise and the fool' in the Book of Proverbs.

[64] *Abr.* 4-6.

a tolerable reality in the lives of virtuous men. Error could be followed by prayers, supplications, and in the ancient tradition, a sacrificial system which restored fellowship with God.[65]

In trying to defend the achievability of his path to virtue, Philo acknowledged the scarcity of living examples. While he often prescribed perfect virtue in absolute terms, he provided a softer definition of what it meant to live virtuously. Perfection was more about quality than quantity of days, and so examples of perfect virtue included those who revealed their character on one good day or through one good action. Further, to be considered virtuous was something of a relative term, so that people who were more virtuous than others could be called virtuous, despite the inevitable presence of vice in their lives if examined closely. Philo exhorted that his readers progress towards perfection of virtue, to the pursuit of the image of those gone before. Yet absolute moral perfection, while a good goal, was probably deemed unlikely. This explains the themes of pursuit, acknowledgement of sin, and repentance.[66] He exhorted goodness in the absolute sense, but probably expected goodness to be lived out in the more common or relative-to-others sense.

Drawing from two well established traditions to portray the path of life, the extent of influence of each depended on the topic and treatise at hand. His very philosophical *Quod omnis probus liber sit* ('Every Good Man is Free') places much responsibility upon the individual for virtue. One must follow the pattern of nature and wisdom in order to reach this end. Philosophy trained the Essenes towards the attainment of virtue. But speaking with a more overtly Jewish perspective, as he does in *De praemiis et poenis* ('Rewards and Punishments'), he allowed more room for God's involvement, sovereignty and deliverance. God was ready to reciprocate man's repentance and good intentions, but did not clearly play a part in leading him to this resolve.

The confusion surrounding the achievability, and God's involvement, in Philo's path of life may be explained by the vastly different approach to such topics across the Judaism-philosophy divide. The former emphasised God's action with human participation; the latter gives emphasis to human activity with the God or gods' endorsement. It might be said that Philo held both perspectives, but it is probably more accurate to say that as a result of this attempt, he held neither.

---

[65] Philo refers to appeasing God by 'prayers and supplications' where we might also expect him to mention sacrifice. The absence of sacrifice may be because as a diaspora Jew, Philo would not have had much experience of the system, even though he referred to it often in his exegetical treatises.

[66] For example, Philo highly esteemed the youth of the Therapeutae community, who were 'pressing on to reach the summit of virtue' (*Contempl.* 72). Virtue was not instantly nor easily attained. Before one reached the summit one had to live with imperfection and simply make progress.

Rewards and Punishments

The Rewards for Virtue

In order to discuss the τέλος of Philo's path of life, it was necessary to discuss the two significant rewards, well-being and fellowship with God. This section will spell-out the other benefits that awaited those who followed Philo's Guide to Life.

In *De praemiis et poenis*, Philo echoed the Torah's promises of health, wealth and progeny as rewards for the virtuous. God's people would have 'abundant production of all necessary things, such as corn, and wine, and oil, and all other productions which are conducive to a comfortable and easy life'.[67]

Further benefits 'for those who follow God and always and everywhere cleave to his commandments' are peace, harmonious society with authoritative rulers, and wealth.[68] Material wealth, while not necessary for contented living, befits the virtuous:

> those who pursue the above-named wealth, who welcome the gifts of nature and not those of empty seeming, who practise frugality and self-restraint, will possess also abundance and more than abundance of another wealth in the shape of delectable food, and that without effort on their part. For it will spring to meet those who are at the same time the most proper, and, in fact, the most nearly related to it and thoroughly worthy of it.[69]

As is discernible from the discussion of the sophists in chapter 5, Philo would more likely associate with the ascetics than the sophists on the matter of wealth and physical comfort. He considered the humble lifestyle of the Therapeutae community, for example, conducive to pious living.[70]

Thus, Philo was by no means a hedonist, nor was he an outright advocate of asceticism.[71] In *Praem.* 118 he concludes the discussion quoted above with a helpful summary:

> These, then, of which we have already spoken, are what are called ἐκτὸς ἀγαθὰ ('external goods'), victory over one's enemies, superiority in war, confirmation of peace, and abundance of those good things which belong to peace, riches, and

---

[67] *Praem.* 107.
[68] *Praem.* 98; cf. 93-100.
[69] *Praem.* 100.
[70] E.g. *Contempl.* 13.
[71] Such insights also act as an interpretive aid for such passages as *Det.* 33-34, where the sophists condemn the lifestyle of the 'so called lovers of philosophy'. For Philo does not resolve the conflict within that passage by sharing his own view. The reader does not know whether he sides with the sophists or the ascetics on this matter. Thus, this passage provides counter balancing evidence, against the emphasis of other passages, that he is also sympathetic to the sophistic view that material well-being is appropriate for the pious. By understanding his position on this matter, we are better able to handle the more difficult passages where he is less revealing of his position.

honours, and authorities, and the praises which always follow those who are successful.[72]

He later states that the bodies of those who strive for virtue will receive

> the gift of complete freedom from disease, and if some infirmity should befall them it will come not to do them injury but to remind the mortal that he is mortal, to humble his over-weening spirit and to improve his moral condition. Health will be followed by efficiency of the senses and the perfection and completeness of every part.[73]

It was in this context that he calls the body 'the congenital and lifelong house of the soul', which God thought it right to make 'well-built and well compacted from foundation to roof, to provide the many things which are necessary and useful for life and particularly for the sake of the mind'. God's intention of blessing, then, encompassed the mind and body. That said, the passage above reveals God's priority for our spiritual health over physical health, since he may allow one's health to suffer to promote spiritual well-being.

The book of Job, which Philo cites on one occasion (*Mut.* 48), counters a simplistic correlation between virtue and prosperity on the one hand, or between sin and suffering on the other. Job was a virtuous man who suffered. So too other Jewish texts oppose such formulaic thinking, such as the observation of the prosperity of the wicked in Psalm 73. In Isaiah 49-53 God's servant would experience much physical and emotional hardship, leading even to his premature death without progeny through execution.[74]

The patriarchs prioritised such God-related blessing over material prosperity. They 'pressed forward to the same τέλος of life, namely, to be pleasing to the Maker and Father of all' (τῷ ποιητῇ καὶ πατρὶ τῶν ὅλων εὐαρεστῆσαι). Such a goal required 'despising all those objects which the generality of men admire: glory, and riches, and pleasure, and laughing at pride'.[75] The personal benefit was to be spared the vanity common to man.[76]

---

[72] *Praem.* 118.
[73] *Praem.* 119.
[74] Nevertheless, these narrow conceptions remained among some Jews in the time of Christ, who challenged them when his disciples asked him, 'Rabbi, who sinned, this man or his parents, that he was born blind?' Jesus answered, 'It was not that this man sinned, nor his parents' (Jn 9:2-3). Similarly in Lk. 13:1-5, 'There were some present at that very time who told [Jesus] about the Galileans whose blood Pilate had mingled with their sacrifices. And he answered them, 'Do you think that these Galileans were worse sinners than all the other Galileans, because they suffered in this way? No, I tell you; but unless you repent, you will all likewise perish. Or those eighteen on whom the tower in Siloam fell and killed them: do you think that they were worse offenders than all the others who lived in Jerusalem? No, I tell you; but unless you repent, you will all likewise perish.'
[75] *Praem.* 24.
[76] *Praem.* 24-25.

Other 'Stoic' rewards included tranquility of mind, and σοφία ('wisdom') which, like reason, led to true ἐλευθερία ('freedom'). Perfect freedom was closely akin to complete independence of action, so that one could stand 'defiant and triumphant over love, fear, cowardice, grief and all such things, as the victor over the fallen in the wrestling bout'. He yearns for the 'freedom whose particular heritage it is that it obey no orders and works no will but its own'. Such a free man, in the 'tossing surge of circumstances'…'bears all that can befall him with a noble courage'—he 'is at once both a philosopher and a free man'.[77]

To summarise, Philo, who stood between both extremes of hedonism and asceticism, maintained a strong cause-and-effect motif in relation to virtue. The virtuous man would usually remain unhurt, since God 'honours virtue and has given it immunity from all designs against it as its proper reward'.[78]

His exegetical work, *De praemiis et poenis,* constrained by his interpretation of the blessings in the Torah, included physical and external elements to his picture of happiness and blessing. When he adopted a philosophical approach, however, as in *Quod omnis probus liber sit,* he was constrained by Stoic thought to say that no such externalities were actually a good at all. In this latter treatise Joseph needed correction for his view that there were three types of good things: 'those pertaining to the outside world, those to the body, and to the soul'.[79]

Overall, an insightful, even if unrealistic, picture of the path *and* goal of Philo's Guide to Life lies in the description of those whom Philo considered lived in accordance with it: the *Therapeutae* community.[80] They demonstrate what true philosophy looked like in practice.

> This then is what I have to say of those who are called Therapeutae, who have devoted themselves to the contemplation of nature, and who have lived in it and in the soul alone, being citizens of heaven and of the world, and very acceptable to the Father and Creator of the universe because of their ἀρετή, which has procured them his love as their most appropriate reward, which far surpasses all the gifts of fortune, and conducts them to the very summit and perfection of εὐδαιμονία.[81]

In addition to these individual rewards, social change would flow from virtuous lives. Moses was a case study for the way blessings upon the pious spill over into their society. He was given authority and honour by 'the all-righteous God, who honours the lovers of piety with independent authority, to the great advantage of all who are associated with them'.[82]

---

[77] *Prob.* 24.
[78] *Praem.* 90.
[79] *Det.* 8.
[80] The Essenes' perfect and happy lives are also held up as a model for imitation in *Prob.* 84-91.
[81] *Contempl.* 90.
[82] *Virt.* 218.

Philo's Guide to Life

The Law promised external blessings of 'victories over enemies, successes in wars, establishments of peace and abundant supplies of the good things of peace, honours and offices and the eulogies accompanying the successful, who receive praise from the lips of all, friends and enemies'.[83] If men's hearts change towards virtue and peace, not only would humanity experience harmony, but even the wild beasts of nature would cease their aggression.[84]

The Punishment for Vice

The flip side of privilege and honour for the virtuous was individual and social κόλασις ('punishment') for the wicked. For the wicked there was 'punishment which affects individuals, houses, cities, countries, nations, and vast regions of the earth'.[85]

The significance of vice and its consequences were highlighted by Philo:

> those who are not totally ignorant would choose to be blinded than see unfitting things, and to be deprived of hearing than listen to harmful words, and to have their tongues cut out to save them from uttering anything that should not be divulged...It is better to be made a eunuch than to be mad after illicit unions.[86]

Why? Because 'all these things, seeing that they plunge the soul in disasters for which there is no remedy, would properly incur the most extreme vengeance and τιμωρία ('punishment')'.[87]

In Stoicism the judgement one received was the natural outworking of poor behaviour, rather than personally inflicted by God. For Philo, the words 'penalty' and 'curses' reflect the calculated engagement of God in proportion to the disobedience.[88] The consequences were not only such internal consequences as hindrance and enslavement, but included physical hardships such as famine and disease that technically did not count for the Stoic.

God's judgement of his own people Israel was not ultimately for their destruction, but reform. He sought to improve the soul as well as the tongue of his people.[89] His judgement benefited not only the victim, but those who witnessed and were thus warned by it. It had both a punitive and correctional function.

What form did judgement take for those who transgressed the Law? Philo provided a summary of how many of the Law's curses (ἀραί), drawn from Israel's history, applied to his first-century setting. First, were the evils (κακοί) of πενία καὶ ἔνδεια ('poverty and deficiency').[90] Families would be destroyed

---

[83] *Praem.* 118.
[84] *Praem.* 88-90.
[85] *Praem.* 7.
[86] *Det.* 175-76.
[87] *Det.* 176.
[88] *Praem.* 157.
[89] *Praem.* 163, 170.
[90] *Praem.* 127; cf. 127, 136.

by it, and cities stripped of their inhabitants.[91] It may have been the lightest of the threatened calamities, but when needs were not met for long periods, the body and soul would waste away in enduring suffering. Within this curse, Philo included war, which was often the reason for such widespread and long-term destitution.[92] Second was slavery, a most 'intolerable evil' to those who were born free. Death was a preferable option for wise men.[93] Third, 'diseases of the body [which would] overpower each limb and part'. Onlookers would be amazed at the victims' change of fortunes, becoming 'nothing but sinews with a thin coating of skin'.[94] These calamities were meant to chasten and reform the victims.[95] Adding further sting to the message of doom upon the Jews was the exaltation of the virtuous proselyte who outperformed the Jew, and who received divine blessing and a place in heaven instead of punishment and curse:

> God receives gladly ἀρετή which grows out of hostility to him, utterly disregarding its original roots, but looking favourably on the whole trunk from its lowest foundation, because it has become useful, and has changed its nature so as to become fruitful (εὐκαρπία).[96]

The Guide to Life in Practice

The Battle for Virtue

Jacob provided Philo with an example of one who battled to be virtuous. For Jacob, 'the applier of knowledge' (ὁ ἀσκητὴς ἐπιστήμης), virtuous living required a daily battle against ἀμαθία ('ignorance') and the ἄλογοι ('irrational') faculties of one's soul.[97] It was a battle in which one's desires and responses had to be brought into accord with reason,[98] and 'perfected through practice'.[99] One should persevere despite battle wounds,[100] difficulties[101] and even 'violent sorrow in the soul'.[102]

The enemy was ἐπιθυμία ('passion, desire, lust'), 'the insidious foe and source of all evils'.[103] Ἐπιθυμία is elsewhere described, using the words of Plato, as τὸ θρεμμάτων ἀπληστότατον ('that most insatiable of animals').[104] If

---

[91] *Praem.* 133.
[92] *Praem.* 132.
[93] *Praem.* 137.
[94] *Praem.* 146.
[95] *Praem.* 148.
[96] *Praem.* 152.
[97] *Det.* 2-3.
[98] *Det.* 4-5.
[99] *Congr.* 45-6; cf. *Cher.* 79-82.
[100] *Contempl.* 72.
[101] *Cher.* 79-82.
[102] *Aet.* 63.
[103] *Virt.* 100.
[104] *Contempl.* 74. See footnote in Colson, *LCL*, who cites Plato, *Timaeus* 70 E.

desires are not kept in check, when stimulated by further 'sensing' of the world, they would surely overwhelm a person. For,

> It is a cruel thing that the inlets of the senses should be opened wide for the torrent of the objects of sense to be poured, like a surging river, into their gaping orifices, with nothing to stay their violent rush. For then the mind is found to be overwhelmed, being wholly absorbed by so vast a wave, and being utterly unable to swim against it, or even to raise its head above it.[105]

With this potential flood always threatening, Philo set out the practical method of maintaining control,[106] in which the final exhortation was to 'contain' oneself: 'So let us make it our earnest endeavour to bind up each opening (στόμιον) which we have mentioned with the unbreakable chains of self-control (ἐγκράτεια)' since

> wretchedness is due to the different parts of the soul having been left loose and gaping and unfastened, but that the fact of their being compacted and tightly bound together contributed to uprightness and life and reason.[107]

A man must contain his desires, preventing their escape towards their object and from acquiring their natural objects. Living in isolation from the world could help in this struggle,[108] particularly for those who had recently come over 'to the ranks of virtue' and were most vulnerable to relapse.[109]

The sense of taste was neither good nor evil; moderation was important.[110] So too sexual organs were created and sexual activity deemed legitimate, according to Philo, as long as it was μετὰ νόμου ('according to the Law'), viz. for procreation, and without impurity.[111]

Emotions played a positive role in this battle. For example, a developed love for God was the powerful force for overcoming the weaker and less noble emotions:

> Thus it is the mind set ablaze by the dazzling vision of the Beautiful, a vision graciously bestowed by God, that ultimately counters the dark glow of the flaming passions and extinguishes them.

In the conflict of emotions, weaker emotions were defeated by stronger ones, and the most powerful force in this battle was the intellectual love of God.[112] Virtue was the divine food, and the scarcity of it was worse than the scarcity of meat and drink.[113] Virtue, 'like a magnet' would draw those who appreciated her:

---

[105] *Det.* 99-100.
[106] *Det.* 101-102.
[107] *Det.* 103.
[108] *Praem.* 17-18.
[109] *Praem.* 21; cf. *Prob.* 78; *Contempl.* 20.
[110] *Det.* 101.
[111] *Det.* 102.
[112] Winston, "Philo of Alexandria on the Rational and Irrational Emotions," 213.
[113] *Det.* 116.

Therefore, my soul, if any of the love-lures of pleasure invite you, turn yourself aside, let your eyes look elsewhere. Look rather on the genuine beauty of virtue, gaze on her continually, till yearning sink into your marrow, till like the magnet it draw you on and bring you nigh and bind you fast to the object of your desire.'[114]

Philo praises those who persistently pursue virtue, because they make the 'soul alone the treasure-house of the good at which they aim, [and] devote themselves to praiseworthy actions'.[115]

The Importance of ἄσκησις ('Practice')

The danger of merely knowing and professing philosophy as opposed to doing it was real, and a classic trait of the sophists among others.[116] For Philo, any assessment of the quality of one's training should include, if not be dominated by, an ethical dimension. Repeated through his work is a close connection between knowledge and application of such knowledge.

The patriarchs *practised* virtue. Abraham was 'the first establisher of the sentiments devoted to God', the first person who crossed over from pride to truth. He was 'self-taught' and had 'self-implanted virtue' and was given joy as a prize.[117] Isaac's antagonists were 'terrified at the greatness and exceeding excellence of his nature in all things'.[118] Jacob was 'made perfect' by ἄσκησις and was 'the practitioner of wisdom'.[119] Despite his rhetorical weakness, Moses could be called 'perfect Moses'[120] on account of his virtuous life, which led to God honouring him as his 'interpreter'[121] to speak the sacred oracles.[122] Joshua too was in all respects morally good.[123]

The Essenes, perhaps reacting to philosophers and sophists who focused on the display of knowledge, intentionally abandoned

> the logical part of philosophy, as in no respect necessary for the acquisition of virtue, to the λογοθῆραι ('word-catchers'); and the natural part, as being too sublime for human nature to master, to those who love to converse about high objects (except indeed so far as such a study takes in the contemplation of the existence of God and of the creation of the universe), they devote all their attention to the moral part of philosophy.[124]

---

[114] *Gig.* 43-44.
[115] *Det.* 35.
[116] *Det.* 74.
[117] *Praem.* 27.
[118] *Det.* 29.
[119] *Det.* 45.
[120] *Det.* 129, 131.
[121] *Praem.* 53.
[122] *Praem.* 1; cf. 53-54; *Virt.* 67; *Det.* 125.
[123] *Virt.* 67.
[124] *Prob.* 80; cf. 84-91. For the three-fold division see also *Agr.* 14ff; and for the Stoic view in which natural theology is included in physics see the Colson's footnotes on *Abr.* 99.

The virtues are defined in a way that precludes one from divorcing knowledge of them from practice. One who has the virtues acts virtuously, since the behaviour was the organic product (γέννημα) of each virtue:

> for out of φρόνησις ('knowledge,' 'good sense') is produced sensible conduct, out of σωφροσύνη ('moderation') modest behaviour, out of εὐσέβεια ('piety') pious demeanour, and from each of the other virtues, the activity that corresponds to it.[125]

The virtues were intrinsically powerful, intended to produce the behavioural manifestation of that which they were.[126]

The end and means to Philo's Guide to Life have been discussed in this chapter with reference primarily to the life that preceded death. The important implications of Philo's view of death and the afterlife will be the subject of the next chapter.

---

[125] *Det.* 114.
[126] *Cher.* 102.

CHAPTER 8

Philo's Guide to Death

Philo was aware of the contention that surrounded death and the life that may or may not follow it. He engaged with what was an internal debate among the Stoics over whether the world was incorruptible or whether there would be a great conflagration.[1] He would have also been well aware of the custom of giving divine honours, and with it the recognition of immortality, to emperors on their accession to the Principate.[2] Seneca the Younger (c. 4 BC – AD 65) would teach that 'It takes the whole of life to learn how to live, and—what will perhaps make you wonder more—it takes the whole of life to learn how to die (*tota vita discendum est mori*).'[3]

In this context of interest and debate surrounding death, Philo drew from his Jewish and Hellenistic traditions to set forth his own Guide to Death as it related to his Guide to Life. He did not compile his thoughts about death in any one treatise, so the approach of this chapter will be to gather an overall picture of his view offered by various texts.

Death and the Afterlife

Immortality through Progeny

Besides the immediate benefits of virtue expressed in Chapter 7, Philo taught that how one lived prior to death had implications for one's progeny:

> But someone may say, What is the use of all these things to one who is not likely to leave heirs and successors behind him? The law, setting as it were the seal to its acts of beneficence, replies: No one shall be without offspring, nor shall there be a barren woman; but all the genuine and sincere servants of God shall fulfill the law of nature as respects the propagation of their species. For the men shall become fathers, and the fathers shall be happy in their offspring, and the women shall be happy mothers of children, so that every house shall be a full company of a numerous family... But no man shall die prematurely or without having fulfilled the legitimate end of his being among those men who observe the laws, nor shall such fail to reach the age which God has allotted to the race of man. But the human being...will eventually arrive at the last of all, that which is near to death,

---

[1] *Aet.* 76-78, 85-90.
[2] Winter, *Philo and Paul among the Sophists*, 42.
[3] Seneca, *De Brevitate Vitae*, 7.3-4.

or rather to immortality; being really and truly happy in his old age, leaving behind him a house happy in numerous and virtuous children in his own place.[4]

Immortality in this instance is happiness in old age, and progeny to live 'in his own place'. This agrees with his teaching about immortality in his treatise, *De aeternitate mundi:*

> The man sows the seeds into a womb as into a field, the woman receives the seed for safekeeping; nature invisibly moulds and shapes each part of the body and soul and bestows upon the race as a whole what individually we were not able to receive, namely immortality. For the race remains forever, though particular specimens perish, a marvel in very truth and the work of God.[5]

Philo's view of immortality often resembled the Sadducees' rather than Pharisees' belief that immortality was attained through one's ancestors, and not through bodily resurrection.[6] The body was mortal and the soul at least longed to be ἀθάνατος ('immortal'):

> but the virtuous man wants but little, being placed on the borders between the immortal and the mortal nature, having wants indeed by reason of his body being mortal, and his freedom from extravagance because his soul is continually longing for immortality.[7]

Life after Death in Heaven or Tartarus

Yet Philo also taught about two potential destinations for the living in the afterlife. The proselyte, for instance, who comes to acknowledge Israel's God, would 'win an honour suited to his merits', membership in οὐρανός ('heaven') that 'was firmly fixed, greater than words dare describe'.

In stark contrast, the nobly born and recalcitrant Israelite would 'be dragged down and carried into Tartarus itself and profound darkness' (πρὸς αὐτὸν τάρταρον καὶ βαθὺ σκότος).[8]

In *De somniis* 1.151, Philo refers to both post-death destinations:

> for the wise have obtained 'Olympus and heavenly country' (τὸν ὀλύμπιον καὶ οὐράνιον χῶρον) as their habitation; having learnt to be continually mounting upwards, but the wicked have received as their share the dark recesses of hell, having from the beginning to the end of their existence practised dying, and having been from their infancy to their old age familiarised with destruction (κακοὶ δὲ τοὺς ἐν Ἅιδου μυχούς, ἐξ ἀρχῆς ἄχρι τέλους ἀποθνῄσκειν ἐπιτετηδευκότες καὶ εἰς γῆρας ἐκ σπαργάνων φθορᾶς ἐθάδες ὄντες).

---

[4] *Praem.* 108-110.
[5] *Aet.* 69.
[6] E.g. Matt 22:23; Mk 12:18; Lk. 20:27; Acts 23:8.
[7] *Virt.* 9-10.
[8] *Praem.* 152. Colson notes on this use of heaven: 'The "place in heaven" (perhaps better "high as heaven") does not of course refer to an afterlife but merely represents the emphatic ἄνω ἄνω, as "Tartarus" the κάτω κάτω.'

Philo refers to τάρταρος ('Tartarus') three other times in his works, depicting a place to which people could be 'dragged down'[9] beyond the limits of earth where evil was banished,[10] or where evil resides and was concealed from light.[11] Though Philo also refers to ᾅδης[12] or Ἅιδης[13] ('Hades') to refer to the shadowy nether world, as in the quotation above, it is difficult to know if he perceived it to be a real place. His mention of it is complicated by what appear hyperbolic statements such as, καὶ γὰρ ὁ πρὸς ἀλήθειαν Ἅιδης ὁ τοῦ μοχθηροῦ βίος ἐστίν ('For indeed [or 'also'], the true hell is the life of the wicked'), which is audacious, murderous, and liable to all kinds of curses.[14]

The Immortality of the Soul

Philo regularly referred to the immortality of the soul. Death separated, and freed, the soul from the body.

> And some time afterwards, when he [Moses] was about to depart from hence to heaven (εἰς οὐρανὸν), to take up his abode there, and leaving this mortal life to become immortal, having been summoned by the Father, who now changed him, having previously been a double being, composed of soul and body, into the nature of a single body, transforming him wholly and entirely into a most sun-like mind.[15]

Likewise in *De virtutibus,* when Moses was about to die, he

> had no tremors at the thought of his own end, but had added other new joys to the old, for he had not only the memory of earlier felicities, which every kind of virtue had given him, filling him to overflowing with delight, but also the hope of coming immortality as he passed from the corruptible (φθαρτός) life to the incorruptible (ἄφθαρτος). Thus with a face beaming with the gladness of his soul, he said brightly and cheerfully, 'The time has come for me to depart from the life of the body.'[16]

The above passages about the afterlife are typical in Philo's corpus: when he wrote about the after-life, it was certainly more in terms of 'the immortality of the soul' than it was 'the resurrection of the body'.[17] Following Greek thought, he refers to it as a παλιγγενεσία ('new birth'),[18] or as a 'second birth in which the soul is free from the body',[19] or as 'another life.'[20]

---

[9] *QE* 2.40.
[10] *Legat.* 49.
[11] Legat. 103.
[12] *Post.* 31; *Mos.* 1.135; 2.281; *Legat.*235.
[13] *Her.* 45, 78; *Congr.* 57; *Somn.* 1.151.
[14] *Congr.* 57.
[15] *Mos.* II. 288.
[16] *Virt.* 67.
[17] Wolfson, *Philo: Foundations of Religious Philosophy*, 1.404.
[18] *Cher.* 32, 114.
[19] *QE* 2.46.
[20] *Qu. in Gen.* III.22; See Wolfson, *Philo: Foundations of Religious Philosophy*, 1.405.

Earth is the dwelling place of mortals, and heaven τὸν δὲ ἀθανάτων οἶκον ('the house of immortals').[21] Moses' death was an illustration of one departing mortality for immortality:

> And when [Moses] had finished his hymn of melodious praise, which was thus in a manner woven together and made up of piety and humanity, he began to be changed and to depart from mortal existence to immortal life, and gradually to feel a separation of the different parts of which he was composed, namely of his body, which was now removed from him like a shell from a fish, from his soul which was thus laid bare and naked, and which desired its natural departure from hence.[22]

Significantly, if Moses' end could be shared by others, the thought of death need not generate fear, but joy.

A further portrayal of death came from its first occurrence in the Bible. Abel, who was slain by Cain, 'is alive with the happy life in God'. For after his death, Abel used his 'voice' to 'cry out'. Appearing to take this metaphor in Genesis literally, Philo asks, 'how could one no longer living speak?'[23] He arrived at this conclusion:

> the wise man, when seeming to die to the corruptible life, is alive to the incorruptible; but the worthless man, while alive to the life of wickedness, is dead to the good life.[24]

And later in the same treatise,

> he that seems to be dead is alive, since he is found acting as God's suppliant and using His voice; whereas he who is supposed to survive has died the death of the soul, being debarred from virtue, the only worthy rule of life.[25]

Cain showed that a man's soul could die while he was still alive. In *De praemiis et poenis* ('Rewards and Punishments'), Philo explained that such a death was far worse than physical death. The first kind of death 'consists in being [physically] dead, which is something either good or indifferent'.[26] There are seemingly no negative implications in this passage for those who have died physically, and no mention of a divine or eschatological judgement. One might cease to be conscious. The second kind of death 'is entirely bad, and more painful because more durable. Death remains with him perpetually.'[27] The latter death was experienced by Cain, who lived 'forever in a state of dying and so to speak suffered a death which is deathless and unending'.[28]

---

[21] *Virt.* 73.
[22] *Virt.* 76.
[23] *Det.* 48.
[24] *Det.* 49.
[25] *Det.* 70.
[26] *Praem.* 70-71.
[27] For this reason, the death penalty should not be considered the end of one's punishment, but 'in the divine court it is hardly the beginning'. *Praem.* 70-71.
[28] *Praem.* 70.

> For the scripture says (Genesis 4:14) that God laid a curse upon the fratricide, so that he should be continually groaning and trembling. Moreover he put a mark upon him, that he might never be pitied by any one, so that he might not die once, but might, as I have said before, pass all his time in dying, amid griefs, and pains, and incessant calamities.[29]

It is difficult to say from this quotation how literally to take this unending state. He may simply mean that he lived a miserable existence while ever he was alive. In this passage he does not mention punishment beyond the grave.

The Relationship between Death and Life

In *Quod omnis probus liber sit* ('Every Good Man is Free'), Philo recalled an occasion when men of a certain city were fighting a losing battle against their invaders. Sensing the imminence of their defeat,

> they drove their women and children each to several homes and there slaughtered them, and after piling the bodies in a heap fired it and slew themselves upon it, thus completing their allotted term as free men inspired by a free and noble resolution.[30]

It is interesting that Philo, who seemed to know little else about the inhabitants of this city, deemed that on the basis of their noble death they lived a virtuous life. They were praised because they 'died with a noble and free spirit'.[31] For if one could face death well, one could face everything else in life well. The Greek root of this thought is made explicit by his quotation of Euripides, who said, 'A man is not a slave if he faces death without fear.'[32] 'For he meant that nothing is so calculated to enslave the mind as a fear of death, arising from an excessive desire of living.'[33] Stated positively, a man is free if he is ready to die.

Philo spoke of the 'sacred arena' (ἱερὸς ἀγών) to describe one's practical exhibition of virtue.[34] He describes the battle for virtue as a deadly contest, war, and fight, with victors, shame and defeat, and those who lose their life 'in a way that can scarcely be raised again'.[35] Some diligently practised virtue. Others, 'unmanly and effeminate, cowardly and weak who fainted before any real danger or trouble came upon them, disgraced themselves, and became the ridicule of the spectators'.[36] To live with no detachment from the senses was to experience a premature death.[37]

---

[29] *Praem.* 72.
[30] *Prob.* 119; cf. Josephus' account of the Sicarii on Masada, *B.J.* 7; esp. 380-406.
[31] *Prob.* 120.
[32] *Prob.* 22.
[33] *Prob.* 22.
[34] *Praem.* 4.
[35] *Praem.* 6.
[36] *Praem.* 4-6.
[37] *Virt.* 11.

In the sophists' argument discussed in chapter 5, from *Quod deterius potiori insidiari soleat*, Philo compared two alternative paths of life which were built upon differing perspectives of death. First was the sophist, who presented his own position through a series of questions, one of which was, 'Did nature create pleasures and enjoyments and the delights that meet us all the way through life, for the dead, or for those who have never come into existence and not for the living?'[38] The sophists' prescience of death led them to enjoy life and its pleasures while they could.[39] Death taught them to live in comfort, and with plenty.

The sophists' defence incorporated a mocking treatment of the miserable alternative. These people, the 'so-called lovers of virtue' (λεγόμενοι φιλάρετοι), were

> almost without exception an obscure people, looked down upon, of mean estate, destitute of the necessaries of life, not enjoying the privileges of subject peoples or even of slaves, filthy, sallow, reduced to skeletons, with a hungry look from want of food, the prey of disease, μελετῶντες ἀποθνῄσκειν ('in training for dying').[40]

Death likewise shaped the 'lovers of virtue' in their approach to life: teaching them to abstain from excess and thereby 'training for dying'.

What did it mean to be 'training for dying'? The sophists used the term to ridicule ascetics because the exclusion from pleasurable things that occurs at death had begun prematurely for them. Their renunciation of these good things was only preparing them for the complete withdrawal of pleasure.

Philo viewed this phrase more positively, however, when he referred, again by adopting a Platonic idea, to those who 'train' (from μελετάω) to die. He was referring to the students of genuine philosophy, who

> from first to last train to die to the life in the body, that a higher existence immortal and incorporeal, in the presence of Him who is Himself immortal and uncreated, may be their portion. But the souls...of the others have held no account of wisdom.[41]

Truly wise people exercised their soul and mind through moderation and study, and thereby exercised the immortal part of them. With a prescience of death, it was folly to live for the sake of our body, 'the dead corpse connected with us' or for 'the things which are even more lifeless than that, such as glory and money and office, and honours'.[42] Philo's caution about the dangers of passion and pleasure, his open condemnation of the sophists' way of life, and his

---

[38] *Det.* 33.
[39] *Det.* 33-34.
[40] *Det.* 34.
[41] *Gig.* 13-14.
[42] *Gig.* 15. Cf. Seneca, who in *De brevitate vitae*, likewise prescribes training for dying. E.g. 14.5-15.1.

emphasis on the soul taking priority over the body, all suggest that he was far closer to the ascetic group than he was to the sophists. He certainly respected the ascetic lifestyle of the Essene and Therapeutae communities.[43] Yet Philo also warned that asceticism for its own sake, like religiosity over genuine worship, was 'fruitless and wearisome'.[44] It oppressed one's soul and body.[45]

His use of the expression 'training for dying' elsewhere discloses his belief that those souls which train for dying will live eternally. Those who sought pleasure and honour for the 'corpse' of the body, were not only living for what was dead, but were deemed already to be dead. They would not experience immortal life after their physical death.[46]

A Messianic Age

Besides the teachings relating to individual bodies and souls, Philo described a future messianic age for Jews and Greeks who had become children of God through repentance.[47] Borgen provides a useful summary of this hope:

> Moses through all his regulations desires to create unanimity, fellowship, unity of mind, blending of dispositions, whereby houses and cities and nations and countries and the whole human race may advance to supreme happiness. These things will, Philo believes, become facts beyond all dispute, if God, even as He gives us the yearly fruits, grants that virtues should bear abundantly.[48]

He adds:

> without using the term 'Messiah,' Philo looks for the possibility of a (non-Davidic) Messiah to come in the form of a 'Man' who is seen as a final commander-in-chief and emperor of the Hebrew nation as the head of the nations.[49]

Whatever the precise nature of the future hope, whether by means of a re-birth of the soul, or a more communal and corporeal kingdom under the Messiah, Philo was certain of a positive future for those who are suffering in the present. There will be joy for the righteous, and special benefits awaiting those who

---

[43] See Philo's extended treatment of these groups in *Quod omnis probus liber sit* and *De vita contemplative*, respectively.
[44] *Det.* 19-21.
[45] *Det.* 19.
[46] *Gig.* 15.
[47] Wolfson, *Philo: Foundations of Religious Philosophy*, 2.257.
[48] Borgen, *Philo of Alexandria – an Exegete for His Time*, 271.
[49] Borgen, *Philo of Alexandria – an Exegete for His Time*, 275-76. It seems the basis of this 'non-Davidic' assumption is simply that the prophecy was sourced in Numbers, which pre-dates David. If my assumption of his reasoning is correct, it is an illogical step to preclude the possibility of it being fulfilled by a Davidic or any other Jewish king on this basis. It would be more accurate to speak of a king who is 'not necessarily' Davidic.

suffer unjustly.[50] The promises Moses made to the twelve tribes of Israel were, in Philo's day, yet to be fulfilled.[51]

Philo speaks of a restoration of God's people at some stage, where God will regather his people from all ends of the earth, so that Israel's glory will blaze out again.[52]

Summary

The task of summarizing Philo's position on death into neat and incontestable conclusions is difficult. As the reader might have perceived, some of the views appear difficult to reconcile with others.[53] In some passages immortality was attained through one's progeny, with no life mentioned where it might have been useful for his argument. While it is not a contradiction that immortality could come both through one's progeny and through the immortality of the soul, Philo seemed unclear about the matter. This is not to say that Philo did not teach about death confidently. It may never have been in his interest to admit uncertainty.

The experiences of Abel and Noah gave Philo boldness to teach that for the virtuous, mortality would be replaced with immortal life—their souls would be with God. Proselytes and the virtuous people of God had this certain hope of heaven.

For the wicked, it is difficult to be certain of Philo's reasons for the annihilation of some, and the afterlife in Tartarus for others. The Stoics of course disagreed about the events that follow death: Zeno differed from Diogenes, who differed from Cleanthes.[54] Citing *Post*. 39, Wolfson suggests that 'awaiting those who live in the way of the impious will be eternal death'.[55] This death may be, as Wolfson argues, death in the figurative sense since in the

---

[50] Williamson, *Jews in the Hellenistic World: Philo*, 213.
[51] *Virt.* 77; *Mos.* II. 228.
[52] *Praem.* 165-172.
[53] This conclusion concurs with Runia's helpful summary: 'The life of the soul continues after death, and both reward and punishment are not confined to this life. This having been noted, it must be stressed that Philo does not give a very concrete picture of life after death. Heaven is portrayed in rather vague terms as a flight of the soul to the celestial realm or to God. Hades is referred to as the place where wicked souls spend their days, but the descriptions are conventional and not very developed. There is nothing in Philo equivalent to the detailed descriptions of hell as portrayed in the later Christian tradition or of the underworld with its punishments as so vividly described in Platonic myths. The major difficulty for Philo is that on the one hand he cannot accept the Platonic doctrine of reincarnation, but that he is also on the other hand not comfortable with the idea that God would punish the wicked for all eternity. So he remains rather vague about the fate of the soul after death and prefers to emphasise that life and death can be experienced in spiritual terms while human beings are alive on this earth.' Runia, "Theodicy in Philo of Alexandria," 600.
[54] Wolfson, *Philo: Foundations of Religious Philosophy*, 1.400.
[55] Wolfson, *Philo: Foundations of Religious Philosophy*, 1.409.

same text Philo also referred to the eternal death to describe the mortality of the wicked. On this basis he suggests that for Philo's mention of post-death punishment should not be interpreted literally. Mortality was the natural end for the wicked, and immortality was a gift given only to the virtuous.[56] Wolfson concludes his study of this subject by saying,

> Thus, according to Philo, there are three places to which immortal souls may go. First, to heaven to be among the angels, which is the place for all the immortal souls. Second, to the intelligible world to be among the ideas, which is the place to which Isaac and Enoch went. Third, to the presence of God, above the intelligible world, which is the place to which Moses went.[57]

Wolfson may be right in much of what he affirms above. It may make sense of Philo's assertion that the after-life was not a matter for fear, but one which was good or indifferent. His labelling of the numerous references to Sheol and Tartarus as 'figurative language' may, however, be too dismissive. His suggestion also requires that there were conflicting principles involved in Philo's portrayal: that God's sovereignty overrides the 'rule' that nothing created can be immortal. Wolfson offers little reason for taking this step.

Further Comments on the Relationship between Death and Life

The perspective that death provided for life is insightful. Borgen rightly observes,

> Thus one aim of Philo's picture of the possible future, is to exhort his contemporary people look [sic] at their own observance of the Laws as a condition for the materialization of their hopes.[58]

The motivation for living well was thus strengthened by one's contemplation of the future. There was little difference in meaning for a Theist between acting in accordance with nature and acting in accordance with God. Compared to annihilationist views, Philo's doctrine of post-death reward and punishment from God increased the implications, and thus motivation, for living well.

---

[56] Wolfson, *Philo: Foundations of Religious Philosophy*, 1.410. Such a view would concur with Chrysippus' teaching that 'only the souls of the wise continue to exist until the general conflagration' (Diogenes, VII, 157). Holding this emphasis of immortality for the virtuous also aligns with Plato who said that those which 'soar upwards back to the place whence they came' are 'the souls of those who have given themselves to genuine philosophy' (Gig. 3.13-14) and that 'immortal life' awaited 'pious men'. Wolfson, *Philo: Foundations of Religious Philosophy*, 1.407.

[57] Wolfson, *Philo: Foundations of Religious Philosophy*, 1.404.

[58] Borgen, *Philo of Alexandria – an Exegete for His Time*, 281.

CONCLUSION

Philo's hermeneutic of applying the Jewish Law to the lives of his first-century audience is fascinating. The Law was first given to a wandering nation in a context of a relationship with YHWH.[59] Having their own land and temple and autonomy made adherence to the Law possible. The audience to whom Philo was appealing, however, even if it could be deemed purely Jewish, was vastly different.

Philo located and expounded some of the significant connecting points between Hebrew thought and Greek philosophy. Some themes lent themselves very easily to this, and others had to be stretched beyond recognition. The easier themes to synthesise included: truth; λόγος (which, conveniently, could mean 'reason' and 'Scripture'); life in accordance with nature and God; virtue and its rewards; as well as the idea that intangible pursuits were better than common pursuits of honour, wealth, and health. His 'Hellenistic Judaism' maintained the requirement of monotheism, in a more complex form, and by focusing on what was held in common most of the details of the Law were made more universally palatable. His focus on such matters as virtue, reason, and piety, for instance, did not separate him from conservative moralists of either tradition.

Philo's choices about clothing, circumcision, and diet would have differentiated Philo from a Stoic, and there were differences in their approach to sources of authority, but in many other respects the life of one who followed Philo's teaching (if there were such people) might look similar to the students of Epictetus. In some such respects, Philo could be said to have successfully shown the harmony between the two traditions.

The τέλος of Philo's prescribed life, following a path established by Moses and developed by Plato, was communion with God brought about by reason and virtue. To be virtuous was to live, both in this life and in the next. Compared to Greek philosophy, Philo's God was notably active in this process, responding to and helping those who determined to be virtuous. His grace and involvement in a man's life would help him avoid unrestrained living, but this should not detract from Philo's emphasis that virtuous living was man's task.

In terms of its achievability, perfection of life might be attained if one had a reasonably loose and general understanding of perfection: a perfection that acknowledged the universal weakness of man; a perfection which incorporated repentance; and a perfection which focused on one's will to be virtuous, rather

---

[59] Hence, the Decalogue in both Exod. 20 and Deut. 5 begin with the introductory formula, 'I am the LORD your God, who brought you out of the land of Egypt, out of the house of slavery.'

than actual performance of virtue. Though he struggled to explain the lack of any virtuous people of his own time, Philo was, overall, convinced that his was the true path of life for Jews and Greeks.

As was discussed in Epictetus' Guide to Life, a first-century enquirer may have had to overcome significant barriers before deeming Philo's views as convincing. Perhaps of most concern in terms of first-century issues was the credibility of the sources and methods by which he derived knowledge. His attempt to show the harmony between Judaism and Greek philosophy led him to significantly compromise both traditions in a way which, it might be said, distorted the teachings of both Moses and Plato.[60]

A conclusion which focuses on these difficulties alone would be unfortunate, however, in light of Philo's *Sitz im Leben*. His inherited view that Moses was the Father of Greek philosophy explains much. And his allegorical interpretation of Moses simply followed a method that was popular among both Jews and Greeks of his day.

Furthermore, the very right of existence for his people was under serious threat. By allegorically reading Jewish Law, he sought to persuade his readers that Greeks and Jews alike sought virtuous lives. The Jewish Law (and Jewish people by implication) was not an obstacle in the way of what is good and virtuous, but a divine gift for assisting all nations towards it. If one remembers Philo's circumstances, and recognises his vested interest in the resonance between Judaism and Hellenism, one is better able to appreciate his corpus as a sincere and impressive work.

---

[60] Cotta's criticism of the Stoics at Cicero's forum was that they taught diverse and discordant notions. He did not need to question the validity of each belief, but showed they are dubious simply because they cannot be all maintained simultaneously. Some Greek thinkers at least expected coherence, and may have balked at Philo's epistemology and interpretive method which lead him to discordant conclusions, even if Philo's methods were those commonly practised by others.

PART III
PETER'S GUIDE TO LIFE AND DEATH

CHAPTER 9
Peter in his First-Century Setting

In the Letter of 2 Peter, Simon Peter[1] set s forth a ὁδός ('road,' 'way' or 'path')[2] of life presented with close reference to death. Not only was Peter's own death imminent, but the destruction of the earth was also to be treated so. A prescience of death and destruction frames Peter's ethical message, and functions as a powerful motivating force.

---

[1] This monograph will mirror the author of 2 Peter's decision to make a strong connection between the letter and the persona of Simon Peter, the fisherman-apostle. The longstanding and inter-related critical debates about authorship, dating, and 2 Peter's relationship with 1 Peter and Jude, while certainly worthy of our acknowledgement, are outside the purview of this thesis. For a survey of the authorship debate see Michael J. Gilmour, "Reflections on the Authorship of 2 Peter," *EvQ* 73 (2001): 291-309. For a shorter, more recent survey see Green, *Jude and 2 Peter*, 139-50. Somewhat helpful is Witherington's challenge of the use of overly restrictive criteria of what constitutes 'authorship' by scholars on both sides of the debate, in Ben Witherington III, *Letters and Homilies for Hellenized Christians: A Socio-Rhetorical Commentary on 1-2 Peter*, vol. II (Nottingham: Apollos, 2007). For our purposes it will suffice to say that the matter of authorship is not *fait accompli*. Some scholars who treat Peter as a possible, if not probable, author of 2 Peter include Schreiner, *1, 2 Peter, Jude: An Exegetical and Theological Exposition of Holy Scripture*; Ruth A. Reese, *2 Peter & Jude* (Grand Rapidse: Eerdmans, 2007), 115-21; Simon J. Kistemaker, *Peter and Jude* (Welwyn: Evangelical Press, 1987); John Phillips, *Exploring the Epistles of Peter: An Expository Commentary* (Grand Rapids: Kregel, 2005); Dick Lucas and Christopher Green, *The Message of 2 Peter & Jude* (Leicester: IVP, 1995), 28-33; Green, *Jude and 2 Peter*, 139-50.

[2] The English words 'road' or 'way' are also acceptable translations of the Greek word ὁδός, and perhaps represent a tighter definition when referring to the physical road. In *Det.* 24, Philo uses interchangeably the terms ὁδός and τρίβος, often translated 'road' and 'path' respectively, in the ethical sense. And he uses them interchangeably in a more physical sense in *Agr.* 94, though is aware of the distinction between the terms in their physical sense (e.g. *Agr.* 102). The use of them as acceptable parallel terms in both their literal and analogous senses can be seen also in the LXX (e.g. Ps. 25:4; Prov. 1:15; 16:17; Isa. 59:8; Jer. 6:16), inter-testamental literature (e.g. Tob. 4:19; Wis. 5:7; 14:3; Bar. 3:21, 23, 31), and the NT (e.g. Mt. 3:3; Mk. 1:3; Lk. 3:4).

This prescience of death is one reason why 2 Peter conveys its message with a sense of urgency, or, as one scholar has posited, 'swiftness and impetuosity'.[3] It was not that there was limited time to compose the letter that necessarily best explains the urgency. Rather, Peter knew that his death meant the loss of an important eyewitness to historical events upon which the growing church was founded.[4] His death would also mean the loss of a shepherding figure for the churches, just as difficult times approached them. The arrival of persuasive false teachers was imminent. The recipients of Peter's letter would soon be presented with an attractive, albeit deadly, alternative path of life.

The path that leads to life, presented positively in chapter 1 and again at the end of chapter 3, forms an inclusio to the book. The false teachers in 2:1 – 3:7 provide the antithesis to Peter's exhortation, and a vivid illustration of the consequences of straying from the path.

Peter uses three different adjectives to describe the path. There was the ἡ ὁδὸς τῆς ἀληθείας ('path of truth') in 2:2, a εὐθύς ὁδός ('right, or straight path') in 2:15, and a ὁδός τῆς δικαιοσύνης ('path of righteousness') in 2:21. Humans had the potential to blaspheme (βλασφημέω) the path of truth (2:2), to 'forsake' it (καταλείπω) and to be led astray (ἐπλανήθην) from the right way (2:15), and for some it would have been better if they had never heard of the way of righteousness because they have subsequently turned back (ὑποστρέφω) from it (2:21). The letter closes with Peter's exhortation to remain steadfast rather than stumble when the false teachers arrive (3:17).

Issues relating to the *Sitz im Leben* of 2 Peter not only assist one's understanding of the letter, but provide important data for comparing the three Guides. This chapter will discuss: Who was Simon Peter, according to the tradition available to us in New Testament?[5] How did the Letter of 2 Peter present him? Who were the recipients of the letter? What were the sources of Peter's thought? How did he attain his views about God, life and death? And, what can be said about the opponents of 2 Peter?

---

[3] Duane Frederick Watson, *Invention, Arrangement, and Style: Rhetorical Criticism of Jude and 2 Peter* (Atlanta: Scholars, 1988), 145-6.

[4] See, for example, 1 Cor. 15:3-8; 2 Pet. 1:12-15.

[5] For various historical reasons the interpretation of 2 Peter has not always been informed by the larger corpus of the Old and New Testaments. Aware that it is a hermeneutical choice, we will nevertheless approach 2 Peter as a work within a 'canon' by consulting as background material the four Gospels, the Book of Acts, and especially 1 Peter, which purports to be written by the same author as 2 Peter. For one presentation of the rationale for reading 2 Peter as part of a broader canon, see Robert W. Wall, "The Canonical Function of 2 Peter," *Biblical Interpretation* 9.1 (2001): 68-74.

Peter in his First-Century Setting

Simeon Peter, a servant and apostle of Jesus Christ

The portrayal of Peter in the New Testament

Prior to meeting Jesus, Συμεὼν Πέτρος ('Simeon Peter')[6] was formerly known by the similar Greek name Σίμων ('Simon'), and worked with his brother Andrew as a fisherman on the Sea of Galilee (Mt. 4:18; Lk. 5:3).[7] Their family business, which employed hired hands (Mk. 1:20) would have put them in the socio-economic 'middle class' of Galilee at the time.[8] Located to the east of the Jordan, their city of origin was Bethsaida, which belonged to the territory of Gaulanitis, a Hellenised region.[9] Besides Aramaic, Greek was well known as a second language, and one which Peter may have needed to converse later with Cornelius the centurion (Acts 10:1-48).[10]

Peter's brother, Andrew, was the first to tell Peter about Jesus, declaring, '"We have found the Messiah" (which means Christ)', Jn. 1:41. Their introduction is recorded briefly by John who writes, '[Andrew] brought [Peter] to Jesus. Jesus looked at him and said, "You are Simon the son of John. You shall be called Cephas"—which means Peter' (σὺ εἶ Σίμων ὁ υἱὸς Ἰωάννου, σὺ κληθήσῃ Κηφᾶς, ὃ ἑρμηνεύεται Πέτρος), Jn. 1:42.[11] Simon Peter was married (Mt. 8:14), though little is known about his wife except that she too was a believer, and travelled with Peter on occasions (1 Cor. 9:5).

Along with James and John, and the Beloved Disciple in John's gospel, Peter had a special place as part of the inner circle within Jesus' twelve disciples (Mt. 17:1; Mk. 14:33; Lk. 8:51), whom he also named apostles (οὓς καὶ ἀποστόλους ὠνόμασεν), Mk. 3:14. In each of the lists of 'the twelve' in the Synoptic gospels, Peter is named first (Mt. 10:2; Mk. 3:16; Lk. 6:14). It is Peter

---

[6] 2 Peter 1:1
[7] Because he is referred to as both Simon and Simeon, there is some question over which name was most original to him. Only in 2 Pet. 1:1 and Acts 15:14 is he referred to as 'Simeon' (Συμεών), the transliterated version of the Hebrew name שִׁמְעוֹן. Cullman raises the possibility, however, that he was simply given the similar-sounding Greek name 'Simon' (Σίμων) from birth, as it seems the case with his brother Andrew (Ἀνδρέας), (17). If his name was Simon from birth, however, it would seem less likely that he would refer to himself as Simeon (a name he never had). It seems more likely that Simeon accepted the Greek name Simon, though occasionally he (and the writer of Acts) made reference to him by his actual name, Simeon. This is implied by Starr, who suggests that the use of Simeon 'perhaps draws attention to the author's life as a Jewish fisherman before he received his nickname from Christ'. Starr, "Sharers in Divine Nature: 2 Peter 1:4 in Its Hellenistic Context", 51.
[8] See Paul Barnett, *Jesus & the Rise of Early Christianity: A History of New Testament Times* (Downers Grove: IVP, 1999), 233.
[9] Barnett, *Jesus & the Rise of Early Christianity*, 232.
[10] Barnett, *Jesus & the Rise of Early Christianity*, 232-33.
[11] Both the Aramaic name 'Cephas' and the Greek name 'Petros' shared the meaning of 'stone' or 'rock.'

whose interactions with Jesus are most prevalent throughout the gospels, and who is presented as an apostle particularly devoted to Jesus (Jn. 6:68; 21:7).[12] As is mentioned in 2 Peter 1:17-18, Peter was with Jesus on the 'holy mountain' when Jesus' body was transfigured, and when the voice from heaven said, 'This is my beloved son, with whom I am well pleased' (Mt. 17:15; Mk. 9:7; Lk. 9:35). Peter was one of the first to the empty tomb, and then the first among the apostles to see the risen Christ (1 Cor. 15:5).

Jesus gave two significant charges to Peter which related to his future function in a church that would soon be born. The first charge was given prior to Jesus' death.

> Blessed are you, Simon Bar-Jonah! For flesh and blood has not revealed this to you, but my Father who is in heaven. And I tell you, you are Peter, and on this rock I will build my church, and the gates of hell shall not prevail against it. I will give you the keys of the kingdom of heaven, and whatever you bind on earth shall be bound in heaven, and whatever you loose on earth shall be loosed in heaven.[13]

Peter will have a foundational role in the establishment of the church (as is detailed in the Book of Acts), and this church will endure throughout the ages.[14]

The second charge given to Peter, building upon the first, came in the post-resurrection and pre-ascension period, in which Jesus said to Simon Peter,

> 'Simon, son of John, do you love me more than these?' He said to him, 'Yes, Lord; you know that I love you.' He said to him, 'Feed my lambs' (βόσκε τὰ ἀρνία μου).
> He said to him a second time, 'Simon, son of John, do you love me?' He said to him, 'Yes, Lord; you know that I love you." He said to him, "Tend my sheep' (ποίμαινε τὰ πρόβατά μου). He said to him the third time, 'Simon, son of John, do you love me?' Peter was grieved because he said to him the third time, 'Do you love me?' and he said to him, 'Lord, you know everything; you know that I love you.' Jesus said to him, 'Feed my sheep' (βόσκε τὰ πρόβατά μου).[15]

It is an emotion-charged interaction between the two men. Peter is grieved by the need to insist he loved Jesus three times, but it was Jesus way of profoundly affirming Peter after his recent and grieving three-fold denial. It also established his love for Jesus as the motivation and manner in which he would care for the good shepherd's (Jn. 10:11-18) sheep. Peter later saw himself as a shepherd of Christ's people, and in 1 Peter 5:1-4, he extends this duty upon the elders of the church. He urges them to 'shepherd the flock of God that is among you, exercising oversight, not under compulsion, but willingly, as God would

---

[12] Though Peter's acts of sincere loyalty were often done in ignorance, and needed to be corrected (Mt. 26:33-34; Mk. 8:33; Lk. 9:33; Jn. 13:6-9, 37; 18:11).
[13] Mt. 16:17-19.
[14] For an early treatment of the various ways the 'keys of the kingdom' passage has been interpreted, see Oscar Cullman, *Peter: Disciple-Apostle-Martyr*, trans. F.V. Filson (London: SCM, 1953), 121; 215-30.
[15] John 21:15-17.

have you; not for shameful gain, but eagerly; not domineering over those in your charge, but being examples to the flock'.

In the book of Acts, Peter is a highly competent and courageous leading figure heavily involved in the formation of what would be known as the Christian church. In c. AD 30-33, immediately after Jesus ascension into heaven (εἰς τὸν οὐρανόν), this embryonic and diverse group of Jews began worshipping Jesus, not only as the Messiah, but as God. Sensing no discontinuity in God's plans for the Jewish people, these monotheists considered it appropriate to worship Jesus, and to continue meeting in the Jerusalem temple to praise God with the other Jews (Lk. 24:52).

At the beginning of Acts the congregated disciples numbered about one hundred and twenty. It was Peter who 'stood up' (from ἀνίστημι) among the believers to instruct them about the way ahead (Acts 1:15-22).[16] And in the confusion created by the events at Pentecost, it was Peter who brought order by instructing the crowd. His speech, though seemingly impromptu, is a logical and persuasive (1:37) interpretation of recent events (including the death and resurrection of Christ, the arrival of the Holy Spirit and the supernatural ability to speak in various languages) in light of various voices in Israel's history (1:17-36).[17] He boldly insists that those who seek forgiveness for their sin respond with repentance and baptism in the name of Jesus Christ (1:38, 40). This speech, which was followed by others in chapters 3 and 4, led to three thousand Jews being baptized and joining the movement (1:41). From this point, Peter continues to have a role of teaching the baptized community (1:42), and before long there are around five thousand believers (4:4). By AD 36, Christians were gathering in Judea, and probably also in Samaria and Galilee.[18]

Despite being ἀγράμματοί καὶ ἰδιῶται (both terms meaning 'uneducated' or perhaps 'laymen'), Peter and with him John, astounded those who were educated (viz. the τοὺς ἄρχοντας καὶ τοὺς πρεσβυτέρους καὶ τοὺς γραμματεῖς ἐν Ἱερουσαλήμ), 4:13; cf. 4:5, 19.[19] Miraculous events surrounded Peter;

---

[16] For other treatments of these speeches which regard them as historically reliable, see F.F. Bruce, *The Speeches in the Acts of the Apostles* (London: 1942); H. Ridderbos, *The Speeches of Peter in the Acts of the Apostles* (London: 1962). For a contrary view see Terence V Smith, *Petrine Controversies in Early Christianity* (Tübingen: Mohr Siebeck, 1985), 152.

[17] For comment upon the NT writers' use of the Old Testament, and their distinctive reading of the OT through the salvation-historical grid, see G.K. Beale and D.A. Carson, eds., *Commentary on the New Testament Use of the Old Testament* (Grand Rapids: Baker, 2007), xxvi.

[18] For a treatment of Peter's life with particular interest in the dating of events, see the chapter entitled 'Peter in Palestine', in Barnett, *Jesus & the Rise of Early Christianity*, 231-45.

[19] To be 'uneducated and common' did not necessarily mean they were not educated in a general sense, but may be a comparative statement, viz. they were not trained in the theological tradition of the elite who opposed them—the rulers, elders, and teachers of the law.

multitudes carried out the sick into the streets and laid them on cots and mats, so that 'as Peter came by at least his shadow might fall on some of them' (5:15). The people also gathered from the towns around Jerusalem, bringing the sick and those afflicted with unclean spirits, and they were all healed' (5:16).

Besides these roles of oversight, teaching and healing, Peter had another significant function to fulfil as the church grew. Attention in the Book of Acts shifts from Peter, the Apostle to the Jews (Galatians 2:7-8), to Paul, the Apostle to the Gentiles (Gal. 2:7-8; cf. Rom. 11:13; 1 Tim. 2:7). Peter assists this rudimentary and largely Jewish movement to become one which welcomes, and becomes predominately comprised of, Gentiles.

Peter served this process of Gentile incorporation through his involvement in the highly significant conversion of the Gentile and Roman Centurion, Cornelius (Acts 10). Later, at the Jerusalem Council (c. 49 AD), Peter again 'stood up' to affirm the validity of full Gentile inclusion into the people of God (Acts 15:7-11). On the basis of Peter's argumentation, drawn from Old Testament prophets (Acts 15:15-17; cf. Amos 9:11-12), as well as the recent miraculous events evidencing God's Spirit indwelling Gentiles (15:12), James offers the accepted resolution to remove, with few exceptions, all cultural hindrances imposed by the Law which prevented the immediate and full inclusion of Gentiles (Acts 15:13-21). With the Gentiles now the focus of the book of Acts, Peter is not mentioned again. Elsewhere in the New Testament are a few incidental references to Peter in Corinthians (1 Cor. 1:12; 3:22; 9:5; 15:5) and Galatians (which mentions his error and Paul's rebuke of him in 2:7-14), as well as the two epistles that bear his name.

During Peter's thirty years of apostolic ministry, he and the church experienced threats from both Jewish and Gentile opposition. The most notable opposition came from King Herod Agrippa, who persecuted the church in the wake of a great disturbance caused by Caligula's anti-Semitism in 37-41.[20] Claudius expelled Jews from Rome in 49, but following his death in 54, the Book of Romans (written c. AD 57)[21] indicates that at least some Jews lived in Rome and were represented in the churches there. 1 Peter reveals Peter's attempt to guide the church through what he described as her 'painful trial' and 'suffering' (4:12; cf. 4:13-18). Clement records that Peter himself suffered 'not one nor two but many trials'[22] before his death, which was probably during what Tacitus describes as the execution of an 'immense multitude' during Nero's pogrom in AD 64. Nero had

> fastened the guilt and inflicted the most exquisite tortures on a class hated for their abominations, called Christians by the populace...Accordingly an arrest was made of all who confessed; then upon their information an immense multitude was convicted....Mockery of every sort was added to their deaths. Covered with the

---

[20] Barnett, *Jesus & the Rise of Early Christianity*, 244.
[21] Douglas J. Moo, *The Epistle to the Romans* (Grand Rapids: Eerdmans, 1996), 3.
[22] 1 Clement 5.4-5.

skins of beasts, they were torn by dogs and perished, or were nailed to crosses, or were doomed to the flames.[23]

In summary, Peter's 'pastoral' responsibility and transparent concern for the recipients of 1 and 2 Peter can be better understood in light of his extraordinary background, and his apostolic duty within the church. Seeing himself as a shepherd who had been shepherded by Christ himself, Peter took seriously the spiritual and eternal well-being of those under his care.

Having sketched a few of the significant moments in Simon Peter's development from fisherman to apostle from the Gospel accounts and the Book of Acts, more attention will now be given to the autobiographical account in 2 Peter.

The Portrayal of Peter in 2 Peter

Peter's self-designation as a bond-servant and apostle of Jesus Christ (δοῦλος καὶ ἀπόστολος Ἰησοῦ Χριστοῦ),[24] if we allow for minor variations, is not peculiar to him.[25] His use of δοῦλος is enlightening. In the New Testament it can refer to a 'slave' or perhaps 'bondservant' to a secular master (e.g. Col. 4:1; Tit. 2:9; Phm. 2:16) or a divine one.[26] In 2 Peter 1:1, it refers to one who serves God, Christ or his people.[27] Indeed, it is used to categorise all of God's people (Rom. 6:18; 1 Pet. 2:16; Rev. 1:1, 11:18, 22:9). Prior to his death Jesus stressed the point that all of his followers must identify themselves as δοῦλοι (John 13:1-17).

Perhaps what can be said about the juxtaposition of δοῦλος with the more overtly prestigious term of ἀπόστολος ('apostle,' 'special messenger'),[28] is that despite the potential to grate against the ears of some Greek recipients, it

---

[23] Tacitus *Annals* 15.44. Cited in Barnett, *Jesus & the Rise of Early Christianity*, 304.

[24] The genitive form of 'Jesus Christ' in the expression, ἀπόστολος Ἰησοῦ Χριστοῦ, could be taken possessively, so that Peter was Jesus Christ's apostle; or it could be taken attributively, so that Peter is an apostle whose message is about Christ. Since both are usually true of NT apostles (e.g. Acts 9:15), there is little reason to drive a wedge between the two.

[25] See Rom. 1:1 and Tit. 1:1.

[26] Ephesians 6:5-6 is an example of both senses being used side-by-side. In this sense, the NT follows the OT; the word עֶבֶד could also be used in relation to a human (e.g. Gen. 20:8) or divine master. God refers to his 'servants' Abraham, Isaac and Jacob (Exod. 32:13), Moses (Deut. 34:5), Samuel (1 Sam 3:9-10) and David (1 Sam. 23:10).

[27] This sense of δοῦλος is intended when used for Phoebe in Rom. 16:1; Paul in Phil. 1:1; 2 Cor. 4:4; Epaphras in Col. 1:7 and 4:12; Tychicus in 4:7; and Timothy in 2 Tim. 2:24-25, where Paul defines how the Lord's servant must live.

[28] The special identity and function of an 'apostle' of Christ did not belong to all 'servants' of Christ, as is implied by such passages as 2 Pet. 3:2; cf. 1 Cor. 12:28; Eph. 3:5; 1 Thess. 2:6. See Kevin Giles, "Apostles before and after Paul," *Churchman* 99.3 (1985): 250-56.

reflected a humility that characterises Peter in both of his letters.[29] This humility should not be confused with weakness, however. Indeed, because of the status attained by slaves who had powerful relations in Roman culture, and because it was a title of honour in the Hebrew Bible and Ancient Near East more broadly to be a servant or slave of the king, it may have added to rather than detracted from their authority and respect within the Christian community.[30] Most influentially for Peter, Jesus' life and death provided the model and mandate for service of God and others (John 13:1-17; 1 Peter 3–4).[31]

Peter's self-designation as a servant and an apostle of Christ matches both the intent and content of his letter—he wrote to serve the recipients' interests (2 Peter 1:12-15) with the authority of a recognised messenger of God (1:16-19, 3:2).

The Recipients of the Letter

Who were the recipients of Peter's letter? There is no scholarly consensus, and opinions follow one's position on authorship—from an audience in the mid-first century AD,[32] to the late-second century AD.[33]

Unfortunately, the actual recipients of the letter cannot be confidently identified. If the common view is correct, that 2 Peter 3:1 is referring to 1 Peter, then the audience could be taken to be the same scattered audience 'in Pontus, Galatia, Cappadocia, Asia, and Bithynia' (1 Pet. 1:1).[34] The lack of particulars in both letters does not preclude the possibility that the recipients of 2 Peter

---

[29] Speaking on a similar issue, Brown *et al* accuse Peter of false humility in 1 Peter 5:1 where 'Peter' speaks of himself as a co-presbyter. Less humble than the other title in 2 Pet. 1:1, as a slave or servant, Brown's comment seems to overlook the custom, and the perceived appropriateness, of humble self-designations even for the apostles. Referring to Peter's self-designation as a servant in 1 Pet. 5:1, Brown's work says, 'We should not be deceived by this modest stance as if the author were presenting himself as their equal. He has already identified his authority as apostolic (1:1); and so the use of "fellow presbyter" is a polite stratagem of benevolence.' It seems an unwarranted statement that misunderstands the nature of NT apostleship, fails to take cognizance of this custom in the other NT writings, and perhaps underestimates the significance of Peter's background, regardless of whether Peter was the actual author or not. It may have been more surprising if Peter asserted his authority without any genuine humility attached. Raymond E. Brown, Karl P. Donfried, and John Reumann, eds., *Peter in the New Testament: A Collaborative Assessment by Protestant and Roman Catholic Scholars* (Minneapolis: Augsburg, 1973), 152.

[30] Dale B. Martin, *Slavery as Salvation: The Metaphor of Slavery in Pauline Christianity* (New Haven: Hale University Press, 1990), 29.

[31] Note also Peter's use of 'Master' (ἐπιστάτης) to address Jesus in Lk. 8:45; 9:33.

[32] See footnote 1 of this chapter for proponents of a first-century setting.

[33] See for example Jonathan Knight, *2 Peter and Jude* (Sheffield: Sheffield Academic, 1995).

[34] Scholars on both sides of the authorship divide view this as likely, as can be seen in the discussion in Richard J. Bauckham, *Jude, 2 Peter* (Waco: Word, 1980), 286.

were in the same region as that of 1 Peter.[35] The uncertainty regarding the provenance of 2 Peter is illustrated by the geographical distances between the educated guesses of scholars; including Rome,[36] Egypt, Asia Minor, Syria, Palestine.[37]

Although many of the Christians were Jews, it was not long before the Christians were rejected by those Jews who rejected Jesus' claim to be the Messiah. Saul's persecution of the believers is early evidence of this, as is Gamaliel II's revision of the twelfth blessing (c. AD 70), which represents a formal rejection of Christians:

> For persecutors let there be no hope, and the dominion of arrogance do Thou speedily root out in our days; and let Christians (*hannozrim*) and *minim* perish in a moment, let them be blotted out of the book of the living and let them not be written with the righteous.[38]

Nationalistic Jews persecuted the Christians in Palestine as early as the 60s, and then again in the 130s.[39]

If 2 Peter is read independently from 1 Peter the recipients can only be described in a very general way: 'to those who have obtained a faith of equal standing with ours by the righteousness of our God and Saviour Jesus Christ' (1:1). If he intended the letter to be widely circulated across Asia Minor, it would make sense to address the recipients in such terms.

With regard to πίστις ('faith') as their identifying feature, it was said to be ἰσότιμος ('of the same kind or value') with 'ours', referring probably to his and the other apostles' faith.[40] The NIV renders this phrase in verse 1 with 'a faith as precious as ours', which captures the intent of the author.[41]

---

[35] Bauckham, *Jude, 2 Peter*.

[36] Bauckham, *Jude, 2 Peter*, 159-62.

[37] Daniel J. Harrington, *1 Peter, Jude and 2 Peter* (Collegeville: Liturgical, 2003), 236.

[38] Cited in Davies, *The Setting of the Sermon on the Mount* (Cambridge: 1964), 275-76.

[39] Wadi Muraba'at in Milik, J., *Une lettre de Simeon Bar Kokheba*, Revue biblique 60 1953. Justin Martyr in *Apol.* 1.31.6 records the flight of the primitive Church to Pella, cf. Eus. *HE* 3.5.3. Cited in Tord Fornberg, *An Early Church in a Pluralistic Society* (Lund: Carl Bloms Boktryckeri, 1977), 136.

[40] Bo Reicke, *The Epistles of James, Peter, and Jude* (Garden City: Doubleday, 1964), 150. In Romans 1:12, another significant apostle, Paul, quite intentionally makes the point that the faith of the Roman Christians was similarly valid as his own, saying: 'that we may be mutually encouraged by each other's faith, both yours and mine'.

[41] Peter and Paul's statements concur with an emphasis on the effectiveness of faith for all who have it. The possession of a belief in that which is true (Tit. 1:13) is important. That said, people can vary in the strength of their faith (Rom. 4:19-20; 12:3; 14:4; 2 Cor. 10:15), but having faith (in God or in Christ) can be said to be equally valid and effective for all, and is more important than the amount of one's faith (e.g. Luke 17:5-6). See also Otto Knoch, "Däs Vermächtnis Des Petrus: Der 2. Petrusbrief," in *Wort Gottes in Der Zeit: Festschrift Karl Hermann Schelkle*, ed. H. Feld and J. Nolte (Patmos: Düsseldorf, 1973), 164.

Despite having a general audience in mind, Peter was confident of the recipients' standing before God and that they were living in a commendable way, as is discernible from the strong expression in verse 13,

> I will always be ready to remind you of these things, even though you already know them (καίπερ εἰδότας), and have been established in the truth which is present with you (στηριγμένους ἐν τῇ παρούσῃ ἀληθείᾳ).[42]

Significant for understanding the function of Peter's ethical exhortations, which will be discussed in more detail later, the recipients were reminded of the way they should live, without any perspicuous indication that they were under-performing and thus in need of rebuke.[43] 2 Peter 3:17 describes them as having a στηριγμός ('steadfastness' or 'secure position').

The Origins of Peter's Message

Where did Peter get his views about God, life and death? Why was he so confident that his message was true, especially about matters in which the philosophic tradition remained rather vague, such as the after-life?[44]

Recent Petrine study has given rise to the view that there were a number of layers of influence at play upon Peter's writing. An in-depth answer to this question which considers each layer is beyond the boundaries of this monograph. Priority will be given to the influence of the Jewish Scriptures as well as Graeco-Roman literature upon his thought, and little attention given to other influences such as the Enochic literature and tradition.[45]

Many commentators have credited Stoicism for at least influencing the ideas presented in 2 Peter.[46] Compared with the repeated and explicit use of OT quotations in 1 Peter, it is often suggested that 2 Peter has drawn on Stoic concepts and terminology to communicate his ideas. Was Peter importing Stoic

---

[42] Translation and italics are those of the NASB.

[43] Contra the sentiments expressed throughout Starr's monograph, which, with little justification suggests correction rather than warning was required for the recipients. This view is difficult to sustain not only in light of chapter 1, but in light of the letter as a whole. Peter used the future tense to speak of the arrival of false teachers (2:1-2), and only commended their behaviour in chapter 3. Starr, "Sharers in Divine Nature: 2 Peter 1:4 in Its Hellenistic Context", 50-51, 53, 64, 227.

[44] Fornberg, *An Early Church in a Pluralistic Society*, 131.

[45] For an in-depth study of the influence of Enochic literature on Judaism, see David R. Jackson, *Enochic Judaism: Three Defining Paradigm Exemplars* (New York: T&T Clark, 2004).

[46] For example, Adams makes the oft-made though incorrect assertion that Peter was 'invoking the Stoic view' when he teaches about the cosmos being destroyed. There may be shared features of their beliefs, but Peter's view, even with its belief in a great conflagration, is as we will see later, hardly the Stoic view. E. Adams, "Where Is the Promise of His Coming? The Complaint of the Scoffers in 2 Peter 3.4," *NTS* 51 (2005): 122.

terminology and concepts into a Christian matrix? To what degree does he owe the contents of this letter to the philosophical tradition?

As a starting point, it is important to understand that for Peter himself, this question of his sources was critically important. He insisted that 'his' message was not his own creation, nor the result of personal reasoning or logic. Besides being a servant and messenger of Jesus Christ, another important self-designation in this regard was ἐπόπτης ('eyewitness'), in 1:16.[47]

As an eyewitness, his primary task was to report the factuality of events pertaining to Jesus Christ, which he refers to as truth (ἀλήθεια, 2 Pet. 1:12; cf. 13-18). He considers it necessary to provide an extended explanation (vv. 16-21) of how he knew what he knew, and as a corollary, why his message should be trusted. He begins,

> For we did not follow sophistic myths (σεσοφισμένοις μύθοις) when we made known to you the power and coming (δύναμις καὶ παρουσία) of our Lord Jesus Christ, but we were eyewitnesses of his majesty (μεγαλειότης).[48]

At the heart of his message, therefore, was the news regarding Christ's power and coming; a message originating not in the schools of philosophy, but from his witness of Christ and his transfiguration.[49]

The transfiguration was significant because it convinced Peter of Christ's majesty and favour with God the Father, the μεγαλοπρεπὴς δόξα ('Majestic Glory'). It was a further attribution of divine honour to Jesus when God said, ὁ υἱός μου ὁ ἀγαπητός μου οὗτός ἐστιν εἰς ὃν ἐγὼ εὐδόκησα ('This is my beloved Son, with whom I am well pleased'), 2 Pet. 1:17. The phrases ἡμεῖς ἠκούσαμεν and σὺν αὐτῷ ὄντες stress how significant it was that he, among others, actually witnessed the events to which he speaks (1:18). To overlook the significance of the transfiguration for Peter's theology and path of life is to miss the source that Peter himself laboured to make known.

Significant as the transfiguration was, it was not the sole basis for believing that his message was credible. Peter did not require them to trust the eyewitnesses alone (1:19), but drew their attention to the prophetic word. Significantly, Peter argued that they had βεβαιότερον τὸν προφητικὸν λόγον ('the made-more-certain prophetic word') on the basis that the descriptions of Christ which they provided had been confirmed by the apostles' eyewitness account (1:19).[50] The prophecy predicted the content of their testimony, and

---

[47] Cf. the similar attitude of John in 1 Jn. 1:1-3.
[48] 2 Pet. 1:16
[49] For discussion on the significance of the transfiguration for 2 Peter's argument, see Starr, "Sharers in Divine Nature: 2 Peter 1:4 in Its Hellenistic Context", 5; Farkasfalvy, "Ecclesial Setting,' 13n.19; cf. Farmer, 'Critical Reflections,' 31-32; Jerome Neyrey, "The Apologetic Use of the Transfiguration in 2 Peter 1:16-21," *CBQ* 42 (1980).
[50] Peter explains the fulfilled and confirmed prophetic word more substantially in his preaching in Acts 2:23, and then again in Acts 3:18 where Peter says, 'But what God

thereby supported their accounts; and conversely, their accounts showed the fulfilment of events that had long before been prophesied, thereby validating the prophecy. Spectacular prophecies had been matched perfectly by spectacular events; it must be ἀπὸ θεοῦ ('from God'), 1:21.

Furthermore, Peter considered the divine origins of his message were supported by their harmony with Paul's writings, which he equated with 'Scripture' (3:15-16). This reference to Paul's writings as Scripture, often used as 'evidence' for late authorship of 2 Peter, is not out of place with respect to other NT texts where God's authority is claimed for their message (e.g. 1 Thess. 2:13; 1 Cor. 15). From the earliest stages of the church, the believers 'devoted themselves to the apostles' teaching' (Acts 2:42). The apostles' teaching would only have become even more precious following the loss of access to them, as believers were scattered throughout the Empire following Stephen's martyrdom.[51]

The author of 2 Peter wanted to be identified with close reference to Christ. He was Christ's apostle, slave and eyewitness; and his years of reflection of how the majestic Christ's transfiguration, death and resurrection had validated, and been validated by, the Old Testament, had clearly shaped his thinking.

Having laid this foundation, many 2 Peter commentaries over the last 150 years were right to observe Hellenistic influences on 2 Peter, even if they were overstated. Käsemann, whose views were incisively corrected by Starr's recent monograph, claimed that 2 Peter had 'smuggled pagan goods into Christian territory', and that 'Hellenistic dualism' characterises Peter's world view.[52] More recently, a helpful recognition of the distinctiveness of Peter's ideas when placed against extant Hellenistic writings, as well as the influence of other Jewish traditions upon his thought, has begun to redress what appears an overly zealous search for Graeco-Roman parallels.

What might be said is that neither Judeo-Christian nor Greek influences are operating to the exclusion of the other. Peter's use of the Koine Greek as the medium for his expression is in itself a reminder that Hellenism influences the entire letter—the question is of course one of degree. The recent examination of

---

foretold by the mouth of all the prophets, that his Christ would suffer, he thus fulfilled.' See also 1 Pet. 1:10-12, which may be referring to such prophecies as found in Isa. 52:13-53:12; Dan. 9:24-26. Certainly, Jesus taught the disciples that his death (Mal. 4:6; Ps. 22:6,7; Isa. 53:2, 3; Dan. 9:26; Zech. 13:7), resurrection (Jn. 20:9; Mt. 22:29; Isa. 53:10-12; and Ps. 16:8-11 cited by Peter in Acts 2:25-32) and subsequent proclamation (Acts 2:32-38; 4:12; 5:31; Gen. 12:3; Ps. 22:27; Isa. 2:2; 49:6; Hos. 2:23; Mal. 1:11) 'is thus written' (οὕτως γέγραπται) in the Scriptures (Lk. 24:45-47).

[51] Paul W. Coleman, *Second Peter and Jude* (Camp Hill: Christian Publications, 2000), 8.

[52] Ernst Käsemann, "An Apologia for Primitive Christian Eschatology," in *Essays on New Testament Themes* (London: SCM, 1964), 179-80, 95. Summary and citations above are those of Starr, "Sharers in Divine Nature: 2 Peter 1:4 in Its Hellenistic Context", 22.

the Greek influence on 2 Peter 1:4 just mentioned, analysed in particular the concept of 'sharing in the divine nature'. Starr concludes that to the Greek readers, Peter would be evoking generally known traditions, and yet at the same time he concludes that these ideas anchor 2 Peter 'most firmly in the epistolary and theological tradition of Pauline Christianity'.[53] It may be that Peter brought to the tradition of Pauline Christianity 'compatible elements from the Hellenistic philosophical tradition particularly as it was voiced by Middle Platonism',[54] meaning that Peter used the concepts and language of the world in which he lived insofar as they were compatible for expressing his decidedly Christian message. About God's role as the righteous judge in 2 Peter, or about walking in God's ways, to cite two thematic examples, Starr determines that '2 Peter's language, while inspired by the language of the Old Testament and Paul, would therefore be broadly accessible'.[55]

Similarly, Peter's use of 'divine power' is not a foreign concept to the New Testament, but the expression itself is unusual. Davids infers from this that

> 2 Peter uses Hellenistic language rather than the more usual language of the rest of the NT. It is the language of his pagan environment, indicating either his own linguistic context or else the background of the people to whom he was trying to communicate.[56]

Such views are only accurate insofar as they recognise the dominating influence of the Jewish and more recent Christ-events as sources. Speaking about the Apostle Paul and the author of 2 Peter (whom he believes was a second-century figure), Fornberg contributes to this discussion:

> The cultural, religious and social differences between Palestine in which Christ taught and the big cities of the Roman Empire (Paul) had the result that Paul could not confine himself to mere repetition of Jesus' teaching. It had to be interpreted into new modes of expression and a new religious vocabulary, in order to win a hearing from the people whom St Paul met. 2 Peter, like e.g. Ignatius and Diognetus, represents a further step in the 'translation' process which is constantly in train, in this case a communication of the Christian message to a more and more 'Hellenistic' society. 2 Peter is one of the most important documents for our knowledge of a fairly early stage in this translation process. It represents a distinctly Christian line, without thereby rejecting those features of the Hellenistic culture which were acceptable. 2 Peter is therefore worthy of much greater attention on the part of the exegetes than it is wont to receive.[57]

---

[53] Starr, "Sharers in Divine Nature: 2 Peter 1:4 in Its Hellenistic Context", 239. Cf. Davids, who observed the concept of sharing in the divine nature in Philo, 4 Maccabees and Josephus, and concludes, 'The picture 2 Peter presents here uses Greek language, but it is far more Jewish than Greek.' Peter H. Davids, *The Letters of 2 Peter and Jude* (Grand Rapids: Eerdmans, 2006), 175.
[54] Starr, "Sharers in Divine Nature: 2 Peter 1:4 in Its Hellenistic Context", 239.
[55] Starr, "Sharers in Divine Nature: 2 Peter 1:4 in Its Hellenistic Context", 232.
[56] Davids, *2 Peter and Jude*, 169.
[57] Fornberg, *An Early Church in a Pluralistic Society*, 148.

It should not be surprising to see various authors and preachers within the New Testament using terms that Greek recipients found at least 'broadly accessible'. The New Testament itself provides clear examples of 'contextualised', or as Fornberg perhaps more liberally calls, 'translated' versions of the gospel message for various audiences. Consider for example, Paul's gospel presentation using agrarian language when in Lystra (Acts 14:15-17) compared to his philosophical argument to the Epicureans and Stoics in the midst of the Areopagus in Athens (Acts 17:22-31).[58] Neither message is overtly Jewish: to those in Lystra he appeals to the God who provides their needs; and to the Athenians he appeals to 'the unknown God' inscribed on one of their altars. Neither presentation even mentions Israel, nor Christ, much less Christ's crucifixion.

Paul saw himself as a highly-credentialed Jew: 'circumcised on the eighth day, of the people of Israel, of the tribe of Benjamin, a Hebrew of Hebrews; as to the law, a Pharisee; as to zeal, a persecutor of the church; as to righteousness under the law, blameless' (Phil. 3:5-6). His letters as well as his sermons in Acts, however, show just how capable even this 'Hebrew of Hebrews' was able to 'translate' his message for a Greek audience. Indeed, the NT presents him as an able communicator in their Hellenistic world. So too it is reasonable to expect that Peter, from Hellenised Judea, and with access to amanuenses (1 Pet. 5:12) had the ability to 'translate' his message into Graeco-Roman concepts and language. The distinctly Christian nature of his message is affirmed not least through its greeting and doxology, which contain high Christological statements that are only comprehensible with close reference to the Jewish Scriptures.[59]

The Opponents in 2 Peter

The attempt to find a known movement with which the false teachers may be associated has proven problematic. To my knowledge, the proposition of this section—that the false teachers are best understood with reference to the Second Sophistic, has not been made.

Although a full historical survey of the problem cannot be achieved within the boundaries of this monograph, some introduction to the issue will be necessary.[60]

For some decades the opponents in 2 Peter have been variously identified. Käsemann's influential study concluded that 2 Peter gives 'the clearest possible testimony to the onset of early Catholicism', while at the same time positing, with others, that Gnostic, or at least proto-Gnostic, characteristics were also

---

[58] Fornberg, *An Early Church in a Pluralistic Society*, 133.
[59] E.g. The four Gospels, and Matthew's in particular, as well as the Book of Romans and Hebrews labour to demonstrate the continuity between Jewish Scripture and their gospel message.
[60] For a helpful survey of this problem, see Green, *Jude and 2 Peter*, 150-59.

present.[61] Both assertions have been gradually put to rest. Neyrey and Fornberg, in particular, undermined the prevalent Gnostic conclusion on the basis of, among other features, the mismatch between Gnostic views of the world's end compared to the scoffers in 2 Peter.[62]

Neyrey offered two alternative possibilities, the first of which was that the teachers were Epicureans, or at least teachers heavily influenced by Epicurean thought. This suggestion has been echoed by many scholars, certainly as a more satisfactory possibility than Gnosticism.[63] More recently, however, the Epicurean thesis has been persuasively rejected by Schreiner (2003) and Green (2008).[64] Both scholars acknowledge the similarities between the opponents and Epicureans, but highlight the problematic differences between them. Some of the problems with the Epicurean theory come when trying to integrate their views with the 'scoffers' of 2 Peter 3:4. The false teachers affirm creation (3:4) whereas Epicurus denied this doctrine (D.L. 10.73-74). And, significantly, they affirm that the world is gradually being destroyed and decaying,[65] not remaining as it has from the beginning of creation' (3:4).

Even while suggesting the Epicureans as the closest known match, Neyrey acknowledged that it is not completely satisfactory. He offered the second suggestion that they simply be called 'scoffers', which is, of course, nothing more than the label given to them in 2 Peter 3:4. Since this term is clearly accurate, however, even though it presents no advancement from the text itself, it is superior to false alternatives. A number of scholars showed a qualified preference for the Epicurean match, though also expressing some discontent

---

[61] Käsemann, "An Apologia for Primitive Christian Eschatology," 195, 80; J.N.D. Kelly, *A Commentary on the Epistles of Peter and of Jude* (London: Adam and Charles Black, 1969), 231. Thiede's less influential suggestion of an Essene community influence has also struggled to gain acceptance, partly on the basis that the Qumran community, the Essenes and Qumran community were not sceptical about such eschatological matters. See Green, *Jude and 2 Peter*, 154-55.

[62] Those who suggest it best to lay aside the Gnostic possibility for identifying the heretics include Fornberg, *An Early Church in a Pluralistic Society*, 31-32; Neyrey, "The Apologetic Use of the Transfiguration in 2 Peter 1:16-21," 506; Bauckham, *Jude, 2 Peter*, 156-57; Donald Guthrie, *New Testament Introduction* (Downers Grove: IVP, 1990), 847-50; Knight, *2 Peter and Jude*, 67; A. Gerdmar, *Rethinking the Judaism-Hellenism Dichotomy: A Historiographical Study of Second Peter and Jude* (Stockholm: Almqvist & Wiksell, 2001), 290; Schreiner, *1, 2 Peter, Jude: An Exegetical and Theological Exposition of Holy Scripture*, 278-79. Cited in Green, *Jude and 2 Peter*, 154.

[63] E.g. Reese, *2 Peter & Jude*, 315; Davids, *2 Peter and Jude*, 133-36; Earl J. Richard, *Reading 1 Peter, Jude, and 2 Peter: A Literary and Theological Commentary* (Macon: Smyth & Helwys, 2000), 315.

[64] Schreiner, *1, 2 Peter, Jude: An Exegetical and Theological Exposition of Holy Scripture*; Green, *Jude and 2 Peter*. Davids, too, recognises a problem of seeing the letter address Epicurean opponents, but dismisses it lightly on the basis that it probably crept in when Peter adapted Jude. Davids, *2 Peter and Jude*, 136.

[65] Lucretius, 2.1170-74; cited in Green, *Jude and 2 Peter*, 157.

with it.[66] Schreiner and Green more decisively separate themselves from the belief in a strong Epicurean influence, preferring to refer to them simply as 'false teachers' or 'scoffers'.[67]

Early Indications of a Sophistic Opposition

Having studied the sophistic opposition faced by Epictetus and Philo, the resemblances between them and the opponents in 2 Peter were striking. Comments made by other scholars in the search for a known group further consolidated this possibility. While referring to the challenge of their identification, for instance, Green asks,

> Can we identify the false teachers' doctrine and praxis with any known system of belief? The attempt to place these people within a particular mould is predicated on models in which consistency of belief among members of a school is assumed. While consistency could be true for some groups, it was not the nature of all.[68]

Epictetus and Philo would agree. After then mentioning the Eclectic movement, Green then refers to the sophists opposed to Philo (citing *Det.* 20-21, 70-71), rightly saying about them:

> Inconsistency in their doctrines and between their doctrine and praxis was their hallmark. We may identify the opponents in 2 Peter as one such group, holding amalgamated beliefs.[69]

Such external observations provided further reason to probe further into a possible sophistic influence. The two groups he mentions, merely as examples of known groups who tolerated inconsistency, were the Eclectics, whose views could be as diverse as the proponents; and the (earlier Greek) sophists, who I would argue not only tolerated inconsistency, but thrived upon it.

Bowersock's work on the influence of the Second Sophistic was developed by others like D.A. Russell, who argued that it had 'a floruit in the latter half of the first century AD'.[70] Our introduction highlighted a renewed appreciation for the Sophistic movement into NT studies, clearly visible in Winter's evaluation of the Sophistic movement's infiltration of the Corinthian church.[71] It was the sophists, rather than Gnostics or Epicureans who best explained the inappropriate attitudes and behaviour of the Corinthian believers. The significant similarities between 2 Peter and Corinthians will be discussed in

---

[66] Others who have taken this 'agnostic' position, to a lesser degree perhaps in the earlier works, include Fornberg, *An Early Church in a Pluralistic Society*, 233; Bauckham, *Jude, 2 Peter*, 156-57.

[67] Cf. Lucas and Green, *The Message of 2 Peter & Jude*, 19-20.

[68] Green, *Jude and 2 Peter*, 157.

[69] Green, *Jude and 2 Peter*, 157.

[70] D.A. Russell, *Greek Declamation* (Cambridge: 1983). Cited in Anderson, *The Second Sophistic: A Cultural Phenomenon in the Roman Empire*, 19.

[71] Winter, *Philo and Paul among the Sophists*.

more detail later, but Rainer Riesner, seemingly unaware of Winter's research, also made a stimulating observation. While seeking clues about the dating of 2 Peter, he observed, 'there are many parallels between the false teaching in 2 Peter and the problems Paul encountered in Corinth, suggesting a possible early date'.[72]

Could it be that our three Guides were faced with a common enemy? On the basis of the growing weight of evidence that it might overcome an impasse in the study of 2 Peter, and because Epictetus and Philo were both opposed to the sophists, it would seem useful to explore this possibility as part of our study of 2 Peter. It will be assumed in this chapter, having seen the sophists at play in Epictetus' and Philo's writings, that the reader will by now be well acquainted with the features of the Second Sophistic.

The Sophists' Approach to History and Knowledge

In a phrase that may have been more heavily loaded with his opponents' identity than previously realised, Peter contrasts his message, grounded in historical events, with any σεσοφισμένος μῦθος ('sophistic myth'), 2 Peter 1:16. Forms of the noun μῦθος appear four other times in the NT, each in the negative sense of a 'myth,' 'fable,' or 'fiction.'[73] The antonyms of μῦθος are the highly significant NT concepts of λόγος and ἀλήθεια.[74] The negative connotation of the noun μῦθος in 2 Peter 1:16 is confirmed by its adjective, σεσοφισμένος, the perfect passive participle of σοφίζω, which denotes something that is 'devised cleverly or craftily,' or perhaps better translated for a classically trained audience, 'sophistic'. 2 Peter 1:16 then naturally reads,

> For we did not follow sophistic myths when we made known to you the power and coming of our Lord Jesus Christ, but we were eyewitnesses of his majesty.

As was observed in the Philonic corpus, by the first century AD, σοφίζω and σοφιστής were terms employed not only in relation to literal sophists, but to actions which resembled 'sophistic' practices more generally, such as the use of persuasive and deceptive arguments, or ingenious contrivances.[75] This common association of 'sophistry' with clever deception can be seen in the much earlier writings of Aristotle's *Organon*. Book 1.1 is titled, *De sophisticis elenchis* ('On Sophistical Refutations') and explains how the philosopher can overcome by true reason and logic the specious arguments of the sophists.

> Let us now discuss sophistic refutations, i.e. what *appear to be refutations* but are really fallacies instead. We will begin in the natural order with the first.

---

[72] Paraphrase of Schreiner, Rainer Riesner, "Der Zweite Petrus-Brief Und Die Eschatologie," in *Zukunftserwartung in Biblischer Sicht : Beiträge Zur Eschatologie : Bericht Von Der 3. Theologischen Studienkonferenz Des Arbeitskreises Für Evangelikale Theologie*, ed. Gerhard Maier (Giessen: Brunnen, 1984), 135.
[73] 1 Tim. 1:4; 4:7; 2 Tim. 4:4; Tit. 1:14; 2 Pet. 1:16.
[74] Friberg.
[75] Liddell-Scott *Lexicon*; cf. Friberg.

> That some reasonings are genuine, while others *seem to be so but are not*, is evident...Those, then, who would be sophists are bound to study the class of arguments aforesaid: for it is worth their while: for a faculty of this kind will make a man *seem* to be wise, and this is the purpose they happen to have in view. Clearly, then, there exists a class of arguments of this kind, and it is at this kind of ability that those aim whom we call sophists. Let us now go on to discuss how many kinds there are of sophistical arguments...[76]

The exposure of the sophists' deceptive techniques by Aristotle can be illustrated later by Dio Chrysostom, who was trained as a sophist but was later 'converted to philosophy' by Musonius.[77] In his Eleventh Discourse, ΤΡΩΙΚΟΣ ΥΠΕΡ ΤΟΥ ΙΛΙΟΝ ΜΗ ΑΛΩΝΑΙ (*Maintaining that Troy was not Captured*), Dio exemplifies the way an event which was well-accepted as historical in the first-century could be persuasively rejected not with historical evidence, but through cleverly-devised, or 'sophistic' argumentation.[78] Plutarch, for instance, accused the Epicureans as being 'sophists and charlatans' (γόης) in this non-literal sense.[79]

The phrase 'sophistic myths' by itself is not reason enough to identify the false teachers with the sophists, since it was a derogatory expression employable to denounce various proponents of allegedly specious arguments. What can be asserted, however, is that whoever these opponents were, their methods are thought by Peter to resemble the contrivances of the sophists, who had the ability to persuasively argue for what was contrary to the truth. Peter's main point, rather, was to assert the historical reliability of his message in contrast to sophistic myths.

Understandably, previous attempts to identify the false teachers have tended to focus almost entirely on 2 Peter 2:1–3:7, where Peter explicitly describes them. Without denying the importance of this, the significance of what may be discreet references to the false teachers in chapters 1 and 3:16-17 may not have been fully appreciated. If they are in fact summary statements, they are probably highly significant – necessarily succinct statements, pregnant with meaning.

Bauckham makes explicit his rejection of 1:16 for being of any assistance for identifying the opponents. He argues that 1:16 only describes the way Peter did not operate, without commenting upon the way the false teachers *did* operate. If anything, he argues, 1:16 reveals the charges made against Peter. In one respect, Bauckham is correct; Peter's statement is a defence. But

---

[76] Aristotle, *On Sophistical Refutations*, 1.
[77] See Moles, "The Career and Conversion of Dio Chrysostom." cf. Dio Chrysostom, "Discourses," in *Loeb Classical Library* (London: William Heinemann), ix-xvi.
[78] Dio derides the sophists, whose 'speeches were devoid of sense' in *Orations* 54.1. Josephus considered sophistry as beguiling and even wicked (*J.W.* 4.2.3). Cited within the helpful treatment of Green, *Jude and 2 Peter*, 217. Recently, scholarship has been divided about the historicity of Troy's capture.
[79] Plutarch, *Moralia*, 1124C.

Bauckham unnecessarily excludes another logical possibility: that it is both a defensive and offensive statement. Indeed if Peter's opponents were not guilty of this very fault in 2 Peter, and not so deserving of precisely that accusation, Bauckham's restrictive reading would be more tenable.

An almost identical passage in Philo supports the claim that Peter was both defending his own position *and* attacking his opponents. In Philo's *De opificio mundi* ('On the Creation of the World'), it was important to Philo, as it was to Peter, that he demonstrate the sound reasoning behind his teaching. He does this in three ways. First, he assured his readers that he is earnest in his task, 'speaking that which is true to the full extent of his ability' (*Opif.* 142; cf. 1). Second, Philo used polarised language to stress the chasm between falsehood and truth, such as ἀψευδέστατα (§142), λογικός ('logic,' §150), and ἀλήθεια (§136). Lastly, in order to express the veracity of his own ideas, he contrasted his own methods with those of the sophists, saying,

> And these things are not mere fabricated myths (ἔστι δὲ ταῦτα οὐ μύθου πλάσματα), in which the race of Poets and Sophists delight (τὸ ποιητικὸν καὶ σοφιστικὸν), but (ἀλλά) are rather types shadowing forth some allegorical truth, according to some mystical explanation.

Peter says, in 1:16:

> For we did not (οὐ) follow sophistic myths (γὰρ σεσοφισμένοις μύθοις ἐξακολουθήσαντες) when we made known to you the power and coming of our Lord Jesus Christ, but (ἀλλ') we were eyewitnesses (ἐπόπται γενηθέντες) of his majesty.

There is a common sentiment between the two texts when they compare their approach to knowledge with those of their opponents. Philo reveals more explicitly that his 'defensive statement' was also used in offence. Coincidentally, perhaps, it is the sophists who are targeted for their indefensible method of arriving at knowledge. Both Guides deny association with the illegitimate approach, followed by the ἀλλά adversative conjunction, and then a positive statement about the reliability of their own approach.

Furthermore, Philo's terminology, within a similar structure to 1:16, shares the noun of 1:16, μῦθος, with the adjective that Peter uses to continue his description in 2 Peter 2:3, πλάστος ('fabricated' or 'fictitious').[80] In 2:3, Peter accuses the false teachers of teaching πλαστοί λόγοι ('fabricated' or 'counterfeit' words), a close echo of Philo's description: μῦθος πλάσμα ('fabricated myths'). Philo then graphically describes sophists in ways reminiscent of 2 Peter 2:

> intemperance trips him up and keeps him down. And he feeds, not on heavenly food, which wisdom offers to contemplative men by means of discourses and opinions; but on that which is put forth by the earth in the varying seasons of the year, from which arise drunkenness and voracity, and licentiousness, breaking

---

[80] LSJ.

through and inflaming the appetites of the belly, and enslaving them in subjection to gluttony, by which they strengthen the impetuous passions, the seat of which is beneath the belly; and make them break forth.[81]

When addressing some of the topics that are also raised in 2 Peter, such as the creation and destructibility of the world and divine providence, Philo chooses to discredit the sophists' epistemology and theory. His treatise dealing with the eternity of the world gives attention to the debate between philosophers and sophists on this topic. Runia explains the debate and Philo's position well:

> The question of the γένεσις/ἀγενησία and φθορά/ἀφθαρσία of the cosmos is one of the most basic questions of philosophy, initiated when man uses his gift of sight to look at the movements of the heavenly beings. It is one of those questions on which philosophers and sophists are bitterly divided, thereby showing the hopelessness of their quest for the truth. Philo's answer is that which he gives in the doxography, and he repeats it over and over again—the cosmos has been created and should in theory come to an end, but is preserved from destruction by the will and providence of its creator. The theory that the cosmos consumes itself and is reborn in an eternally recurring cycle is nothing but myth-making τερατολογία. A distinction is made between the heavenly beings who receive direct immortality, and man in the sublunary sphere, who as an individual perishes but as a race receives immortality. As biblical exegete Philo discusses on numerous occasions the theme of divine punishment applied on a cosmic scale, but always in terms of natural disasters or θεήλατα in parts of the cosmos, and not in terms of a universal eschatological perspective. Those who do consider the cosmos un-created and eternal fail to recognize God's providence and are filled with godless arrogance. Such were the builders of the tower of Babel, who were duly punished with total confusion.[82]

From Philo's perspective it should not be said, as some were saying, that the cosmos cannot undergo destruction on the basis that there is no internal or external cause mighty enough to destroy it (*Aet.* 20-24).[83] In this regard Philo and Peter (as expressed in 2 Peter 3:4-7) are of one mind. Life as it had been known from the creation could be decisively brought to a close by the Creator. But in both Philo's and Peter's mind, even if God brings enormous destruction upon the world, he does not intend to annihilate it altogether. Philo's reason for this view comes from his exegesis of Genesis 1:1-2; Peter's came from the account of the flood, but his view that fire would be the means probably also came from references to it in the Law and Prophets, as well as Christ's own teaching. Deuteronomy 32:22, as one example, speaks of a terrible fire which devours the earth, but may leave the world intact for recreation:

> For a fire has been kindled in my anger,
> one that burns to the depths of Sheol.
> It will devour the earth and its harvests,
> and sets on fire the foundations of the mountains.

---

[81] Philo, *Opif.* 158.
[82] Runia, "Philo's 'De Aeternitate Mundi': The Problem of Its Interpretation," 132.
[83] Runia, "Philo's 'De Aeternitate Mundi': The Problem of Its Interpretation," 137.

Zephaniah 1 and 3 provide more detailed and lengthy prophecies of destructive fire that will consume the 'all the earth', before a renewal.

It appears that a sophistic opposition is certainly not out of the question in the important matter of their scepticism surrounding the world's judgement. This is significant because it has been this matter which rightly brought undone the Gnostic and Epicurean hypotheses. At the very least, Philo's engagement with the sophists and philosophers demonstrates that this matter was a hot topic for the sophists. Holding views opposed to Philo's and the Stoics', they no doubt ridiculed such views as part of skilfully setting forth their own 'fabrications'.

Returning to 2 Peter 1:16, whether or not Peter intended an accusatory element to be understood from 1:16, his intense and extended invective in chapters 2:1-3:7, 16-17 certainly reiterate the same charges as might be intimated in 1:16. As it happens, the false teachers would secretly bring in destructive heresies (2:1), blaspheme the way of truth (2:2), 'exploit [the Christians] with pretensions' (2:3),[84] and abandon the 'right way' by sharing the madness of Balaam (2:15-16).

Besides the above evidence drawn from chapter 2, our suggestions that chapter 1:16 is a preliminary (or at least preparatory) comment for his invective against the false teachers, and that the false teachers resemble the sophists in their artful distortion of truth, are further supported by Peter's similar summary statement of them in chapter 3:16-17, which echoes what he has said of the false teachers in 2:1–3:7 (and 1:16).

Not unlike those who cleverly devise myths, they intentionally 'twist' or 'distort' (στρεβλόω) the plain (even if difficult) meaning of Paul's letters as well as 'the other scriptures' (3:16). 'To misunderstand is one thing; to *distort* is quite another, and that is the problem Peter tackles.'[85] Such distortions for the sake of deception were unacceptable for genuine seekers of truth, such as philosophers. But Peter may have chosen this phrase because it expressed, in essence, the sophists' trademark practice.

Resonance between the Opponents in 2 Peter and the 'Sophists' among the Ante-Nicene Fathers

Although 2 Peter is very brief compared to the writings of Epictetus and Philo, a large proportion of it is dedicated to the description of the false teachers. We do not suggest that the false teachers were sophists per se, but that the Sophistic movement was an important layer of influence upon their teaching and lifestyle.

---

[84] Following Winter, *Philo and Paul among the Sophists*, 80-94, Green observes, 'Peter's denunciation again echoes Philo's accusation of the sophists as those who not only are corrupt and seek to get gain out of others, but who also use deception as a means to their ends.' Green, *Jude and 2 Peter*, 244.

[85] Lucas and Green, *The Message of 2 Peter & Jude*, 152.

But how could we know whether or not the language used to describe the false teachers is actually describing sophistic qualities? The sophists' profile developed in chapters 1 (Epictetus) and 4 (Philo) can inform our thinking, but the task was slightly easier for those chapters because of their repeated mention and sometimes direct identification of the sophists.

In the case of the Petrine epistles, the possibility of cross-checking other Petrine references to the sophists is of course absent. The possible sophistic 'imprints' in 2 Peter will need to be compared with external sources, preferably where other Christians counter sophists. One such source, Paul's first letter to the Corinthians, will be discussed shortly. The source for our immediate attention, however, though admittedly late (mid-second to the fourth century AD), is the literature generated by the Ante-Nicene Fathers (a selection of which is in the Appendix), since some of them also named and described the false-teachers as 'Sophists'.

While the inclusion of the Ante-Nicene Fathers (mid $2^{nd} - 4^{th}$ century) may seem to be anachronistic (depending on one's dating of 2 Peter), it is significant that the instances in the New Testament were not the last time Christian writers confronted false teachers bearing a sophistic imprint. The purpose of their inclusion is not to argue that Peter opposed sophistic opposition on the basis that later Christians did. Rather, the literature is included to point out the resonance between the description of the unnamed opponents in 2 Peter, with the opponents repeatedly described as 'sophists' (both in a literal and non-literal sense) by the Ante-Nicene Fathers.

It is important to realise that the σοφισταί of later Christian writers could at times be referring to sophists in the literal sense. The Sophistic movement was still very much alive for much of this time.[86] It is soon obvious, however, that they, like others (including Epictetus and Philo) had done for many centuries, use the term 'sophistic' and 'sophist' in the non-literal sense, and usually pejoratively, for anyone they deemed fitted the sophist mould. Arian and his followers were regular victims of this label. As in earlier centuries, notable features of a 'sophist' included rhetorical ability, intentional deception of others, deliberate misinterpretation of Scripture as a proof text, as well as libertine living. These 'sophists' posed a threat to the undiscerning who were the least established in the truth. It is possible that Peter's polemic against sophist-like behaviour was, with Paul's letter to the Corinthians, a forerunner and guide for many later Christian writers.

Working through the letter of 2 Peter, it will be possible to demonstrate the vast number of connections with the sophist-like behaviour of his opponents, with the sophist-like behaviour of false teachers from the second century

---

[86] Swain suggests the Second Sophistic period was between AD 50-250. Swain, *Hellenism and Empire: Language, Classicism, and Power in the Greek World, AD 50-250*, 1. It was in the late 230s that Philostratus wrote *Lives of the Sophists*, Whitmarsh, *The Second Sophistic*, 4.

onwards. The 'cf.' references below indicate an instance where a church father said something the same or similar in relation to false teachers that he had identified was a 'sophist' or was engaged in 'sophistry' (or, more precisely, when they used terms such as σοφιστής, σόφισμα, and σοφιστικός).

Beginning at 2 Peter 1:3-4, Peter emphasises three traits of the recipients which were highly sought after by later 'sophists': δύναμις, 'power' (cf. Clement, *Strom.* 1.8.1); γνῶσις / ἐπίγνωσις, 'knowledge' (cf. Clement, *Strom.* 6.15.10; 7.7.13); and δόξα, 'glory' (cf. Clement, *Strom.* 1.8.1; 7.15.12). Peter affirms that to those with πίστις (1:1-2; significantly, this was a trait *not* highly regarded by sophists or philosophers – see Clement, *Strom.* 2.2.2) in Christ, an effective and divine power had been given, making moral excellence possible (1:3-4). In 2 Peter, a true knowledge of Christ, which goes hand in hand with precious faith (1:1), constitutes a standing from which one will not fall (2 Pet. 1:10; cf. Clement, *Strom.* 6.10.3). That is, by faith, the believers had received that which later 'sophists' sought.

The sophists by contrast promised a way of life that claimed to be powerful for moral transformation, but was deemed by Peter and others to be *powerless* (cf. Irenaeus, *Adv. haer.* 3.24.2). Their knowledge was spurious, not based on truth (cf. Clement, *Strom.* 2.2.2). The heretics have some knowledge of Christ (2 Pet. 2:20) and yet do not live according to their knowledge, lacking also the traits exhorted in 1:5-7. As a consequence, Peter describes them as 'ineffective and unfruitful' in their knowledge (1:8); nearsighted and blind (1:9), and unprotected from falling (1:10) away from the path of life.

In 2 Peter 1:16, Peter contrasts the reliability of his message with the 'sophistic myths' of others (cf. Minucius Felix, *Oct.* 31.1; Ireneaus, *Adv. haer.* 4.2.2; Clement, *Strom.* 1.8.1; 7.15.12; Tertullian, *De anima* 3; Origen, *C. Cels.* 3.39; and Athanasius refers to 'Arian's fables' in the context of sophistic persuasion in Athan., *Ar.* 1.6). Certainly in the early church the reliability of the apostles (cf. Iren. *Adv. haer.* 3.5.1; Tatian, *Orat.* 33) and Christian practices (cf. Minucius Felix, *Oct.* 31.1) were questioned by the sophists. Disinterested in spurious myths, Peter simply conveyed the events he saw (1:16), and heard (1:18) when they were 'with him' [Christ] on the holy mountain. Peter's word confirmed the prophetic word, which, importantly from a Greek perspective, was more ancient than the sophists' source (cf. Tatian, *Orat.* 35; 36; 40; Tert. *Apol.* 47.1), and which provided 'a light shining in a dark place'. Those who reject this new testimony, built upon ancient divine prophecies (1:19-21) remain in the darkness (cf. Iren. *Adv. haer.* 3.5.1; 3.24.2).

For those who believe, the time is coming when the day dawns and the 'morning star arises in your hearts' (1:19). The underappreciated beauty of Peter's inclusion of this particular Old Testament prophecy (one of the notably few in 2 Peter), lies in the identity of the prophet from whom it came. Balaam, the one presented by Philo as the archetypal sophist,[87] was the prophet who first

---

[87] See my treatment of Philo and the σοφισταί in Chapter 5.

used the 'star' metaphor for Israel's Messianic figure (Num. 24:17; cf. Rev. 2:14). Since he was a prophet, Balaam too would have spoken from God as he was 'carried along by the Holy Spirit' (1:21), and knew enough about God to make his folly inexcusable. The fact that he should have known better is the very charge Peter wishes to lay against the false teachers when he compares their abandonment of the right way (1:15) with that of Balaam in 2:15. Just like the sophists, Balaam 'loved gain from wrongdoing' (ὃς μισθὸν ἀδικίας ἠγάπησεν) and his direction equated with such 'madness' (παραφρονία; cf. Tatian, *Orat.* 22; 33) that his donkey was used to correct and 'restrain' him (2:16). Truth, even from the lips of a donkey, is superior to falsehood from the more outwardly impressive, professional mouthpiece.

Despite these possible allusions to the opponents in chapter 1, the clearest description of them emerges when it is Peter's overt intent, in 2:1–3:7 and in 3:14-17.

The Christian Fathers engaged in fierce polemic against those who were trained sophists, as well as those who merely acted like them. Athanasius and Marcellus of Ancyra, for example, were opposed by Asterius 'the Sophist' (died c. 341), one of the founders and most prominent representatives of the Arian movement.[88] Sophistry was Asterius' profession, and while he may have ceased to work as a σοφιστής professionally following his conversion to Arian Christianity,[89] Athanasius' reference to him as 'advocate of the heresy' suggest he was still very much using his sophistic training to promote heterodox views of Christ.[90]

The italicised characteristics from the quotations from 2 Peter below resonate not only with the sophists' qualities as described by Epictetus and Philo, but with those described as sophists by later Christian writers.

> But there arose false prophets also among the people, as among you also there shall be false teachers (ψευδοδιδάσκαλοι; cf. references to sophists as false teachers in Tatian, *Orat.* 22, 40; Gregory, *Orat.* 1.13), who shall secretly bring in destructive heresies (cf. Irenaeus, *Adv. haer.* 5.20.2), *denying* (ἀρνέομαι) even the Master that bought them (cf. sophists who deny the Lord in Athan. *Ar.*, 2.32-33; 14.37) bringing upon themselves swift destruction (ἀπώλεια). And many will follow (καὶ πολλοὶ ἐξακολουθήσουσιν; cf. the 'sophists'' appeal to large followings, Tatian, *Orat.* 22) their sensuality (ἀσέλγεια), and because of them the way of truth (ὁδὸς τῆς ἀληθείας cf. Clement, *Strom.* 1.5.2) will be blasphemed (βλασφημηθήσεται – for the common charge of sophists as those who blaspheme see Irenaeus, *Adv. haer.* 3.24.2; 5.20.2). And in their greed (πλεονεξία) they will exploit (ἐμπορεύομαι; Clement, *Strom.* 1.8.4) you with false words (πλαστὸς

---

[88] For a helpful introduction to the life and works of Asterius the Sophist, see Wolfram Kinzig, *In Search of Asterius: Studies on the Authorship of the Homilies on the Psalms*, (Göttingen: Vandenhoeck & Ruprecht, 1990), 14-21. See, also George A Kennedy, *Greek Rhetoric under Christian Emperors* (Princeton: Princeton University Press, 1983).

[89] As per Socrates, the church historian, in *Hist. eccl.* 1.36.

[90] Athan, *Ar.* 1.30. See Kinzig, *In Search of Asterius*, 14-15.

λόγος). Their condemnation (κρίμα) from long ago is not idle, and their destruction (ἀπώλεια) is not asleep.

Switching freely between the wicked of ancient to modern times in 2:10, Peter continues their portrayal, this time with more vivid terms, presumably because he was familiar with contemporary examples. They are described in the following ways in 2 Peter:

2:10 – 'bold and self-willed' (τολμηταὶ αὐθάδεις) cf. Irenaeus, *Adv. haer.* 5.20.2.

2:10 – 'irrational animals' (ἄλογον ζῷον) cf. Clement, *Strom.* 2.2.2; Origen, *De princ.* 1.8.4.

2:12 'blasphemers about matters of which they are ignorant' (ἐν οἷς ἀγνοοῦσιν βλασφημοῦντες) cf. Irenaeus, *Adv. haer.* 5.20.2; Clement, *Strom.* 1.8.1; 7.15.11; Origen, *C.Cels.* 4.25; Athan. *Ar.* IV.1.9.

2:13 – they 'count it pleasure to revel' (from τρυφή) in the daytime' (and are shameless, cf. Clement, *Strom.* 2.2.2; 3.19.4).

2:13 – they 'revel in their deceptions' (ἐντρυφῶντες ἐν ταῖς ἀπάταις, cf. the sense of Sophists' revelry in Origen, *C. Cels.* 3.39; Athan, *Ep. Aeg. Lib.* 9; *Ar.* 90, and for their deceit in particular see Clement. *Strom.* 1.6.3; 7.9.2; 7.15.11; Gregory, *Orat.* 1.13; Tatian, *Orat.* 22.1).

2:13 – while they feast (συνευωχέομαι) with you (not observed in the Ante-Nicene Fathers, but present in Paul's letter to the Corinthians, and discussed later in this chapter).

2:14 – those with eyes full of adultery (ὀφθαλμοὺς ἔχοντες μεστοὺς μοιχαλίδος) cf. Tatian, *Address to the Greeks,* 22.

2:14 – insatiable (ἀκατάπαυστος) for sin (ἁμαρτία) cf. Clement, *Strom.* 3.19.4.

2:14 – are trained (from γυμνάζω) in 'greed' 'covetousness' or perhaps 'exploitation' (πλεονεξία) cf. Clement, *Strom.* 2.2.2.

2:18 – speaking loud boasts of folly (ὑπέρογκα γὰρ ματαιότητος φθεγγόμενοι) cf. Clement, *Strom.* 1.3.1; 7.7.13.

2:19 – They promise them freedom (ἐλευθερίαν αὐτοῖς ἐπαγγελλόμενοι), but they themselves are slaves of corruption (αὐτοὶ δοῦλοι ὑπάρχοντες τῆς φθορᾶς) cf. Clement, *Strom.* 1.3.1; 3.19.5; Origen, *C. Cels.* 4.25; Athan, *Decr.* 18.

2:20 – For if, after they have escaped the defilements of the world (ἀποφυγόντες τὰ μιάσματα τοῦ κόσμου) through the knowledge of our Lord and Savior Jesus Christ, they are again entangled (cf. the entangling effects of sophistry in Clement, *Strom.* 2.2.2) in them and overcome (πάλιν ἐμπλακέντες ἡττῶνται), the last state has become worse for them than the first.

2:22 – What the true proverb says has happened to them: "The dog (κύων) returns to its own vomit (cf. Athanasius comparison with vomit for heretics in Athan. *Ar,* 2.30), and the sow (ὗς), after washing herself, returns to wallow in the mire (βόρβορος) cf. the mud of the sophists' heresy in Clem. *Protr.* 10.3-5; Cyprian, *Ep.* 74.23; and the dog and swine returning to Arian's sophistic views in Athan. *Ar.* 29.

3:3 – scoffers will come in the last days with scoffing (ἐμπαιγμονῇ ἐμπαῖκται) cf. the sophists known as scoffers in Clement, *Strom.* 1.3.1; Tatian, *Orat.* 22.1; and Athanasius refers to 'this Arius jesting on such matters as on a stage' in Athan., *Ar.* 1.7.

3:4-5 – They will say, "Where is the promise of his coming? For ever since the fathers fell asleep, all things are continuing as they were from the beginning of creation." For they deliberately overlook this fact (Λανθάνει γὰρ αὐτοὺς τοῦτο θέλοντας), that the heavens existed long ago, and the earth was formed out of water and through water by the word of God', 3:4-5 (for the sophists' enjoyment of captious and vain argumentation, cf. Clement, *Strom.* 1.22; 1.8.1. As we saw in Philo's interaction with the sophists in his *The Eternity of the World*, the philosophers and sophists were particularly eager to contest matters pertaining to the destruction of the earth).

3:16 – Twisting Paul's words, (cf. the sophists doing so in Athan. *Ar.* 14.37).

One of the well-recognised methods employed in sophistic argumentation was undermining the opposition's case by arguing from probability. This technique sought to demonstrate that one's proposition is more *likely* to be true than the opponents. The classic example of this method, in the ancient tradition was the defence provided by the little man when charged of beating a larger man. The little man defends his innocence by arguing,

> 'It is not likely (probable) that I would do so,' he would reply, 'for the bigger man is stronger than I am and would defeat me. Since I would know that, I would not anger him by hitting him.'[91]

Ballif and Moran argue that this approach

> to argument can be described as rhetorical more than typically philosophical. That is, the sophistic, rhetorical approach to disputation is to assert that there is no objective (and/or accessible) standard of truth to which one can appeal to determine the truthfulness of claims; rather, one appeals to probability, to conventional values, and to the judgment of the public opinion, which will determine the 'truth' of any case. Philosophers and philosophically prone rhetoricians, such as Plato, however, fiercely denounced the Sophists, with their rhetorical strategies and presuppositions, as liars, as flatterers, as word stylists without substance, and as lovers of the appearance (of truth) rather than of the reality (of truth). Even more rhetorically oriented philosophers, such as Aristotle, condemned sophistry as fallacious argument, as illogical.[92]

At the close of his letter, in what may be a succinct summary of the sophistic nature of the opponents, Peter expresses contempt for their manipulation of the scriptures to make it support their false teaching. The ignorant and unstable (οἱ

---

[91] The summary of this well-known classical line of argument, gleaned from the writings of Aristotle, Cicero, and Quintilian is offered in James J. Murphy et al., *A Synoptic History of Classical Rhetoric* (Mahwah: Hermagoras, 2003), 19.

[92] Michelle Ballif and Michael G. Moran, "Introduction," in *Classical Rhetorics and Rhetoricians: Critical Studies and Sources*, ed. M. Ballif and M.G. Moran (Westport: Praeger, 2005), 7.

ἀμαθεῖς καὶ ἀστήρικτοι) 'twist' (στρεβλόω) Paul's writings to their own destruction, as they do the other Scriptures (cf. the distortion or 'twisting' of Scripture see Tatian, *Orat.* 41; Tertullian, *De carne Chr.* 23.1; Origen, *De princ.* 1.8.4; Clement, *Strom.* 3.19.4; Irenaeus, *Adv. haer.* 1.9.1, 4; Athan, *Ep. Aeg. Lib.* 2.8; *Ar.* 2.30). You therefore, beloved, knowing this beforehand, take care (cf. the need to protect oneself from their heresy in Clement, *Strom.* 1.5.1) that you are not carried/lead away (συναπάγω) with the error of lawless people (τῶν ἀθέσμων) and lose your own stability (στηριγμός)', 2 Pet. 3:16-17.

What then can we conclude from the linguistic and thematic echoes between Peter's polemic and that of later Christians against 'sophists' of their own day? Could they simply be the way false teachers of various kinds were described? Against this conclusion, not all false teachers share these features, as exemplified by other New Testament writings. Most of the false teachers described in the New Testament and by the Ante-Nicene Fathers do not match the sophistic profile. The alleged features of both sophists and 'sophists' include: their priority for argumentation over truth and their captious arguments; their unashamed intent to deceive; their libertine living and greed; their particular scepticism about the destruction of the world; their lack of interest in a consensus regarding any matter, particularly eschatological matters.

We have been examining descriptions that are far narrower than a generic type of false teacher, or even 'scoffer'. The scoffers of 2 Peter lived and acted in particularly 'sophistic' ways. It was when the Ante-Nicene Fathers deemed that their opponents were acting like 'sophists' that overwhelming similarities of response emerge with the 2 Peter descriptions. It may be that the later Christians, aware of the sophistic opposition in 2 Peter and Corinthians (not to mention other authors like Philo), intentionally borrowed their descriptions and insults. At the least, they were, like Peter, adopting the caricatures and language used by anti-sophistic polemicists.

To say that Peter's opponents *were* sophists because they behaved like sophists may be to outrun the evidence. What can be affirmed, however, is that if the false teachers were not trained sophists, they had been significantly influenced by the Sophistic movement and are best described with reference to it.

Further Similarities between the Polemic of 2 Peter and 1 Corinthians

One of the biggest threats against the believers in the New Testament is false teaching, and it comes in various forms. In the Gospels, the opposition of the Jews is given primary attention as the claims of Jesus to be the Jewish Messiah are proclaimed and debated. In the book of Acts, the nature of the opposition reflects the general movement of the book's attention from Jerusalem and Judea into the Roman world. Numerous New Testament authors reveal something of their opposition, often from Jewish interest groups, as in Galatians and

Philippians. The threat of physical persecution by local and Roman authorities is indicated in such books as 1 Peter, Hebrews and the Book of Revelation.

Paul's letter to Titus bears some resemblance with 2 Peter with respect to their sophist-like deception as well as Paul's response for overcoming their influence (2:1-15), but the major difference is their Jewish traits, with mention of the 'circumcision party' (1:10) and their fascination with 'Jewish myths' (1:13). John's letters (1 Jn. 2:26-29), as well as Paul's second letter to Timothy provide warnings that resonate with 2 Peter about deceitful, loveless, libertine teachers who would seek to lead the believers astray. For example, 2 Tim 4:3-4 says,

> For the time is coming when people will not endure sound teaching, but having itching ears they will accumulate for themselves teachers to suit their own passions, and will turn away from listening to the truth and wander off into myths (τοὺς μύθους ἐκτραπήσονται).

It may be expected, though it cannot be argued in depth here, that the cultural changes brought about by the Second Sophistic as it spread through the Empire was having a discernible influence within these various church contexts.

It is to Paul's first letter to the Corinthians, however, that we will give most attention, for two reasons. First, the sophistic presence in Corinthians has already been well established by Winter *et al.*[93] Second, it is in 1 Corinthians that there are striking and numerous similarities. This cannot be developed in length here, nor will we extend our glance into the rich fields of 2 Corinthians, but it is important to highlight some of the characteristics in the Corinthians setting that warrant further investigation.

By way of introduction, Paul, also writing to a largely Greek audience to the church in Corinth, sought to lay forth the plain historical truth vis-à-vis the impressive 'lofty speech or wisdom' that some were anticipating (1 Cor. 2:4). In both letters he felt it necessary to remind them, as did Peter, that his is a divine message, not one of human wisdom or invention:

> εἰ δὲ καὶ ἰδιώτης τῷ λόγῳ, ἀλλ' οὐ τῇ γνώσει, ἀλλ' ἐν παντὶ φανερώσαντες ἐν πᾶσιν εἰς ὑμᾶς.
> Even if I am unskilled in speaking, I am not so in knowledge; indeed, in every way we have made this plain to you in all things.[94]

In 1 Cor. 1-3 there is an emphasis on themes such as true versus pretentious wisdom, where folly and craftiness characterise his opposition, as can be seen in such phrases as 'for he catches the wise in their craftiness' (τοὺς σοφοὺς ἐν τῇ πανουργίᾳ αὐτῶν), 3:9. Like Peter (1:17-21), Paul is self-effacing in the revelation process, being a servant and steward (ὑπηρέτης καὶ οἰκονόμος). There is a significant contrast in their behaviour; his opponents indulge now, and seek honour and the trappings of blessing. Paul, by contrast, lives in a way

---

[93] As mentioned earlier in this section, but also in the Introduction.
[94] 2 Cor. 11:6

that they would deem a pitiable life of labour and hardship (ch. 4; cf. the very similar observation in Philo, *Det.* 33-34). They are arrogant (cf. 2 Pet. 2:10), and their impressive speech does not compare with divine power (4:19-20; cf. 2 Pet. 1:3; 2:19). Their sexual immorality is such that they act in ways that are 'not tolerated even among the pagans' (5:1; cf. 2 Peter 2, where the false teachers in 2 Peter who live in defiance even of classical virtues such as piety and moderation). Rather than feel shame about this, they equate such behaviour with their supposed liberty and freedom in Christ (6:12; cf. 2 Pet. 2:18-19). Both 1 Corinthians and 2 Peter have an emphasis on true knowledge (1 Cor. 1:18-31; cf. 2 Pet. 1:12, 16-21). Forms of γνῶσις appear ten times in 1 Corinthians which is more than any other book; and 3 times in 2 Peter, which is the highest concentration of occurrences, and not including the four occurrences of ἐπίγνωσις. Despite this emphasis on true knowledge from God, both letters insist that knowledge is inadequate if not accompanied by love (1 Cor. 8:1-3; 16:14; cf. 2 Pet. 1:5-7).[95] Paul does not follow the Sophists' custom of peddling his wisdom for personal gain. Instead, he relinquishes his right to be supported by the Corinthians, and does what a sophist would consider demeaning, and unrewarding, by working with his own hands to provide for his needs (1 Cor. 9:3-18 cf. the sophist-like greed seen in 2 Pet. 2:14). Peter and Paul promote self-control over licentious living, and felt they must distinguish themselves from their opponents by acting in the interests of the believers (1 Cor. 9:19-22; cf. 2 Pet. 1:12-15). Problems at the meal setting are described in both letters, probably because loveless behaviour was obvious in that setting. In one group, 'One goes hungry, another gets drunk' (1 Cor. 11:21); and in the other group the false teachers revel 'in their deceptions while they feast with you' (2 Pet. 2:13). Both letters provide their readers with a reminder and clear statement of historical events, brought by the apostles' testimony which must be accepted by the community of faith (1 Cor. 15:3-8; cf. 2 Pet. 1:16-17; 3:2ff.). The eschatology of each author in particular was challenged: some 'say that there is no resurrection from the dead' (1 Cor. 15:13) and others 'scoff at the promise of Christ's return' (2 Pet. 3:4).

Both Paul and Peter work to undermine a spirit of comparison between believers. Paul does so by reminding them that they have received that which they might be tempted to boast about, from God and not from their own effort (1 Cor. 4:7); as well as instructing them that each member of the body of Christ is important (12:12-26). Similarly, Peter asserts that in their most valuable possession, πίστις, they have all 'obtained a faith of equal standing' with his own, removing any basis for comparison or rivalry.

The geographical details of the two letters further extend the possibility of a sophistic influence upon both groups. Both authors were aware of the other's

---

[95] The word ἀγάπη appears only once in 2 Peter, but its position after γνῶσις and in the ultimate position in the list of traits reflects the NT's attribution its place as the highest of traits. For further comment, see the discussion of traits in Chapter 11.

life and ministry: Paul mentions Peter's custom of travelling with his wife (1 Cor. 9:5) and that Peter was first to see Christ after his resurrection (15:5). And Peter was clearly familiar with Paul's writings and the way they were being intentionally misinterpreted (2 Pet. 3:16). Writing to Corinth from Ephesus in Asia Minor, Paul says in 1 Cor. 16:19, 'The churches of Asia send you greetings.' He had been in contact with Galatia (1 Cor. 16:1 cf. 1 Pet. 1:1), and passes on greetings from Asia more broadly (1 Cor. 16:19 cf. 1 Pet. 1:1). Since the other letter alluded to in 2 Peter 3:1 is normally taken to refer to 1 Peter, 2 Peter also was also probably intended for the same region of churches in Asia Minor (c. AD 64-5), ten or so years after Paul had written the letter now known as 1 Corinthians from Asia Minor (c. AD 54)[96] which dealt with sophistic problems in Corinth. Thus it is quite plausible, indeed likely, that Peter was well aware of Paul's struggle with the sophists in Corinth, even if he had not already engaged directly with them himself.

The recipients of 2 Peter, if they resided in the places listed in 1 Peter, may have comprised Christian Jews who were part of the community evicted from Rome by Claudius in AD 49, many of whom appear to have settled in these Roman colonies established by Claudius in northern Turkey.[97] Further research might shed light on the extent to which Corinth was a point of intersection for believers (including Paul and Peter) on the route from Rome (where Peter mainly worked) to these cities. Such a situation would help to explain layers of Jewish, Roman, and Corinthian cultural, theological and linguistic influences on 2 Peter and on the Christians in the colonies to which it was written.

Further, Ephesus and Smyrna, also in Asia Minor, would become two of the three centres of the Second Sophistic, as Bowersock observes:

> From the abundant evidence for the origins of sophists and the cities (other than Rome) in which they taught, it is not difficult to make out which were the great sophistic centres. Above all ranked Athens, Smyrna, and Ephesus. These three cities produced many of the eminent sophists of the second century and received most of the others at some time during their careers.[98]

Since Bowersock's work in 1969, more has been unearthed to show that sophistic influences clearly observable in the second century (thanks largely to Philostatus' *Vitae sophistarum*) were also present in the first century AD. 2 Peter may provide evidence that the sophists' prominence in Asia Minor was also a first-century phenomenon, even if in its infancy.

---

[96] Anthony C. Thiselton, *The First Epistle to the Corinthians: A Commentary on the Greek Text* (Grand Rapids: Eerdmans, 2000), 31-32.

[97] I am grateful to David Jackson, whose own research led him to raise the possible connections made in this paragraph through personal correspondence. For a helpful treatment of the exiles of the διασπορά in relation to 1 Peter 1:1, see Karen H. Jobes, *1 Peter* (Grand Rapids: Baker, 2005), 32ff.

[98] Bowersock, *Greek Sophists in the Roman Empire*, 17.

Lastly, in terms of similarities between the two letters, both apostles considered it important to 'remind' their audience of the gospel that was earlier received by them (1 Cor. 15:1, 11; 2 Pet. 1:12-15; 3:1-2). For both authors, the influence of persuasive teachers advocating licentious lifestyles was a danger; 'bad company ruins good morals' (1 Cor. 15:33), and according to Peter, 'many will follow their sensuality' (2 Pet. 1:2). Both groups were encouraged to remain 'steadfast,' 'immovable' and 'productive' in God's service (1 Cor. 15:58; cf. 2 Pet. 1:10; 3:17), and both authors commended the believers in their walk, but insisted that they must walk carefully (1 Cor. 16:13; 2 Pet. 3:17).

To summarise our comparison of 2 Peter with Corinthians, there are compelling parallels between the false teachers of 2 Peter and the problems Paul faced in Corinth. The parallels extend beyond the similarities between the false teachers. Also similar are the detrimental effects upon the believers, the apostles' emphasis on divine origins of their plainly presented message, the remedy to confront the threat, and ethical admonitions which accompany right knowledge.

Conclusions

This section sought to gain an understanding of Simeon Peter. His documented rise was quite remarkable, beginning in a fishing boat on the Sea of Galilee and concluding with a central role in the spread of Christianity. According to the Gospel accounts, Jesus' purposes for Peter were announced in their first encounter, and then uncomfortably driven home during their last recorded conversation. Peter's self-perception was shaped by the shepherding role which Jesus first modelled, and then passed on. Deeply convinced that the Scriptures were fulfilled with the life, death and resurrection of Christ, Peter also saw his function to be part of what yet remained unfulfilled—the proclaiming of that message to every nation (Mt. 28:18-20; Lk. 24:46-47).

The motive leading to the composition of 2 Peter as far as is evident from the New Testament texts generally, and from 2 Peter in particular, stem from Peter's sense of his Christ-given function as shepherd. He seeks to feed and tend to the needs of God's flock, strengthening their resolve to remain in the truth.

Peter was clearly convinced that his message was true. A significant influence among many for Peter was the time he spent in direct contact with his Rabbi, the θεός-ἄνθρωπος, Jesus Christ. While with Jesus on 'the holy mountain', Peter himself heard the voice from heaven which memorably affirmed God's pleasure in Jesus. For Peter, this also confirmed his belief in the Jewish Scriptures and their predictions relating to Jesus Christ. Jesus' clarity about such matters as life and death was conferred to Peter, his apostle. In Acts and in the letters of 1 and 2 Peter, Peter spoke with great authority and in significant detail about the way to live and the events which follow one's death.

Lastly, we noted already but will further observe that while Peter's knowledge came from Jewish Scripture and other Jewish writings, and from his years with Messiah Jesus, he demonstrates an awareness also of the Hellenistic world in which he lived. With little reason to doubt that Peter was an able communicator in light of Luke's account in the Book of Acts, it is unsurprising that he may, in his later years, express himself in a way that was accessible to a broad audience.

CHAPTER 10
Peter's Guide to θεός

The Person of θεός

Although technical formulations of the doctrine of the Trinity were still centuries away, the disciples and early church were founded upon such 'Trinitarian' formulations as is present in Jesus' commission to his disciples:

> All authority in heaven and on earth has been given to me. Go therefore and make disciples of all nations, baptizing them in the name of the Father and of the Son and of the Holy Spirit.[1]

The latent foundations for the profound Trinitarian doctrine were already laid in the Jewish Scriptures (e.g. Gen. 1:1-2, 26; Isa. 9:6, 45:21 read in light of 53:11), and in the Gospel accounts, Peter's awareness of Jesus' divinity develops.[2]

In Matthew 14:33, Peter, the monotheistic Jew,[3] worshiped Jesus. On another occasion Peter says to Jesus as though to God himself, 'Depart from me, for I am a sinful man, O Lord' (ἔξελθε ἀπ' ἐμοῦ, ὅτι ἀνὴρ ἁμαρτωλός εἰμι, κύριε).[4] Likewise, in the Book of Acts, Peter said, 'Let all the house of Israel therefore know for certain that God has made him both Lord and Christ, this Jesus whom you crucified' (Acts 2:36).

In 1 and 2 Peter this three-person understanding of God is again affirmed.[5] The transfiguration account in 2 Peter clearly reveals a divine Father-Son conception. And although the Holy Spirit is mentioned only once, a divine function, if not divine being, is explicit: 'men spoke from God as they were carried along by the Holy Spirit' (2 Peter 1:21).

---

[1] Matt. 28:18-19. Peter's encounter with Father, Son and Spirit at Jesus' baptism was also significant enough to be recorded in all four Gospels (Matt. 3:16-17; Mk. 1:9-11; Lk. 3:21-22; and expressed differently in Jn. 1:32-34).

[2] See, for example, Mt. 16:16; 22:41-45; Mk. 8:29; Lk. 9:20; Jn. 11:27; Acts 9:34; cf. Jn. 20:28; Acts 7:59.

[3] As would have been reinforced by such accounts as in Matt. 4:10; Mk 12:29-30; and Lk. 4:8.

[4] Lk. 5:8, echoing the wording of Isa. 6:5.

[5] 1 Peter begins with the words, 'according to the foreknowledge of God the Father, in the sanctification of the Spirit, for obedience to Jesus Christ' (1:2).

The first chapter of 2 Peter is loaded with references to the Godhead, containing more than chapters 2 and 3 combined.[6] Jesus' divinity is implicit, if not explicit, in a few verses in 2 Peter. The first verse of chapter 1 (which has parallels in 1:11; 2:20; 3:2, 18) is almost certainly an explicit reference to Christ's divinity, referring to one person and not two when it says: τοῦ θεοῦ ἡμῶν καὶ σωτῆρος Ἰησοῦ Χριστοῦ ('our God and Savior Jesus Christ').[7] Remarkably, in the next verse, the two persons are distinguished: 'God and Father' and 'Jesus Christ'. Jesus is identified with God, as being God; and Jesus is described as distinct from the Father.

This dual perspective of God as one person, and yet more than one person, is further reflected by Peter's use of the word 'Lord' (κύριος) to refer to both God and Jesus. Some of the fourteen occurrences clearly refer to Christ (e.g. 2 Pet. 1:8, 14, 16), and others appear to refer to the Father (e.g. 2 Pet. 2:9, 11), but it is not immediately obvious in some verses to whom the title refers, and the word 'Lord' could refer to one and the other, and perhaps to both (2 Pet. 3:2, 8-9). For theological reasons, the author was not averse to this ambiguity.[8]

---

[6] Four of the seven occurrences of θεός in 2 Pet. occur in chapter 1; as do seven of the nine references to Ἰησοῦς. In addition to proper names, 2 Pet. 1 also refers to God indirectly with such terms as θεῖος (used twice only, in 1:3,4), υἱός (only in 1:17), the Majestic Glory (μεγαλοπρεπὴς δόξα, only in 1:17), as well as the personal pronoun.

[7] Contra Neyrey, who rejects the translation 'of our God and Savior Jesus Christ' for a rendering which requires more intervention: 'our God and Jesus Christ the Savior'. Two of his three reasons for rejecting what might be considered a more natural reading on the basis of grammatical argumentation alone, are based on an alleged lack of precedent for such expression in the NT. His argument that it is unlikely because it is 'rare' in the NT, however, is an unfortunate one if it flattens on principle forms of expression that are rare. Indeed, we might be surprised greatly if there were not rare expressions and perspectives across the writings of any of the NT authors. This allowance for individuality of expression should be especially 'permitted' for 2 Pet. because, as Neyrey himself states (57), it contains fifty-seven words that are not found elsewhere in the New Testament. Neyrey's other reason depends upon his view that the author of 2 Peter intended a parallel between this distinction in the persons of God in verse 1, with what is a clearer two-person description of God and of Christ in v. 2. Reese's view, however, that the author is juxtaposing two complementary truths is more feasible on the bases of grammatical norms, pre-existing theology (as is demonstrated above), the NT canon, and even in light of the exalted claims made about Jesus in 2 Peter itself. If Neyrey is wrong, as we contend, 2 Pet. 1:1-2 is less redundant in expression, and provides a theological gem for NT theologians that aligns with the broader claims for Christ in 2 Peter. For more detailed grammatical argumentation for our case, see the discussion in Robertson, *A Grammar of the Greek New Testament in the Light of Historical Research* (Leicester: Hodder & Stoughton, 1919), 785-86; J.H. Moulton, *A Grammar of N.T. Greek* (1908), 1.84. Cf. the study of Σωτήρ in P. Wendland, *ZNTW* 5 (1904); Reese, *2 Peter & Jude*, 132.

[8] Another example of this interesting question of ambiguous identity comes in the text-critical questions of Jude 5, which relates to the use of Lord, God, Jesus, or combinations thereof. Following the strong attestation of the uncial fragments,

Peter's Guide to θεός

Furthermore, the divinity of Christ can also be deduced from the elevated place that he has beside God the Father in Peter's schema. Peter writes of the 'knowledge of God and of Jesus our Lord' as though the two are equally significant if not equivalent (2 Pet. 1:2, 9). In verse 11 the eternal kingdom is that of 'our Lord and Saviour Jesus Christ'. Peter speaks of Jesus Christ's 'majesty' (1:16), and his receipt of 'honour and glory from the Father'. Concluding the letter, Peter's doxology expresses the desire that Christ receive eternal glory, a desire normally reserved for God alone (as in such texts as Rev. 4:11):

> But grow in the grace and knowledge of our Lord and Savior Jesus Christ. To him be the glory both now and to the day of eternity (αὐτῷ ἡ δόξα καὶ νῦν καὶ εἰς ἡμέραν αἰῶνος). Amen.

There are many other ways in which Christ and/or God the Father are portrayed in 2 Peter. He has 'glory and excellence' (1:3), is the 'giver of precious and very great promises' (1:4), is distinct in nature from the corruption that is in the world (1:4), is the possessor of an eternal kingdom (1:11), and communicated to Peter directly (1:14). Christ is one who has power and who came to earth (1:16), appeared in 'majesty' (1:16) and received honor and glory from God the Father, the Majestic Glory (1:17). Grace, knowledge and peace are found in Jesus Christ (1:2; 3:18).

The Work of θεός in 2 Peter

With the above references to God combined, it is evident that God has an essential place not only in the overall message of 2 Peter 1, but in each of the three sections within the chapter. A closer look at the subjects covered by Peter in chapter 1 explain the many references to God. Firstly, in the salutations the author and his audience are defined by their relationship to God (1:1-2). Second, in order to enunciate the believers' current standing and their way ahead for the future, God is included as the acting agent as well as the giver of final rewards (1:3-11). Thirdly, because Peter is stressing the divine origin and authority of his message, God is necessarily of central importance (1:12-21).

The ways Peter chose to describe God are also significant for his literary purposes. His moral perfection (1:2-3), communicative ability (1:1, 4, 14, 16-21), and glory and majesty (1:3, 16-17) dominate chapter 1. Such traits of God

---

Alexandrinus and Vaticanus, the ESV went against other popular translations (though expressing a phenomenon similar to 1 Cor. 10:4) to attribute, remarkably, the Exodus rescue to Jesus: 'Now I want to remind you, although you once fully knew it, that Jesus, who saved a people out of the land of Egypt, afterward destroyed those who did not believe.' *The Greek New Testament* (1998). See, also, Bruce Metzger, *A Textual Commentary on the Greek New Testament* (Stuttgart: United Bible Society, 1994), 657. Ignatius, who died c. 117 AD, wrote plainly of Christ as God when he wrote, 'our God, Jesus the Christ, was conceived by Mary'. Ignatius, *Epistle to the Ephesians* 18.2.

help us to understand the basis for his anger and judgement in chapters 2–3. Confronted with gross immorality, a defiant attitude towards his word, the 'majestic' God becomes understandably active in judgement against it. A life lived in opposition to the God of chapter 1 is tolerated only temporarily, as chapters 2 and 3 elucidate. Christ's coming will bring with it the condemnation (2:2) and destruction of the false teachers (2:3, 12). Their destruction is 'not asleep' (2:3). On his word (3:5), he will judge the ungodly as surely as he condemned Sodom and Gomorrah (2:6) and brought a deluge upon the world in which people perished (3:6). And on his word (3:7) he will at an unexpected moment (3:10) bring judgement and destruction upon the ungodly again, this time by fire upon the heavens and earth (3:7, 10).

In chapter 2 the judgement motif dominates, but God's role as the rescuer is juxtaposed, the effect of which is to generate two vastly different categories in which a person can live in relationship with God. God 'preserved' Noah, a herald of righteousness (2:5), and he 'rescued righteous Lot' (2:7), both accounts confirming God's ability to 'rescue the godly from trials' (2:9). One's response to his word is the basis upon which they are categorised; some scoff and will perish; others persist in their belief that God will fulfil his promises about returning (3:2-4) and about judgement (3:8-10).

Peter presents God as standing behind his letter as one ready and able to judge all of those who reject its message about life and death. After all, Peter's message was in continuity with the OT prophets, and 'the commandment of the Lord and Saviour'. Significantly, Peter asserts that this very message came 'through your apostles' (3:2), which included his own message (1:1). 2 Peter claims to be more than a letter *about* God's word to his people; it claims to *be* God's word (cf. 1:19), stemming from God's desire that people be saved (3:15).

God's role did not finish with judgement, nor even with sparing the righteous from judgement. He would also deliver those who had repented from indifference or faithlessness, and were actively waiting (3:12, 13), into the new heavens and new earth (3:13).

2 Peter has as its foundation the person and work of God the Father, Jesus Christ the Son, and to a lesser degree in this letter, the Holy Spirit (1:1-2, 21). Why did Peter give such significant attention to his God? The reasons are manifold. God was the source of his message, had provided the way to life of which Peter was a herald, was strengthening those with faith to remain pure and to be fruitful, would bring believers into his eternal kingdom upon their death, and would punish the unrepentant.

Humanity in Relation to God

We have posited that 2 Peter 1 is best understood, and perhaps only understood, with close reference to the rest of the letter.[9] The contrasts provided within the entire letter of the two groups in relation to God are a good example of this. On the one hand, the picture provided by chapter 1 is of those who have faith in Christ (1:1, 5), which shapes their attitude to the promises of God (1:4).[10] They recognise the power of God's word (3:5-7) and see the delay of God's coming as an opportunity for repentance (3:9) and salvation (3:15). On the other hand, there is a group who have no such trust in God, nor his promises or word. They scoff at the promise of Christ's coming (3:4), and see his delay as a reason for disbelief (3:4).

The believers are those who remember Peter's words (1:12-15; 3:1-2) and who do not overlook God's activity in the world (3:8). Unbelievers are those who forget (1:9), and deliberately overlook God's actions in the past (3:5).

Believers have escaped the corruption of the world (1:4). By contrast, unbelievers are slaves of corruption (2:19). Their experience of life can be compared with vomit and mire (2:22). They will not escape such a regrettable end, but are 'entangled and overcome' (2:20), and will be 'caught and destroyed' (2:12, cf. 14).

Believers are the 'beloved' (3:1, 8, 14, 17) who will be given a grand entrance into the eternal kingdom (1:11); unbelievers are accursed children (2:12) to be 'destroyed in their destruction' (2:12).

Believers' are to be without spot or blemish (3:14); unbelievers *are* blots and blemishes (2:13).

Believers can expect fruitful and productive lives to flow out of commendable behaviour (1:8); far from productive, unbelievers seek to gain

---

[9] This has been a point missed by numerous commentaries, particularly those which see 2 Peter as the product of a somewhat clumsy redactor, who sought to bring together various sources into a pseudonymous work. The scholar who assumes that his or her role is to critique the work of a redactor, is more likely to find 'evidence' to support his or her expectations, viz. signs of their redaction which seems to include errors, incompetence, or disunity between sections of the letter. Such a premise has characterised Petrine scholarship for over a century. See, for example, the commentary of Charles Bigg, *A Critical and Exegetical Commentary on the Epistles of St. Peter and St. Jude* (Edinburgh: T&T. Clark, 1901). A more recent example is Jonathan Knight's study of 2 Peter, who claims that Peter was embarrassed by the non-fulfilment of Christ's return. Such comments diametrically oppose the author's own attitude, at least as we have it recorded. Knight, *2 Peter and Jude*, 72.

[10] The promises to which Peter referred may be the prophetic word (1:19); or the promise of his coming (3:4) and the new heavens and new earth (3:13); or perhaps even to all of the above since each of these elements are promised in the Scriptures (e.g. Isaiah 2, 11, 52-56, 65-66; Jer. 31; Mic. 5; Mal. 4). The book of 1 Peter is certainly aware of these aspects of the promise, claiming that within the message of the prophets were promises concerning 'Christ and the glories that would follow' (1 Pet. 1:11), or in short-hand, it was a message 'about this salvation' (περὶ ἧς σωτηρίας), 1 Pet. 1:10-12.

from wrongdoing (2:15), they are waterless springs, mists driven by a storm (2:17).

Further, Peter's methodology is intentionally contrasted with the methodology of the false teachers. Peter's approach appeals to one's reasoning or cognitive functions as a point of entry, referring regularly to knowledge, truth and faith. He contends that his message is reasonable in light of ancient and recent events in order that they might have certainty. Like Paul's message, Peter uses the medium of a letter which can be stored, memorised and considered by its recipients (1:12-15; 3:1-2). His goal is to consolidate the faith of his people, described as making them 'steady and sure' (1:10), so that they may be stable (3:17) and protected from falling (1:10). False teachers by contrast, acting out of greed (2:3), seek to win over their audience by that which is sensual (2:18), pleasurable (2:13) and sinful (2:14). Their hope is to 'entice unsteady souls' (2:14) and to 'entice by sensual passions of the flesh those who are barely escaping from those who live in error' (2:18). They are 'ignorant and unstable' people who have not only gone astray morally, but also doctrinally; they live in error (3:17) and distort the truth. They 'twist' Paul's writings and the other scriptures (3:16). False teachers revel in their deceptions (2:13; 3:17). Paul wrote according to the 'wisdom' that was given to him (3:15), and Peter's message likewise came from God (1:16). The false teachers by contrast are not wise and their message is not divine; they transmit 'cleverly devised myths' and their 'wisdom' is comparable to the madness of Balaam (2:15-16).

Can Mayor's assertion that 2 Peter lacks the warmth of 1 Peter be maintained, simply because of the significant attention 2 Peter gives to describing and condemning the false teachers?[11] To believe so is to inadequately appreciate the function that condemnation has in 2 Peter. There were wolves among the sheep, and Peter's aggressive response was shepherd-like. Indeed, the distressing warnings of Peter to his 'beloved' express his deep interest in their welfare.

We are now ready to understand the path of life that Peter, following Jesus, sets forth for his readers.

---

[11] For Mayor, the perceived difference in warmth, which he later calls 'personality' is the most compelling reason (more than vocabulary or Greek style) to reject the possibility that both 1 and 2 Peter were written by the one author. He argues, 'On the whole I should say that the difference of style is less marked than the difference in vocabulary, and that again less marked than the difference in matter, while above all stands the great difference in thought, feeling, and character, in one word of personality.' Joseph B Mayor, *The Epistle of Saint Jude and the Second Epistle of Saint Peter* (Grand Rapids: Baker, 1965), 105. Such warmth of personality, however, has been here observed in 2 Peter, albeit expressed differently for a different context.

CHAPTER 11

Peter's Guide to Life

It has been argued that Jesus Christ was a significant source for much of Peter's thought about God. As we shall now see, Christ's teachings also shaped Peter's views about what constitutes a life well lived.

What will be Peter's focus? According to Davids, his focus will follow that of Jesus: 'The question that 2 Peter, following Jesus, has answered is, "Who will enter, and what will enable that person to enter?'[1] It is this notion of entering, or commencing one's journey on the path of life, that we are now ready to consider in closer detail.

Entry into Life

Having outlined the historical, and now the literary context in which 2 Peter was written, we are ready to better understand the details of his Guide to Life and Death. The place to begin this investigation is 2 Peter 1:1-2.

> [1] Συμεὼν Πέτρος δοῦλος καὶ ἀπόστολος Ἰησοῦ Χριστοῦ τοῖς ἰσότιμον ἡμῖν λαχοῦσιν πίστιν ἐν δικαιοσύνῃ τοῦ θεοῦ ἡμῶν καὶ σωτῆρος Ἰησοῦ Χριστοῦ, [2] χάρις ὑμῖν καὶ εἰρήνη πληθυνθείη ἐν ἐπιγνώσει τοῦ θεοῦ καὶ Ἰησοῦ τοῦ κυρίου ἡμῶν.
>
> Simeon Peter, a servant and apostle of Jesus Christ, To those who have obtained a faith of equal standing with ours by the righteousness of our God and Saviour Jesus Christ: [2] May grace and peace be multiplied to you in the knowledge of God and of Jesus our Lord.[2]

At the beginning of 2 Peter 1, before any exhortations are given, the recipients learn that they have already arrived at a most satisfactory destination. They

> have obtained a faith (πίστις) of equal standing with ours by means of (or 'for' or 'in')[3] the righteousness of our God and Saviour Jesus Christ' (ἐν δικαιοσύνῃ τοῦ θεοῦ ἡμῶν καὶ σωτῆρος Ἰησοῦ Χριστοῦ), v.1.

Also giving them a common bond is their 'knowledge (ἐπίγνωσις) of God and of Jesus our Lord' (v. 2).[4] His audience are defined by their two fundamental

---

[1] Davids, *2 Peter and Jude*, 190.
[2] Translation from the ESV.
[3] Reese sees that the faith is 'by means of' God's righteousness, and while probably correct, the alternative renderings of the dative construction could be similarly supported by canonical texts. Reese, *2 Peter & Jude*, 131.

traits: a valuable faith, and a knowledge of God and of Jesus Christ. Both are from God. Verse 3 affirms that their knowledge of Christ did not come as a result of disciplined investigation, but through his 'divine power' (θεῖος δύναμις) and because Jesus himself 'called' (from καλέσαντος) them to his own glory and excellence.[5] Hence Jesus Christ was called the Saviour (σωτήρ), v. 1. This group had thus benefited from what came ἐν δικαιοσύνῃ τοῦ θεοῦ and stood to enjoy ongoing benefits with multiplied χάρις καὶ εἰρήνη ('grace and peace'), v. 2.

Γνῶσις and ἐπίγνωσις are significant terms in 2 Peter. Forms of these two nouns, each usually translated 'knowledge,' appear seven times. Ἐπίγνωσις makes up four of these occasions (out of 20 in the NT), and may have a slightly stronger force than γνῶσις.[6] The word, which has a directional quality to it, is aimed at 'perceiving, discerning, or recognising' its specific object.[7] Each time it is used in 2 Peter, its object is either God or Christ (1:2, 3, 8; 2:20).[8] The knowledge that Peter is referring to throughout the Epistle could therefore be taken to mean 'knowing Jesus (or God) and growing in that knowledge'.[9]

In his book, *The Problem of Knowledge*, Raoul Mortley suggests this dual emphasis on faith and knowledge were responsible for Christianity becoming known as 'the Way' (e.g. Acts 9:2; 19:9, 23; 24:14, 22), since it was essentially an 'epistemological movement, in which the 'way' (like the Hermetic 'way') is constituted by knowing, or believing, a body of doctrine, and in which this response of knowing or believing itself constitutes a major religious experience'.[10] There may be some validity to this view, but besides knowledge, one's behaviour was clearly important in 2 Peter and the NT. Furthermore, the basic Jewish metaphor of walking in the דֶּרֶךְ ('way' or 'path') of the Lord (e.g. Gen. 18:19; Deut. 5:33; Prov. 8:20, 15:9-10), as well as Jesus' claim, ἐγώ εἰμι ἡ ὁδός ('I am the Way,' Jn. 14:6), should inform this discussion.

---

[4] On its own among the translations, the NIV, perhaps to match the expression in verse 3, translates the phrase in verse 2, ἐν ἐπιγνώσει τοῦ θεοῦ, as 'through our knowledge of God' The ESV, NASB, ERB, NKJ, YLT all translate the ἐν simply as 'in'. By using the word 'through' the NIV is committing to the instrumental dative. The English word 'in' is probably the better choice since, like the Greek ἐν, it can refer to the locative without precluding the instrumental sense.

[5] It is difficult to see who the subject of these verbs is, though Reese argues convincingly that it refers to Christ as the antecedent of αὐτός. Davids holds a similar view, simply because Christ is the most proximate antecedent. Davids, *2 Peter and Jude*, 170. As we have noticed from the theology expressed in verses 1 and 2, Peter may be content to allow ambiguity to exist about whether he is referring to God the Father, or to 'our God and Saviour Jesus Christ'.

[6] For a more detailed discussion see Robert E. Picirelli, "The Meaning of 'Epignosis'," *EvQ* 47.2 (1975): 85-93.

[7] Reese, *2 Peter & Jude*, 132.

[8] Picirelli, "The Meaning of 'Epignosis'," 85-93.

[9] Reese, *2 Peter & Jude*, 133.

[10] R.J. Mortley, *The Problem of Knowledge in Late Antiquity* (The Center, 1978), 1.

Less helpful is Sidebottom's assertion that in Peter knowledge 'takes the place of Pauline "faith" and is something different'.[11] While the latter may be conceded, viz. that there is a difference between Paul's faith and Peter's knowledge, the idea that it 'takes the place' of faith seems spurious on the basis that 1 and 2 Peter maintain a Paul-like priority on the importance of faith (e.g. 1 Pet. 1:7-9; 5:9; 2 Pet. 1:1, 5).[12] A better explanation for Peter's emphasis on knowledge in 2 Peter is the imminent arrival of false teachers who would target believers' knowledge of Christ (e.g. 2 Pet. 2:1-2).

2 Peter 1:3 begins with Ὡς, which might be translated 'because', or 'seeing that'.[13] Peter uses verses 3-4 as a bridge to shift from God's activity to that of the believers. For with the news that all things that pertain to ζωὴν καὶ εὐσέβειαν ('life and piety') had been granted to them, came the responsibility to live accordingly (vv. 5-11). One could not apportion blame for failure to God, since he had given all that one needed, nor for this reason could believers give up as though the task was beyond them.

How are the believers given access to this new ability? Again, it is διὰ τῆς ἐπιγνώσεως τοῦ καλέσαντος ἡμᾶς. The process is somewhat difficult to pin down in verses 1-4, due to a number of potentially instrumental, or partially instrumental, datives. Some of the factors contributing to their blessed state include the work of God and of Christ, the righteousness of God and Christ, God's glory and goodness, their knowledge of God and of Jesus Christ, and divine power. As the text continues there are still more causal forces contributing to their transformation: it is through the promises of God, and their partaking in the divine nature (v. 4).

In what sense is Peter meaning that believers share in the divine nature? What can be affirmed are the moral implications (v. 4b) whereby they had 'escaped from the corruption that is in the world because of sinful desire' (ἐπιθυμίᾳ φθορᾶς), brought about by spiritual changes as explained in 1 Peter (e.g. 1 Pet. 1:2; 3:18; 4:14) and by Paul in such passages as Romans 5-8. Peter is presenting the case for two sets of circumstances in which people could live: under the influence of τῆς ἐν τῷ κόσμῳ ἐν ἐπιθυμίᾳ φθορᾶς ('the corruption that is in the world because of lusts'); or in a new situation in which, by implication, these forces otherwise common to humanity are non-possessive of them. The recipients of 2 Peter have escaped (from ἀποφεύγω) the former to enjoy the latter, and now experience Christ's empowering presence.

This does not mean that they are deified, but that Christ's life and moral excellence, through their spiritual union with him (as in Jn. 14:16-20; 15:1-10 or Rom. 8:5-11), now characterises them, even if their response to this change is still imperfect. The 'sharing in the divine nature' thus refers to their new and

---

[11] E.M. Sidebottom, *James, Jude and 2 Peter* (London: Nelson, 1967), 106.
[12] Further, as has been seen in the sketch of 1 Cor., Paul emphasised knowledge rather than faith when his topic demanded it.
[13] Friberg, *Lexicon*.

spiritual life in Christ, which has led to a transformed inner and ethical nature, as is made clear by the end of v. 4.[14]

Further, the supplements to faith also play a part in the process, making them fruitful and effective, confirming their calling and election, and assuring them that they 'will be furnished with (from ἐπιχορηγέω) a rich welcome into the eternal kingdom'. The verb ἐπιχορηγέω is used in vv. 5 and 11, a repetition which seems to suggest reciprocity, though God provides more liberally than the recipients deserve: they seek to supplement their faith, and God will richly bestow on them an eternal kingdom.[15] This is highlighted by the point already made that God changes their very nature and empowers virtuous living.

In these first verses Peter describes salvation in striking ethical terms; there is much more to God's work on believers' behalf than being forgiven of sins and justified before him.[16] In fact, such concepts used repeatedly by Paul are not in focus here. Salvation is announced in terms that forcefully communicate a spiritual and ethical transformation, involving participation in the divine nature, and an escape from the world's corruption (1:3-4).

In 2 Peter there is an interplay between God's role and the person's role for one's progress on the path of life. Starr aptly represents the thrust of 2 Peter 1, and expresses well the tension between divine and human roles:

> the initial knowledge of Christ in his capacity as sovereign and rescuer inaugurates the Christ believer on a journey intended to give him safe passage through the coming eschatological judgment into Christ's eternal kingdom. The Christ believer's well-being is dependent on his sharing in divine nature, seen at present in the taking on of moral virtues (Christ's righteousness and virtue) and seen ultimately in the rescue from corruption and the world's destruction (Christ's glory and eternity).[17]

The believer's part is certainly crucial, but the credit for one's progress belongs to God. His reward for believers is far beyond what is commensurate with their contribution.

---

[14] In his monograph on this topic, Starr appears to underestimate the connections between the phrase 'sharers in the divine nature' with such promises of the OT and Jesus that God would be present or abide with his people by his Spirit (e.g. Ezek. 36:24-27; John 14 and Mt. 28:20; 1 Pet. 1:2; 3:18; 4:14), and with the wider NT emphasis on a believer's union with Christ. He appears to interpret it to be a primarily ethical and relatively impersonal ethical change that can increase by degrees. He says, for example, 'either a person is without the knowledge of Christ and part of the world's pattern of desire-leading-to-decay, or else a person has the knowledge of Christ and has fled the world's pattern and is sharing to an ever greater degree in divine nature'. Peter Starr, "Sharers in Divine Nature: 2 Peter 1:4 in Its Hellenistic Context", 48.

[15] Starr, "Sharers in Divine Nature: 2 Peter 1:4 in Its Hellenistic Context", 49.

[16] Davids, *2 Peter and Jude*, 156.

[17] Starr, "Sharers in Divine Nature: 2 Peter 1:4 in Its Hellenistic Context", 49.

Continuing on the Path of Life

Peter depicts the believers' new life as a journey along a path. There is the potential to stumble and fall on one's way to God's kingdom, and the journey's end is depicted as God's rich welcome into his eternal kingdom.[18] How should one walk well on this path to arrive at the intended end? What did Peter's Guide to Life look like in terms of one's behaviour?

The Supplements of Faith

As has been discussed with reference to other parts of chapter 1, 2 Peter 1:5-7 in particular was intended to be read with close reference to chapters 2 and 3. Unfortunately, few commentators adequately express the interpretive assistance that these chapters provide.[19] Seeking to understand verses 5-7 for example, it is certainly beneficial to consider how the vocabulary is used by NT authors as well as other contemporary writers. Useful as such reference points are, any such study which fails to grasp the importance of 1:5-7 within Peter's immediate argument (as has often been the practice) unnecessarily rends the text out of its most enlightening literary context.

Peter's instruction might be compared with a vaccine, the implementation of which increases one's protection. The protective function of the list of seven supplements to faith in 1:5-7 is explicitly made in verses 10-15, and then again by his portrayal of those who live according to the antonyms of these traits, most concentrated in 2:10-15. Peter sought to protect his recipients from the end awaiting those who have renounced Christ. It is difficult to find scholarly works in recent decades which are cognizant of the relationship between these traits and the immoral alternatives spelled out in chapters 2 and 3. Chapters 2 and 3 provide the interpretive key for chapter 1, and particularly verses 5-7.

Verse 5 begins with an interesting construction, containing the particles Καὶ ... δὲ, and the adverbial phrase αὐτὸ τοῦτο. A construction not unique to Peter (see Xenophon, *An.* 1.9.21; Plato, *Prot.* 310e), it could be rendered, 'For this very reason, then', and marks a clear connection and progression of thought.[20]

---

[18] Davids, *2 Peter and Jude*, 189.

[19] The source critical (and perhaps pseudonymous) reading of 2 Peter seems to carry with it a predisposition to perceive contrastive material as problematic, or as 'evidence' of different sources. Many have suggested, for instance, that chapters 1 and 2 were composed by different authors. This assumption seems to be partly responsible for many to overlook what I have suggested are intentional connections and contrasts which bind the letter together. David Runia makes a similar observation in relation to Philonic studies, arguing that those who doubt Philo's authorship of *De aeternitate mundi* are prone to treat the pseudonymous author as incompetent, which results in misinterpretation: 'It should be noted that all the proponents of the work's inauthenticity had an extremely low regard for its author's abilities.' Runia, "Philo's "De Aeternitate Mundi": The Problem of Its Interpretation," 107.

[20] Kelly, *A Commentary on the Epistles of Peter and of Jude*, 305-306. Cf. Gingrich, *Lexicon* and *LSJ*.

It connects with some force the intangible events accompanying their salvation (vv. 3-4), with the ethical exhortations in verses 5-7. The sense is that, because they shared in the divine nature, they were to make every effort to supplement their faith with the following traits, which are arranged here to show the important repetition of the ἐν τῇ ... τὴν ... construction.

Καὶ αὐτὸ τοῦτο δὲ σπουδὴν πᾶσαν παρεισενέγκαντες ἐπιχορηγήσατε
ἐν τῇ πίστει ὑμῶν τὴν ἀρετήν,
ἐν δὲ τῇ ἀρετῇ τὴν γνῶσιν,
ἐν δὲ τῇ γνώσει τὴν ἐγκράτειαν,
ἐν δὲ τῇ ἐγκρατείᾳ τὴν ὑπομονήν,
ἐν δὲ τῇ ὑπομονῇ τὴν εὐσέβειαν,
ἐν δὲ τῇ εὐσεβείᾳ τὴν φιλαδελφίαν,
ἐν δὲ τῇ φιλαδελφίᾳ τὴν ἀγάπην.

For this very reason, make every effort to supplement
your faith with virtue,
and virtue with knowledge,
and knowledge with self-control,
and self-control with steadfastness,
and steadfastness with godliness,
and godliness with brotherly affection,
and brotherly affection with love.

The exhortation to ἐπιχορηγέω ('add to' or 'supplement') their πίστις with various other traits reiterates Peter's assertion that πίστις was already theirs (v. 1; cf. 1 Pet. 1:3-7). It is a foundation for all that follows—sharing in the divine nature, or joining the path of life, begins with one's πίστις. The other traits, however, are for those already on the road, as supplements to πίστις. That being so, the supplements are non-essential for entry, and could not be expected in new believers nor in those who had not begun on the path. Only faith in Christ was required to enter. The other traits were then prescribed and anticipated, but only from this forgiven (v. 9) and empowered (vv. 1-4) position.

This has important implications for the standard of behaviour required by Peter's Guide to Life. It can be said on the one hand that continual progression and moral perfection is required; progress is esteemed by Peter as it was in other first-century philosophies. And yet on the other hand, the minimum requirement for entry onto the path is simply faith in Christ. It is only from this point that an increase in the traits which are absent or at least deficient is expected. Distinguishing Peter from many other ethicists is the strong affirmation that believers had *already arrived* at a most favourable position in God's eyes before they began to progress in behaviour. To have joined the path of Christ was the enormous leap, and to make progress on the road was then a natural expectation in light of the empowering spiritual presence that God had given.

This does not deny the importance of human effort, which is strongly expressed through the participle παρεισενέγκαντες. The two prefixes *par-* and *eis-* function to strengthen the stem, i.e. 'bring to bear every effort'.[21] Believers were to pursue with zeal and earnestness (σπουδή) the life marked out by Peter. A similar expression of the cooperation between God and his people in this pursuit can be seen in Philippians 2:12-13, where Paul says to his recipients, 'work out your own salvation with fear and trembling, for it is God who works in you, both to will and to work for his good pleasure'.

With divine empowerment and assurance believers should be 'applying all diligence' to supplement their πίστις. Some unhelpfully speak of these traits as a list of 'virtues' in verses 5-7.[22] While the label of 'virtues' might be fitting in other contexts to describe such traits, it is unnecessarily confusing in a situation where one of these 'virtues' is ἀρετή ('virtue'). Much better is the noun 'supplement', which can be derived from the verb ἐπιχορηγέω, or even 'qualities' (ESV) or 'traits', which then provide a suitable translation for showing the connection with the ταῦτα ('these things') in verses 9, 10, and 12.

An additional problem in the discussion relating to these verses occurs when they are uncritically treated as a set of eight virtues. The relationship that exists between faith and these supplements is lost if faith is numbered with them without comment.[23] Least confusion arises by seeing the seven supplements as being added to the foundation of faith, which fits well with Peter's further reference to these supplements in verses 9, 10 and 11.

These three verses (1:5-7) have generated a wide variety of scholarly opinion, which are tied to theories regarding the dating and authorship of 2 Peter. From where has the author drawn this list and its arrangement? How are we to discern the relationship between these supplements?

Fornberg cites this passage to argue that the 'list of virtues in 2 Pet. 1:5-7 is dependent for its form and its content on Stoic originals'.[24] Bauckham likewise notes that verses 5-7 differ from NT ethical lists 'both in terminology, since it employs a vocabulary with extensive parallels in Greek popular philosophy, and in form, as the author uses a device called *sorites* (also known as a *climax* or *gradatio*) in which each virtue is repeated to yield a logical progression'.[25] A *sorites* is 'a set of statements which proceed, step by step, through the force of

---

[21] Harrington, *1 Peter, Jude and 2 Peter*, 244.
[22] See, for example Charles, Virtue Amidst Vice: The Catalog of Virtues in 2 Peter 1; Davids, *2 Peter and Jude*, 177-78; Reese, *2 Peter & Jude*, 136; Kelly, *A Commentary on the Epistles of Peter and of Jude*.
[23] Mayor is willing to speak of both 'the octave of virtues' (cxiii) when referring to each quality named in verses 5-7, but later speaks of 'the seven virtues' when speaking more technically of their relationship to faith. For him, faith 'is the gift of God already received; to this must be added [the seven virtues]'. Mayor, *The Epistle of Saint Jude and the Second Epistle of Saint Peter*, 93.
[24] Fornberg, *An Early Church in a Pluralistic Society*, 138.
[25] Bauckham, *Jude, 2 Peter*, 174-75.

logic or reliance upon a succession of indisputable facts, to a climactic conclusion, each statement picking up the last key word (or key phrase) of the preceding one'.[26] The *sorites* form was widely used and recognised among the early Christian period, as is evidenced by their extracanonical writings.[27] The Pastor of Hermas' *Visions* says,

> For from Faith arises Self-restraint; from Self-restraint, Simplicity; from Simplicity, Guilelessness; from Guilelessness, Chastity; from Chastity, Intelligence; and from Intelligence, Love.[28]

More recently, Davids observed that the language of 2 Peter 1:5-7 'belongs to the Hellenistic world rather than to the Hebrew/Aramaic world'.[29] His reason is that it bears significant differences from 'Jewish lists',[30] and raises further questions.

Firstly, were these verses compared with similar [Jewish] Christian writings, such as Romans 5:3-5.[31] Secondly, and most helpfully, is there a way we can discern why Peter chose these traits over others? A survey of the commentaries reveals that this issue has not been adequately grasped. For instance, in his influential commentary, Richard Bauckham says about these traits,

> Of the author's selection of virtues, other than πίστις and ἀγάπη we can only say that he has chosen virtues familiar from the Stoic and popular philosophical ethics of the Hellenistic world, some of them very general in meaning, to give a general impression of the kind of virtuous life the Christian faith should foster.[32]

Mystery surrounds Peter's choice of these particular traits, and it is a matter we will address as we look at each in turn.

It will be the proposed in this chapter that these particular traits were intended to do much more than 'give a general impression' of the Christian life, and that together they have quite a specific function. They appear, as indicated earlier, to be a thoughtfully concocted vaccine, given to protect his recipients from the imminent arrival of false teachers. The antithesis of these traits were being demonstrated by the false teachers and mockers in chapters 2 and 3. A few commentaries approach an appreciation of this point, and link some of the

---

[26] H.A. Fischel, "The Uses of Sorites (*Climax, Gradation*) in the Tannaitic Period," *HUCA* 44 (1973): 175. Cited in Bauckham, *Jude, 2 Peter*, 175.

[27] E.g. *1 Clem.* 1.2; 62.2; 64.1; *2 Clem.* 4.3; Herm. *Mand.* 6.1.1; 8.9; 12.3.1; *Sim.* 9.15.2; *Barn.* 2.2-3; *Act. Verc.* 2; *Acts John* 29. See Bauckham, *Jude, 2 Peter*, 174-75.

[28] Pastor of Hermas, *Vis.* 3.8.7.

[29] Davids, *2 Peter and Jude*, 179.

[30] Davids, *2 Peter and Jude*, 179.

[31] The *sorites* was a form used in Hellenistic lists, but the *sorites* in Rom. 5:3-5 warns against isolating 2 Pet. 1 from other New Testament texts on the basis of this form. Paul writes, καυχώμεθα ἐν ταῖς θλίψεσιν, εἰδότες ὅτι ἡ θλῖψις ὑπομονὴν κατεργάζεται, ἡ δὲ ὑπομονὴ δοκιμήν, ἡ δὲ δοκιμὴ ἐλπίδα. ἡ δὲ ἐλπὶς οὐ καταισχύνει ('we rejoice in our sufferings, knowing that suffering produces endurance, and endurance produces character, and character produces hope, and hope does not put us to shame).

[32] Bauckham, *Jude, 2 Peter*, 185.

virtues with some of the problems, but in a cursory way with some and not with all of the traits.[33]

Something Bauckham does highlight in the above quotation is an observation which benefits his commentary; he makes the helpful distinction between the more narrow philosophic use of Greek words and their 'very general' meaning. That ἀρετή may not have easily been separated from its narrower philosophical connotations, however, probably explains the near-absence of it in the NT.[34]

> Doubtless because of its Greek connotations – virtue as the achievement of human excellence, rather than as obedience to God – it is rarely used in the LXX or in the NT (only here and Phil 4:8 in the moral sense), and only slightly more common in the Apostolic Fathers (2 Clem. 10:1; Herm. *Mand.* 1:2; 6:2:3; 12:3:1; *Sim.* 6:1:4; 6:2:3; 8:10:3).[35]

It was with the more general sense that Paul used the term among a list of others in Philippians 4, perhaps because the general sense would be clear in that context.

Before delving into the nature of each of the seven 'supplements,' the way in which these terms stand in relationship requires discussion.[36] Is it the case that the believer pays no attention to ἀγάπη but only on ἀρετή, and then, having mastered this, moves through the list until he or she reaches ἀγάπη?

The purpose of Peter's construction was not to generate such a strict temporal sequence. Rather, it was intended to show that one cannot stop with virtue, nor with knowledge; but each supplement is necessary for a Christian to reach maturity. In Peter's schema, although God is active, the array of traits are not automatically infused into believers; significant effort is required.[37]

Each trait can now be considered in turn.

Πίστις had a far wider semantic domain than simply 'faith,' though is an adequate choice for translation choice in the context of 2 Peter. In the NT it could connote more broadly 'the [Christian] faith, doctrine', (Jd 3, 20); 'conviction'; 'good conscience' (Rom. 14:22-23); 'assurance, or proof' (Ac

---

[33] Most notable for making this connection and linking the positive trait with its negative counterpart in 2 Pet. 2 is Lucas and Green, *The Message of 2 Peter & Jude*. Gene Green, likewise, perceives this important connection between the traits and the vices, referring to the traits as an 'antidote'. See Green, *Jude and 2 Peter*, 191.

[34] Philo, as we observed in Chapters 6 and 7, had no such qualms about using ἀρετή freely for his ethical teaching, and this can be explained by his particular view of the harmony between the two traditions. He saw ἀρετή as a point of contact between the two traditions rather than a threat against the nature of Scriptural ethics.

[35] Bauckham, *Jude, 2 Peter*, 185.

[36] The translations diverge on this matter. The NIV translates the phrase, παρεισενέγκαντες ἐπιχορηγήσατε ἐν τῇ πίστει ὑμῶν τὴν ἀρετήν, ἐν δὲ τῇ ἀρετῇ τὴν γνῶσιν, 'add to your faith goodness; and to goodness, knowledge' and so on.

[37] Davids, *2 Peter and Jude*, 179.

17.31); and 'promise' (1 Tm 5.12).³⁸ In the case of 2 Peter, and in agreement with the usage in 1 Peter 1, the terms 'faith', 'trust', 'belief', or even 'conviction' fit the context.

More helpful for understanding the nature of faith, and its importance, is the portrayal of the faith-less characters in chapters 2 and 3. Faith defines the recipients, and might be considered in 2 Peter as an antonym of 'scoffing' (3:3). Those with faith will value the promises made by God. Peter's faith enables him to regard them as 'precious and very great promises' (1:4). The person of faith will also recognise the need to heed God's word (3:5-7). Unperturbed by the scoffing and mocking of the faithless (3:4), they will see the so-called 'delay' as a reason not to doubt (3:4), but as an indication of God's patience so that people will repent (3:9) and find salvation (3:15).

Ἀρετή, often rendered 'virtue' is translated in various ways across Bible versions, perhaps because of the inadequacy of any one English word to capture what was a loaded term. Liddell and Scott provide the broad definition of 'goodness, excellence, of any kind'.³⁹ A virtuous act could include those performed in a military conquest. In classical literature the virtues are often referred to in the plural to denote the four cardinal virtues, or to any number of others. Aristotle said, 'The components of virtue are justice, courage, self-control, magnificence, magnanimity, liberality, gentleness, practical and speculative wisdom'.⁴⁰

In the Apocryphal Wisdom of Solomon the four cardinal virtues (σωφροσύνη, φρόνησις, δικαιοσύνη, and ἀνδρεία) flow out of ἀρετή itself.⁴¹ Even if Peter never left Palestine, he would have been aware of the cardinal virtues. Accordingly, he could use the term to convey moral excellence in a general sense, but informed the readers' interpretation of it by connecting it closely with the nature of God and of Christ (2 Pet. 1:3, 17).⁴²

---

[38] The much earlier lexicon of Hesychius likewise demonstrates a broad semantic domain with his choice of the synonym ἀπόδειξις, which relates to a showing forth, an exposition or even publication. This corresponds to the orators' use of πίστις to refer to '*a means of persuasion, an argument, proof,* such as used by orators, Plat., etc', as observed by Liddell & Scott. Other definitions cited in Barclay Newman, *A Concise Greek-English Dictionary of the New Testament* (Stuttgart: United Bible Societies, 1971).

[39] *LSJ*. Other translations reflect this by rendering ἀρετή with 'goodness' (NIV) and 'moral excellence' (NASB).

[40] Aristotle, *Rhetoric* 1366B.

[41] Davids, *2 Peter and Jude*, 178.

[42] Of the five occurrences of ἀρετή in the NT, four are in the Petrine Epistles. Of these, three appear in 2 Pet. 1, two regard virtue as an ethical trait (v. 5), and the other (v. 3) to refer to the praiseworthiness or excellence of God (as it does also in 1 Pet. 2:9). This latter sense resembles those in the LXX, where ἀρετή and ἔπαινος, both rendered 'praise', are closely aligned, almost synonymous. Ἀρετή appears six other times in the LXX, five times in relation to God's 'honour' or 'praises' (Hab 3:3; Zech 6:13; Isa 42:12; 43:21; 63:7) and once relating to the praise of a thing (Esth 4:17). In the LXX

It is difficult to say why 2 Peter 1 is the only place where this more narrow use of ἀρετή occurs in both the LXX and NT. Scholars note the rarity of the word in the NT, but few suggest possible reasons for this.[43] The NT more frequently uses καλός and ἀγαθός to prescribe certain traits (James 3:13; Tit. 1:17; 2:7). In contexts when one might expect the use of ἀρετή, as in Titus 3:8, it is absent:

> The saying is trustworthy, and I want you to insist on these things, so that those who have believed in God may be careful to devote themselves to good works (ἵνα φροντίζωσιν καλῶν ἔργων προΐστασθαι). These things are excellent and profitable (ταῦτά ἐστιν καλὰ καὶ ὠφέλιμα) for people.

Likewise, in Philemon 14 Paul writes,

> but I preferred to do nothing without your consent in order that your goodness (τὸ ἀγαθόν σου) might not be by compulsion but of your own accord.[44]

Did Paul avoid the language of ἀρετή because of the possible associations it held with civic self-promotion?[45] Being born in Tarsus, which was a centre of philosophic learning, and comfortable among philosophers (Acts 17) we might have expected Paul to have used the term much more frequently. His sole use of ἀρετή (in Philippians 4:8), however, occurs in what might be considered a very 'safe' place—its narrower meaning being avoided by its placement among seven other terms with overlapping semantic domains. It can be posited that it is for this reason of distinction from secular philosophy that Paul and other NT writers preferred the more generic terms denoting 'good' such as καλός, ἀγαθός

ἔπαινος has a similar meaning (see 1 Chr 16:27; Ps 21:4, 26 in the LXX) to that of ἀρετή, where 'praise' is the normal English translation. One example of ἀρετή in the LXX is in Isa. 42:8, which translates וּתְהִלָּתִי , with ἀρετάς μου: ἐγὼ κύριος ὁ θεός τοῦτό μού ἐστιν τὸ ὄνομα τὴν δόξαν μου ἑτέρῳ οὐ δώσω οὐδὲ τὰς ἀρετάς μου τοῖς γλυπτοῖς. In the NT, however, the ἔπαινος and ἀρετή denote related yet distinct meanings. In the NT, ἔπαινος occurs only in the letters attributed to Paul (Rom. 2:29; 1 Cor. 4:5; 2 Cor. 8:18), in each case conveying the idea of praise or praiseworthiness, not to moral virtue. In Phil. 4:8, where ἀρετή and ἔπαινος appear together, both the 'praiseworthy' and 'moral goodness' sense of ἀρετή could be intended at once, since things that are virtuous in the moral sense could also be considered praiseworthy: 'Finally, brothers, whatever is true, whatever is honourable, whatever is just, whatever is pure, whatever is lovely, whatever is commendable, if there is any excellence (εἴ τις ἀρετή), if there is anything worthy of praise (καὶ εἴ τις ἔπαινος), think about these things' (ESV translation). Returning to 1 Pet. 2:9, the word ἔπαινος may have been equally fitting. Indeed, the NIV translates τὰς ἀρετὰς in this verse as 'the praises', again suggesting there is an overlapping semantic domain, where ἀρετή can be used in place of ἔπαινος to convey praise, praiseworthiness or excellence, but we do not see ἔπαινος used to convey the ideas that ἀρετή does in 2 Peter, which we might consider the behavioural or moral qualities of a person.

[43] E.g. Harrington, *1 Peter, Jude and 2 Peter*, 245.
[44] Phm. 1:14
[45] For a detailed discussion of this topic, see the dissertation by Brian. W. Powell, "Did Paul Believe in Virtue" (PhD Thesis, Macquarie University, 1995).

and forms of these words such as ἀγαθωσύνη (the fruit of the spirit, 'goodness', in Gal. 5:22).[46]

Cranfield likewise suggests Greek virtue 'was too dominantly anthropocentric to be easily assimilated to biblical thinking'.[47] Virtue could refer to a person of 'consummate excellence or merit within a social context',[48] and it may have been this outward dimension which was avoided in preference for words that incorporate one's internal character and lack of concern for public recognition.[49] Jesus cautioned his disciples, 'Beware of practicing your righteousness before other people in order to be seen by them, for then you will have no reward from your Father who is in heaven' (Matt. 6:1). It was an instruction that undermined the basis of the benefactor-client social structure, which saw favours repaid with recognition, and thus was a primary motivation for doing good.

If the word ἀρετή was avoided for such reasons, was Peter less concerned than Paul (and perhaps the other NT writers) about avoiding it? For Peter chose it over the alternatives, not only relating to human excellence or virtue (2 Peter 1:5), but also in relation to God's attributes, where ἔπαινος might have been expected (1 Pet. 2: 9 and 2 Pet. 1:3). It is probably safe to assume that as a letter writer hoping to communicate effectively, Peter chose the language that he deemed apposite for his distinct purpose and recipients. Additionally, Peter's prior use of virtue to refer to God's character in verse 3 may have limited the potential in verse 5 of a corrupted, and as Cranfield says, 'anthropocentric' meaning as it related to public recognition. The virtue in verse 5 has been informed by a knowledge of Christ (v. 2) and accords with the virtuous nature of God (vv. 3-4).

More helpful still, the false teachers' lack of virtue in chapter 2 reveals the significance for its inclusion in 1:5. There are numerous terms used of the false teachers which Peter may have intended as antonyms of ἀρετή.[50] They are entangled in the μίασμα ('defilement', 'shameful deed' 2:20) of the world, and do acts of ἀδικία ('unrighteousness', 'wrongdoing' in 2:13, 15) and παρανομία ('transgression', 'crime' in 2:16). A conscious pursuit of ἀρετή is part of the

---

[46] Cf. Hebrews 10:24
[47] C.E B. Cranfield, *1 and 2 Peter and Jude* (London: SCM, 1960), 178.
[48] See BAGD.
[49] The outward dimension of ἀρετή can be seen in the definition offered in LSJ: 'reward' of excellence, 'distinction,' or 'fame;' 'displayed great deeds' (cf. Hes. Op. 313; Sapph. 80; Pi. N. 5.53; S. Ph. 1420; Pl. Smp. 208d.)
[50] *LSJ* offers good reason for seeing κακία as the antonym of ἀρετή when used to refer in general to 'moral virtue' or 'excellence' (X. *Mem.* 2.1.21; cf. Pl. *R.*500d; *Lg.* 963a; D.60.17; Arist. *EN* 1102; *Pol.* 1295). 2 Pet. does not use κακία, but does describe the final state of the wrongdoers as being χείρονα τῶν πρώτων (meaning 'more κακός' than the first state), in 2:20. This could mean simply 'worse' (ESV) or 'worse off' (NIV), but it could also be a moral judgement of being in a 'more evil' or 'more wicked' state than they were earlier, perhaps because of their increased culpability.

defence against the temptations of desire which began, and later characterised, the life of those who departed from the right way.

Following ἀρετή is γνῶσις ('knowledge'). Like πίστις, γνῶσις requires an object. Was Peter referring primarily to knowledge of God (as in 2 Pet. 3:18; Phil. 3:8)? In 1 Corinthians 8:6-7, Paul speaks of the knowledge that there is only one God; something he said is known 'to us' (ἡμῖν), 'but which is not known to all' (Ἀλλ' οὐκ ἐν πᾶσιν ἡ γνῶσις), v.7. There is probably no compelling reason to restrict γνῶσις to knowledge of the divine here, however, since elsewhere Peter uses γνῶσις more broadly when exhorting husbands to treat their wives κατὰ γνῶσιν, by which he means to have consideration for them. The knowledge to which Paul refers does not always refer directly to God, but true knowledge would flow from a right understanding of God and his world (2 Cor. 10:5; 11:6; 1 Tim. 6:20).

Again, chapters 2–3 are insightful for interpreting chapter 1; the cost of ignorance on display there explains what Peter meant by knowledge, and why he included it. Firstly, knowledge would help believers to recognise and reject 'sophistic myths' and 'destructive heresies' that would be circulated (1:16; 2:1). The teachers' alternative message will be attractive, and 'the way of truth will be blasphemed' by the pseudo-γνῶσις, or 'false words' (πλαστοῖς λόγοις), 2:3. Knowledge countered ignorance and with it, vulnerability and instability on the path of life, as is explicit in 3:17-18:

> You therefore, beloved, knowing [about the ignorant and unstable, v. 16] beforehand, take care that you are not carried away with the error of lawless people and lose your own stability. [18] But grow in the grace and γνῶσις of our Lord and Saviour Jesus Christ.

In addition to knowledge, the addressees were to have ἐγκράτεια: 'self-control', 'mastery over oneself', or 'temperance'. Nominal, adjectival and verbal forms of the ἐγκράτ- stem appear only eight times in the NT,[51] but it was a key term in Greek ethics since Plato and Aristotle, and denoted 'self-control in all matters affecting the senses'.[52]

As people who have escaped from the corruption in the world because of sinful desire, this trait was deemed attainable. Again, the importance of ἐγκράτεια in Peter's schema becomes clear only in consultation with chapters 2–3, where Peter describes the fate of those who lack it. Traits of the unbelievers include sensuality (2:2) and sensual conduct (v. 7). They are irrational creatures of instinct (v. 10) who 'pleasure to revel in the daytime' (v. 13) and who have 'eyes full of adultery' (v. 14). They are insatiable for sin (v. 14) and have 'hearts trained in greed' (v.14). Without a trace of self-control,

---

[51] Though its occurrences are few in the NT, it is a highly esteemed trait, being part of Paul's presentation before Felix in Acts 24:25; as well as a fruit of the Spirit in Gal. 5:23.

[52] For further comment of its Hellenistic usage, see comments in J.N.D. Kelly, *Peter and Jude*, 23; Davids, *2 Peter and Jude*, 180.

they simply follow their own sinful desires (3:3). Resisting impious allurements is the ability, expressed negatively, of those who are now empowered to live lives in 'holy conduct and godliness' (ἁγίαις ἀναστροφαῖς καὶ εὐσεβείαις), 2 Pet. 3:11.[53]

The next trait, ὑπομονή ('perseverance' or 'steadfastness') was a highly esteemed trait for philosophers, and for Stoics in particular. In Stoic and Christian literature, perseverance was important for bearing trials and discouragement, but in 2 Peter it is given special pointedness by the impatience of some sceptics, and the need to wait patiently for the *parousia* of Christ (2 Pet. 3:3-14).[54] For this very reason, a most pressing realm in which one must persevere is in knowledge. The believers were urged to 'remember' and 'continue' to know and believe what they already knew (e.g. 1:12-15; 3:1-2). But perseverance extends beyond the cognitive matters. Perseverance would show itself not only by the duration of one's waiting, but also by the manner in which one waited. As they wait for the coming day of God (3:12) and for the new heavens and new earth (3:13), they would be prepared to face those who scoff (3:3). Perhaps significantly, ὑπομονή precedes εὐσέβεια (godliness or piety) in both of Peter's lists; in 1:5-7 as well as 3:8-13. Their waiting was to be done ἐν ἁγίαις ἀναστροφαῖς καὶ εὐσεβείαις ('in lives of holiness and godliness'), v. 11.

Perhaps the most striking reason to persevere is given in chapter 2, where we learn that those who would endanger the church once belonged to it. The false teachers once had 'the knowledge of our Lord and Saviour Jesus Christ' (v. 20). At one time they knew the way of righteousness (v. 21a), but had since turned back from it (v. 21b). They had become sceptics, and as a result of this 'progression' from what they formerly believed, they were probably well equipped to raise troubling questions for those who believed. The importance of perseverance therefore should not be understated. Would the recipients remain distinct from those who are now unbelievers? Or would the recipients lack perseverance and join their ranks? Peter is confident of the former in their case, and his letter was written to make their resistance more likely (1:12-15; 3:1-3, 17).

εὐσέβεια, rendered 'godliness' or 'piety' was also a common Hellenistic virtue. It pointed to the appropriate attitude towards one's authorities: the gods, dead ancestors, and family or parents.[55] Philo and Josephus regularly mention εὐσέβεια as one of their many virtues.[56] As is the case in other Jewish writings,

---

[53] Paul observes that like athletes, Christ's people should demonstrate ἐγκράτεια (1 Cor. 9:25).When Paul is speaking to Felix and his Jewish wife Drusilla about faith in Jesus Christ (περὶ τῆς εἰς Χριστὸν Ἰησοῦν πίστεως), he speaks of three subsidiary matters: δικαιοσύνη, ἐγκράτεια and κρίμα (Acts 24:25). ἐγκράτεια was a fruit of the Spirit in Gal. 5:23.

[54] Kelly, *A Commentary on the Epistles of Peter and of Jude*, 307.

[55] Davids, *2 Peter and Jude*, 181.

[56] They refer to it 162 times and 102 times, respectively.

εὐσέβεια had a God-ward dimension (e.g. Philo, *Spec. leg.* 2.63; *Det.* 155; *Plant.* 135; Josephus, *Antiquities* 9.2; *Autobiography* 1.14).[57] Davids may be right to suggest that, on the basis that it appears in only one other NT ethical list (in 1 Tim. 6:11), it shows the author had a tendency to select vocabulary which appealed to a Hellenistic audience.[58]

Its prevalence in Acts (when speaking only to Jews in 3:12) and the Pauline epistles, however, prohibits us from subscribing fully to Davids' point, since it was clearly an important trait for NT writers and for Jews more generally. Despite only two appearances in NT ethical lists, forms of the word appear twenty-two times in the NT, and thirty-six times if we include the negative form ἀσέβεια (ungodliness, impiety). Nevertheless, we are left with the fact that the eight occurrences of the positive and negative form in the short letter of 2 Peter is disproportionately high. We concur that this is partially explained by his appeal to a Gentile readership. But more centrally it is to be explained by the subject matter and particular context into which it was written. Peter's inclusion of it in his list in 1:5-7 is followed by extensive description of the ἀσεβῶν 'ungodly ones' who will be among them (2 Pet. 2:5, 6; 3:7 cf. 1 Pet. 4:18).

Φιλαδελφία referred in the Hellenistic world to the love for one's brother or sister—to be brotherly or sisterly.[59] In the NT, the noun appears three times in the Petrine epistles (1 Peter 1:22; twice in 2 Peter 1:7), and six times in total (in three verses: Rom. 12:10; 1 Thess. 4:9; Heb. 13:1), to refer to the love or affection for ones fellow believer in Christ.[60] Its appearance would not surprise one who is accustomed to Greek ethics. What may be surprising, however, is the way Peter (and Paul, following Jesus) extends familial love to benefit a much larger 'family' of believers (e.g. Matt. 12:48-50). Soon after this trait is prescribed (in 2 Pet. 1:10), Peter addresses the recipients with the phrase, διὸ μᾶλλον, ἀδελφοί ('Therefore, brothers'), providing an immediate illustration of this familial bond. Later, Christian apologists recorded the scorn pagans held towards Christians for treating each other as family (Lucian, *Peregrinus* 13; Minucius Felix, *Oct.* 31.8; Tertullian, *Apology* 39).[61]

---

[57] Davids, *2 Peter and Jude*, 181.
[58] Davids, *2 Peter and Jude*, 168.
[59] LSJ.
[60] Louw-Nida, *Lexicon*
[61] Davids argues that Christian φιλαδελφία is 'that same familial love [as that of the non-Christian Graeco-Roman context] extended to the whole Christian community'. Davids, 183. While we agree that (in light of 4 Macc. 13:19-27; Philo, *Joseph* 218; Josephus, *Ant.* 2.161; *War.* 1.275, as well as the later apologists' texts that he cites), Peter *was* extending the concept beyond one's family, it does not follow that it was the same in nature and quality, and not 'Christianised' to some extent. A text from Tertullian, which Davids himself cites, argues that it was not merely the extent, but the nature of φιλαδελφία that was being re-defined by the Christian community. In Tertullian's *Apology* 39 he writes, 'we are regarded as having less claim to be held true brothers, that no tragedy makes a noise about our brotherhood, or that *the family*

Peter's inclusion of φιλαδελφία need not be a mystery, nor should it be seen as evidence that Peter was to a peculiar extent reaching into the Graeco-Roman world to borrow ethical terminology. Like the other traits, φιλαδελφία had a function of protecting the faith and fruitfulness of the recipients in their particular context. First, φιλαδελφία would keep them from resembling the false teachers, since it could not coexist with their antithetical behaviour. These teachers, rather than having familial concern, had a destructive effect upon those around them (2:1). They had 'hearts trained in greed' and it was out of this greed that they would exploit (2:2) and deceive even those with whom they shared a table (2:13). Second, and more speculatively, a community in which each believer practised φιλαδελφία might be more resilient to heresy and temptation, since the way each person progressed on the path of life would become the concern of all.

Unlike the preceding traits, ἀγάπη is a more distinctly Christian ethical trait, being prevalent in the NT but extremely rare in Greek virtue lists.[62] Jesus gave special attention to love when he said, 'This is my commandment, that you love one another as I have loved you' (John. 15:12). Paul and Peter emphasised love in a way that reiterated the emphases of the Law and of Jesus: that the two greatest commandments are the love of God and of one's neighbour. By doing this one fulfils the requirements of the Law (Lev. 19:18, 34; Dt. 6:5; 11:1; Matt. 22:37-39; Mark 12:30-31; Luke 10:27; Rom. 13:9-10). It was in this trait of love that Peter failed (John 18:17-27), and then was uncomfortably questioned about, three times (John 21:15-17).[63]

It is interesting that in both of the Petrine epistles, φιλαδελφία and the ἀγάπ-stem are juxtaposed, since their semantic domains overlap to a considerable degree. Like φιλαδελφία, ἀγάπη can also denote brotherly-love (e.g. 1 Cor. 13). In both of Peter's letters the exhortation to have ἀγάπη follows φιλαδελφία.[64] 1

---

possessions, which generally destroy brotherhood among you, create fraternal bonds among us. One in mind and soul, we do not hesitate to share our earthly goods with one another. All things are common among us but our wives' (italics mine). According to this view, family property was the cause of breakdown among those who would otherwise enjoy φιλαδελφία. By contrast, Christians unrelated by birth were brought closer together by property; their unique attitude to possessions fostered φιλαδελφία (exemplified in Acts 2:45-46).

[62] Outside the NT, ἀγάπη was used to denote the love between a husband and wife, and between God and man. *LSJ;* cf. Bauer, *op. cit.*, 5; Dupont, *op. cit.*, 397; cited in Fornberg, *An Early Church in a Pluralistic Society*, 100. See, also, Davids, *2 Peter and Jude*, 184; cf. E. Stauffer, "Agapaō ktl" in TDNT.

[63] Ἀγάπη was used to some degree also in the inter-testamental Jewish literature, such as in *Ep. Arist.* 229, which speaks of ἀγάπη as the gift of God. See also *Pss. Sol.* 18:3; *T. Gad* 4:7; 5:2 and *T. Benj.* 8:2. Fornberg, *An Early Church in a Pluralistic Society*, 100.

[64] A similar emphatic sense for loving one another may be seen in Paul's command and immediately reiterated command to 'rejoice' (χαίρετε) in Phil. 4:1, 'Rejoice in the Lord always. I will say it again: Rejoice!' (Χαίρετε ἐν κυρίῳ πάντοτε· πάλιν ἐρῶ χαίρετε). Unlike Peter, however, Paul defies convention to avoid repetition by simply

Peter 1:22 says, 'Having purified your souls by your obedience to the truth for a sincere brotherly love (φιλαδελφία), love one another (ἀλλήλους ἀγαπήσατε) earnestly from a pure heart'.[65] There is not a problem of redundancy here; Peter adds ἀγάπη to φιλαδελφία so that they would love more earnestly, but also more widely, since ἀγάπη was more obviously to extend beyond familial boundaries.

The ultimate position of love also gives it emphasis. Paul places it first (Gal. 5:22), or last (1 Cor. 13:3; 16:14) on numerous occasions for this reason. Its importance is seen by his insistence that if one has faith, knowledge, generosity and self-sacrifice without love, the former are considered worthless (1 Cor. 13:1-3; cf. 1 Cor. 8:1). Colossians 3:12-14 is quite explicit about love's superior position, perhaps earning it the right to be called the chief Christian trait:

> Put on then, as God's chosen ones, holy and beloved, compassionate hearts, kindness, humility, meekness, and patience, bearing with one another and, if one has a complaint against another, forgiving each other; as the Lord has forgiven you, so you also must forgive. And above all these put on love, which binds everything together in perfect harmony.

In 2 Peter, love intimately joins God and his people.[66] God referred to Jesus Christ as 'my beloved Son' (ὁ υἱός μου ὁ ἀγαπητός μου), 1:17. This love is echoed by Peter (in a similar way to that of Paul and John's epistles) for his recipients when he addresses them directly in chapter 3. He refers to them in the vocative as his 'beloved' (ἀγαπητοί) in 3:1, 8, 14, 17; and in verse 15 refers to 'our beloved brother Paul' (ἀγαπητὸς ἡμῶν ἀδελφὸς Παῦλος). Peter expresses his love for them, and his desire that they love one another.

Love, which has a central place in NT ethics, was used by Peter to complete the portrayal of the life which shares in the divine nature. Since ὁ θεὸς ἀγάπη ἐστίν ('God is love'), ἀγάπη should surely characterise his people (2 Pet. 1:7; cf. 1 John 4:8, 16).

Summary

In summary, the seven supplements to faith in 2 Pet. 1:5-7 are each vitally important for Peter's audience in their dangerous context. Together, the traits would prevent them from falling (1:10) from the path of life. In verses 1-4, Peter provided the believers with a reason for confidence that their

---

repeating the same verb. Indeed, in Philippians he uses the stem χαίρ- eleven times, and there are three other verses which contain the verb twice (in Phil. 1:18; 2:17; 2:18). Peter appears to be seeking a similar emphasis in 1 and 2 Peter, but by the more conventional use of synonyms.

[65] For this reason, Harrington's assertion is untenable, that ἀγάπη refers to 'love for God' in this verse simply to avoid redundancy on the basis that φιλαδελφία precedes ἀγάπη. Harrington, *1 Peter, Jude and 2 Peter*, 245.

[66] The love which characterises the relationship between God and his people is also clear throughout 1 Pet. E.g. 1:8; 2:17; 3:8; 4:8, 12; 5:6, 10.

transformation had begun and was divinely empowered; and verses 5-7 gave them the direction needed to actively cooperate with God in their ongoing transformation.

The *sorites* containing seven supplements was not intended to provide a strict logical progression,[67] since it takes excessive manoeuvring to demonstrate such.[68] That said, the overarching framework of the eight traits parallel the Christian triad of πίστις ('faith'), ελπίς ('hope') and ἀγαπή ('love'), as in 1 Corinthians 13, if we allow ὑπομονή to represent hope (as it does in 1 Thess. 1:3; 5:8).

Why did Peter choose these traits out of all of those available to him? Firstly, it should be recognised that each supplement was used elsewhere by NT authors, suggesting that Peter was using 'Christian' terminology which also operated in a Gentile environment, rather than simply borrowing 'virtues' from the philosophical world.[69]

Secondly, each trait was chosen because of its protective function in the context of false teachers, so that the believers would never fall (1:10) from the path of life. Thus, chapters 2 and 3 provide an important hermeneutical key for chapter 1 (and vice versa). The scoffers (in 2 Pet. 3) and the allurements of the world offered by false teachers (in ch. 2) could be resisted and rejected by a person who protects her 'precious' faith (1:1) in Christ by supplementing it with these seven traits. Faith is the starting point, but without the supplements which transform the believers' thinking and behaviour, as individuals and as a community, they remain vulnerable to being 'carried away by the error of lawless men and falling from [their] secure position' (2 Pet. 3:17; cf. 2:1, 18). Each trait adds something significant, and while the last two traits are similar conceptually, the addition of ἀγάπη to φιλαδελφία adds breadth, depth and emphasis to Peter's command to love.

Having discussed the nature of the exhortations, it is important to consider the positive and negative repercussions for those who obey and disobey. To what end would their efforts lead them? Would the rewards be commensurate with the believers' effort?

The Consequences of How One Lives: Two Ways to Live and Die

In 2 Peter 1, Peter is urging believers to employ their wills and energy, to make 'all the more effort' to cooperate with the divine presence, direction and empowerment through their ἐπίγνωσις of Jesus Christ (v. 8). They are to pursue the traits that are, and will continue to, keep them from being ineffective and unfruitful. That this protection was a present reality for them is lost somewhat

---

[67] Davids, *2 Peter and Jude*, 178.
[68] Green's attempt provides one such example. See Michael Green, *2 Peter and Jude* (Nottingham: IVP, 1985; 2009), 86-91.
[69] Fornberg 1977; Davids 2006. See Fornberg, *An Early Church in a Pluralistic Society*, 100.

by most Bible translations by the insertion of 'if' and a future tense into verse 8, though a future aspect is certainly intended by the imperatives and the future tense in verse 10. 2 Peter 1:8 would be better translated as follows:

> For these qualities, which are yours and are increasing, are keeping you from being ineffective and unfruitful in the knowledge of our Lord Jesus Christ.

Alliteration is effected by the clustering of alpha privatives in 2 Peter. In verse 8, believers will be neither ἀργὸς οὐδὲ ἄκαρπος ('unproductive nor unfruitful'). Conversely, for the wicked in chapter 2 it is their destruction that is οὐκ ἀργεῖ (lit. not not-working, or 'not idle'), and rather than enjoying fruitfulness, they are πηγαὶ ἄνυδροι ('springs without water').

It has been argued, albeit briefly, that Peter's emphasis on the supplement of love was drawn from his time with Jesus. So too the agricultural analogy of growth and fruitfulness was prominent in the OT (Isa. 5; Ezek. 19; Jer. 17:5-8; Ps. 1), Jesus' teachings (e.g. Mt. 3:8-10; 7:16-20; 12:33; 21:19-43; Mk. 11:13-18; Lk. 3:8-9; 6:43-44; 13:6-9; Jn. 15:2-8, 16; cf. 1 Pet. 2:9-12; 2 Pet. 1:4) as well as other NT writings (Rom. 7:4-5; Gal. 5:22; Eph. 5:9; Phil. 1:11; Col. 1:6, 10; Jam. 3:17).

Peter argues that indifference to the seven traits is incongruous with gratitude to God for his forgiveness (1:9). Though some believers may have considered this indifference an unlikely possibility, he points out in chapter 2 that such people exist. They had been 'bought' and yet now deny the master who bought them' (v. 15). They previously escaped the corruption of the world, but then returned to it (v. 20). This hypothetical apathy among believers who were well established (1:10), combined with the portrayal of false teachers, provides a precautionary barb in the exhortation. There were living examples of those who once belonged, but did not take their progress seriously, and lived according to the vices.

With the false teachers occupying a large portion of 2 Peter, the importance of the way believers lived, rather than simply what they believed, is made clear (perhaps matching the clarity of the strong point made in Jam. 2:14-24).

The New Testament Epistles share this emphasis on behavioural change (e.g. Jam. 2:26; 1 Jn. 1:5-6), and link this with resembling God (e.g. 1 John 1:5-7). In Romans 8:28-30, Paul uses the language of 'image' or 'likeness' (εἰκών) rather than 'nature' to describe one's progress towards resembling Christ. 1 Peter teaches that God's character is to be demonstrated by his people when he says, 'You shall be holy, for I am holy' (1:16; cf. Lev. 11:44). The ever increasing resemblance is one of the goals of Peter's path of life, made possible by the presence of God by his Spirit in his people.

A second goal is seen in verse 11, namely, a rich entrance into a second life. The promise begins with the adverbial construction linking the outcome with the prescribed path: οὕτως γὰρ ('For in this way') 'there will be richly provided for you an entrance into the eternal kingdom of our Lord and Saviour Jesus Christ'.

It might be said, therefore, that the richly provided entry is in some way conditional upon them continuing to supplement their faith. Again, the performance expected by Peter must be informed by his positive statement about their current status. He was not rebuking them for poor performance, but, on the contrary, reminding them to continue growing in these important qualities, as is seen in verses 12-13;

> Therefore I intend always to remind you of these qualities, though you know them and are established in the truth that you have. I think it right, as long as I am in this body, to stir you up by way of reminder.

This is the second time Peter has written to 'stir up their sincere minds by way of reminder' (3:1). It is to prepare them to withstand the enticements of those who will seek to deceive them (2:1).

Conclusions

Rather than demanding moral perfection as the way to fellowship with God, Peter is satisfied that they already experience such fellowship. The sentiments of 2 Peter 1 resemble the exhortation in Hebrews 10:34-39. There the author begins with warm affirmation, an exhortation to persevere, followed by an optimistic certainty about their current standing. The author's certainty is based upon their παρρησία ('confidence', v. 35), and πίστις ('faith', vv. 38, 39). Interestingly, both texts were written to address a context where the alleged delay of Christ's return and opposition had the potential to unsettle believers' confidence and faith:

> For you had compassion on those in prison, and you joyfully accepted the plundering of your property, since you knew that you yourselves had a better possession and an abiding one. Therefore, do not throw away your confidence, which has a great reward. For you have need of endurance (ὑπομονή), so that when you have done the will of God you may receive what is promised. For, 'Yet a little while, and the coming one will come and will not delay; but my righteous one shall live by faith, and if he shrinks back, my soul has no pleasure in him.' But we are not of those who shrink back and are destroyed, but of those who have faith and preserve their souls.[70]

The themes of confidence, endurance, receiving what is promised, and living by faith are the themes of 1 and 2 Peter, the first letter in a context of persecution and the second in a context of scoffing. The thrust of 2 Peter is that the recipients, who have a valuable faith in Christ and await a rich welcome into an eternal kingdom, are to seek to live consistently with their convictions, because in so doing they would enjoy ongoing certainty regarding their future,

---

[70] Heb. 10:34-39.

and fruitfulness in God's service. In the next chapter, further attention will be given to Peter's teaching about death and the events which follow it.

CHAPTER 12

Peter's Guide to Death

Peter's Own Death: The Putting off of the Body

Despite its succinct nature, Peter's self-disclosure regarding his own death in chapter 1 is very significant.[1] 2 Peter 1:13-14 express Peter's attitude to his own death. First, his body was only a temporary dwelling:

> I think it right, as long as I am in this σκήνωμα (literally 'tabernacle,' 'tent,' or 'dwelling place'), to stir you up by way of reminder; knowing that the putting off of my dwelling will be soon (εἰδὼς ὅτι ταχινή ἐστιν ἡ ἀπόθεσις τοῦ σκηνώματός μου), as our Lord Jesus Christ made clear to me.

The phrase, 'as long as I am in this dwelling' implies that the 'I' of his statement continues to exist after Peter leaves the temporary dwelling, his body, behind.

Second, in verse 14, Peter speaks without apparent fear regarding what he considered was his imminent death. He anticipated his death on the basis of what Jesus 'made clear' or 'indicated' (δηλόω). Jesus' description in John 21:18-19 may have ensured that Peter would recognise the times: perhaps he experienced the combination of old age and compulsion, as was very possible during Nero's persecution of Roman Christians.[2]

> 'Truly, truly, I say to you, when you were young, you used to dress yourself and walk wherever you wanted, but when you are old, you will stretch out your hands, and another will dress you and carry you where you do not want to go.' (This he said to show by what kind of death he was to glorify God.)

If these were indeed the words of Jesus to which Peter referred, Peter had overcome any fears regarding the execution that awaited him. Though this execution-style end for Peter was certainly an undesirable way to die, he projects no fear or self-concern whatsoever, but rather a concern that his

---

[1] Some who read 2 Pet. as a pseudonymous work have also highlighted the force of the author's portrayal of Peter as an elderly man. Starr following Bauckham, suggests three reasons for this: 'to give a final reminder of Christ's promises; to affirm again the traditional eschatology; and to point to the apostolic teaching as sure access to understanding the gospel and the scriptures'. See Starr, "Sharers in Divine Nature: 2 Peter 1:4 in Its Hellenistic Context", 52; Richard J. Bauckham, "Pseudo-Apostolic Letters," *JBL* 107 (1988): 477.

[2] Lucas and Green, *The Message of 2 Peter & Jude*, 68-69.

'beloved' recipients remember to live well after his ἔξοδος ('departure'), 2 Pet. 1:15.

With some awareness of Peter's attitude to his own death, it will be helpful to understand the broad schema into which Peter viewed his own 'end' and relatedly, his 'goal' or 'purpose' (τέλος). It will become apparent as we do so that this short letter is by no means an exhaustive presentation of Peter's belief about the cosmic and personal end. His views can also be gleaned from his first letter, and 'all of the letters' of Paul, which speak of the end in ways that were endorsed by Peter (2 Pet. 3:16). 2 Peter should thus be treated as a supplement to the perspective offered by these Christian sources.

The τέλος according to Peter

The τέλος for those without faith

2 Peter continues the sentiment of 1 Peter that the πάντων δὲ τὸ τέλος ἤγγικεν ('The end of all things is at hand'), 1 Pet. 4:7. Scoffers will question the eschatological judgement of God upon the world because of a perceived delay in bringing it about (2 Pet. 3:3-10). The reaction of various groups to Christian eschatology was mixed. Some rejected and showed disdain for the Christian belief in resurrection for the dead.[3] While other groups conceived of a resurrection or post-death life of the soul, there was no equivalent to Christ's Parousia.[4] Peter assures his audience that regardless of others' disbelief, God will come, and with his coming (3:4, 12) will be cataclysmic world events (3:5-13).

Peter presents all people as belonging to one of two groups, whose respective ends could not be further apart. They can be distinguished in various ways: the repentant and unrepentant (3:17); those scoffing at his coming (3:3) and those waiting for his coming (3:13); those with faith, with knowledge of God and of Christ (1:1-2) and established in the truth (v. 12), and those without such faith, knowledge and truth (2:1); those who share in the divine nature, and those who still live in a world corrupted by sinful lust (1:4); those who live in accordance with faith and with recognition of their cleansing from past sins (1:5-8); and those who are not living lives founded upon faith.

Peter's view of the end is complicated somewhat by the especially damning end he describes for a sub-group of unbelievers—the apostate false teachers. They once associated with the repentant group on the right path, but now clearly belong to the group awaiting judgement.

The mention of their 'escape', and 'knowledge' of Christ (2 Pet. 2:20), closely resembles Peter's description of the recipients in 2 Peter 1:2, 4. They

---

[3] A later example is the handling of the martyrs of Lyons in 177. Following the martyrs' cremation, their ashes were scatted in the Rhone to destroy any hope of their resurrection. Min Felix, *Oct.* 8.5

[4] Fornberg, *An Early Church in a Pluralistic Society*, 135.

were subsequently, however, entangled and defeated by the defilements of the world (2:20). They abandoned what would have provided their σωτηρία ('salvation'), 3:15. They turned back (from ὑποστρέφω) from their life of repentance (μετάνοια, 3:9; cf. 2:21). These people belong to the unrepentant group, though were more culpable because they deliberately chose to return to the 'vomit' or 'mud' after enjoying a more privileged position (2:22).[5]

In one sense, those who are now living in an unrepentant way, whether they broke from it in the past or have never repented, share the same fate unless they come to lasting repentance. Peter spells out the impending judgement of God upon them. Noah's generation, who perished (from ἀπόλλυμι) by water, is an illustration of the ἡμέρα κρίσις ('day of judgement') that will bring ἀπώλεια ('destruction') upon the ungodly, only this time the destruction will be of οἱ ... οὐρανοὶ καὶ ἡ γῆ ('the heavens and earth') and it will be by πῦρ ('fire'), 3:6-7. The 'day of the Lord' which brings fire with it will come unexpectedly upon the world (3:10). The fire will be intense, causing even the 'heavens to pass away with a roar', and the heavenly bodies to melt as they are burned up and dissolved (3:10, 12), and the earth and the works that are done on it will be laid bare' (3:10). Such catastrophic events do not imply that the earth will be annihilated. Rather, it will experience severe, destructive forces as evil is judged, in preparation for renewal.[6]

In another sense, the end for those who have repented and then returned to their former way of life is worse. They share the same reason to fear the general eschatological judgement, but Peter is more explicit about the judgement awaiting this sub-group of the ungodly (2:6). They 'are bringing upon themselves swift destruction' (2:1); they are condemned and their destruction is not asleep (2:3); they await the same fate as the sinning angels, who were cast into hell and committed to chains of gloomy darkness until the final judgement (2:4; cf. 2:9). The destruction of the cities Sodom and Gomorrah further illustrate what will happen to them (2:6). They will be 'destroyed in their destruction' (v. 12), and will 'suffer wrong as the wage of their wrongdoing' (v.13). They are 'accursed children' (v. 14) for whom 'the gloom of utter darkness has been reserved' (v. 17). As they live, they live as slaves to corruption (v. 19), and their death, though it may be similar to the death awaiting others', is more vividly depicted.

---

[5] The proverbs of the dog and the sow are may be examples of Peter's method of drawing upon both Jewish and Greek images. Sidebottom's contention that swine did not appear in Jewish proverbs seems overstated at best, on the basis of their appearance in Prov. 11:22; Matt. 7:6; and Lk. 15:15-16). This particular swine metaphor in 2 Pet., which appears in *The Story of Ahikar* 8.18, was probably Assyrian in origin, but well-known to the Greeks, as is indicated by Democritus' use of it (Clem. Alex: *Protrpt.* 75). Sidebottom, *James, Jude and 2 Peter*, 117.

[6] For the view that the world is not destroyed completely, but is 'laid bare,' see Davids, *2 Peter and Jude*, 157; 286-88, cf. Bauckham, *Jude, 2 Peter*, 317-21.

Peter's description of the end for the angels is interesting. Aware of the place of imprisonment for the Titans in Greek mythology, Peter uses the verbal form of τάρταρος ('Tartarus'), instead of the more regular NT term γέεννα ('Gehenna' or 'hell'). Three references to Tartarus appear in the LXX (Prov. 30:16; Job. 40:20; 41:24), but in the NT it is a *hapax legomenon*. It was the place of imprisonment for angels, but for humans no such imprisonment is mentioned.[7]

There appear to be two stages of judgement in Peter's eschatology. Firstly, those who have died continue to be kept bound in 'Tartarus' or 'hell' (as is discernible from the phrase: 'but cast them into hell and committed them to pits of darkness, reserved for judgment' (ἀλλὰ σειραῖς ζόφου ταρταρώσας παρέδωκεν εἰς κρίσιν τηρουμένους, 2:4), until the final judgement occurs. The final judgement is the time for which Peter employs the terminology of fire, dissolution, and passing away of the heavens and the earth. Such is the τέλος for the unrepentant.

In summary, Peter's description of the end for the unrepentant is mediated through graphic language of a fiery destruction. Though some of the details pertaining to these matters are unspecified, what is unmistakable is that it is an end to be avoided, as Jesus' likewise earnestly taught (e.g. Mt. 5:9; Mk. 9:47). Compared to other views of the after-life in Peter's time, this Guide to Death carried with it a stern warning for those who disregard it. One's response to Peter's Lord, Jesus, had eternal implications.

The τέλος for those with Faith

Peter is confident of a vastly more desirable end for his audience. Their faith is of equal standing to the apostle Peter's (1:1). They are recipients of grace and peace (1:2), and they know God's Son and Saviour, Jesus Christ (1:2, 11; 3:18). A clear statement of their end is provided in 2 Peter 1:11: they will enjoy a 'richly provided' entrance 'into the eternal kingdom of our Lord and Saviour Jesus Christ'. Just as God would enact judgement upon the wicked, so he would richly welcome those with faith in Christ.

What did Peter mean by an entrance into a 'kingdom'? Peter most likely sourced ideas of God's eternal kingdom from the attention given to it in the Jewish Scriptures (1 Sam. 13:13; 2 Sam. 7:13; 1 Chron. 17:14; 1 Chron. 28:7; Ps. 45:6; Dan. 2:44; 6:26) as well as from the teaching of Christ in the Gospels and Acts (Lk. 1:33; 22:30; Acts 1:3). The preaching of Paul was summarised as 'proclaiming the kingdom' (Acts 20:25; cf. 14:22; 28:31). The kingdom was a subject about which Paul (Rom. 14:7; 1 Cor. 6:9; 1 Cor. 15:24, 50; Gal. 5:21; Eph. 5:5; Col. 4:11; 1 Thess. 2:12; 2 Thess. 1:5; 2 Tim. 4:18) and other NT authors (Heb. 1:8; Jam. 2:5; Rev. 1:6, 9; 5:10) gave significant attention in their letters. Paul's writings, like the Gospels (Lk. 22:29-30; John 18:33-39), show that the 'kingdom of God' was not to be distinguished from the 'kingdom of

---

[7] Davids, *2 Peter and Jude*, 157.

Christ'. Paul refers to the 'kingdom of Christ and God' (Eph. 5:5), and says that the Father has 'transferred us to the kingdom of his beloved Son' (Col. 1:13; cf. 2 Tim. 4:1; Rev. 11:15). The link between the kingdom of the Father and that of the Son was drawn from the Old Testament (e.g. Ps. 45:6; cf. Heb. 1:8), and would be revealed when God's enemy is thrown down (Rev. 12:10).

The idea of a welcome is also present in other NT texts, as in Matthew 25:34: 'the King will say to those on his right, "Come, you who are blessed by my Father, inherit the kingdom prepared for you from the foundation of the world"'. Matthew's gospel also significantly develops the idea of the 'kingdom of God', referring to it as οὐρανός ('heaven') or ἡ βασιλεία τῶν οὐρανῶν ('the kingdom of heaven'), as in Matthew 7:27.[8]

Having considered something of the development of the idea of 'kingdom', as well as its prevalence in the thought of other NT writers, we might not be surprised at Peter's focus on it. More noteworthy is Peter's description of this place as ἡ αἰωνία βασιλεία ('the kingdom of the age' or 'the eternal kingdom'), an expression unique to this verse in the NT.[9] Peter did not use the phrase 'eternal kingdom' in 1 Peter, but he did speak of truths that together can be succinctly summarised with 'eternal kingdom'. He refers to the believers, for example, as a 'chosen race, a royal priesthood, a holy nation, a people for his own possession (1 Pet. 2:9). This royal people have eternal life (1:4, 23), in heaven (3:22), and are richly rewarded by Christ at his return (1:5, 7, 13; 4:13; 5:1, 4). It is possible that 2 Peter 1:10 was intended as a succinct phrase which recalls the more detailed portrayal provided in 1 Peter.[10]

In his image of the 'new heavens and the new earth' Peter is speaking of a re-creation of all that God made in the beginning (Gen. 1:1). The first and last chapters of the Bible describe the creation and new creation respectively. It has

---

[8] The 'kingdom of heaven' plays a dominant role in the gospel according to Matthew, being mentioned throughout the letter in 33 places: 3:2; 4:17; 5:3, 10, 19f; 7:21; 8:11; 10:7; 11:11f; 13:11, 24, 31, 33, 44f, 47, 52; 16:19; 18:1, 3f, 23; 19:12, 14, 23; 20:1; 22:2; 23:13; 25:1. In the LXX and NT, οὐρανός, refers to the 'space above the earth, including the vault arching high over the earth from one horizon to another, as well as the sun, moon, and stars—'sky'. Οὐρανός is also represented in the Scriptures as a dwelling place of certain supernatural beings, for the various stars and constellations were associated with supernatural forces (such as στρατιὰ τοῦ οὐρανοῦ, literally 'the army of heaven,' in Acts 7.42). Johannes P. Louw and Eugene A. Nida, *Greek-English Lexicon of the New Testament Based on Semantic Domains* (New York: United Bible Societies, 1988).

[9] In the LXX translation of Dan. 4:33, the phrase βασιλεία αἰωνία is used, perhaps with a less-developed sense of 'eternal' or 'everlasting' than that of Peter, since it could be taken in the generational sense of one's progeny: 'his kingdom is an everlasting kingdom, and his power to all generations'. The earliest examples following 2 Peter's use of βασιλεία αἰωνία come in Aristides, *Apol.* xvi; and Clem. *Hom.* x.25. Mayor, *The Epistle of Saint Jude and the Second Epistle of Saint Peter*, 98.

[10] A similar verse is 1 Pet. 5:4: 'And when the Chief Shepherd appears, you will receive the crown of glory that will never fade away.'

often been claimed that Peter drew on Stoic ideas of world conflagration followed by further life. But Peter's images are best understood in light of the larger storyline of Scripture (e.g. Zeph. 3). The fire is the promised agent of judgement (3:7), like the flood (vv. 5-6), but leading to a more permanent renewal of humanity and earth (vv. 10-13). Peter depicts God's people being welcomed into a second, permanently good, creation: καινοὺς δὲ οὐρανοὺς καὶ γῆν καινὴν ('a new heaven and a new earth')...ἐν οἷς δικαιοσύνη κατοικεῖ ('in which righteousness dwells'), 3:13. God will once again have close communion with his people, without the tarnishing effects of sin and death, reigning as king over his righteous people forever.

This is the promised end of chapters 1 and 3, though Peter's description differs in each according to his purpose. In 2 Peter 1 (and 1 Peter 1) the author emphasises the eternally satisfying reward for enduring in faith and conduct. Chapter 3 emphasises the destructive fire that inaugurates this restored life with God, because it is this act of judgement and 'coming' that dramatically and permanently vindicates those who patiently waited among the scoffers.

Summary

The picture of the end in 2 Peter has a function in Peter's argument that extends beyond mere interest. It serves as a powerful motivating agent in a letter that is seeking to inspire behavioural outcomes. This view of death and the afterlife is fundamental for the ability to live well in the present. Peter's Guide to Death thus forms the basis for his Guide to Life.

The two ultimate destinations could not be further apart. The choices one makes in this life determine one's existence in the next. Peter's intent is made explicit when he writes,

> Since everything will be destroyed in this way, what sort of people ought you to be? You ought to live holy and godly lives...But in keeping with his promise we are looking forward to a new heaven and a new earth, where righteousness dwells.[11]

These observations accord with similarly confronting teachings about the two final states in the NT, including those of Jesus (e.g. Mk. 9:43-47; Lk. 12:4-5; Jn. 3:36), Paul (e.g. Rom. 6:23), 1 Peter (1 Pet. 4:2-5, 17) and others (e.g. Heb. 9:27; Rev. 21:1-8). In Matthew 25, for example, 'the King will say to those on his right, "Come, you who are blessed by my Father, inherit the kingdom prepared for you from the foundation of the world"' (v. 34). But 'to those on his left he will say, "Depart from me, you cursed, into the eternal fire prepared for the devil and his angels"' (v. 41).

Within the group who are not trusting in Christ, there are those who seem to have been influenced by the Second Sophistic. At one stage they walked with

---

[11] 2 Pet. 3:11-12 (NIV).

Christ's people but have since strayed from the path of life. About such people Peter gives an outlook darker than he did for those who never belonged.

The stakes are high, and Peter wants those in the blessed category to remain there. To remain on his path of life requires activity, not passivity. Peter urges the recipients of his letter to make every effort to supplement their faith with seven preserving traits (vv. 5-7), leading to effectiveness and fruitfulness (v. 8); the affirmation of their calling and election (v. 10); and the avoidance of stumbling on the path (v.10). They are to live in expectation that Christ will return as he promised (3:13), desiring to be found without spot or blemish, and at peace (3:14). The end awaiting this sub-group is a rich welcome into the eternal kingdom of Jesus Christ (1:11).

CONCLUSION

2 Peter sets forth a path of life with close reference to death. It contains no problematic divergence (in terms of such matters as theology or vocabulary) from 1 Peter, nor from other NT formulations of the Christian life. That is not to say that some themes are given more or less emphasis than others.

For Peter, knowledge is given a significance which approaches the importance of the related trait of faith, though the two are in no sense rivals. Faith built upon knowledge of Christ is not only the way to begin on the path of life, but also the way to continue upon it. The preserving function of knowledge was especially pertinent for a community of believers who were to be infiltrated by proponents of a false, though persuasive, alternative 'knowledge'. The prescriptions in chapter 1 and at the end of chapter 3 are best understood by the contrasting path of the wicked in 2:1-3:7. Peter's paraenesis provides the ethical antithesis, which when combined with true knowledge would act as a vaccine for those on the path of life. The shepherd's 'beloved' were on the right path, and he wanted them to remain upon it.

Like other NT authors, Peter conveys absolute confidence in the validity of his teaching. The reason in Peter's case, and to capture Peter's emphasis, was that he himself heard the very voice of God. He was clearly convinced that what he wrote was true, and would thus benefit all who believed it. This message had Old Testament antecedents, which were to be understood in light of the events surrounding the life, death and resurrection of his Lord and friend, Jesus the Messiah. Intending to benefit an audience much larger than those acquainted with the history of Israel, however, Peter presents his message through concepts and language that the Jewish and Gentile world would understand.

2 Peter has a sobering awareness of the temptations that people will experience to stray from the path of life, but overall his Guide to Life and Death is characterised by a pervading sense of hope that the believers will reach their desired end. This hopeful tone can be attributed to a number of factors.

Firstly, Peter's audience were deemed to be already living in alignment with his prescribed way. They were urged to simply continue doing what they were doing. Peter's positive evaluation of their current performance suggests that perfection was not expected. They were to continue in their present direction and intention to live holy and godly lives (3:11). Far from being rare or even extraordinary traits that might foster disillusionment, such as asceticism, perfect detachment or perfection in any other area, Peter's stated objectives are more than attainable; they are actually being attained. Neither perfect performance nor progress were conditions for arriving at the end.

Secondly, Peter assured them that God was empowering them to do exactly what they must do and were doing. God had effected a transformation within them that enabled them to escape the behavioural patterns that once enslaved them. They would have ongoing divine help.

Thirdly, the basis for Peter's message and his commendation of the believers was intentionally grounded on an authority greater than Peter himself. He claims that his message shares the same authority as the Scriptures, and that these truths and promises came from the θεός-ἄνθρωπος, Jesus Christ (1:1-2; cf. 16-21). Peter sought to further validate his Guide to Life and Death by claiming solidarity with Paul (3:15-16) and the other apostles (1:16-19).

Lastly, the individual believer would be supported by the 'family' of believers. Such traits as love, added to brotherly love was to characterise the group. Outright individuality was thereby proscribed in favour of a deep concern for the progress of others.

Our assertion that 2 Peter is a hopeful letter represents a further point of contact between it and 1 Peter. 1 Peter 1:3-5 says,

> Blessed be the God and Father of our Lord Jesus Christ! According to his great mercy, he has caused us to be born again to a living hope through the resurrection of Jesus Christ from the dead, to an inheritance that is imperishable, undefiled, and unfading, kept in heaven for you, who by God's power are being guarded through faith for a salvation ready to be revealed in the last time.[12]

Despite the present suffering of his recipients, he assured them in terms reminiscent of 2 Peter, 'the God of all grace, who has called you to his eternal glory in Christ, will himself restore, confirm, strengthen, and establish you' (1 Pet. 5:10).

With an equally hopeful outlook for the believers in 2 Peter, Peter explains how they are to wait well for Christ's return. Those who heeded Peter's Guide to Life and Death would, at the end of their fruitful lives, be richly welcomed into the eternal kingdom. Those who did not had starkly contrasting prospects.

---

[12] 1 Pet. 1:3-5.

PART IV

RESONANCE AND DISSONANCE IN THE THREE GUIDES TO LIFE AND DEATH

CHAPTER 13
The Three Guides Compared

How might Cicero have reflected on the forum attended by the representatives of three traditions? With their opinions still fresh in his mind pertaining to a topic of great interest to him, he would have been well placed to not only identify points of resonance between them, but to consider how they differed on those same matters.

The purpose of this chapter is to reflect on the three Guides in a like manner. Under a number of headings which represent points of agreement between the Guides, differences between them on these very matters will be discussed.[1]

The Three Guides' *Sitz im Leben*

Three Different Responses to a Common Enemy

Each of the Guides contended with those who, following a sophistic approach, were deemed to be setting forth a baseless and ultimately unfruitful alternative ὁδός of life. The Guides were concerned that their opponents might skilfully lure people away from a superior way. The enemy shared many features, but the Guides' responses were unique.

Epictetus targeted the various alternative forms of philosophy being advocated, with the sophists and Epicureans receiving the most severe criticism. The overwhelming concern that Epictetus had with the sophists was their complacency in putting their knowledge into practice. Although he usually pitied those who lacked ὀρθὸς λόγος ('true reason'), he had little tolerance for those who engaged in deceit and sophistic fallacies. Unlike οἱ πολλοί or the ἰδιῶται, the sophistic opponents deliberately lived in a way contrary to nature, and were calculated in their deceit. In such a context of deceptive argumentation, rhetoric was an important facet of the philosophers' training—a

---

[1] Since this section represents a summary of Parts I-III, most citations of primary sources have not been repeated.

slothful approach could lead to defeat in public debate, which meant that the inferior wisdom of sophists might be construed by the audience as superior.

In a context where orators were praised and rewarded with honour and wealth, many students came to Epictetus seeing philosophy as a means to this end. Epictetus trained them in sophisms, logic, argumentation, and persuasive oratory, but this was all for a more substantial end than merely ἐπίδειξις ('display'). It equipped them not only to develop their powers of reason, but to publicly counter the sophists who sought to discredit Stoic philosophy as a legitimate path of life.

Philo likewise was keenly aware of the sophists with their persuasive techniques and lack of regard for truth. Epictetus considered it quite rudimentary to study their ways so that they might be overcome, and although Philo saw the importance of having some people trained with this rhetorical ability, his counsel was to simply avoid arguing with them—persuasive oratory was the sophists' specialty after all. The fatal mistake of virtuous Abel was his entrance into a contest for which he was ill-prepared against his wicked brother Cain. Possessing ἀρετή ('virtue') was not enough to defeat the sophists, and entering a contest with them as the weaker opponent was worse than unproductive; it was fatal.

Like Epictetus, who did not deny the power of rhetoric, Philo stressed the importance of the presentation *of truth* rather than mere presentation. Sophistry promised ἐλευθερία, but was powerless to help one escape the πάθη ('passions') that were part of the Graeco-Roman world. Worse than failing to free a person from the πάθη, the sophists managed to justify a life which indulged them. They taught the virtues, but lived according to the vices.

Philo's struggle was to convince Alexandrians and the world beyond of the Law's significance, and to keep the Jews from apostasy. The sophists were irritating in their resistance, not because of any particular political agenda so much as a typically sophistic one.

Peter alluded to his opponents when stating, in defence and offence, 'we did not follow σεσοφισμένοις μύθοις ('sophistic myths') when we made known to you the power and coming of our Lord Jesus Christ' (2 Pet. 1:16). Sophistic myths were the antithesis of Peter's eyewitness testimony which accorded with, and further confirmed, Scripture. Sophistic influences had poisoned the Corinthian church's reception of the outwardly unimpressive Apostle Paul. In Paul's mind, however, an even greater problem was the sophists' derailment of the believers, from Christ as God's display of wisdom, towards human displays of wisdom. Sharing geographical ties with Paul in Asia Minor, Peter was probably well aware of the sophistic threat, and wrote to protect the believers in Asia Minor from its influence.

As in Epictetus and Philo, so too in 2 Peter the teachers with sophistic characteristics were worse than wrong; their error was craftily πλαστός ('fabricated'). They were very able to persuade an audience by twisting (from στρεβλόω) the Scriptures and Paul's writings to create fine-sounding myths.

Arrogantly claiming to have knowledge, they promised freedom (ἐλευθερία) to their audience while they themselves were slaves (δοῦλοι) to corruption.

Peter, like the other two Guides, seemed willing to contend with his opponents at least in writing. His first level of defence against them was a detailed and condemning description of them, so that they would be readily identified as false teachers (ψευδοδιδάσκαλοι) on arrival (2 Pet. 2:1-3:7). Their methods were also exposed so that his readers, by walking according to the prescribed traits in chapters 1 and 3, might be a community built upon φιλαδελφία ('brotherly love') and ἀγάπη ('love'), with a heresy-resistant πίστις ('faith') because of its moorings to sound γνῶσις / ἐπίγνωσις ('knowledge'). They would be disinterested in libertine living on account of their interest in ἀρετή ('virtue'), ἐγκράτεια ('self-control'), ὑπομονή ('perseverance'), and εὐσέβεια ('godliness'). The immediate benefits that the false teachers offered would be inconsequential in light of the new heavens and new earth for which his recipients eagerly awaited (2 Pet. 3).

Peter did not comment about the wisdom or otherwise of publicly debating with sophistic natured opposition. Instead, he showed the believers how to resist (individually and corporately) being 'carried away with the error of lawless people and lose [their] own stability' (3:17).

The extent to which the three Guides prescribe engagement with their opponents may be in proportion to their philosophical moorings, and the importance they placed on public debate. Historically, of course, the Stoics held an important place in this sphere. Perhaps because of the philosophical content of his views, Philo felt it important that they could at least be represented, or perhaps defended, by able rhetors. Peter, in both of his letters, seeks to fortify the faith of the believers, but with seemingly little importance attached to public debate. Though there were some examples of Christians engaged in the public defence of their views against various opponents (e.g. Paul's speeches in Acts 14, 17, 22-25), it may not have been until the second-century AD that Christians, perhaps with Philo's writings at their side, adopted more overtly philosophical language.[2] By the time of the Ante-Nicene Fathers, the Christians vigorously engaged, through their writings at least, with 'sophistic' opposition.

Three Responses to Internal Problems within their Communities

Each of the Guides experienced difficulty and frustration, but it was not only from outside their communities.

Epictetus expressed dismay about his students' inability to live according to Stoic principles. Some approached his school with an unacceptable motive, namely, to receive the education necessary for ascending the social ladder.

---

[2] See discussions of this development in Runia, *Philo in Early Christian Literature: A Survey*; Robert L. Wilken, "The Christians as the Romans (and Greeks) Saw Them," in *Jewish and Christian Self-Definition*, ed. E.P. Sanders (London: SCM, 1980).

Epictetus simply longed to 'see a living Stoic', by which he meant a contemporary who practised living in accordance with philosophy and reason.

Philo gave relatively little attention to the success or otherwise of his intended audience. He did, however, indicate the moral imperfection of his own people by emphasizing God's grace (χάρις), forgiveness (or perhaps 'forgetfulness': ἀμνηστία), and their need for repentance (μετάνοια). The perfectly virtuous lives of the patriarchs were esteemed because their performance was in a different league to most others. He demanded a lofty standard of behaviour, and promised much to those who approached it. God would certainly help those who pursued ἀρετή.

In his second letter, Peter recognised the problem of apostasy within the church. Those who threatened the stability of believers were those who had earlier claimed fellowship with Christ and his church. The recipients themselves received no rebuke from Peter since they were standing firm in the truth, but his exhortations imply the possibility of apostasy. He stressed the importance of knowledge of, and faith in, Jesus Christ, and reminded them of the divine power which would assist them to be free of worldly corruption.

Three who called for Ethics that Exceeded Social Norms

Each Guide was unimpressed by the ethical norms in the world around them, but spoke of this problem in different ways.

Perhaps influenced by his own experience of exile from Rome, Epictetus felt free to challenge the social structures and behavioural standards of Roman life. He lacked fear and unquestioning respect for powerful people, wealth and other external things. From the distance of Nicopolis, his lectures demonstrated that he was free to speak his mind and even ridicule the men of rank who visited him. His saw οἱ πολλοί as miserable creatures who simply followed the impulses of their desire for things indifferent, and who paid no attention to matters of real importance. As a consequence, the world was plagued with problems such as rivalry, unbridled desire, suffering, grief, and fear, which rob it of true happiness (εὐδαιμονία). Besides pity, they could be shown a better way by those who lived according to reason (λόγος).

Philo was certainly unimpressed by the lax moral norms of Alexandrian society, but of greater concern to him was the possibility of Jewish apostasy when Jews, like his brother and nephew, assimilated and prospered under Roman rule. Rather than simply urge Jews to return to a traditional form of Judaism, however, Philo focused on a way forward that was inclusive for Greeks as well as Hellenised Jews: all should seek ἀρετή and renounce κακία ('vice'). Those who lived virtuously, and so had communion with God were to be esteemed. Sages of other nations approached wisdom, but the Law of Moses would provide a more powerful θεραπεία ('cure') to the ills of the world if its pre-eminence was fully recognised. If the Greek world recognised that the Septuagint was God's gift to the nations, and that Plato was Moses Atticising, virtue would overcome κακία in the world.

The Three Guides Compared

Peter asserted that his recipients had escaped the 'corruption that is in the world because of lust' (1:4) which was exemplified by the false teachers. The believers were given a new, divinely empowered way to live, which was quite foreign to the world around them. They could entrust themselves to God, who would judge their oppressors, and 'restore, confirm, strengthen, and establish' them (1 Pet. 5:10; cf. 2 Pet. 3:11-18). Peter expressed no hope for the moral transformation of those who remained outside his tradition.

An Emphasis on Ethical Implications

Epictetus' lectures placed much emphasis upon ethics, and confronted an apparently common conception that it was sufficient to 'learn' philosophy without the ἄσκησις ('application') of it. Across his *Discourses,* he presented a fulsome picture of how the life of a Stoic might look in practice. Epictetus wanted his students to demonstrate their knowledge by showing indifference to that which truly was indifferent, and in particular, in the face of pain or death. There was nothing impressive about those who could simply recite poetry or syllogisms.

Philo emphasised behavioural change by pointing to the Law, which clearly guided and empowered people to live according to reason. In *Quod deterius potiori insidiari soleat* he countered those who reinvented philosophy to fit their lifestyle and passions. Knowledge (γνῶσις) for Philo would be shown in the virtuous life that one lives.

Peter placed great importance upon the way one lived. His followers were to add to their faith virtue, to virtue, knowledge, to knowledge, self-control, to self-control, perseverance, to perseverance, godliness, to godliness, brotherly kindness, and to brotherly kindness, love (2 Pet. 1:5-7). Growing in these traits would not only protect them from the fruitlessness of the false teachers, but would keep believers from falling from their privileged position. The false teachers were the antithesis of all that Peter taught, having fallen on account of their misguided knowledge and shameful behaviour. A believer, on the other hand, had all that was needed for life and godliness, a fact which not only forbade excuses, but empowered progress as a partaker (κοινωνός) of the divine nature (θεῖος φύσις).

A Comparison of Three Guides to θεός

Three Descriptions of θεός as the Source of Knowledge

For each of our Guides, philosophy or knowledge came from θεός. Stoicism at the time of Epictetus was marked by divergent views pertaining to the precise nature of θεός. Epictetus was aware of the views of earlier influential Stoics and Greek philosophers, and was comfortable to incorporate many of them. His extant writings focus on what were the broadly accepted views, and were more interested in the implications of theology than identifying precisely the camp to which he belonged. Following the observations of Cotta in Cicero's *De natura deorum,* we observed that the views of earlier Stoics were mutually exclusive, and that Epictetus' use of this tradition led him to views about God that were likewise incoherent.

God was the starting place of philosophy because it was by understanding the ποιήσας (Creator) of the world that one could understand the nature of things. The world was the philosopher's classroom, since God was perceptible in what he had made and clearly deserved recognition and praise from reasoning creatures.

Besides θεός, Epictetus refers to God as Ζεύς, and often uses the plural θεοί to refer to the gods. His name was not as critical as his function as the Creator and the source of λόγος. Epictetus' inclusion of God in his various discussions was usually of an instrumental nature. The study of God was good for its own sake, but Epictetus usually moved from ontological discussion to arrive at his desired ethical point. Supporting this observation, the *Encheiridion*, which intended to outline his essential teachings, gives God no concentrated attention. Nevertheless, Epictetus' high esteem and devotion to God and the gods is difficult to dispute.

For Epictetus, the extent that one lived according to λόγος was the extent to which one would be assimilated into the being of God, and could be said to become a god. In this way, θεός was not only the starting place for philosophers, but was also their τέλος in the sense that they assimilated with, and became, part of God.

Philo too taught that there was no greater good than λόγος. Reason made a person resemble θεός; but for Philo one did not become God. Philo shared Epictetus' conviction that knowledge began with God, but such knowledge was most clearly found in the Laws of Moses.

Compared to Epictetus, Philo was far more rigid about the correct identification of θεός as being the God of Israel, though he only rarely mentioned the τετραγράμματον (*YHWH*), in *Mos.* 2.115. As a concession to this, it was argued that the rigidity of Philo's insistence that Israel's God was the only true god was somewhat compromised in his more philosophical works. Philo's vast exegetical works presuppose his esteem for the Law, which was only surpassed by his admiration for the God who produced it. The θεός of the Jews was the source of γνῶσις, and essential to Philo's τέλος of life, which was to have κοινωνία with him.

For Peter, knowledge also began with θεός, but the process by which God revealed knowledge differed from the way it did for both Philo and Epictetus. When Peter assured his readers of the truth of his message, he referred to Philo's source, the Hebrew Scriptures. By insisting that his views of God were from God himself, he by implication would likely exclude 'natural' or philosophic sources as suspect at best, insisting that certainty about divine things required a message clearly inspired by God (the Holy Spirit) himself. Being 'carried along by the Holy Spirit', the prophets predicted the arrival of an even clearer witness, the Son of God who was God himself. Peter was thus taught directly by the θεός-ἄνθρωπος, Jesus Christ, and became his apostle. Part of an apostolic band, Peter equated their eyewitness testimony with Scripture as a legitimate source of divine truth. Their γνῶσις of God, and the πίστις which it produced, was the foundation for their standing on the path of life.

To summarise, each Guide deemed θεός to be the source of γνῶσις, and the starting point for understanding how one was to live in the world. The similarities beyond this, however, are limited. Significant differences existed in the process they followed for arriving at knowledge as well as in the role of knowledge in one's life.

Three Formulations of the τέλος in Relation to θεός

θεός had a central place in the formulation of each Guide's τέλος. For Epictetus, right reason (ὀρθὸς λόγος) led to freedom (ἐλευθερία), both of which were given by God. The goal of life which included the attainment of these two things, could thus be equated with following θεός.

Philo's formulation was similar. His τέλος, which included a life of virtue, happiness, joy and freedom, had God at its centre. Ultimately, the ideal life is one which imitates God and involves fellowship with him.

A significant difference between these two τέλη, however, was that although Epictetus spoke in unusually theistic terms for a Stoic, θεός was reason (λόγος), and inseparable from creation. To know θεός was to know and live in harmony with the world. But when Philo spoke of communion with θεός, he was referring to the God who was a person. He was distinct from his creation and not only able, but desirous, to have a real relationship. God spoke and heard prayers; there was a two-way communication between man and God not far removed from the depth of intimacy expressed in the Psalms.

Peter likewise inherited Jewish conceptions of θεός, and accordingly gave him the central position in his τέλος. Faith in Christ (Χριστός, who is θεός), and knowledge of him was the entry point, but it was also more than that. Knowledge of Christ is a theme which introduces and closes the letter of 2 Peter; believers are to 'grow in the grace and knowledge of our Lord and Saviour Jesus Christ. To him be the glory both now and to the day of eternity' (2 Pet. 3:18). God's δόξα ('glory'), and the appropriate recognition of it by his people was the keen interest of God's apostle. Eternal life is described with this relationship in mind—believers would be given a rich welcome 'into the eternal kingdom of our Lord and Saviour Jesus Christ' (1:11). Those who denied God by rejecting his word and his path (in chs. 2 and 3) received Peter's invective. Peter could be said to share some of Philo's emphases, but presented them more sharply, through his intimate knowledge of, and κοινωνία with, Jesus who is God.

Three Descriptions of θεός as Good and Powerful

First-Century Guides to Life and Death

Our three Guides would have agreed that θεός is good and powerful. There are considerable differences, however, in the way this was conceived.

Epictetus taught quite persuasively about the power of θεός as discernible from his role as creator and sustainer of all life. His inherent goodness was clear, and was to lead people into unceasing praise and contentment. Early in Epictetus' formulation of Stoicism, however, he explained the limitations of God's power, and the significant implications. God's limited power explained the presence of evil in the world. He was unable to prevent or restrain it, nor could he give people the power to avoid hardship themselves. It was upon this premise that Stoicism was built. Man's greatest pursuit was to live in harmony with this reality: to consider those things which are beyond God's control and ours as matters of indifference (ἀδιάφορα). God's power was seen in the way he equipped people with λόγος. They could be content with their lot and free, not from the world's problems altogether, but from the problems affecting them.

Philo also believed in a powerful and benevolent God, and like Epictetus, he gave attention to God's creative work, his gift of life and of everything that is good. God's attributes are described positively and negatively in Jewish and Platonic language.

Compared to Epictetus' θεός, however, Philo's θεός is more active. Unlike Plato's θεός, Philo's God performed miracles. He engaged in purging evil and promoting virtue in his world. He was the 'Lover of virtue' and used his power to this end, turning some of the wicked towards virtue, and actively judging others. Philo struggled, however, to present a cogent theodicy, arguing somewhat simplistically that God 'is the cause of good things only; and of nothing that is bad'.[3] The presence of evil was not entirely explained when describing God's goodness and power.

Peter shared some of the Jewish aspects of Philo's presentation of God's goodness and power, though his presentation lacked the same philosophic style and vocabulary. Peter highlighted God's righteousness, glory, excellence, power, and majesty. Peter's God was very active in engaging with, and even overcoming, the world. On a macro level, he would return to judge the world at his appointed time, and warned the world to repent (μετανοέω, 2 Pet. 3:9) and find salvation (σωτηρία, 3:15). On a micro level, he gave individuals knowledge of, and faith in, himself, and then indwelled and empowered them to live morally transformed lives. His goodness and power provided an escape from the world's corruption, building a virtuous community that would live forever in his kingdom, where righteousness dwells.

Peter did not fully explain the presence of evil in the world of a good and powerful God. The devil, who 'prowls around like a roaring lion, seeking someone to devour' (1 Peter 5:8) is certainly partly responsible, but the reason for God's creation of him, and patience towards him, is not explained. A partial

---

[3] *Conf. Ling*, 180.

and latent answer may be found not only in the impending judgement, but in the τέλος of God's plan for creation in 2 Peter. The τέλος of a redeemed eternal community who had knowledge of God's grace, and who would forever appreciate his salvation from the world's corruption through the death of his Son, may to some degree explain the presence of an enemy and circumstances from which they would be rescued.

A Comparison of Three Guides to Life

Three Descriptions of the ὁδός of Life

Each of our Guides prescribe a particular path (ὁδός) of life. Epictetus' path is quite comprehensible if one grasps his key concepts. Προαίρεσις was a favourite word of Epictetus used to refer to one's 'moral purpose' or 'volition.' It is part of 'us' in the deepest sense, is always wholly under control, and untouchable by people or circumstances. Untouchable, invincible, and a slave to nobody in the sphere that he controls, the philosopher could experience true freedom (ἐλευθερία): 'He is free who lives as he wills.'[4] Freedom from hindrance was sometimes equated with experiencing εὐδαιμονία.

Supporting this idea, Epictetus provided other principles which were necessary for enjoying freedom of volition. One must study the three τόποι, and give particular attention to the topic of ὄρεξις καὶ ἔκκλισις ('desire and aversion'). To desire anything outside of one's volition is foolish, as it is to be averse to anything taking place that might take place; since by so doing, one becomes as vulnerable as one's ability to control circumstances. Related to this idea, philosophic conceptions of ἀγαθός and κακός must replace common definitions. Outside the sphere of volition, there is nothing either ἀγαθός or κακός. Everything but one's *response* to life is a matter of indifference (ἀδιάφορα).

In all of this, Epictetus' ethics communicate the importance of ἀρετή, and the obligations that come with being a citizen, father, neighbour, or husband. But his commitment to volition made him at least appear personally, or perhaps emotionally, distant in these relationships.

On certain matters Philo's teaching resonates very closely with the teaching of Epictetus. Borrowing Stoic ideas, Philo explained that human desire must be limited to something that cannot be frustrated: namely, progress in ἀρετή and that which proceeds from it. Philo says, 'the wise man only desires such things as proceed from virtue, in which it is impossible for him to be disappointed.'[5] Both Epictetus and Philo would agree, therefore, that the wise only seek that which was attainable, but they differed slightly in the object of their sole pursuit: Epictetus sought to perfect his volition, and Philo to perfect his virtue.

---

[4] *Diss.* IV.1.1.
[5] *Prob.* 60.

Having said this, their views overlapped. Epictetus esteemed the virtuous life, and Philo considered it valuable to live well in relation to one's volition. The difference between the two Guides on volition and virtue was not over their validity so much as the form it took and the emphasis each received. In his philosophical treatise, *Quod omnis probus liber sit,* Philo borrows much of the volition conceptual framework developed by the Stoics, but then inserts the notion of Law-prescribed virtue to re-define it. In so doing, the well-recognised volition concept in the Greek world became the vehicle for expressing, in philosophical terms, the importance of a virtuous life. For to be virtuous was in Philo's mind the same as being obedient; and living according to reason was the same as living in accordance with the truth, or Law.

For Peter, entry onto the path of life also included knowledge and truth, but also, uniquely, faith (πίστις). Peter was able to commend the believers for their present standing on the basis of their faith in the person of Jesus Christ, which they obtained (from λαγχάνω) from the God who granted this gift (δῶρον) to them. Since God was the primary agent for their blessing and salvation in both 1 and 2 Peter, faith (not volition, virtue, nor even progress) was the basis for blessing.

The believers' place on the path of life was more clearly due to God's provision than their wisdom or good intentions. And further distinguishing Peter from Epictetus and Philo was the confidence of arrival for those who were already on the path. It was largely assumed that those on the path were established in the truth (1:12), and would arrive at the end. Peter does emphasise the importance of the believers' effort to arrive at this end, but this was not to earn it so much as to protect it.

The Three Guides provided some indication as to how achievable their respective paths of life were to follow. Each of them demanded great effort and perseverance. This was a topic of great significance among thinkers of their period.

Cicero, for instance, explained that there was no difference in *degree* with regard to wisdom or the good, either one has it or one does not. Just as a person drowns whether he is a mile or an inch below the water surface, 'similarly one who has made some progress towards virtue is in no less misery than the one who has made no progress'.[6] Seneca likewise argued that 'he who makes progress is still numbered with the fools'.[7]

Whether or not he was aware of Cicero's concern, this study of Epictetus highlighted a troubling tension that runs throughout his *Discourses.* Epictetus longed to see a sage, someone resembling the great Socrates, who lived according to reason. But he despaired of ever seeing one, and acknowledged the unbearable weight of the philosopher's task. He acknowledged the chasm

---

[6] Cicero, *De Fin.* 3.28; translation of Starr, "Sharers in Divine Nature: 2 Peter 1:4 in Its Hellenistic Context", 162.

[7] Seneca, *Ep.* 75.8.

between the potential benefits of philosophy and the reality that few, if any, had ever approached it.

As mentioned previously, θεός reduced the field of man's concern to merely living in accordance with his own volition. This was his responsibility entirely to achieve, and perhaps possible in theory, but beyond him in experience. Progress (προκοπή) was often stated as the goal, and would have made the path more achievable if failure were tolerable—but it was not. As a result, Oldfather observed the frustration in Epictetus' life. He perceived in Epictetus the 'truly pathetic longing as of tired men for a passive kind of happiness, an ill-defined yearning to be "saved" by some spectacular and divine intervention'.[8]

On occasion, Philo's standard was almost identical to that of Epictetus, and his sage was equally elusive. This was expressed in similar language, where absolute detachment from external circumstances was necessary. At other times, and most commonly, this high standard was expressed through historical Jewish figures, such as the patriarchs, who lived perfectly virtuous lives. Unfortunately, there were no such people in Philo's generation to observe, besides perhaps in the highly idealised portrayal of an ascetic community called the *Therapeutae*.

When Philo was challenged by his contemporaries about the impossibility of his prescribed path, he reduced the demands to being more virtuous than others. A further significant concession Philo made that Epictetus did not, is seen in the place he gave to themes such as human weakness, repentance, sacrifice, forgiveness for wrongdoing, as well as God's ἡμερότης ('mercy' or perhaps 'gentleness') and χάρις ('grace'). By his mercy, God responded when one sought to live according to ἀρετή—he actively cooperated and strengthened one in this pursuit. There was a heavy responsibility for self-transformation, but a place given to God to perfect what was lacking. Because of God's mercy, Philo seemed hopeful overall that his path was effective for arriving at his τέλος.

As Peter introduced his path of life he reiterated a feature of the Christian message which was being preached by the apostles of Christ, viz. σωτηρία ('salvation') or δικαιοσύνη ('righteousness') was not a reward for one's own effort but freely given on the basis of Christ's work on his or her behalf. In this way, faith came to prominence, since it was by believing the message that one was rewarded (e.g. Jn. 3:16; Rom. 10:9; 2 Pet. 1:1). This is implied in the introduction and throughout 2 Peter, as well as in the introduction of 1 Peter which addressed the exiles who were 'elected'

> according to the foreknowledge of God the Father, in the sanctification of the Spirit, for obedience to Jesus Christ and for sprinkling with his blood: May grace and peace be multiplied to you. Blessed be the God and Father of our Lord Jesus Christ! According to his great mercy, he has caused us to be born again to a living hope through the resurrection of Jesus Christ from the dead, to an inheritance that is imperishable, undefiled, and unfading, kept in heaven for you, who by God's

---

[8] Oldfather, *Epictetus: The Discourses*, xxvii.

power are being guarded through faith for a salvation ready to be revealed in the last time.[9]

The 'foreknowledge' of θεός described here extends well beyond the conceptions of Epictetus or Philo in terms of the 'fate' of humans.[10] God was clearly the agent responsible for the state of 'the elect' who were chosen by him. Grace, mercy, and Christ's work were responsible for their inheritance.

The idea that God was the responsible agent for salvation might have 'startled' or 'bewildered' Epictetus and Philo, as Paul's message did the Athenian Stoic philosophers (Acts 17). According to Peter, it was simply by believing his message, that common people (οἱ πολλοί) or the laymen (ἰδιῶται) to whom Epictetus referred, could become those who actually 'followed' Peter's God. Likewise, the wicked man (φαῦλος) of Philo could be effortlessly deemed a virtuous man by Peter's θεός, as did the criminal being crucified next to Jesus. A number of Jesus' parables show the resistance of Jewish Pharisees to accept that any prerequisite goodness was unnecessary for inclusion into God's people (e.g. Lk. 18:10-14).

The 'elusive sage' phenomenon in Epictetus and Philo was discussed, and in one sense the perfect Christian sage was also absent from Peter's writings. In a far more prominent sense, however, the Christian sage was far from elusive: he was Christ himself, the key figure of every NT author. Likewise, in 1 and 2 Peter, Christ's people were conferred with Christ's virtue by association (2 Peter 1:3; cf. v. 5). The recipients of 2 Peter were to make every effort in their lives, but they had in a more dominant sense already arrived at a τέλος comparable to that for which the other Guides were striving. Peter's sense of arrival seems strong indeed if it were acceptable to substitute the NT 'blessings' enjoyed by the believers (such as peace and joy) with Epictetus' and Philo's longing for happiness (εὐδαιμονία). The same can be said if Peter's present enjoyment of union with God were deemed comparable to the assimilation into, and κοινῶνια with, θεός, which was being pursued by Epictetus and Philo respectively. In Christ, believers were treated by θεός as though they were without moral blemish, and already enjoyed unbroken fellowship with him.[11]

---

[9] 1 Pet. 1:2-5.

[10] An interesting comparative study could be made between these three Guides understanding of providence, or perhaps 'fate'. Regrettably, though we have touched on it at various places, this question is beyond the limits of this monograph.

[11] It could be argued that Peter is providing an 'easier' standard than Epictetus or Philo because 2 Pet. may have been addressing a less sophisticated audience than the other two—a simpler standard for simpler people. Though the audience may well have been simpler, the trouble with this suggestion is the absence in the NT of any more difficult standard for entry into life with God for more 'advanced' believers; the way onto this path appears to be the same as the way to proceed upon it—with πίστις in Christ. Indeed, Paul (in Romans and Corinthians) repeatedly counters libertine behaviour among Christians by re-emphasising the grace of God for their salvation—

A Comparison of Three Guides to Death

Each Guide chose to incorporate death into their message, but the reasons and methods for doing so differed. Death had a significant place in Epictetus' *Discourses*. The point most emphasised about death was that it was not to be feared. This was because: it was nothing more than a return to the elements from which we came; Socrates called death by soft names and approached death confidently; death was inevitable and natural for all of creation and thus fear represented a senseless opposition to the way things were; death was like a mask (μορμολύκεια), which had a tendency to scare those who were ignorant of its true nature.

Besides being a reflection of the importance of a right view of death, the numerous persuasive arguments that Epictetus devoted to death may reflect just how difficult it was for students to adopt his indifference towards it. Indeed, Epictetus explicitly acknowledged how difficult it was to be indifferent towards death, particularly at the time of application. He admitted that 'we' naturally seek a pardon, or any other way to escape the threat of death. Because the application of philosophy was much more difficult than the theory of it, the philosopher's progress was most visible outside the classroom when tested by exile or illness, or by the most difficult trial of life—one's death.

For Epictetus, the topic of death was structurally important in that it held his overall philosophy together. First, death was the door that was always open, meaning that life need not ever become unbearable; freedom was always available. Similarly, the man who was unafraid of death need not fear any circumstance that might lead him to take his own life. Confidence towards death is thus important because it enabled philosophers to be free from what the untrained deem 'fearful' events in life, such as poor health, torture, imprisonment or exile. One was free to the extent that one was confident about death, and so a philosopher was to be always training for dying.

If Epictetus' students were to be convinced that it was reasonable to be solely concerned for their volition, they must be convinced that it works in life's most difficult circumstance. The matter of death became the matter on which Epictetus made philosophy stand or fall. He showed that since it stands in death it would stand in life.

Furthermore, imagining oneself on the verge of death provided a helpful window by which one could evaluate how one is living in relation to reason. If a man had to justify himself before θεός after his death, what would his defence look like? Such reflection enabled even youths to look at their lives in retrospect. For Epictetus, what was true in life was crystallised by the

---

not to excuse immorality, but to motivate a more appropriate response to God's kindness. Elders and leaders are to be chosen on the basis of an exemplary standard of behaviour (e.g. 1 Tim. 3; 1 Pet. 2), but standards are in place in order that they fulfil their role adequately, not as the basis for their salvation.

perspective of death. He shared with his students his desire to face death knowing that he adequately, indeed perfectly, lived in accordance with λόγος.

The place Philo gave to death and that which follows death is also of great significance in his overall message, even if it did not have the same structural importance that it had for Epictetus.[12]

Philo's schema of the afterlife meant that for most people, bodily death was not to be feared. Unless given the gift of immortality, death was a natural end for the wicked. The descent of some to ᾅδης ('Hades') or Τάρταρος ('Tartarus') was mentioned on a few occasions, but not enough to take away from his overall emphasis on the mortality of the wicked. The worst kind of death was experienced by those who are governed by their senses while still alive in the body. They suffer a premature death, being displeasing to God, and cut off from virtue and its rewards.

Like Epictetus, Philo reflected upon death to learn about life. Moses' death taught him a number of things. First, as was the case with Epictetus' use of Socrates' death, one need not live in fear of it. Second, the death of Moses, like that of Socrates, helped him to see what was important while he lived. Third, and in a way which represents a divergence from Epictetus' use of Socrates' death, Moses not only lacked the fear of death, but eagerly anticipated the life that would follow it. Epictetus aimed for indifference towards death; Philo taught that the contemplation of death may even be a source of joy for those who live.

The most significant function of death and the afterlife for Philo was its motivational function. Like Epictetus, Philo says that the way we die shows the quality and praiseworthiness of our life.[13] And although the rewards for the virtuous include happiness (εὐδαιμονία) in this life, they also extend beyond this life into immortality, clarifying further what is important in the present life. The soul and body of the virtuous are transformed so that they become an immortal 'sun-like mind'. Some indication of heaven (οὐρανός) was given, though the more essential benefit of virtuous living was communion with God, which begins now.

There were immediate implications for living according to virtue or vice, obedience or disobedience. But Philo's inclusion of death, followed by either judgement or immortality, added motivational weight to follow his path.

---

[12] In his more philosophic works, however, the nature of death becomes more structurally important for Philo's formulation of how to live. Like Epictetus, Philo insisted that death was nothing to be feared if one pursues ἀρετή, and it provided an essential and ubiquitous escape route which guarantees one's freedom.

[13] Catharine Edwards demonstrates from various sources that the nobility of one's death communicated one's nobility in life. Gladiators, for example, 'were celebrated in Roman culture not only because they knew how to kill, but also because they knew how to die'. Catharine Edwards, *Death in Ancient Rome* (London: Yale University Press, 2007), 46; cf. 5-13.

Peter approached death with a similar respect for its importance, but the reason why it is significant differs from the philosophic reason given by Epictetus, and to a lesser extent, Philo.

Firstly, he drew attention to his own imminent death, and confidently taught that life extends beyond the departure from one's tent (σκήνωμα) of a body. The path of life that he has been advocating has very real implications for the moment of departure.

Interestingly, and perhaps significantly, all three of our Guides draw attention to the death of their 'sage': Socrates, Moses, and Jesus. Peter (esp. in 1 Peter) draws attention to the death of his 'sage' when he describes the honourable way Jesus faced his death (1 Pet. 2:13-23). Persecution and death were not to be feared, nor was revenge to be sought, but like Christ one could entrust oneself to him who judges justly, and so be content to face death.

The death of Jesus Christ for Peter was more significant than simply providing a model for his followers, however. Jesus' death showed the extent of his love for his 'friends' (John 15; 2 Cor. 5:14), as well as Jesus' confidence in God's superintending power over life and death (1 Pet. 2:23; cf. Lk. 23:43, 46). Further, his death was the means by which God could declare righteous all of those who have faith in Christ (1 Pet. 1:18-19; 2:24). For Peter and the other apostles, Jesus' resurrection gave further significance to his death. Among other things, it provided the basis for Peter's own confidence that life surely follows death.

Compared to the emphasis given to Christ's death in 1 Peter through numerous explicit references, death has a less overt presence in the message of 2 Peter. His death (and resurrection) does, nonetheless, have an important structural and motivational function as an assumed reality. Indeed, the *gravitas* of the book is attributable in no small measure to the imminence of death and the afterlife which pervades each chapter. The faith which begins chapter 1 relates to confidence in the Christ who died and was raised again. Christ's death and life is thus foundational for Peter's Guide to Life and Death. In 2 Peter 2, despite the present prosperity and self-indulgent lifestyle of the false teachers, the fact that there was ultimately no good future in defying God is abundantly clear in light of their destruction. Likewise, in chapter 3, benefits of living with faith in Christ certainly existed in the present, but the rewards would be most fully realised in the events that follow one's death, or Christ's return.

Both 1 and 2 Peter rely heavily on the fulfilment of promises that were, in the opinion of many, spurious. If the persecutors and mockers were right, and there was neither blessing nor destruction following death, the logic of both letters would collapse, as would the basis for any behavioural change. Peter's recipients were to be pitied, mocked even, if the life for which they suffer (1 Peter) and wait (2 Peter) would not come to pass.

CHAPTER 14

Conclusion

What interesting outcomes might result from a 'Ciceronian forum' consisting of a Roman Stoic, an Alexandrian Jew and a Christian apostle from Galilee? To what extent did their views of θεός, life and death converge or diverge? What can be said of the sophistic opposition that they faced and the way in which they overcame it?

Three Guides facing Sophistic Opposition

It unexpectedly emerged in the course of this monograph that the three Guides faced an enemy with common features, reflecting the movement that spread rapidly throughout the Roman Empire during the Julio-Claudian and Flavian period known as the Second Sophistic. Each of the Guides were motivated by, and responded in unique ways to, the threat posed by this opposition.

Each of the Guides observed that their opponents rejected sound reason and truth in favour of more immediate fame and influence and pleasure. The close proximity of these deceitful teachers to each of the Guides and their followers is reflected in the vehement polemical style with which each Guide sets forth his superior path, in each case shaped quite explicitly as the antithesis to the proponents and promoters of the Second Sophistic.

All three present their case with sound reasoning based upon their own philosophical or theological presuppositions, but the way this looks for each one is different. Epictetus trained all of his students to treat as indifferent (ἀδιάφορα) the things for which the sophists strove, and he drilled his students in sophistic argumentation, so that they would be prepared for debate. Similarly, Philo argued that it is only things that pertain to the soul that are good and should be sought, rather than seeking the trappings of life that the sophists clearly enjoyed. Such knowledge of the truth did not guarantee Philo's audience victory over the sophists, however. Some from among them at least should be trained in rhetoric to defeat them at their own game; all others should avoid entering any contest. Peter sought to defend his people by reinforcing their faith in, and knowledge of, Jesus the Christ, whose rewards would extend into eternity. The list of traits in 2 Peter 1:5-7 was carefully crafted to render the teaching of the sophists unacceptable, and their alternative lifestyle repulsive.

Conclusion

Three Guides to θεός

Each Guide's theology was determinative for his Guide to Life and Death. Common threads in their theologies were observed: the three authors share the view that θεός is good, powerful, and central to their task of arriving at knowledge. But beyond these similarities significant differences emerged in what each Guide means when they describe θεός.

Epictetus' view of θεός could be described as being complex and incoherent, and strikingly theistic compared to other Stoics. It is clear, however, that God's power is painfully short of being absolute. He has enabled man to experience freedom (ἐλευθερια) by living according to reason (λόγος), and so (in a way which differs from Philo's and Peter's ideas) to assimilate with God who is perfect reason. Philosophy, therefore, is the vehicle for closing this divine-human gap. Men of reason were to seek and test philosophy, and were left to their own God-given ability to live in accordance with it. To the extent that they could do so, they would experience the freedom and happiness (εὐδαιμονία) that God intended.

Philo also used Greek philosophical concepts of θεός, but integrated them into what is most essentially a Hebrew theology. The philosophy is broadly that of first-century Platonism, but he also draws upon Stoic ideas in his more philosophical treatises. Though one could also learn about God from the Greek poets and philosophers, God revealed himself most clearly in the Law (νόμος) of Moses. One obeys God by obeying the Law, and in so doing cooperated with God's intention that the world be a place of virtue (ἀρετή). Those who were virtuous would enjoy the end (τέλος) of worshipping God, having fellowship with him, and so experiencing happiness (εὐδαιμονία).

Like Philo, Peter builds upon a Jewish view of θεός. Rather than drawing heavily on philosophical ideas, however, Peter was profoundly shaped by his time as a disciple of the Rabbi, Jesus Christ. According to Peter, Jesus revealed in himself the very person of God, and modelled how one was to walk on the path of life. Jesus thus provided the grid through which Peter formed his views about God, the Jewish Scriptures (including the Laws of Moses expounded by Philo), and things pertaining to life and death. God had clearly spoken to reveal his will, and actively empowered those who believed him to live in a way which resembles his own 'divine nature' (θεῖος φύσις). God would bless those who had fellowship with him through their faith (πίστις) in Christ, and would judge those who rejected Jesus' claims.

Three Guides to Life

Epictetus' Guide to Life promised much, but by his own concession, it was a very difficult path. Freedom was as attainable as one's capacity to live according to reason, which meant living in a detached way to everything external to one's volition (προαίρεσις). But one's inability to consistently live according to reason proved a hindrance in his overall philosophy. Although some recent discussions have emphasised progress (προκοπή) rather than perfection (τέλειος) as the Stoic goal, this would not sit easily with Epictetus. He does indeed prescribe progress, but also refuses to relinquish the goal of actually living in accordance with reason. This unattainable pursuit created a sense of despair for Epictetus, perhaps because it struck at the heart of the Stoic principle that one pursues only what is attainable, or 'up to us' (ἐφ᾽ ἡμῖν). Living in accordance with reason seemed wise because it was attainable in theory, and yet it was beyond him when it came to practice (ἄσκησις). Epictetus lamented the absence of any living sage:

> So, although we are unable even to fulfil the profession of a man, we take on the additional profession of the philosopher—so huge a burden (τηλικοῦτο φορτίον)! It is as though a man who was unable to raise ten pounds wanted to lift the stone of Aias.[1]

Philo likewise conceived the path of life to involve attaining perfection, but instead of focusing on volition, he asserted that one must live in accordance with perfect virtue. According to Philo's critics at least, the attainment of this was unheard of. When pushed by his critics to explain the absence of any living sage, Philo reluctantly softened the standard so that he could provide examples of virtuous people. Ideas drawn from the Law, such as the inevitability of human imperfection and God's mercy to forgive the repentant, provided Philo with a precedent for hope that his path was possible, and therefore viable. The extent to which Philo allowed a place for divine assistance to overcome human weakness (even in his philosophical treatises), is the extent to which he deviated, whether consciously or not, from Stoic and more generally Platonic philosophy that otherwise deeply influenced him.

Peter also addresses this common question of human imperfection by focusing on Jesus Christ's virtue (ἀρετή). Since Jesus was both θεός and saviour (σωτήρ), he was the 'sage' of absolute importance. His virtue was both definitively and progressively communicable to those who had faith in him. The value of progressing, or 'abounding' (from πλεονάζω) in knowledge (γνῶσις) and virtue, was the protective function it played for one's faith in Christ – keeping one from falling from the 'right way' (εὐθὺς ὁδός). For this reason, Peter was unique among the three Guides in his commendation of his audience for living according to the way he set forth. By their faith they had already, in the most significant sense, attained what was required of them. Peter's condemnation of the false teachers is a real warning for the believers, however, that although a morally perfect life may not be required from each of them to reach the goal or end (τέλος), the alternative path of faith-less and ungodly (ἀσεβής) living was the path to destruction (ἀπώλεια).

Each Guide deemed his own path to be superior to the way of the common people (οἱ πολλοί), who lived in ignorance of it. Each Guide claimed that their

---

[1] *Diss.* II.9.22.

own path was better than known alternative philosophies. And each claimed, in different ways, to possess true reason or even truth (ἀλήθεια).

Three Guides to Death

The theme of death (θάνατος) had a significant place in each Guide's formulation of the path of life. Their views pertaining to death were not expressed merely for interest-sake, but because of death's function in their overall philosophy. The contemplation of death instructed one for life, and provided a motivation for ethical progress. Beyond these similarities, significant differences emerged in the detail of how and why each Guide considered it important to teach about death and that which follows it.

Epictetus' view of death helped one to experience freedom and well-being. Since one would simply return to the elements at death, there was no need to fear what was commonly considered the worst and most fearful event. Socrates' fearless approach to death was a powerful demonstration of this truth. The benefits of knowing about death ended at death for Epictetus, however, because there was no reward, punishment, or even consciousness beyond it.

Philo shared some of the perspectives of Epictetus about death on the basis of his Hellenistic background. He stands, as has often been the case in this study, somewhere between Epictetus and Peter. On the one hand, Philo, like Epictetus, described the rewards and judgements of God in ways that barely extended beyond this life. On the other hand, following broadly Jewish concepts he casted a vision for a post-death life which may be with God for some, and separated from him for others. Philo was uncertain of the details, but based on the experience of Moses as well as tenets of Platonism, he expressed much hope in the immortality of virtuous souls.

Like Philo, Peter thought it important to understand death for living in the present, but to a greater degree. The death of importance for Peter was that of Christ. His death, coupled with his resurrection, provided both the model for facing death as well as a basis for confidence that life follows it. Death was the departure from one's tent of a body, and a gateway into the 'eternal kingdom' (αἰωνία βασιλεία), meaning that the consequences of one's life would only become fully apparent after death. Peter urged his recipients to hold this strong post-death focus while still alive—they were to 'hasten' and 'wait' for it. In many respects, new life with God and the associated benefits had already begun for believers through their spiritual union with the resurrected Jesus, yet a more final arrival awaited them in 'the new heavens and new earth, where righteousness dwells' (2 Pet. 3:13).

To summarise, the presence of each Guide in this comparative study, which bears some resemblance to the forum held in Cicero's *De natura deorum*, has enabled us to better appreciate each Guide's own views, as well as the tradition each represents, in matters of Life and Death.

If it were possible to sit the Guides down together, as was the case in Cicero's work, these three Guides might have had quite a harmonious conversation—if harmony was their intent. There are many points of contact on which they could have chosen to focus and agree. They could have spoken passionately together about θεός their creator, sustainer, and guide, who is good, powerful, and worthy of their lives and praise. They could have lamented together the folly of the world, which lives out of harmony with θεός, reason or truth. They could have agreed about the importance of living with virtue, and agreed that death need not be feared.

If the Guides came to the discussion seeking to compare the substance and detail of their views, however, they would have found immediate and numerous differences, and on the most significant topics. They held mutually exclusive views about the 'person' and work of θεός, about the way to enter and remain upon the path of life, and about where the path ends. Is it by listening to Socrates, Moses, or Jesus Christ that one could live, and die, well?

Though a superficial resonance may be claimed to exist between the three Guides, significant dissonance emerges in the most critical matters when subjected to closer examination.

Appendix: 'Sophistic' Opposition in Ante-Nicene Fathers

Athanasius

Epistula encyclical ad episcopos Aegypti et Libyae

9 For instance, let them ask the Greeks, who have been their instructors (for it is a word of their invention, not Scripture), and when they have been instructed in its various significations, then they will discover that they cannot even question properly, on the subject which they have undertaken...Further, Asterius, the unprincipled Sophist, the patron too of this heresy, has added in his own treatise, that what is not made, but is, is 'unoriginate'.

Orationes contra Arianos 2.32-33

32. It is plain from this that the Arians are not fighting with us about their heresy; but ... their real fight is against the Godhead Itself. For if the voice were ours which says, 'This it My Son', small were our complaint of them; but if it is the Father's voice, and the disciples heard it, and the Son too says of Himself, 'Before all the mountains He begat me', are they not fighting against God, as the giants...so in like manner about the Son's Godhead, what has been above said is sufficient, and it becomes superfluous, or rather it is very mad to dispute about it, or to ask in an heretical way, How can the Son be from eternity? or how can He be from the Father's Essence, yet not a part? since what is said to be of another, is a part of him; and what is divided, is not whole. *33* These are the evil sophistries of the heterodox; yet, though we have already shewn their shallowness, the exact sense of these passages themselves and the force of these illustrations will serve to show the baseless nature of their loathsome tenet.

Ar. 3.2.

But now let us see what Asterius the Sophist says, the retained pleader for the heresy. In imitation then of the Jews so far, he writes as follows; 'It is very plain that He has said, that He is in the Father and the Father again in Him, for this reason, that neither the word on which He was discoursing is, as He says, His own, but the Father's, nor the works belong to Him, but to the Father who gave Him the power.' Now this, if uttered at random by a little child, had been excused from his age; but when one who bears the title of Sophist, and professes universal knowledge, is the writer, what a serious condemnation does he deserve! And does he not show himself a stranger to the Apostle, as being puffed up with persuasive words of wisdom, and thinking thereby to succeed in deceiving, not understanding himself what he says nor whereof he affirms?

Ar. 14.37

This they have not confined to words, but Arius composed in his Thalia, and the Sophist Asterius wrote, what we have stated above, as follows: 'Blessed Paul said not that he preached Christ, the Power of God or the Wisdom of God', but without the addition of the article, 'God's power' and 'God's wisdom' thus preaching that the proper Power of God Himself which is natural to Him, and co-existent in Him ingenerately, is something besides, generative indeed of Christ, and creative of the whole world, concerning which he teaches in his Epistle to the Romans

Ar. 2.28

For thus the Sophist Asterius, on the strength of having learned to deny the Lord, has dared to write, not observing the absurdity which follows...But to speak thus of the Word of God, is not the part of Christians but of Greeks.

Ar. 1.6-7

These are portions of Arius' fables as they occur in that jocose composition. Who is there that hears all this, nay, the tune of the Thalia, but must hate, and justly hate, this Arius jesting on such matters as on a stage? who but must regard him, when he pretends to name God and speak of God, but as the serpent counselling the woman? who, on reading what follows in his work, but must discern in his irreligious doctrine that error, into which by his sophistries the serpent in the sequel seduced the woman?

Irenaeus

Adversus haereses 1.9.1

You see, my friend, the method which these men employ to deceive themselves, while they abuse the Scriptures by endeavouring to support their own system out of them. For this reason, I have brought forward their modes of expressing themselves, that thus thou mightest understand the deceitfulness of their procedure, and the wickedness of their error.

Adv. haer. 1.9:4

Then, again, collecting a set of expressions and names scattered here and there [in Scripture], they twist them, as we have already said, from a natural to a non-natural sense.

Adv. haer. 3.5.1

Neither did His disciples make mention of any other God, or term any other Lord, except Him, who was truly the God and Lord of all, as these most vain Sophists affirm that the apostles did with hypocrisy frame their doctrine according to the capacity of their hearers, and gave answers after the opinions of their questioners, fabling blind things for the blind, according to their blindness; for the dull according to their dullness; for those in error according to their error.

Adv. haer. 3.24.2
Alienated thus from the truth, they do deservedly wallow in all error, tossed to and fro by it, thinking differently in regard to the same things at different times, and never attaining to a well-grounded knowledge, being more anxious to be Sophists of words than disciples of the truth. For they have not been founded upon the one rock, but upon the sand, which has in itself a multitude of stones. Wherefore they also imagine many gods, and they always have the excuse of searching [after truth] (for they are blind), but never succeed in finding it. For they blaspheme the Creator, Him who is truly God, who also furnishes power to find [the truth]; imagining that they have discovered another god beyond God, or another Pleroma, or another dispensation. Wherefore also the light which is from God does not illumine them, because they have dishonoured and despised God

Adv. haer. 4.1:5
[T]hose things are clearly shown to be false which these deceivers and most perverse Sophists advance, maintaining that the being whom they have themselves invented is by nature both God and Father; but that the Demiurge is naturally neither God nor Father, but is so termed merely by courtesy (*verbo tenus*), because of his ruling the creation, these perverse mythologists state, setting their thoughts against God

Adv. haer. 4.2.2
What Father will those men have us to understand [by these words], those who are most perverse Sophists of Pandora? Whether shall it be Bythus, whom they have fabled of themselves;

Adv. haer. 5.20.2
Those, therefore, who desert the preaching of the Church, call in question the knowledge of the holy presbyters, not taking into consideration of how much greater consequence is a religious man, even in a private station, than a blasphemous and impudent Sophist. Now, such are all the heretics, and those who imagine that they have hit upon something more beyond the truth, so that by following those things already mentioned, proceeding on their way variously, in harmoniously, and foolishly, not keeping always to the same opinions with regard to the same things, as blind men are led by the blind, they

shall deservedly fall into the ditch of ignorance lying in their path, ever seeking and never finding out the truth

Tatian the Assyrian

Oratio ad Graecos 1.2

Yet those who eagerly pursue it shout lustily, and croak like so many ravens. You have, too, contrived the art of rhetoric to serve injustice and slander, selling the free power of your speech for hire, and often representing the same thing at one time as right, at another time as not good. The poetic art, again, you employ to describe battles, and the amours of the gods, and the corruption of the soul.

Orat. 22:1

And of what sort are your teachings? Who must not treat with contempt your solemn festivals, which, being held in honour of wicked demons, cover men with infamy? I have often seen a man – and have been amazed to see, and the amazement has ended in contempt, to think how he is one thing internally, but outwardly counterfeits what he is not – giving himself excessive airs of daintiness and indulging in all sorts of effeminacy; sometimes darting his eyes about; sometimes throwing his hands hither and thither, and raving with his face smeared with mud; sometimes personating Aphrodite, sometimes Apollo; a solitary accuser of all the gods, an epitome of superstition, a vituperator of heroic deeds, an actor of murders, a chronicler of adultery, a storehouse of madness, a teacher of cynaedi, an instigator of capital sentences; and yet such a man is praised by all. But I have rejected all his falsehoods, his impiety, his practices, in short, the man altogether. But you are led captive by such men, while you revile those who do not take a part in your pursuits. I have no mind to stand agape at a number of singers, nor do I desire to be affected in sympathy with a man when he is winking and gesticulating in an unnatural manner. What wonderful or extraordinary thing is performed among you? They utter ribaldry in affected tones, and go through indecent movements; your daughters and your sons behold them giving lessons in adultery on the stage. Admirable places, forsooth, are your lecture-rooms, where every base action perpetrated by night is proclaimed aloud, and the hearers are regaled with the utterance of infamous discourses! Admirable, too, are your mendacious poets, who by their fictions beguile their hearers from the truth!

Orat. 33.1

Therefore I have been desirous to prove from the things which are esteemed honourable among you, that our institutions are marked by sober mindedness, but that yours are in close affinity with madness. You who say that we talk nonsense among women and boys, among maidens and old women, and scoff at us for not being with you, hear what silliness prevails among the Greeks.

Orat. 35.1
The things which I have thus set before you I have not learned at second hand. I have visited many lands; I have followed rhetoric, like yourselves; I have fallen in with many arts and inventions; and finally, when sojourning in the city of the Romans, I inspected the multiplicity of statues brought thither by you: for I do not attempt, as is the custom with many, to strengthen my own views by the opinions of others, but I wish to give you a distinct account of what I myself have seen and felt. So, bidding farewell to the arrogance of Romans and the idle talk of Athenians, and all their ill-connected opinions, I embraced our barbaric philosophy. I began to show how this was more ancient than your institutions

Orat. 36.1
But let Homer be not later than the Trojan war; let it be granted that he was contemporary with it, or even that he was in the army of Agamemnon, and, if any so please, that he lived before the invention of letters. The Moses before mentioned will be shown to have been many years older than the taking of Troy

Orat. 40.1
Therefore, from what has been said it is evident that Moses was older than the ancient heroes, wars, and demons. And we ought rather to believe him, who stands before them in point of age, than the Greeks, who, without being aware of it, drew his doctrines [as] from a fountain. For many of the Sophists among them, stimulated by curiosity, endeavoured to adulterate whatever they learned from Moses, and from those who have philosophised like him, first that they might be considered as having something of their own, and secondly, that covering up by a certain rhetorical artifice whatever things they did not understand, they might misrepresent the truth as if it were a fable.

Clement of Alexandria

Stromata 1.1.22
Because there is great danger in divulging the secret of the true philosophy to those, whose delight it is unsparingly to speak against everything, not justly; and who shout forth all kinds of names and words indecorously, deceiving themselves and beguiling those who adhere to them. 'For the Hebrews seek signs,' as the apostle says, 'and the Greeks seek after wisdom.'

*Strom.*1.3.1
There is a great crowd of this description: some of them, enslaved to pleasures and willing to disbelieve, laugh at the truth which is worthy of all reverence,

making sport of its barbarousness. Some others, exalting themselves, endeavour to discover calumnious objections to our words, furnishing captious questions, hunters out of paltry sayings, practisers of miserable artifices, wranglers, dealers in knotty points, as that Abderite says: 'For mortals' tongues are glib, and on them are many speeches; And a wide range for words of all sorts in this place and that.' And 'Of whatever sort the word you have spoken, of the same sort you must hear.' Inflated with this art of theirs, the wretched Sophists, babbling away in their own jargon; toiling their whole life about the division of names and the nature of the composition and conjunction of sentences, show themselves greater chatterers than turtle-doves; scratching and tickling, not in a manly way, in my opinion, the ears of those who wish to be tickled.

Strom. 1.3.3
'Such a hive of Sophists have you examined.' And similarly Iophon, the comic poet, in Flute-playing Satyrs, says: 'For there entered a band of sophists, all equipped.' Of these and the like, who devote their attention to empty words, the divine Scripture most excellently says, 'I will destroy the wisdom of the wise, and bring to nothing the understanding of the prudent.'

Strom. 1.5.1
Perchance, too, philosophy was given to the Greeks directly and primarily, till the Lord should call the Greeks. For this was a schoolmaster to bring 'the Hellenic mind,' as the law, the Hebrews, 'to Christ.' Philosophy, therefore, was a preparation, paving the way for him who is perfected in Christ.

Strom. 1.5.2
'Now,' says Solomon, 'defend wisdom, and it will exalt thee, and it will shield thee with a crown of pleasure.' For when thou hast strengthened wisdom with a cope by philosophy, and with right expenditure, thou wilt preserve it unassailable by Sophists. The way of truth is therefore one.

Strom. 1.6.3
'For hatred,' says Solomon, 'raises strife, but instruction guardeth the ways of life;' in such a way that we are not deceived nor deluded by those who are practised in base arts for the injury of those who hear. 'But instruction wanders reproachless,' it is said. We must be conversant with the art of reasoning, for the purpose of confuting the deceitful opinions of the Sophists.

Strom. 1.8.1
But the art of sophistry, which the Greeks cultivated, is a fantastic power, which makes false opinions like true by means of words. For it produces rhetoric in order to persuasion, and disputation for wrangling. These arts, therefore, if not conjoined with philosophy, will be injurious to every one. For Plato openly called sophistry 'an evil art'. And Aristotle, following him,

demonstrates it to be a dishonest art, which abstracts in a specious manner the whole business of wisdom, and professes a wisdom which it has not studied. To speak briefly, as the beginning of rhetoric is the probable, and an attempted proof the process, and the end persuasion, so the beginning of disputation is what is matter of opinion, and the process a contest, and the end victory. For in the same manner, also, the beginning of sophistry is the apparent, and the process twofold; one of rhetoric, continuous and exhaustive; and the other of logic, and is interrogatory. And its end is admiration. The dialectic in vogue in the schools, on the other hand, is the exercise of a philosopher in matters of opinion, for the sake of the faculty of disputation. But truth is not in these at all. With reason, therefore, the noble apostle, depreciating these superfluous arts occupied about words, says, 'If any man do not give heed to wholesome words, but is puffed up by a kind of teaching, knowing nothing, but doting about questions and strifes of words, whereof cometh contention, envy, railings, evil surmisings, perverse disputings of men of corrupt minds, destitute of the truth.'

*Strom.*1.8.4
For the saving Word is called 'wholesome', He being the truth; and what is wholesome (healthful) remains ever deathless. But separation from what is healthful and divine is impiety, and a deadly malady. These are rapacious wolves hid in sheep-skins, men-stealers, and glozing soul-seducers, secretly, but proved to be robbers; striving by fraud and force to catch us who are unsophisticated and have less power of speech.

*Strom.*1.8.5
'Often a man, impeded through want of words, carries less weight in expressing what is right, than the man of eloquence. But now in fluent mouths the weightiest truths they disguise, so that they do not seem what they ought to seem,' says the tragedy. Such are these wranglers, whether they follow the sects, or practise miserable dialectic arts. These are they that 'stretch the warp and weave nothing,' says the Scripture; prosecuting a bootless task, which the apostle has called 'cunning craftiness of men whereby they lie in wait to deceive'.

*Strom.*1.8.2
You see how he is moved against them, calling their art of logic—on which, those to whom this garrulous mischievous art is dear, whether Greeks or barbarians, plume themselves—a disease.

Strom. 2.2.2
For it is not spurious words which those inspired by God and those who are gained over by them adduce, nor is it snares in which the most of the Sophists entangle the young, spending their time on nought true. But those who possess the Holy Spirit 'search the deep things of God', that is, grasp the secret that is

in the prophecies. 'To impart of holy things to the dogs' is forbidden, so long as they remain beasts. For never ought those who are envious and perturbed, and still infidel in conduct, shameless in barking at investigation, to dip in the divine and clear stream of the living water...But faith, which the Greeks disparage, deeming it futile and barbarous, is a voluntary preconception the assent of piety.

Strom. 3.19.4

Seeing, however, that these heretics, and the followers of Prodicus, who wrongfully call themselves gnostics, claimed a practical indulgence in all manner of disgusting profligacies, he convicts them by arguments derived from right reason and from the Scriptures, and by human laws as well. Further, he exposes the folly of those who pretended that the less honourable parts of man are not the work of the Creator, and overwhelms their presumption by abundant argument, exploding, at the same time, their corruptions of the sacred text of the Scriptures.

Strom. 3.19.5

To relieve himself of a more particular struggle with each individual heresy, he proceeds to reduce them under two heads: Those who teach a reckless mode of life, and those who impiously affect continence. To the first, he opposes the plain propriety and duty of a decorous way of living continently; showing, that as it cannot be denied that there are certain abominable and filthy lusts, which, as such, must be shunned, therefore there is no such thing as living 'indifferently' with respect to them. He who lives to the flesh, moreover, is condemned; nor can the likeness and image of God be regained, or eternal life be ensured, save by a strict observance of divine precepts. Further, our author shows that true Christian liberty consists, not, as they vociferate, in self-indulgence, but, on the contrary, is founded in an entire freedom from perturbations of mind and passion, and from all filthy lusts.

Strom. 6.2.4

But not to protract the discourse further, in our anxiety to show the propensity of the Greeks to plagiarism in expressions and dogmas, allow us to adduce the express testimony of Hippias, the Sophist of Elea, who discourses on the point in hand, and speaks thus: 'Of these things some perchance are said by Orpheus, some briefly by Musaeus; some in one place, others in other places; some by Hesiod, some by Homer, some by the rest of the poets; and some in prose compositions, some by Greeks, some by Barbarians. And I from all these, placing together the things of most importance and of kindred character, will make the present discourse new and varied.'

Strom. 6.10.3

Now David cried, 'The righteous shall not be shaken for ever'; neither, consequently, by deceptive speech nor by erring pleasure. Whence he shall never be shaken from his own heritage. 'He shall not be afraid of evil tidings'; consequently neither of unfounded calumny, nor of the false opinion around him. No more will he dread cunning words, who is capable of distinguishing them, or of answering rightly to questions asked. Such a bulwark are dialectics, that truth cannot be trampled under foot by the Sophists.

Strom. 6.10.6
Therefore the truth that appears in the Hellenic philosophy, being partial, the real truth, like the sun glancing on the colours both white and black, shows what like each of them is. So also it exposes all sophistical plausibility. Rightly, then, was it proclaimed also by the Greeks: 'Truth the queen is the beginning of great virtue.'

Strom. 6.15.10
Knowing and learning, not from the Sophists, but from God Himself, what is well-pleasing to Him, we endeavour to do what is just and holy. Now it is well-pleasing to Him that we should be saved; and salvation is effected through both well-doing and knowledge, of both of which the Lord is the teacher.

Strom. 7.7.13
Having got to this point, I recollect the doctrines about there being no necessity to pray, introduced by certain of the heterodox, that is, the followers of the heresy of Prodicus. That they may not then be inflated with conceit about this godless wisdom of theirs, as if it were strange, let them learn that it was embraced before by the philosophers called Cyrenaics.

*Strom.*7.9.2
Whatever, therefore, he has in his mind, he bears on his tongue, to those who are worthy to hear, speaking as well as living from assent and inclination. For he both thinks and speaks the truth; unless at any time, medicinally, as a physician for the safety of the sick, he may deceive or tell an untruth, according to the Sophists.

Strom. 7.15.11
Now, of those who diverge from the truth, some attempt to deceive themselves alone, and some also their neighbours. Those, then, who are called wise in their own opinions, who think that they have found the truth, but have no true demonstration, deceive themselves in thinking that they have reached a resting-place. And of whom there is no inconsiderable multitude, who avoid investigations for fear of refutations, and shun instructions for fear of condemnation. But those who deceive those who seek access to them are very

astute; who, aware that they know nothing, yet darken the truth with plausible arguments.

Strom. 7.15.12
But, in my opinion, the nature of plausible arguments is of one character, and that of true arguments of another. And we know that it is necessary that the appellation of the heresies should be expressed in contradistinction to the truth; from which the Sophists, drawing certain things for the destruction of men, and burying them in human arts invented by themselves, glory rather in being at the head of a School than presiding over the Church?

Tertullian

De idolatria 9
After the Gospel, you will nowhere find either Sophists, Chaldeans, enchanters, diviners, or magicians, except as clearly punished. 'Where is the wise, where the grammarian, where the disputer of this age? Hath not God made foolish the wisdom of this age?'

De anima 3
The fault, I suppose, of the divine doctrine lies in its springing from Judaea rather than from Greece. Christ made a mistake, too, in sending forth fishermen to preach, rather than the Sophist. Whatever noxious vapours, accordingly, exhaled from philosophy, obscure the clear and wholesome atmosphere of truth, it will be for Christians to clear away, both by shattering to pieces the arguments which are drawn from the principles of things (I mean those of the philosophers) and by opposing to them the maxims of heavenly wisdom—that is, such as are revealed by the Lord; in order that both the pitfalls wherewith philosophy captivates the heathen may be removed, and the means employed by heresy to shake the faith of Christians may be repressed.

De anima 28
If, indeed, the Sophist of Samos is Plato's authority for the eternally revolving migration of souls out of a constant alternation of the dead and the living states, then no doubt did the famous Pythagoras, however excellent in other respects, for the purpose of fabricating such an opinion as this, rely on a falsehood, which was not only shameful, but also hazardous.

De carne Christi 23.1
We discover, then, what the sign is which is to be spoken against – the conception and the parturition of the Virgin Mary, concerning which these Sophists say: 'She a virgin and yet not a virgin bare, and yet did not bear'; just as if such language, if indeed it must be uttered, would not be more suitable even for ourselves to use! For 'she bare', because she produced offspring of her

own flesh and 'yet she did not bear', since she produced Him not from a husband's seed; she was 'a virgin,' so far as (abstinence) from a husband went, and 'yet not a virgin', as regards her bearing a child. There is not, however, that parity of reasoning which the heretics affect: in other words it does not follow that for the reason 'she did not bear', she who was 'not a virgin' was 'yet a virgin', even because she became a mother without any fruit of her own womb. But with us there is no equivocation, nothing twisted into a double sense. Light is light; and darkness, darkness; yea is yea; and nay, nay; 'whatsoever is more than these cometh of evil'. She who bare (really) bare; and although she was a virgin when she conceived, she was a wife when she brought forth her son.

Apologeticus pro Christianis 47.1
Unless I am utterly mistaken, there is nothing so old as the truth; and the already proved antiquity of the divine writings is so far of use to me, that it leads men more easily to take it in that they are the treasure-source whence all later wisdom has been taken. And were it not necessary to keep my work to a moderate size, I might launch forth also into the proof of this. What poet or Sophist has not drunk at the fountain of the prophets?

Origen

Contra Celsus 2.31
He next charges the Christians with being 'guilty of sophistical reasoning, in saying that the Son of God is the Logos Himself'. And he thinks that he strengthens the accusation, because 'when we declare the Logos to be the Son of God, we do not present to view a pure and holy Logos, but a most degraded man, who was punished by scourging and crucifixion'.

C. Cels. 3.39
And we have confidence also in the intentions of the writers of the Gospels, observing their piety and conscientiousness, manifested in their writings, which contain nothing that is spurious, or deceptive, or false, or cunning; for it is evident to us that souls unacquainted with those artifices which are taught by the cunning sophistry of the Greeks (which is characterised by great plausibility and acuteness), and by the kind of rhetoric in vogue in the courts of justice, would not have been able thus to invent occurrences which are fitted of themselves to conduct to faith, and to a life in keeping with faith. And I am of opinion that it was on this account that Jesus wished to employ such persons as teachers of His doctrines, viz., that there might be no ground for any suspicion of plausible sophistry, but that it might clearly appear to all who were capable of understanding, that the guileless purpose of the writers being, so to speak, marked with great simplicity, was deemed worthy of being accompanied by a diviner power, which accomplished far more than it seemed possible could be

accomplished by a periphrasis of words, and a weaving of sentences, accompanied by all the distinctions of Grecian art.

C. Cels. 4.25
And although a man may be an orator like Demosthenes, yet, if stained with wickedness like his, and guilty of deeds proceeding, like his, from a wicked nature; or an Antiphon, who was also considered to be indeed an orator, yet who annihilated the doctrine of providence in his writings, which were entitled Concerning Truth, like that discourse of Celsus—such individuals are notwithstanding worms, rolling in a comer of the dung-heap of stupidity and ignorance. Indeed, whatever be the nature of the rational faculty, it could not reasonably be compared to a worm, because it possesses capabilities of virtue. For these adumbrations towards virtue do not allow of those who possess the power of acquiring it, and who are incapable of wholly losing its seeds, to be likened to a worm.

Gregory Thaumaturgus

Oratio Panegyrica 1.13
For a mighty thing and energetic is the discourse of man, and subtle with its sophisms, and quick to find its way into the cars, and mould the mind, and impress us with what it conveys; and when once it has taken possession of us, it can win us over to love it as truth; and it holds its place within us even though it be false and deceitful, overmastering us like some enchanter, and retaining as its champion the very man it has deluded.

Origen

De Principiis 1.8.4
...sink into the condition of irrational animals, either large or small; and in support of these assertions they generally quote some pretended statements of Scripture, such as, that a beast, to which a woman has unnaturally prostituted herself, shall be deemed equally guilty with the woman, and shall be ordered to be stoned; or that a bull which strikes with its horn, shall be put to death in the same way; or even the speaking of Balaam's ass, when God opened its mouth, and the dumb beast of burden, answering with human voice, reproved the madness of the prophet. All of which assertions we not only do not receive, but, as being contrary to our belief, we refute and reject. After the refutation and rejection of such perverse opinions, we shall show, at the proper time and place, how those passages which they quote from the sacred Scriptures ought to be understood.

Minucius Felix

Octavius 31.1

And of the incestuous banqueting, the plotting of demons has falsely devised an enormous fable against us, to stain the glory of our modesty, by the loathing excited by an outrageous infamy, that before inquiring into the truth it might turn men away from us by the terror of an abominable charge. It was thus your own Fronto acted in this respect: he did not produce testimony, as one who alleged a charge, but he scattered reproaches as a rhetorician. For these things have rather originated from your own nations.

Cyprian

Epistles of Cyprian 74.23

What, then, is to be made of what is written, 'Abstain from strange water, and drink not from a strange fountain', if, leaving the sealed fountain of the Church, you take up strange water for your own, and pollute the Church with unhallowed fountains? For when you communicate with the baptism of heretics, what else do you do than drink from their slough and mud; and while you yourself are purged with the Church's sanctification, you become befouled with the contact of the filth of others?

Bibliography

Adams, E. "Where Is the Promise of His Coming? The Complaint of the Scoffers in 2 Peter 3.4." *NTS* 51 (2005): 106-22.

Adams, Sean A. "The Tradition of Peter's Literacy: Acts, 1 Peter, and Petrine Literature." In *Peter in Early Christianity*, edited by Helen K. Bond and Larry W. Hurtado. Grand Rapids: Eerdmans, 2015.

Aland, Barbara, Kurt Aland, Johannes Karavidopoulos, Carlo M Martini, and Bruce M Metzger, eds. *The Greek New Testament*. 4th Revised ed. Stuttgart: Deutsche Bibelgesellschaft, 1998.

Aland, Kurt, Donald Guthrie, A.Q. Morton, and et al., eds. *The Authorship and Integrity of the New Testament*. London: SPCK, 1965.

Alesse, Francesca, ed. *Philo of Alexandria and Post-Aristotelian Philosophy*. Edited by Francesca Calabi and Robert Berchman. Vol. 5, Studies in Philo of Alexandria. Leiden: Brill, 2008.

Alexander Jr, Manuele. "The Art of Periodic Composition in Philo of Alexandria." In *The Studia Philonica Annual: Studies in Hellenistic Judaism*, edited by David T. Runia, 133-50. Atlanta, Georgia: Scholars Press, 1991.

Alexander, T. Desmond, and Brian S. Rosner, eds. *New Dictionary of Biblical Theology*. Downers Grove: IVP, 2000.

Algra, Keimpe. "Epictetus and Stoic Theology." In *The Philosophy of Epictetus*, edited by Theodore Scaltsas and Andrew S. Mason, 32-55. New York: OUP, 2007.

Anderson, Graham. *Sage, Saint, and Sophist: Holy Men and Their Associates in the Early Roman Empire*. New York: Routledge, 1994.

—. *The Second Sophistic: A Cultural Phenomenon in the Roman Empire*. New York: Routledge, 1993.

—. "The Second Sophistic: Some Problems of Perspective." In *Antonine Literature*, edited by Russell, 91-110. Oxford, 1990.

Arnold, E.V. *Roman Stoicism*. Cambridge, 1911.

Ballif, Michelle, and Michael G. Moran, eds. *Classical Rhetorics and Rhetoricians: Critical Studies and Sources*. Westport, Conn.: Praeger, 2005.

—. "Introduction." In *Classical Rhetorics and Rhetoricians: Critical Studies and Sources*, edited by M. Ballif and M.G. Moran, 1-13. Westport, Conn.: Praeger, 2005.

Barclay, John M.G. *Jews in the Mediterranean Diaspora: From Alexander to Trajan (323 B.C.E – 117 C.E)*. Edinburgh: T&T Clark, 1996.

Barclay, John M.G., and Simon J. Gathercole, eds. *Divine and Human Agency in Paul and His Cultural Environment*. Edited by John M.G. Barclay, Early Christianity in Context, Library of New Testament Studies. New York: T&T Clark, 2006.

Barclay, William. *The Letters of James and Peter*. 2003 ed. Louisville: Westminster John Knox Press, 1958.

Barnes. *Logic and the Imperial Stoa*. Leiden: Brill, 1997.

Bibliography

Barnett, Paul. *Jesus & the Rise of Early Christianity: A History of New Testament Times*. Downers Grove: IVP Academic, 1999.
Bartlett, John, ed. *Jews in the Hellenistic and Roman Cities*. London and New York: Routledge, 2002.
Barton, Carlin. *The Sorrows of the Ancient Romans*. Princeton, 1993.
Bauckham, Richard J. "2 Peter: A Supplementary Bibliography." *JETS* 25 (1982): 91-93.
—. "2 Peter: An Account of Research." *ANRW* 2.25.5 (1988): 3713-52.
—. "The Delay of the Parousia." *TynB* 31 (1981): 3-36.
—. *Jesus and the Eyewitnesses: The Gospels as Eyewitness Testimony*. Michigan: Eerdmans, 2006.
—. *Jude, 2 Peter*, Word Biblical Commentary. Waco: Word, 1980.
—. "Life, Death, and the Afterlife in Second Temple Judaism." In *Life in the Face of Death: The Resurrection Message of the New Testament*, edited by R. Longenecker, 80-95. Grand Rapids: Eerdmans, 1998.
—. "Pseudo-Apostolic Letters." *JBL* 107 (1988): 469-94.
Beale, G.K., and D.A. Carson, eds. *Commentary on the New Testament Use of the Old Testament*. Grand Rapids: Baker Academic, 2007.
Benko, Stephen. *Pagan Rome and the Early Christians*. London: Batsford, 1985.
Betz, Otto. "The Concept of the So-Called 'Divine Man' in Mark's Christology." In *Studies in New Testament and Early Christian Literature: Essays in Honor of Allen P. Wikgren* (*NovT, Suppl. 33*), edited by Allen Paul Wikgren and David Edward Aune. Leiden: Brill, 1972.
Bigg, Charles. *A Critical and Exegetical Commentary on the Epistles of St. Peter and St. Jude*. Edinburgh: T&T Clark, 1901.
Billings, T.H. "The Platonism of Philo Judaeus." diss. Chicago, 1919.
Birnbaum, Ellen. "Philo on the Greeks: A Jewish Perspective on Culture and Society in First-Century Alexandria." In *The Studia Philonica Annual*, edited by David T. Runia and Gregory E. Sterling. Providence, RI: Brown Judaic Studies, 2001.
—. "Portrayals of the Wise and Virtuous in Alexandrian Jewish Works: Jews Perceptions of Themselves and Others." In *Ancient Alexandria between Egypt and Greece*, edited by W.V. Harris and G. Ruffini, 125-60. Leiden and Boston: Brill, 2004.
Bolt, Peter G. "Life, Death, and the Afterlife in the Greco-Roman World." In *Life in the Face of Death: The Resurrection Message of the New Testament*, edited by R. Longenecker, 51-79. Grand Rapids: Eerdmans, 1998.
Bonhöffer, Adolf. *Epictet Und Die Stoa*. Stuttgart: Enke, 1890.
Borgen, Peder. *Early Christianity and Hellenistic Judaism*. Edinburgh: T&T Clark, 1996.
—. "Philo of Alexandria – a Systematic Philosopher or an Eclectic Editor? An Examination of His *Exposition of the Laws of Moses*." *Symbolae Osloenses* 71.1 (1996): 115-34.
—. *Philo of Alexandria – an Exegete for His Time*. Leiden: Brill, 1997.
—. "Philo of Alexandria. A Critical and Synthetical Survey of Research since

World War II." In *ANRW II*, 1984.

—. *Philo, John and Paul: New Perspectives on Judaism and Early Christianity*, Brown Judaic Studies. Atlanta, Georgia: Scholars Press, 1987.

—. "The Sabbath Controversy in John 5:1-18 and Analogous Controversy Reflected in Philo's Writings." In *The Studia Philonica Annual: Studies in Hellenistic Judaism*, edited by David T. Runia, 209-21. Atlanta, Georgia: Scholars Press, 1991.

Bowersock, G.W. *Greek Sophists in the Roman Empire*. Oxford: Clarendon Press, 1969.

Bowie, E.L. "The Importance of the Sophists." In *Yale Classical Studies*, 29-59 Cambridge: CUP, 1982.

—. "Philostratus: The Life of a Sophist." In *Philostratus*, edited by E.L. Bowie and J. Elsner, 19-32. Cambridge: CUP, 2009.

Brennan, Tad. *The Stoic Life: Emotions, Duties, and Fate*. New York: OUP, 2005.

Brennan, T., and C. Brittain. *Simplicius: On Epictetus' Handbook 27-53*. Ithaca and London: Duckworth and Cornell, 2002.

Brower, Kent E., and Andy Johnson, eds. *Holiness and Ecclesiology in the New Testament*. Grand Rapids: Eerdmans, 2007.

Brown, John. *Parting Counsels: An Exposition of 2 Peter 1*, Geneva Series Commentary. Chatham: Banner of Truth, 1856; reprint 1980.

Brown, Raymond E., Karl P. Donfried, and John Reumann, eds. *Peter in the New Testament: A Collaborative Assessment by Protestant and Roman Catholic Scholars*. Minneapolis: Augsburg, 1973.

Bruce, F.F. *Paul: Apostle of the Heart Set Free*. Grand Rapids: Eerdmans, 1977.

—. *The Speeches in the Acts of the Apostles*. London, 1942.

Brueggemann, W. "A Convergence in Recent Old Testament Theologies." *JSOT 18* 18 (1980): 3-10.

Brunt, P.A. "The Bubble of the Second Sophistic." *BCIS* 39 (1994): 25-52.

Burkhardt, H. *Die Inspiration Heiliger Schriften Bei Philo Von Alexandrien*. Basel: Giessen, 1988.

Calvin, John. *Commentaries on the Catholic Epistles*. Grand Rapids: Eerdmans, 1948.

Carr, David. "The Cardinal Virtues and Plato's Moral Psychology." *Philosophical Quarterly* 38.151 (1988): 186-200.

Carson, D.A. "2 Peter." In *Commentary on the New Testament Use of the Old Testament*, edited by G.K. Beale and D.A. Carson, 1047-62. Grand Rapids: Baker Academic, 2007.

—. "Divine Sovereignty and Human Responsibility in Philo: Analysis and Method." *Novum Testamentum* XXIII.2 (1981): 148-64.

Carter, Elizabeth. *The Moral Discourses of Epictetus*. London: J.M. Dent & Sons, 1910.

Caulley, Thomas Scott "The False Teachers in Second Peter." *Studia Biblica et Theologica* 12 (1982): 27-42.

Chadwick, Henry. "Enkrateia." *RAC* 5 (1962): 343-65.

Chae, D.J. *Paul as Apostle to the Gentiles*. Feltham: Paternoster, 1997.
Charles, J.D. *1-2 Peter, Jude*. Scottdale, PA: Herald, 1999.
—. "The Language and Logic of Virtue in 2 Peter 1:5-7." *BBR* 8 (1998): 55-73.
—. *Virtue Amidst Vice: The Catalog of Virtues in 2 Peter 1*. JSNTSup. Sheffield: Sheffield Academic, 1997.
Charlesworth, James H. "Pseudonymity and Pseudepigraphy." In *Anchor Bible Dictionary*, 540-41. New York: Doubleday, 1992.
Charlesworth, Martin Percival. *Five Men: Character Studies from the Roman Empire*. Vol. VI, Martin Classical Lectures. Cambridge: Harvard University Press, 1936.
Childs, Brevard. *The New Testament as Canon: An Introduction*. Philadelphia: Fortress, 1984.
Cicero. "De Natura Deorum." In *Cambridge Greek and Latin Classics*, edited by Andrew R. Dyck. Cambridge: CUP, 2003.
—. *De Natura Deorum*. Translated by H. Rackham, LCL. Cambridge, Mass.: Harvard University Press, 1933.
Clark, Gillian, and Tessa Rajak. "Introduction: Philosophy and Power." In *Philosophy and Power in the Graeco-Roman World*, edited by Gillian Clark and Tessa Rajak, 1-10. Oxford and New York: OUP, 2002.
Clarke, Andrew D., and Bruce W. Winter, eds. *One God, One Lord: Christianity in a World of Religious Pluralism*. 2nd ed. Grand Rapids and Carlisle: Baker and Paternoster, 1992.
Clark-Soles, Jaime. *Death and the Afterlife in the New Testament*. London and New York: T&T Clark, 2006.
Cohen, Naomi. *Philo Judaeus: His Universe and Discourse*. Edited by M. Augustin and M. Mach. Vol. 24, Beataj. Frankfurt am Main: Peter Lang, 1995.
Colardeau, Théodore. *Étude Sur Épictète*. Paris: A. Fontemoing, 1903.
Coleman, Paul W. *Second Peter and Jude*, The Deeper Life Pulpit Commentary. Camp Hill, PA: Christian Publications, 2000.
Colish, Marcia L. *The Stoic Tradition from Antiquity to the Early Middle Ages*. Leiden: Brill, 1985.
Cooper, John M. "The Relevance of Moral Theory to Moral Improvement in Epictetus." In *The Philosophy of Epictetus*, edited by Theodore Scaltsas and Andrew S. Mason, 9-19. New York: OUP, 2007.
Corbelli, Judith A. *The Art of Death in Graeco-Roman Egypt*. Princes Risborough: Shire, 2006.
Corley, B. "Interpreting Paul's Conversion – Then and Now." In *The Road from Damascus*, edited by R. Longenecker, 1-17. Grand Rapids: Eerdmans, 1997.
Craddock, Fred B. *First and Second Peter and Jude*. Louisville, Kentucky: Westminster John Knox Press, 1995.
Cranfield, C.E.B. *1 and 2 Peter and Jude*. London: SCM, 1960.
Crivelli, Paolo "Epictetus and Logic." In *The Philosophy of Epictetus*, edited by Theodore Scaltsas and Andrew S. Mason, 20-31. New York: OUP, 2007.
Cullman, Oscar. *Peter: Disciple-Apostle-Martyr*. Translated by F.V. Filson.

London: SCM, 1953.
Davids, Peter H. *The First Epistle of Peter*, The New International Commentary on the New Testament. Grand Rapids: Eerdmans, 1990.
—. *The Letters of 2 Peter and Jude*, Pillar New Testament Commentary. Grand Rapids: Eerdmans, 2006.
—. "Peter." In *Dictionary of the Bible*, edited by David Noel Freedman, 1035-36. Grand Rapids: Eerdmans, 2000.
Davies, W.D.,. *The Setting of the Sermon on the Mount*. Cambridge, 1964.
de Silva, David. *Honor, Patronage, Kinship, and Purity: Unlocking New Testament Culture*. Downers Grove: IVP, 2000.
Delia, Diana. "Philo's Alexandria (Book Review). "*International Journal of the Classical Tradition* 7.2 (2000): 283.
Didymus, Arius. *Arius Didymus: Epitome of Stoic Ethics*. Edited by Arthur J. Pomeroy. Atlanta, Georgia: Society of Biblical Literature, 1999.
Dillon, J.M. *The Middle Platonists: A Study of Platonism 80 B.C. To A.D. 220*. London: Duckworth, 1977.
Dillon, J.T. *Musonius Rufus and Education in the Good Life*. Lanham, Maryland: University Press of America, 2004.
Dobbin, Robert F. *Epictetus Discourses Book I*. Oxford: Clarendon, 1998.
Droge, Arthur J., and James D. Tabor. *A Noble Death : Suicide and Martyrdom among Christians and Jews in Antiquity*. 1st ed. San Francisco: HarperSanFrancisco, 1992.
Drummond, James. *Philo Judaeus, or the Jewish-Alexandrian Philosophy in Its Development and Completion*. 2 vols. London: Williams and Norgate, 1888.
Duff, R.A. "Virtues and Vices (Book). "*Philosophical Quarterly* 30.118 (1980): 86-88.
Dumbrell, William. *The Search for Order: Biblical Eschatology in Focus*. Grand Rapids: Baker, 1994.
Dunnett, W.M. "The Hermeneutics of Jude and 2 Peter: The Use of Ancient Jewish Traditions." *JETS* 31 (1988): 287-92.
Dyck, Johnathan. "Philo, Alexandria and Empire: The Politics of Allegorical Interpretation." In *Jews in the Hellenistic and Roman Cities*, edited by John Bartlett. London and New York: Routledge, 2002.
Easton, B.S. "New Testament Ethical Lists." *JBL* 51 (1932): 1-12.
Edwards, Catharine. *Death in Ancient Rome*. London: Yale University Press, 2007.
—. "Senecan Philosophy (Reading Seneca: Stoic Philosophy at Rome) (Book Review)." *Classical Review* 57.1 (2007): 118(3).
Elliot, J.H. *I-Ii Peter, Jude*, Acnt. Minneapolis: Augsburg, 1982.
Engberg-Pedersen, Troels. "Paul, Virtues, and Vices." In *Paul in the Greco-Roman World*, edited by J. Paul Sampley, 608-33. Harrisburg, P.A.: Trinity Press International, 2003.
Epictetus. *Discourses*. Translated by W.A. Oldfather, LCL. Cambridge: Harvard University Press.
Ewin, R.E. "Loyalty and Virtues." *Philosophical Quarterly* 42.169 (1992): 403.
Ferguson, Everett. *Backgrounds of Early Christianity*. Grand Rapids:

Eerdmans, 1987.
Fischel, H.A. "The Uses of Sorites (*Climax, Gradation)* in the Tannaitic Period." *HUCA* 44 (1973): 119-51.
Fitzgerald, John T., ed. *Passions and Moral Progress in Greco-Roman Thought*, Routledge Monographs in Classical Studies. London and New York: Routledge, 2008.
Fitzmyer, Joseph. "The Name Simon." In *Essays on the Semitic Background of the New Testament*, 105-12. SBLSBS 5. Missoula, MT: Scholars Press, 1974.
Forbes, Christopher. "Paul and Rhetorical Comparison." In *Paul in the Greco-Roman World*, edited by J. Paul Sampley, 134-71. Harrisburg, P.A.: Trinity Press International, 2003.
Fornberg, Tord. *An Early Church in a Pluralistic Society*, Coniectanea Biblica: New Testament Series 9. Lund: Carl Bloms Boktryckeri, 1977.
Fossum, Jarl. "Social and Institutional Conditions for Early Jewish and Christian Interpretation of the Hebrew Bible, with Special Regard to Religious Groups and Sects." In *Hebrew Bible / Old Testament: The History of Its Interpretation*, edited by Magne Sæbø, 239-55. Göttingen: Vandenhoeck & Ruprecht, 1996.
Frick, Peter. *Divine Providence in Philo of Alexandria*. Edited by Martin Hengel and Peter (a:) Schafer, Texts and Studies in Ancient Judaism. Tübingen: Mohr Siebeck, 1999.
Galloway, Lincoln E. *Freedom in the Gospel: Paul's Exemplum in 1 Cor 9 in Conversation with the Discourses of Epictetus and Philo*. Leuven: Peeters, 2004.
Garland, Robert. *The Greek Way of Death*. Ithaca, New York: Cornell University Press, 1985.
Gerdmar, A. *Rethinking the Judaism-Hellenism Dichotomy: A Historiographical Study of Second Peter and Jude*, Coniectanea Biblica: New Testament Series. Stockholm: Almqvist & Wiksell, 2001.
Gerhardsson, Birger. *Memory and Manuscript: Oral Tradition and Written Transmission in Rabbinic Judaism and Early Christianity*, Acta Seminarii Neotestamentici Upsaliensis. Copenhagen: Ejnar Munksgaard, 1961.
Giles, Kevin. "Apostles before and after Paul." *Churchman* 99.3 (1985): 241-56.
Gill, Christopher. "The School in the Roman Imperial Period." In *The Cambridge Companion to the Stoics*, edited by Brad Inwood, 33-58. New York: CUP, 2003.
Gill, David W.J., and Conrad Gempf, eds. *The Book of Acts in Its Graeco-Roman Setting*. Edited by Bruce W. Winter. Vol. 2, The Book of Acts in Its First Century Setting. Grand Rapids and Carlisle: Eerdmans and Paternoster, 1994.
Gilmour, Michael J. "Reflections on the Authorship of 2 Peter." *EvQ* 73 (2001): 291-309.
—. *The Significance of Parallels between 2 Peter and Other Early Christian Literature*. Edited by M.A. Powell, Academia Biblica. Atlanta: Society of

Biblical Literature, 2002.

Glatzer, Nahum N., ed. *The Essential Philo.* New York: Schocken, 1971.

Goldhill, Simon, ed. *Being Greek under Rome: Cultural Identity, the Second Sophistic and the Development of Empire.* Cambridge: CUP, 2001.

Goldingay, John. "The 'Salvation History' Perspective and the 'Wisdom' Perspective within the Context of Biblical Theology." *EvQ* 51 (1979): 194-207.

Goodenough, Erwin R. *An Introduction to Philo Judaeus.* Oxford: Basil Blackwell, 1962.

Green, Gene L. *Jude and 2 Peter*, Baker Exegetical Commentary on the New Testament. Grand Rapids: Baker Academic, 2008.

Green, Michael. *2 Peter and Jude.* 2009 ed, Tyndale New Testament Commentaries. Nottingham: IVP, 1985.

Guhl, E., and W. Koner. *The Romans: Their Life and Customs.* London: Senate, 1994.

Guthrie, Donald. *New Testament Introduction.* Downers Grove, Illinois: IVP, 1990.

Hadot, Pierre. *Philosophy as a Way of Life: Spiritual Exercises from Socrates to Foucault.* Oxford Blackwell, 1995.

Hankinson, R.J. "Stoic Epistemology." In *The Cambridge Companion to the Stoics*, edited by Brad Inwood, 59-84. New York: CUP, 2003.

Harrington, Daniel J. *1 Peter, Jude and 2 Peter.* Vol. 15, Sacra Pagina. Collegeville, Minnesota: Liturgical, 2003.

Hay, David M. "Philo's References to Other Allegorists." In *Studia Philonica*, 1979/80.

—. "Philo's View of Himself as an Exegete." In *The Studia Philonica Annual: Studies in Hellenistic Judaism*, edited by David T. Runia, 40-52. Atlanta, Georgia: Scholars Press, 1991.

Hays, Richard B. *The Moral Vision of the New Testament: A Contemporary Introduction to New Testament Ethics.* San Francisco: Harper Collins, 1996.

Helyer, Larry R. *The Life and Witness of Peter.* Downers Grove: IVP Academic, 2012.

Hengel, Martin. *Saint Peter: The Underestimated Apostle.* Translated by Thomas H. Trapp. Grand Rapids: Eerdmans, 2010.

—. *The Hellenization of Judaea in the First Century after Christ.* London: SCM, 1989.

—. *Judaism and Hellenism : Studies in Their Encounter in Palestine During the Early Hellenistic Period.* London: SCM, 1974.

Henten, J.W. van, and Friedrich Avemarie. *Martyrdom and Noble Death: Selected Texts from Graeco-Roman, Jewish, and Christian Antiquity*, The Context of Early Christianity. London; New York: Routledge, 2002.

Higginson, Thomas W. "The Works of Epictetus. Consisting of His Discourses, in Four Books, the Enchiridion, and Fragments. A Translation from the Greek Based on That of Elizabeth Carter." Boston: Little, Brown, and Co., 1865.

Hijmans. *Askesis: Notes on Epictetus' Educational System.* Assen: von

Gorkam, 1959.

Hillyer, Norman. *New International Biblical Commentary: 1 and 2 Peter, Jude*. Edited by W. Ward Gasque. Peabody, MA: Hendrickson, 1992.

Hock, Ronald F. ""By the Gods, It's My One Desire to See an Actual Stoic": Epictetus' Relation with Students and Visitors in His Personal Network." *Semeia* 56 (1991): 121-42.

Hope, Valerie M. *Death in Ancient Rome: A Sourcebook*. Abingdon: Routledge, 2007.

Hopkins, Keith. *Death and Renewal*. Cambridge: CUP, 1983.

Horsley, G.H.R., ed. *New Documents Illustrating Early Christianity*. Vol. 2. Sydney: Macquarie University Ancient Documentary Research Centre, 1982.

House, Paul R. *Old Testament Theology*. Downers Grove: IVP, 1998.

Hübner, Hans. "New Testament Interpretation of the Old Testament." In *Hebrew Bible / Old Testament: The History of Its Interpretation*, edited by Magne Sæbø, 332-72. Göttingen: Vandenhoeck & Ruprecht, 1996.

Hudry, Jean-Louis. "Self: Ancient and Modern Insights About Individuality, Life, and Death." *Philosophical Quarterly* 57.229 (2007): 686-88.

Bond, Helen K. and Hurtado, Larry W., ed. *Peter in Early Christianity*. Grand Rapids: Eerdmans, 2015.

Ierodiakonou, Katerina. "The Philosopher as God's Messenger." In *The Philosophy of Epictetus*, edited by Theodore Scaltsas and Andrew S. Mason, 56-70. New York: OUP, 2007.

Inwood, B., ed. *The Cambridge Companion to the Stoics*. New York: CUP, 2003.

Inwood, Brad. *Ethics and Human Action in Early Stoicism*. Oxford: OUP, 1985.

Jackson, David R. *Enochic Judaism: Three Defining Paradigm Exemplars*. New York: T&T Clark, 2004.

James, M.R. *The Second Epistle General of Peter and the Epistle of Jude*, Cambridge Greek Testament for Schools and Colleges. Cambridge: CUP, 1912.

Jeffers, James S. *The Greco-Roman World of the New Testament*. Downers Grove: IVP, 1999.

Jobes, Karen H. *1 Peter*, Baker Exegetical Commentary on the New Testament. Grand Rapids, MI: Baker Academic, 2005.

Johnson, L.T. "Conflict and Christian Self-Definition." *Bible Translator* 25 (1987): 215-19.

Johnston, David. "The Jurists." In *The Cambridge History of Greek and Roman Political Thought*, edited by C. Rowe and Malcolm Schofield, 616-32. Cambridge: CUP, 2000.

Josephus. *The Works of Josephus: Complete and Unabridged*. Translated by William Whiston. Peabody, MA: Hendrickson, 1987.

Judge, Edwin A. *The First Christians in the Roman World : Augustan and New Testament Essays*. Edited by James R. Harrison. Tübingen: Mohr Siebeck, 2008.

Judge, Edwin A. *Social Distinctives of the Christians in the First Century: Pivotal Essays by E.A. Judge*. Edited by David M. Scholer. Massachusetts: Hendrickson, 2008.

Käsemann, Ernst. "An Apologia for Primitive Christian Eschatology." In *Essays on New Testament Themes*, 169-95. London: SCM, 1964.

Kelly, J.N.D. *A Commentary on the Epistles of Peter and of Jude*. London: Adam and Charles Black, 1969.

Kennedy, George A. *Greek Rhetoric under Christian Emperors*. Princeton: Princeton University Press, 1983.

Kent, J.H. *Corinth: Inscriptions 1926-1960*. Princeton: The American School of Classical Studies at Athens, 1966.

Kinzig, Wolfram. *In Search of Asterius: Studies on the Authorship of the Homilies on the Psalms*, Forschungen Zur Kirchen - Und Dogmengeschischte 47. Göttingen: Vandenhoeck & Ruprecht, 1990.

Kistemaker, Simon J. *Peter and Jude*. Welwyn, Hertfordshire: Evangelical Press, 1987.

Knight, Jonathan. *2 Peter and Jude*. Edited by A.T. Lincoln, New Testament Guides. Sheffield: Sheffield Academic, 1995.

Knoch, Otto. "Däs Vermächtnis Des Petrus: Der 2. Petrusbrief." In *Wort Gottes in Der Zeit: Festschrift Karl Hermann Schelkle*, edited by H. Feld and J. Nolte, 65-81. Patmos: Düsseldorf, 1973.

Köstenberger, A.J., and P.T. O'Brien. *Salvation to the Ends of the Earth*. Ebbw Vale, Wales: Apollos, 2001.

Kraftchick, S.J. *Jude, 2 Peter*, Abington New Testament Commentaries. Nashville: Abington, 2002.

Kümmel, W.G. *Introduction to the New Testament*. London: SCM, 1975.

Kyle, Donald G. *Spectacles of Death in Ancient Rome*. London and New York: Routledge, 1998.

Laertius, D., and R.D. Hicks. *Lives of Eminent Philosophers*: William Heinemann, 1925.

Lee, Simon S. *Jesus' Transfiguration and the Believers' Transformation : A Study of the Transfiguration and Its Development in Early Christian Writings*. Tübingen, Germany: Mohr Siebeck, 2009.

Leisegang, H. "Der Gottmensch Als Archetypus." *ErJb 18 [Aus der Welt der Urbilder: Sonderband für C.G. Jung zum fünfundsiebzigsten Geburtstag, 26. Juli 1950]* (1950): 9-45.

Leithart, Peter J. *The Promise of His Appearing: An Exposition of Second Peter*. Moscow, Idaho: Canon, 2004.

Leonhardt-Balzer, Jutta. *Jewish Worship in Philo of Alexandria*, Texte Und Studien Zum Antiken Judentum. Tübingen: Mohr Siebeck, 2001.

Lévy, Carlos. "Philo's Ethics." In *The Cambridge Companion to Philo*, edited by Adam Kamesar, 146-74. New York: CUP, 2009.

Liddell, Henry George, and Robert Scott. *A Greek-English Lexicon*. 9 ed. Oxford: Clarendon, 1990.

Llewelyn, Stephen R. "The Epitaph of a Student Who Died Away from Home." In *New Documents Illustrating Early Christianity*, edited by Stephen R.

Bibliography

Llewelyn. Grand Rapids: Eerdmans, 1998.

Long, A.A. *Epictetus: A Stoic and Socratic Guide to Life*. Oxford: Clarendon, 2002.

———. *From Epicurus to Epictetus: Studies in Hellenistic and Roman Philosophy*. Oxford: Clarendon, 2006.

———. *Hellenistic Philosophy: Stoics, Epicureans, Sceptics*. Second ed. Berkeley and Los Angeles: University of California Press, 1986.

———, ed. *Problems in Stoicism*. New York: OUP, 1971.

———. "Soul and Body in Stoicism." *The Center for Hermeneutical Studies* 36 (1980).

———. *Stoic Studies*. Cambridge: CUP, 1996.

Louw, Johannes P, and Eugene A Nida. *Greek-English Lexicon of the New Testament Based on Semantic Domains*. 2nd ed. New York: United Bible Societies, 1988.

Lucas, Dick, and Christopher Green. *The Message of 2 Peter & Jude*. Edited by John Stott, The Bible Speaks Today. Leicester: IVP, 1995.

Lutz, C. "Musonius Rufus: The Roman Socrates." *Yale Classical Studies* 10 (1947): 1-147.

Mack, Burton L. "Philo and Exegetical Traditions in Alexandria." *ANRW* 2.21.1 (1984): 242ff.

Marshal, H. "A New Understanding of the Present and the Future: Paul and Eschatology." In *The Road from Damascus*, edited by R. Longenecker. Grand Rapids: Eerdmans, 1997.

Martin, Dale B. *Slavery as Salvation: The Metaphor of Slavery in Pauline Christianity*. New Haven: Hale University Press, 1990.

Mayor, Joseph B. *The Epistle of Saint Jude and the Second Epistle of Saint Peter*. Grand Rapids: Baker, 1965.

McLaren, James S. *Power and Politics in Palestine: The Jews and the Governing of Their Land 100 Bc-Ad 70*, Jsntsupp 63. Sheffield: Sheffield Academic, 1991.

Meade, David G. *An Investigation into the Relationship of Authorship and Authority in Jewish and Early Christian Tradition*. Grand Rapids: Eerdmans, 1986.

———. *Pseudonymity and Canon: An Investigation into the Relationship of Authorship and Authority in Jewish and Earliest Christian Tradition*. Grand Rapids: Eerdmans, 1986.

Meeks, Wayne A. *The Moral World of the First Christians*. Philadelphia: Westminster, 1986.

Mendelson, Alan. *Philo's Jewish Identity*, Brown Judaic Studies. Atlanta: Scholars Press, 1988.

———. *Secular Education in Philo of Alexandria*. Cincinnati: Union College Press, 1982.

Metzger, Bruce. *The Canon of the New Testament: Its Origin, Development, and Significance*. Oxford: Clarendon, 1987.

———. *A Textual Commentary on the Greek New Testament*. 2nd ed. Stuttgart: United Bible Society, 1994.

Michaels, J. Ramsay. *1 Peter*, Word Biblical Commentary. Waco: Word, 1988.
Miller, Robert J. "Is There Independent Attestation for the Transfiguration in 2 Peter?" *NTS* 42 (1996): 620-25.
Modrzejewski, J.M. *The Jews of Egypt: From Ramses II to Emperor Hadrian.* Princeton, 1997.
Moffatt, James. *The General Epistles: James, Peter, and Judas*, The Moffatt New Testament Commentary. London: Hodder and Stoughton, 1947.
Moles, J.L. "The Career and Conversion of Dio Chrysostom." *Journal of Roman Studies* 68 (1978): 79-100.
Moltmann, Jürgen. *The Coming of God.* Translated by Margaret Kohl. Minneapolis: Fortress, 1996.
Moo, D.J. *2 Peter, Jude*, NIV Application Commentary. Grand Rapids: Zondervan, 1996.
—. *The Epistle to the Romans*, New International Commentary on the New Testament. Grand Rapids: Eerdmans, 1996.
Mortley, R.J. "The Past in Clement of Alexandria: A Study of an Attempt to Define Christianity in Socio-Cultural Terms." In *The Shaping of Christianity in the Second and Third Centuries: Jewish and Christian Self-Definition*, edited by E.P. Sanders, 186-200. Philadelphia: Fortress, 1980.
—. *The Problem of Knowledge in Late Antiquity*, Protocol Series of the Colloquies of the Center: The Center, 1978.
Moulton, J.H. *A Grammar of N.T. Greek.* Vol. I, 1908.
Munck, J. *Paul and the Salvation of Mankind.* Norwich: SCM, 1959.
Murphy, James J., Richard A. Katula, with, Forbes I. Hill, and Donovan J. Ochs. *A Synoptic History of Classical Rhetoric* 3rd ed. Mahwah, N.J.: Hermagoras, 2003.
Nash, Ronald H. *The Gospel and the Greeks: Did the New Testament Borrow from Pagan Thought?* Phillipsburg, New Jersey: P&R, 2003.
Newman, Barclay. *A Concise Greek-English Dictionary of the New Testament.* Stuttgart: United Bible Societies, 1971.
Neyrey, Jerome. *2 Peter, Jude: A New Translation with Introduction and Commentary*, The Anchor Bible. New York: Doubleday, 1993.
—. "The Apologetic Use of the Transfiguration in 2 Peter 1:16-21." *CBQ* 42 (1980): 504-19.
—. "The Form and Background of the Polemic in 2 Peter." *JBL* 99 (1980).
Neyrey, Jerome H. "The Form and Background of the Polemic in 2 Peter." *Journal of Biblical Literature* 99.3 (1980): 407-31.
Niehoff, Maren. *Philo on Jewish Identity and Culture*, Texte Und Studien Zum Antiken Judentum. Tübingen: Mohr Siebeck, 2001.
Nikiprowetzky, Valentin. *Le Commentaire De L'écriture Chez Philon D'alexandrie*, Alghj 11. Leiden, 1977.
O'Brien, Peter T. *Introductory Thanksgivings in the Letters of Paul.* NovTSup 49. Leiden: Brill, 1977.
Oldfather, W.A. *Epictetus: The Discourses as Reported by Arrian, the Manual, and Fragments* 2 Vols, LCL. Cambridge: Harvard University Press, 1925-28.

Bibliography

Pearce, Sarah J.K. *The Land of the Body: Studies in Philo's Representation of Egypt.* Tübingen: Mohr Siebeck, 2007.
Pearson, Sharon Clark. *The Christological and Rhetorical Properties of 1 Peter*, Studies in Bible and Early Christianity. Lewiston, New York: Edwin Mellen, 2001.
Perkins, Judith. *Roman Imperial Identities in the Early Christian Era.* London and New York: Routledge, 2009.
Perkins, Pheme. *Peter: Apostle for the Whole Church.* Edited by D. Moody Smith, Studies on Personalities of the New Testament. Edinburgh: T&T Clark, 2000.
Phillips, John. *Exploring the Epistles of Peter: An Expository Commentary.* Grand Rapids: Kregel, 2005.
Philo. *The Works of Philo: Complete and Unabridged.* Translated by C.D. Yonge. Peabody, MA: Hendrickson, 1993.
Picirelli, Robert E. "The Meaning of 'Epignosis'." *EvQ* 47.2 (1975): 85-93.
Plutarch. "Virtue and Vice." In *Moralia*, 93-104. Cambridge, MA: Harvard University Press, 1928.
Powell, Brian. W. "Did Paul Believe in Virtue." Macquarie University, 1995.
Radice, Roberto. "Observations on the Theory of the Ideas as the Thoughts of God in Philo of Alexandria." In *The Studia Philonica Annual: Studies in Hellenistic Judaism*, edited by David T. Runia, 126-34. Atlanta, Georgia: Scholars Press, 1991.
Rea, J. "A Student's Letter to His Father: *P.Oxy.* Xviii 2190 Revised." *ZPE* 99 (1993): 75-88.
Reese, Ruth A. *2 Peter & Jude*, The Two Horizons New Testament Commentary. Grand Rapids / Cambridge: Eerdmans, 2007.
—. "Holiness and Ecclesiology in Jude and 2 Peter." In *Holiness and Ecclesiology in the New Testament*, edited by Kent E. Brower and Andy Johnson, 326-42. Grand Rapids: Eerdmans, 2007.
Reicke, Bo. *The Epistles of James, Peter, and Jude.* Garden City: Doubleday, 1964.
Reydams-Schils, G.J. *The Roman Stoics: Self, Responsibility, and Affection*: University of Chicago Press, 2005.
Richard, Earl J. *Reading 1 Peter, Jude, and 2 Peter: A Literary and Theological Commentary.* Macon: Smyth & Helwys, 2000.
Ridderbos, H. *The Speeches of Peter in the Acts of the Apostles.* London, 1962.
Riesner, Rainer. "Der Zweite Petrus-Brief Und Die Eschatologie." In *Zukunftserwartung in Biblischer Sicht : Beiträge Zur Eschatologie : Bericht Von Der 3. Theologischen Studienkonferenz Des Arbeitskreises Für Evangelikale Theologie*, edited by Gerhard Maier, 124-43. Giessen: Brunnen, 1984.
—. *Paul's Early Period: Chronology, Mission Strategy, Theology.* Grand Rapids: Eerdmans, 1998.
Rife, Joseph L. "The Deaths of the Sophists: Philostratean Biography and Elite Funerary Practices." In *Philostratus*, edited by E.L. Bowie and J. Elsner, 100-30. Cambridge: CUP, 2009.

Rist, John M. "The Stoic Concept of Detachment." In *The Stoics*, edited by John M. Rist, 259-72. Berkeley and Los Angeles: University of California Press, 1978.
—. *Stoic Philosophy*. Cambridge: CUP, 1969.
—. *The Stoics*. Berkeley and Los Angeles: University of California Press, 1978.
Roberts, C.H. "The Greek Papyri." In *The Legacy of Egypt*, edited by J.R. Harris. Oxford: Clarendon, 1971.
Robertson. *A Grammar of the Greek New Testament in the Light of Historical Research*. Leicester: Hodder & Stoughton, 1919.
Robinson, J. Armitage. *St. Paul's Epistle to the Ephesians*. London: James Clarke, 1903.
Roots, Peter. "Is Stoicism Internally Consistent?" *Stoic Voice Journal*, 1 (2000).
Roskam, Geert. *On the Path to Virtue: The Stoic Doctrine of Moral Progress and Its Reception in (Middle-) Platonism*, Ancient and Medieval Philosophy. Leuven: Leuven University Press, 2005.
Rowe, C.J. *Plato*. Brighton: Harvester, 1984.
Runia, David T. "Eudaimonism in Hellenistic-Jewish Literature." In *Shem in the Tents of Japhet: Essays on the Encounter of Judaism and Hellenism*, edited by James L. Kugel, 131-58. Leiden: Brill, 2002.
—. *Exegesis and Philosophy: Studies on Philo of Alexandria*. Hampshire: Variorum, 1990.
—. "Further Observations on the Structure of Philo's Allegorical Treatises." *Vigiliae Christianae* 41.2 (Jun., 1987): 105-38.
—. "God and Man in Philo of Alexandria." *JTS* 39 (1988): 48-75.
—. "How to Read Philo." *Nederlands Theologisch Tijdschrift*, 40 (1986): 185-98.
—. "Philo and Hellenistic Doxography." In *Philo of Alexandria and Post-Aristotelian Philosophy*, edited by Francesca Alesse, 13-54. Leiden: Brill, 2008.
—. *Philo in Early Christian Literature: A Survey*. Edited by Aschkenasy et al. Vol. 3, Compendia Rerum Iudaicarum Ad Novum Testamentum. Assen: Van Gorcum, 1993.
—. "Philo of Alexandria and the Greek *Hairesis*-Model." *Vigiliae Christianae* 53 (1999): 117-47.
—. *Philo of Alexandria and the Timaeus of Plato*, Philosophia Antiqua. Leiden: Brill, 1986.
—. "Philo of Alexandria in Five Letters of Isidore of Pelusium." In *The Studia Philonica Annual: Studies in Hellenistic Judaism*, edited by David T. Runia, 295-319. Atlanta, Georgia: Scholars Press, 1991.
—. "Philo's 'De Aeternitate Mundi': The Problem of Its Interpretation." *Vigiliae Christianae* 35.2 (Jun., 1981): 105-51.
—. "Philo's Reading of the Psalms." In *In the Spirit of Faith: Studies in Philo and Early Christianity in Honor of David Hay*, edited by D.T. Runia and G.E. Sterling, 102-21. Providence: Brown Judaic Studies, 2001.
—. "The Reward for Goodness: Philo, De Vita Contemplativa 90." In *Wisdom*

and Logos: Studies in Jewish Thought in Honor or David Winston edited by David T. Runia and Gregory E. Sterling, 3-18. Atlanta, 1997.

—. "The Theme of Flight and Exile in the Allegorical Thought-World of Philo of Alexandria." In *The Studia Philonica Annual*, edited by David T. Runia and Gregory E. Sterling, 1-24. Atlanta: SBL, 2009.

—. "Theodicy in Philo of Alexandria." In *Theodicy in the World of the Bible*, edited by Antti Laato and Johannes C. de Moor, 576-604. Leiden: Brill, 2003.

—. "Where, Tell Me, Is the Jew...?: Basil, Philo and Isidore of Pelusium." *Vigiliae Christianae* (1992): 172-89.

Russell, D.A. *Greek Declamation*. Cambridge, 1983.

Sandbach, F.H. *The Stoics*. Edited by M.I. Finley, Ancient Culture and Society. London: Chatto & Windus, 1975.

Sandelin, Karl Gustav. "Philo's Ambivalence Towards Statues." In *Spha*, 2001.

Sandmel, Samuel. *Philo of Alexandria: An Introduction*. Oxford: OUP, 1979.

Scaltsas, Theodore, and Andrew S. Mason, eds. *The Philosophy of Epictetus*. New York: OUP, 2007.

Schofield, Malcolm. "Epictetus: Socratic, Cynic, Stoic." *Philosophical Quarterly* 54.216 (2004): 448-56.

Schreiner, T.R. *1, 2 Peter, Jude: An Exegetical and Theological Exposition of Holy Scripture*, New American Commentary. Nashville: Broadman & Holman, 2003.

Schultz, R.L. "Unity or Diversity in Wisdom Theology? A Canonical and Covenantal Perspective." *TynB* 48.2 (1997).

—. "Unity or Diversity in Wisdom Theology? A Canonical and Covenantal Perspective." *Tyndale Bulletin* 48.2 (1997).

Schürer, Emil. *The Literature of the Jewish People in the Time of Jesus*. 4 vols. New York: Schocken, 1972.

Scott, Alan B. *Origen and the Life of the Stars: A History of an Idea*. Oxford: Clarendon, 1991.

Seddon, Keith. *Epictetus' Handbook and the Tablet of Cebes: Guides to Stoic Living*. London: Routledge, 2005.

Sedley, David. "The School, from Zeno to Arius Didymus." In *The Cambridge Companion to the Stoics*, edited by Brad Inwood, 7-32. New York: CUP, 2003.

Seeley, David. *The Noble Death : Graeco-Roman Martyrology and Paul's Concept of Salvation*. Sheffield: JSOT, 1990.

Segal, Alan F. *Life after Death : A History of the Afterlife in the Religions of the West*. New York: Doubleday, 2004.

Sevenster, J.N. "The Roots of Pagan Anti-Semitism in the Ancient World." *Supplements to Novum Testamentum* 41 (1975): 145-49.

Sharp, Douglas S. *Epictetus and the New Testament*. London: Charles H. Kelly, 1914.

Shroyer, Montgomery J. "Alexandrian Jewish Literalists." *JBL* 55 (1936): 261-84.

—. "Paul's Departure from Judaism to Hellenism." *Journal of Biblical*

Literature 59.1 (1940): 41-49.
Sidebottom, E.M. *James, Jude and 2 Peter*. The New Century Bible Commentary. London: Nelson, 1967.
Sidebottom, Harry. "Philostratus and the Symbolic Roles of the Sophist and Philosopher." In *Philostratus*, edited by E.L. Bowie and J. Elsner, 69-99. Cambridge: CUP, 2009.
Siegert, Folker. "Early Jewish Interpretation in a Hellenistic Style." In *Hebrew Bible / Old Testament: The History of Its Interpretation*, edited by Magne Sæbø, 130-97. Göttingen: Vandenhoeck & Ruprecht, 1996.
—. "Philo and the New Testament." In *The Cambridge Companion to Philo*, edited by Adam Kamesar, 175-209. New York: CUP, 2009.
Skidmore, Clive. *Practical Ethics for Roman Gentlemen: The Work of Valerius Maximus*. Exeter, Devon: University of Exeter Press, 1996.
Smith, Terence V. *Petrine Controversies in Early Christianity*. Tübingen: Mohr Siebeck, 1985.
Snyder, John. "A 2 Peter Bibliography." *JETS* 22 (1979): 265-67.
Sorabji, Richard. "Epictetus on *Proairesis* and Self." In *The Philosophy of Epictetus*, edited by Theodore Scaltsas and Andrew S. Mason, 87-98. New York: OUP, 2007.
Spicq, C. *Les Épîtres De Saint Pierre*, Sources Bibliques. Paris: Gabalda, 1966.
Stanton, G.R. "Sophists and Philosophers: Problems of Classification." *AJP* 94 (1973): 350-64.
Starr, James M. "Sharers in Divine Nature: 2 Peter 1:4 in Its Hellenistic Context." Almqvist & Wiksell 2000.
Stemberger, Günter. "Exegetical Contacts between Christians and Jews in the Roman Empire." In *Hebrew Bible / Old Testament: The History of Its Interpretation*, edited by Magne Sæbø, 569-86. Göttingen: Vandenhoeck & Ruprecht, 1996.
Stephens, William O. *Stoic Ethics: Epictetus and Happiness as Freedom*. London: Continuum, 2007.
Sterling, Gregory E. ""the Queen of the Virtues": Piety in Philo of Alexandria." In *Spha*, edited by David T. Runia and Gregory E. Sterling, 103-24, 2006.
—. "'The School of Sacred Laws': The Social Setting of Philo's Treatises." *Vigiliae Christianae* 53 (1999): 148-64.
Stern, Menahem, ed. *Greek & Latin Authors on Jews & Judaism with Introductions: Translations & Commentary*: Lubrecht & Cramer, 1974-84.
Stough, Charlotte. "Stoic Determinism and Moral Responsibility." In *The Stoics*, edited by John M. Rist. Berkely and Los Angeles: University of California Press, 1978.
Strange, Steven K., and Jack Zupko, eds. *Stoicism: Traditions and Transformations*. New York: CUP, 2004.
Struck, Peter. *The Birth of the Symbol: Ancient Readers at the Limits of Their Texts*. Princeton, N.J.: Princeton University Press, 2004.
Swain, S.C.R. *Hellenism and Empire: Language, Classicism, and Power in the Greek World, AD 50-250*. New York: OUP, 1996.
Tcherikover, V. "Prolegomena." In *Corpus Papyrorum Judaicarum*, edited by

V Tcherikover and A Fuks, 1-111. Cambridge: Harvard University Press, 1957.

Thiselton, Anthony C. *The First Epistle to the Corinthians: A Commentary on the Greek Text*, The New International Greek Testament Commentary. Grand Rapids: Eerdmans, 2000.

Tobin, Thomas H. "Romans 10:4: Christ the Goal of the Law." In *The Studia Philonica Annual: Studies in Hellenistic Judaism*, edited by David T. Runia, 272-80. Atlanta, Georgia: Scholars Press, 1991.

Toynbee, J.M.C. *Death and Burial in the Roman World*. Edited by H.H. Scullard, Aspects of Greek and Roman Life. London: Thames and Hudson, 1971.

Trapp, Michael B. *Philosophy in the Roman Empire: Ethics, Politics and Society*. Aldershot, Hampshire, England: Ashgate, 2007.

Van Gemeren, W. *The Progress of Redemption*. Grand Rapids: Zondervan, 1988.

Van Geytenbeek, A.C. *Musonius Rufus and Greek Diatribe*. Assen, Netherlands: Royal VanGorcum, 1962.

Völker, W. *Fortschritt Und Vollendung Bei Philon Von Alexandrien: Eine Studie Zur Geschichte Der Frömmigkeit*, Text Und Untersuchungen 49.1. Leipzig, 1938.

Wall, Robert W. "The Canonical Function of 2 Peter." *Biblical Interpretation* 9.1 (2001): 64-81.

—. *The New Testament as Canon: A Reader in Canonical Criticism*. Sheffield: Sheffield Academic, 1992.

Wallace, Daniel B. *Greek Grammar Beyond the Basics: An Exegetical Syntax of the New Testament*. Grand Rapids: Zondervan, 1996.

Wardy, Robert. "The Stoic Life: Emotions, Duties, and Fate. (Book Review)." *Classical Review* 57.2 (2007): 355-57.

Watson, Duane Frederick. *Invention, Arrangement, and Style: Rhetorical Criticism of Jude and 2 Peter*, SBLDS. Atlanta: Scholars Press, 1988.

Webb, Robert L. and Watson, Duane F., ed. *Reading Second Peter with New Eyes: Methodological Reassessments of the Letter of Second Peter*. Edited by Mark Goodacre, Library of New Testament Studies 382: T&T Clark, 2010.

Westermann, C. *Roots of Wisdom*. Louisville: Westminster John Knox, 1995.

Whitmarsh, Tim. "'Greece Is the World': Exile and Identity in the Second Sophistic." In *Being Greek under Rome: Cultural Identity, the Second Sophistic and the Development of Empire*, edited by Simon Goldhill, 269-305. Cambridge: CUP, 2001.

—. *Greek Literature and the Roman Empire: The Politics of Imitation*. New York: OUP, 2001.

—. *The Second Sophistic*. Vol. 35, New Surveys in the Classics. Oxford / New York: OUP, 2005.

Whittaker, Molly. *Jews & Christians: Graeco-Roman Views*. Vol. 6, Cambridge Commentaries on Writings of the Jewish & Christian World 200BC to AD200. Cambridge: CUP, 1984.

Wiedemann, T. *Adults and Children in the Roman Empire*. London: Routledge, 1989.
Wilken, Robert L. "The Christians as the Romans (and Greeks) Saw Them." In *Jewish and Christian Self-Definition*, edited by E.P. Sanders, 100-25. London: SCM, 1980.
Williams, B. *Ethics and Limits of Philosophy*. London, 1985.
Williamson, Ronald. *Jews in the Hellenistic World: Philo*. Edited by P.R. Ackroyd, A.R.C. Leaney and J.W. Packer, Cambridge Commentaries on Writings of the Jewish & Christian World 200bc to Ad200. Cambridge: CUP, 1989.
—. *Philo and the Epistle to the Hebrews*. Leiden: Brill, 1970.
Wilson, L. "The Place of Wisdom in Old Testament Theology." *RTR* 49 (1990): 60-69.
Winston, David. "Aspects of Philo's Linguistic Theory." In *The Studia Philonica Annual: Studies in Hellenistic Judaism*, edited by David T. Runia, 109-25. Atlanta, Georgia: Scholars Press, 1991.
—. "Philo of Alexandria on the Rational and Irrational Emotions." In *Passions and Moral Progress in Greco-Roman Thought*, edited by John T. Fitzgerald, 201-20. London and New York: Routledge, 2008.
—. *Philo of Alexandria: The Contemplative Life, the Giants, and Selections*. Edited by Richard J. Payne, The Classics of Western Spirituality. Ramsey, New Jersey: Paulist P, 1981.
—. "Phil's Ethical Theory." *ANRW* II.21.1 (1984): 409-14.
—. "Sage and Super-Sage in Philo of Alexandria." In *Pomegranates and Golden Bells : Studies in Biblical, Jewish and near Eastern Ritual, Law, and Literature in Honor of Jacob Milgrom*, edited by David P. Wright, David Noel Freedman, Avi Hurvitz and Jacob Milgrom, 815-24. Winona Lake, Ind: Eisenbrauns, 1995.
Winter, Bruce W. *After Paul Left Corinth: The Influence of Secular Ethics and Social Change*. Grand Rapids: Eerdmans, 2001.
—. "On Introducing Gods to Athens: An Alternative Reading of Acts 17.18-20." *TynB* 47 (1996): 71-90.
—. *Philo and Paul among the Sophists*. 2 ed. Grand Rapids: Eerdmans, 2002.
—. "Public and Private: Early Christians and Religious Pluralism." In *One God, One Lord: Christianity in a World of Religious Pluralism*, edited by Andrew D. Clarke and Bruce W. Winter. Grand Rapids and Carlisle: Baker and Paternoster, 1992.
—. *Seek the Welfare of the City*. Grand Rapids: Eerdmans, 1994.
Witherington III, Ben. *Letters and Homilies for Hellenized Christians: A Socio-Rhetorical Commentary on 1-2 Peter*. Vol. II. Nottingham: Apollos, 2007.
Wolfson, Harry Austryn. *Philo: Foundations of Religious Philosophy in Judaism, Christianity, and Islam*. 2 vols. Cambridge: Harvard University Press, 1968.
Wolter, M. "Der Reichtum Gottes." *Jahrbuch für biblische Theologie* 21 (2006): 145–60.
Wolters, Al. "'Partners of the Deity': A Covenantal Reading of 2 Peter 1:4."

Bibliography

    CTJ 25.1 (1990): 28-44.
Wright, W.C. *The Lives of the Sophists*: Heinemann, 1968.
Xenakis, Iason. *Epictetus: Philosopher-Therapist*. The Hague: Martinus Nijhoff, 1969.
Zeyl, D. "Socratic Virtue and Happiness" *Archiv für Geschichte der Philosophie* 64 (1982): 227.
Zimmerli, W. "The Place and Limit of Wisdom in the Framework of the Old Testament Theology." *Scottish Journal of Theology* 17 (1964): 146-58.

Author index

Adams, E., 154
Adams, S., 4
Algra, K., 38, 43
Anderson, G., 2, 160
Arnim, von, 58

Ballif, M., 170
Barclay, J.M.G., 80
Barnes, J., 15
Barnett, P., 147, 149, 150, 151
Bauckham, R.J., 152, 153, 159, 162, 189, 190, 191, 204, 206
Beale, G.K., 149
Benedeum, J., 20
Bigg, C., 179
Birnbaum, E., 80, 93
Bonhöffer, A., 73
Borgen, P., 4, 79, 80, 83, 92, 94, 95, 96, 110, 122, 140, 142
Borkhardt, H., 93
Bowersock, G.W., 2, 3, 33, 34, 159, 173
Brennan, T., 12
Brown, R.E., 151, 152
Brueggemann, W., 99
Bruce, F.F., 149
Brunt, P.A., 34

Carson, D.A., 5, 149
Carter, E., 13, 29, 42, 72
Charles, J.D., 5, 189
Cohen, N., 110
Colardeau, T., 32
Coleman, P.W., 156
Colish, M.L., 12
Cooper, J.M., 3
Cranfield, C.E.B., 193, 194
Cullman, O., 147, 148

Davids, P.H., 156, 157, 159, 183, 184, 186, 189, 190, 191, 192, 195, 196, 197, 198, 199, 200, 206, 207
Davies, W.D., 153

Dillon, J.M., 79, 97
Dillon, J.T., 15
Dobbin, R.F., 32
Donfried, K.P., 151

Edwards, C., 226

Fischel, H.A., 189
Fitzgerald, J.T., 117
Fornberg, T., 153, 154, 157, 158, 159, 189, 198, 200, 205

Gerdmar, A., 159
Geytenbeek, A.C. Van, 25
Giles, K., 150
Gill, C., 11, 15, 16, 22, 28, 29, 52
Gilmour, M.J., 146
Goldhill, S., 86
Goldingay, J., 99
Goodenough, E.R., 4, 80, 81, 84, 94, 95, 104, 107
Green, C., 146
Green, G.L., 5, 8, 24, 146, 158, 159, 160, 162, 165, 190, 191, 204
Green, M., 199
Guthrie, D., 159, 165

Hadot, P., 15, 76
Harrington, D.J., 153, 188, 193, 198
Harrison, J.R., 21
Hay, D.M., 80, 84, 95
Helyer, L., 5, 8
Hengel, M., 4
Higginson, T.W., 13, 70
Hijmans, B.L., 15
Hock, R.F., 24, 30
Horsley, G.H.R., 20

Ierodiakonou, K., 16
Inwood, B., 52

Jackson, D.R., 154
Jobes, K.H., 174
Johnston, D., 11
Judge, E.A., 5

Käsemann, E., 156, 158
Kelly, J.N.D., 158, 187, 189, 195, 196
Kennedy, G.A., 168
Kinzig, W., 168
Kistemaker, S.J., 146
Knight, J., 152, 159, 181
Knoch, O., 153

Lee, S.S., 5
Leisegang, H., 122
Leonhardt-Balzer, J., 83, 117
Llewelyn, S.R., 13
Long, A.A., 7, 12, 13-14, 15, 16, 22, 23, 29-30, 32, 40, 44, 45, 55, 58, 65, 72, 73, 76
Louw, J.P., 208
Lucas, D., 146, 165, 190, 204
Lutz, C., 25, 26, 30, 54, 56

Martin, D.B., 152
Mayer, J.B., 182, 189, 208
Mendelson, A., 81, 101, 105
Metzger, B., 178
Modrzejewski, J.M., 80
Moles, J.L., 22, 162
Moo, D.J., 150
Moran, M.G., 170
Mortley, R.J., 4, 83, 84, 184
Moulton, J.H., 178
Muraba'at, W., 153
Murphy, J.J., 170

Newman, B., 191
Neyrey, J., 155, 158, 159, 179
Nida, E.A., 208
Niehoff, M., 80
Nikiprowetzky, V., 78, 104
Oldfather, W.A., 13, 16, 19, 23, 28, 39, 48, 55, 56, 71, 73, 222, 223

Pearce, J.K., 83, 96
Picirelli, R.E., 184
Phillips, J., 146
Powell, B.W., 193

Radice, R., 96
Rea, J., 85
Reese, R.A., 146, 159, 179, 183, 184, 189
Reicke, B., 153
Reumann, J., 152
Richard, E.J., 159
Ridderbos, H., 149
Riesner, R., 160
Rist, J.M., 73
Roberts, C.H., 85
Rowe, C.J., 89
Runia, D.T., 6, 8, 78, 79, 84, 88, 93, 94, 95, 97, 98, 100, 103, 104, 106, 107, 110, 112, 113, 141, 163, 164, 187, 215
Russell, D.A., 160

Sandbach, F.H., 12, 13, 14, 15
Sandbel, S., 81, 104
Sandelin, K.G., 96
Schreiner, T.R., 5, 146, 159
Schultz, R.L., 99
Seddon, K., 52
Sedley, D., 11, 12
Sidebottom, E.M., 184, 203
Smith, T.V., 149
Snyder, J., 5
Sorabji, R., 50
Stanton, G.R., 34
Starr, J.M., 5, 147, 154, 155, 156, 157, 185, 186, 204, 222
Stauffer, E., 198
Sterling, G.E., 84, 110
Swain, S.C.R., 1, 166

Tcherikover, V., 80, 83
Thiselton, A.C., 173

Wall, R.W., 146
Watson, D.F., 146
Wendland, P., 178
Westermann, C., 99
Whitmarsh, T., 1, 2, 34, 166
Wilken, R.L., 212
Williams, B., 112
Williamson, R., 80, 81, 106, 110, 114, 120, 122, 141
Wilson, L., 99
Winston, D., 78, 96, 98, 100, 103, 1110, 111, 116-117, 122, 131
Winter, B, 2, 22, 34, 35, 36, 38, 43, 52, 84, 85, 89, 111, 134, 160, 165, 172
Witherington, B., III, 146
Wolfson, H.A., 83, 95, 96, 100, 101, 104, 105, 110, 116, 121, 122, 136, 141, 142, 143
Wolter, M., 104

Xenakis, I., 23, 32-33

Yonge, C.D., 101

Zeyl, D., 89
Zimmerli, W., 99

Indexes

Persons index

Biblical
Abel, 137, 141, 213
Abraham, 112, 114, 115, 121, 132, 151
Agrippa, 150
Andrew, 147

Balaam, 89, 167, 182

Cain, 137, 214
Christ, Jesus, 127, 147, 182
Claudius, 150, 174
Cornelius, 150

David, 115, 118, 151

Enoch, 115, 142
Epaphras, 151

Gamaliel II, 153

Isaac, 115, 132, 142, 151

Jacob, 115, 130, 132, 151
James, 147, 150
Job, 115, 127
John, 147, 149
Joshua, 114, 132

Lot, 179

Mary, 179
Moses, 6, 78, 84, 92, 96, 97, 98, 99, 100, 106, 114, 115, 116, 128, 132, 136, 137, 140, 142, 143, 144, 151, 216, 226, 229, 231, 232

Noah, 114, 141, 181, 206

Paul, 150, 151, 153, 156, 158, 160, 165, 169, 170, 172, 173, 174, 181, 182, 185, 186, 193, 194, 196, 198, 199, 207, 214, 215, 224
Peter, 1, 3, 4-5, 6, 145, 214, 215, 216, 217, 218, 219, 220, 222, 223, 224, 225, 226, 228-232
Pharisees, 224
Phoebe, 151

Samuel, 151
Stephen, 156

Timothy, 151
Tychicus, 151

Others
Anaxagorus, 71
Antiochus of Ascalon, 97
Antony, Mark, 79
Apollonius of Tyana, 12, 18
Arian, 166
Aristides of Pergamon, 35
Aristippus, 71
Aristo, 44
Aristotle, 32, 83, 92, 95, 96, 161, 162, 170, 192, 195
Arius, 169
Arrian, 3, 14, 22, 31, 38
Asterius, 168
Athanasius, 167, 168, 169, 170
Athenodotus, 25
Atticus, Herodes (of Athens), 115
Augustus, Caesar, 3, 20, 31, 80
Aurelius, Marcus, 3, 12, 14, 22, 28

Balbus, Quintus Lucilius, 1, 38, 41, 43, 44, 46

Caesar, Julius, 20
Caligula, 83, 105, 150

267

Celsus, 23
Chrysippus, 11, 12, 12n.9, 14, 15, 32, 43, 44, 58, 72, 101, 142
Cicero, 1, 12n.9, 14, 21, 38, 41, 41n.25, 43, 44, 45, 48, 51, 63-64, 114, 120, 170, 213, 217, 222, 231, 232
  De natura deorum, 1, 12n.9, 14n.18, 38, 43, 54, 63-64, 231
Clement, 166, 167, 168, 169, 170
Cleanthes, 11, 14, 20, 43, 44, 50, 72, 141
Clearchus of Soli, 96
Clement, 150
Cleopatra, 79
Cotta, Gaius, 1n.1, 12, 44, 46, 51, 56, 144
Cyprian, 169

Daphnus, M. Aurelius, 52
Democritus, 101
Demosthenes, 34
Didymus, Arius, 14
Dio Chrysostom, 162
Diogenes Laertius, 12, 14
Diogenes of Babylon, 44, 46
Diogenes of Melos, 38
Diogenes the Cynic, 34, 62, 71, 72, 141
Diognetus, 157
Dio of Prusa (Dio Chrysostom), 21, 25, 25, 85, 92
Domitian, 4

Empiricus, Sextus, 14
Ennius, 19
Epaphroditus, 22-23
Epictetus, 1, 2, 3, 4, 5, 6, 6n.21, 7, 9, 11-77, 79, 85, 120, 143, 144, 160, 161, 165, 166, 168, 213, 214, 215, 216, 217, 218, 219, 220, 221, 222, 223, 224, 225, 228-232, background, 22-24, *Contra Celsus*, 23, *Discourses*, 3, 7, 21, 22, 24, 26, 31, 33, 34, 35, 37, 38-39, 49, 70, 217, 224; *Encheiridion*, 7, 16, 18-19, 38, 39, 49, 62, 218, *Of Personal Adornment*, 35, Style and delivery, 31-33
Epicurus, 13n.9, 101, 159
Euphrates of Tyre, 25
Euripides, 138
Euthydemus, 18

Felix, Minucius, 167, 198
Flaccus, 2n.7, 8, 79
Fronto, 25

Gaius, 79, 80
Galen, 14
Gregory, 168, 169

Hadrian, 35
Heracleitus, 72
Heracles, 25
Hesiod, 83, 92
Himerius, 25
Homer, 55, 83, 98, 107

Ignatius, 157, 178
Irenaeus, 167, 168, 170
Italicus, 19-20

Josephus, 96, 138, 196
Julian, 25n.91
Justin, 25n.91

Lucius, 25-26

Marcellus of Ancyra, 168
Martyr, Justin, 153

Nero, 25, 79, 150, 204
Numenius, 84

Octavian, 79
Odysseus, 25n.91
Origen, 167, 168, 169, 170
Origenes, 25n.91

Panaetius, 12
Persaeus, 44
Philo, 1, 2, 3, 4, 5, 6, 6n.21, 7-8, 9, 78-144, 156, 160, 161, 162, 163, 164, 165, 166, 167, 168, 169, 171, 172, 191, 196, 214, 215, 216, 217, 218, 219, 220, 221, 222, 223, 224, 225-226, 228-232; *De Abrahamo*, 8, 124; *De aeternitate mundi*, 8, 91, 92, 135; *De opificio mundi*, 162, *De praemiis et poenis*, 8, 119, 125, 126, 128, 137; *De Sacrificiis Abelis et Caini*, 111; *De somniis*, 135; *De virtutibus*, 8, 110-111, 124, 136; *De vita contemplativa*, 8, 82, 123, 140; *Quis rerum divinarum heres sit*, 88; *Quod deterius potiori insidiari soleat*, 8, 85, 89, 91, 118, 139, 217; *Quod Deus sit immutabilis*, 8; *Quod omnis probus liber sit*, 8, 97, 125, 128, 138, 140, 221
Philostratus, 1, 12n.9, 18, 35n.149, 174
Plato, 12n.9, 73, 76, 78, 84, 95, 96, 97, 105, 116, 142n.57, 144, 187, 195, 216
Plautus, 19-20
Pliny, 25, 25n.91
Plutarch, 14, 24n.85, 49, 162
Posidonius, 12, 43n.51
Protagoras, 38
Pyrrho, 36n.158

Quintilian, 76n.36, 170n.91

Rufus, Musonius, 3, 7n.22, 9, 14, 15, 15n.21, 17-18, 22, 23n.79, 24, 25-30, 36, 54, 55, 56n.64, 57, 59n.77, 70n.3, 76, 162

Seneca the Younger, 13, 14, 31, 72, 134, 139, 222

Silvanus, 9
Simplicius, 23
Socrates, 6n.21, 12, 17, 20, 22, 25, 25n.91, 45, 53, 61, 62, 70, 71, 73, 82, 92, 222, 224, 226, 231, 232
Sophocles, 8n.24
Strabo, 12

Tacitus, 25n.91
Tatian, 167, 168, 169, 170
Tertullian, 167, 170, 196, 198
Theodorus of Cyrene, 38
Tiberius, 79, 80
Timocrates of Heracleia, 25
Titans, the, 206

Valleius, Gaius, 1n.1, 44
Vespasian, 25
Vitellius, 25

Xenophon, 187

Zeno, 11, 12, 14, 20, 43, 43n.51, 44, 97, 99, 141
Zeus, 16-17, 39, 40n.15, 41, 45, 53, 218

Scripture index

Old Testament

Genesis
1:1   208
1:1-2   164, 177
1:26   177
4:14   138
5:22   115n.8
5:24   115n.8
12:3   155n.50
17:1   103
18:19   184
20:8   151n.26

Exodus
20   143n.59
20:3   105n.24
20:4   95
32:13   151n.26

Leviticus
10:16   121
11:44   201
19:18   198
19:34   198
26:40-42 121

Numbers
24:17   167

Deuteronomy
5   143n.59
5:8   95
5:26   105n.24
5:33   184
6:5   198
11:1   198
14   120n.40
30:10   120
32:22   165
34:5   151n.26

1 Samuel
3:9-10 151n.26
13:13   207
23:10   151n.26

2 Samuel
7:13   207

1 Chronicles
16:27   192n.42
17:14   207
28:7   207

Esther
4:17   192n.42

Job   99, 127
1:1   115n.8
40:20   207
41:24   207

Psalms 93
1   99, 200
21:4   192n.42
21:26   192n.42
22   118n.32
22:6-7 155n.50
22:27   155n.50
23   6n.21
25:4   145n.2
45:6   207
49   99
51   119n.32, 122n.51
67:4   6n.21
73   99, 127
119   122n.51

Proverbs 99, 124
1:7   99
1:15   145n.2
6:6   99
6:34-35 99
8:20   184
9:6   99
11:22   206n.5
15:9-10 183
16:17   145n.2
30:16   206

Ecclesiastes 99

Isaiah
2   180n.10
2:2   155n.50
5   199
6:5   177n.4
9:6   177
11   181n.10
42:8   192n.42
42:12   192n.42
43:21   192n.42
44:6-20 105n.24
45:21   177
49:6   155n.50
49-53   127
52-56   181n.10
52:13-53:12 155n.50
53:2   155n.50
53:3   155n.50
53:10-12 155n.50
53:11   177
59:8   145n.2
63:7   192n.42
65-66   181n.10

Jeremiah
6:16   145n.2
17:5-8 200
31   181n.10

Ezekiel
19   200

36:24-27   186n.14

Daniel
2:44   207
4:33   208n.9
6:26   207
9:24-26   155n.50
9:26   155n.50

Hosea
2:23   155n.50

Amos
9:11-12   150
15:12   150
15:13-21   150

Micah
5   181n.10

Habakkuk
3:3   192n.42

Zephaniah
1   164
3   164, 208
3:5-6   208
3:7   208
3:10-13   208
3:13   209

Zechariah
6:13   192n.42
13:7   155n.50

Malachi
1:11   155n.50
4   181n.10
4:6   155n.50

Intertestamental literature

Baruch
3:21   145n.2

3:23   145n.2
3:31   145n.2

Tobias
4:19   145n.2

Wisdom
5:7   145n.2
14:3   145n.2

New Testament

Matthew   30n.123
3:2   208n.8
3:3   145n.2
3:8-10   200
3:16-17   177n.1
4:10   177n.3
4:17   208n.8
4:18   147
5:3   208n.8
5:9   207
5:10   208n.8
5:19   208n.8
6:1   193
7:6   206n.5
7:16-20   200
7:21   208n.8
7:27   208
8:11   208n.8
8:14   147
10:2   147
10:7   208n.8
11:11   208n.8
12:33   200
12:48-50   197
13:11   208n.8
13:24   208n.8
13:31   208n.8
13:33   208n.8
13:44   208n.8
13:47   208n.8
13:52   208n.8
14:33   177
15:14   6n.21

16:16   177n.2
16:17-19   148n.13
16:19   28n.8
17:1   147
17:15   148
18:1   208n.8
18:3   208n.8
18:23   208n.8
19:12   208n.8
19:14   208n.8
19:23   208n.8
20:1   208n.8
21:19-43   200
22:2   208n.8
22:23   135
22:29   155n.50
22:37-39   198
22:41-45   176n.2
23:13   208n.8
23:16   6n.21
23:24   6n.21
25:1   208n.8
25:34   208, 209
25:41   209
26:33-34   148n.12
28:18-20   175, 177n.1
28:20   186n.14

Mark
1:3   145n.2
1:9-11   177n.1
1:20   147
3:14   147
3:16   147
8:29   177n.2
8:33   148n.12
9:7   148
9:43-47   209
9:47   207
11:13-18   200
12:18   135
12:29-30   177n.3
12:30-31   198
14:33   147

Luke
1:33   207
1:76-79   6n.21
2:24-52   149
3:4   145n.2
3:8-9   201
3:21-22   177n.1
4:8   177n.3
5:3   147
5:8   177n.4
6:14   147
6:43-44   201
8:45   152n.31
8:51   147
9:20   177n.2
9:33   148n.12, 152n.31
9:35   148
10:27   198
12:4-5   209
13:1-5   127
13:6-9   201
15:15-16   206n.5
17:5-6   153n.41
18:10-14   224
20:27   135
22:29-30   207
22:30   207
23:43   227
23:46   227
24:44   93n.107
24:45-47   155n.50
24:46-47   175

John
1:32-34   177n.1
1:41   147
1:42   147
3:16   223
3:36   209
6:68   148
9:2-3   127
10:11   6n.21
10:11-18   148
11:27   177n.2
13:1-17   151

13:6-9   148n.12
14   186n.14
14:6   184
14:16-20   185
15   227
15:1-10   185
15:2-8   201
15:12   198
15:16   201
16:13   6n.21
18:11   148n.12
18:17-27   198
18:33-39   207
20:9   155n.50
20:28   177n.2
21:7   148
21:15-17   6n.21, 148n.13, 198
21:18-19   204

Acts   30n.123
1:3   207
1:15-22   149
1:17-36   149
1:37   149
1:38   149
1:40   149
1:41   149
1:42   149
2:23   155n.50
2:25-32   155n.50
2:32-38   155n.50
2:36   177
2:42   156
2:45-46   197n.61
3:12   196
3:18   155n.50
4:4   149
4:5   149
4:12   155n.50
4:13   4, 149
4:19   149
5:15   149
5:16   149
5:31   155n.50
7:42   211n.8

7:59   177n.2
9:2   184
9:15   151n.24
9:34   177n.2
10   150
10:1-48   147
14   215
14:15-17   157
14:22   207
15:7-11   150
15:14   147
15:15-17   150
17   193, 215, 224
17:22-31   158
17:31   191
19:9   184
19:23   184
20:25   207
22–25   215
23:8   135
24:14   184
24:22   184
24:25   195n.51, 196n.53
28:31   207

Romans
1:1   151n.25
1:12   153n.40
2:15   92n.104
2:29   192n.42
4:19-20   153n.41
5–8   185
5:3-5   190
6:18   151
6:23   209
7:4-5   201
8:5-11   185
10:9   223
11:13   150
12:3   153n.41
12:10   197
13:9-10   198
14:4   153n.41
14:7   207
14:22-23   191

16:1   151n.27

1 Corinthians
1–3   172
1:12   150
1:18-31   172
2:4   172
3:9   172
3:22   150
4:5   192n.42
4:7   173
4:19-20   172
5:1   172
6:9   207
6:12   172
8:1   199
8:1-3   172
8:4-5   105n.24
8:6-7   194
9:3-18   173
9:5   147, 150, 173
9:19-22   173
9:25   195n.53
10:4   178n.8
11:21   173
12:12-26   173
12:28   151n.28
13   198, 199
13:1-3   199
13:3   198
15   156
15:1   174
15:3-8   146n.4, 173
15:5   148, 150, 173
15:13   173
15:24   207
15:33   174
15:38   174
15:50   207
16:1   173
16:6   92n.104
16:13   174
16:14   172, 198
16:19   173

2 Corinthians
1:13   92n.104
4:4   151n.27
5:14   225
8:18   192n.42
10:5   195
10:10   59n.79
10:15   153n.41
11:6   172n.94, 193

Galatians   171
2:7-8   150
2:7-14   150
5:21   207
5:22   193, 198, 201
5:32   195n.51, 196n.53

Ephesians
3:5   151n.28
5:5   207
5:9   201
6:5-6   151n.26

Philippians   171
1:1   151n.27
1:11   201
1:18   199n.64
2:17   199n.64
2:18   199n.64
3:5-6   158
3:8   194
4   191
4:8   191, 192n.42, 193

Colossians   30n.123
1:6   201
1:7   151n.27
1:10   201
1:13   207
3:12-14   199
4:1   151

4:7   151n.27
4:11   207
4:12   151n.27

1 Thessalonians
1:3   198
2:6   151n.28
2:12   207
2:13   156
4:9   197
5:8   199

2 Thessalonians
1:5   207

1 Timothy
2:7   150
3   224
5:12   191
6:11   196
6:20   195

2 Timothy
2:24-25   151n.27
4:1   207
4:3-4   171
4:18   207

Titus
1:1   151n.25
1:10   171
1:13   153n.41, 170
1:17   193
2:1-15   171
2:7   193
2:9   151
3:8   193
3:12   31n.124

Philemon
14   192

Hebrews   171
1:8   207
9:27   209
10:34-39   203

10:35 203	2:24 227	1:3 172, 178n.6, 179, 183n.4, 184, 185, 192, 194, 223
10:38 203	3:8 199n.66	
10:39 203	3:18 185, 186n.14	
13:1 197	3:22 208	
13:20 6n.21	4:2-5 209	1:3-4 166, 185, 186, 187, 194
	4:7 205	
James	4:8 199n.66	1:3-11 179
2:5 207	4:12 150, 199n.66	1:4 156, 178n.6, 179, 181, 185, 192, 205, 216
2:14-24 201	4:13 208	
2:26 201	4:13-18 150	
3:13 193	4:14 185, 186n.14	1:5 181, 185, 186, 187, 192n.42, 194, 225
3:17 201	4:17 209	
	4:18 197	
1 Peter 9, 145n.1, 171	5:1 152n.29, 152n.29, 208	1:5-7 167, 173, 187, 189, 190, 196, 197, 198, 209, 217, 228
1:1 151n.29, 152, 173, 191	5:1-4 6n.21, 148	
	5:4 6n.21, 208, 208n.10	
1:1-4 188		1:5-8 205
1:2 177n.5, 185, 186n.14	5:6 199n.66	1:5-11 185
	5:8 220	1:7 197, 199
1:2-5 223	5:9 185	1:8 167, 181, 184, 200, 209
1:3 186n.14	5:10 199n.66, 212, 217	
1:3-5 212		1:9 167, 179, 189, 201
1:3-7 188	5:12 3, 158	
1:4 201, 208		1:10 166, 167, 174, 181, 189, 197, 199, 200, 201, 209
1:5 208	2 Peter 2, 5, 8, 9, 145, 171	
1:7 208		
1:7-9 185	1 5, 5n.16, 162, 179, 186, 192n.42, 195, 202, 209, 211	
1:8 199n.66		1:10-15 187
1:9 1888		1:11 178, 179, 181, 186, 189, 201, 207, 210, 219
1:10-12 155n.50, 181n.10	1:1 8, 147n.6, 147n.7, 151, 152, 152n.29, 166, 179, 180, 181, 183, 184, 185, 200, 207, 223	
1:11 181n.10		
1:13 208		1:12 155, 172, 189, 205, 222
1:16 201		1:12-13 201
1:18-19 227		1:12-15 146n.4, 152, 173, 174, 181, 196
1:22 197, 198	1:1-2 166, 178n.7, 179, 180, 183, 205, 212	
1:23 208		
2 224		1:12-21 179
2:9 192n.42, 194, 208	1:1-4 199	1:13 153
	1:2 174, 179, 183, 184, 194, 205, 207	1:13-14 204
2:9-12 201		1:13-18 155
2:13-23 226		1:14 178, 179, 204
2:16 151		
2:17 199n.66	1:2-3 179	
2:23 227		

1:15 167, 201, 204
1:16 155n.48, 161, 162, 163, 164, 165, 167, 178, 179, 182, 195, 214
1:16-17 173, 179
1:16-18 8
1:16-19 152, 212
1:16-21 155, 172, 179, 212
1:17 155, 178n.6, 179, 192, 199
1:17-18 148
1:17-21 172
1:18 155, 167, 178
1:19 155, 180, 181n.10
1:19-21 167
1:20 201
1:21 156, 167, 177, 179
2 172, 177, 187, 200, 227
2:1 195, 198, 200, 202, 205
2:1–3:7 211, 215
2:2 195, 198
2–3 195
2:1 165, 206
2:1-2 154n.43, 185
2:1–3:1 165
2:1–3:7 146, 162, 164-165, 167
2:2 146, 165, 178
2:3 163, 165, 179, 180, 182, 195, 206
2:4 206, 207
2:5 180, 197
2:6 180, 197, 206
2:7 180, 195
2:9 178, 180, 193n.42, 206
2:10 168, 172, 195
2:10-15 187
2:11 178
2:12 168, 179, 181, 206
2:13 169, 173, 181, 182, 194, 195, 198, 206
2:14 169, 173, 182, 195, 206
2:15 146, 167, 181, 194
2:15-16 165, 182
2:16 167, 194, 195
2:17 181, 206
2:18 169, 182, 200
2:18-19 172
2:19 152, 169, 172, 206
2:20 167, 169, 178, 184, 194, 196, 205
2:21 146, 196, 205
2:22 169, 206
3 177, 187, 199, 200, 209, 211, 215, 227
3:1 9, 152, 173, 199, 201
3:1-2 174, 181, 196
3:1-3 196
3:2 151n.28, 152, 178, 180
3:2-4 180
3:3 169, 192, 195, 196, 205
3:3-10 205
3:3-14 196
3:4 159, 174, 181, 192, 205
3:4-5 169
3:4-7 164
3:5 180
3:5-7 181, 192
3:5-13 205
3:6 180
3:6-7 206
3:7 180, 197
3:8 181, 199
3:8-9 178
3:8-10 180
3:8-13 196
3:9 181, 192, 205, 220
3:10 180, 206
3:11 182, 195, 196, 211
3:11-12 209n.11
3:11-18 217
3:12 180, 196, 205, 206
3:13 180, 181n.10, 196, 205, 210, 232
3:14 181, 199, 210
3:14-17 167
3:15 180, 181, 182, 192, 205, 220
3:15-16 156, 212
3:16 165, 169, 174, 205
3:16-17 162, 165, 170
3:17 146, 154, 174, 181, 182, 196, 199, 200, 205, 215
3:17-18 195
3:18 178, 179, 194, 207, 218
5:12 9
1 John

1:1-3   155n.47
1:5-6   201
1:5-7   201
2:26-29 171
4:8   199
4:16   199

Jude   145n.1
3   191
20   191

Revelation   170
1:1   151
1:6   207
1:9   207
2:14   168
4:11   179
5:10   207
7:17   6n.21
11:15 207
11:18 151
12:10 207
21:1-8 209
22:9   151

Subject index

Alexandria, 81, 84, 96
anti-Semitism, 150
apostasy, 216
apostle(s), 147, 151, 151n.28, 156, 167, 175, 180
application, 58-60
asceticism, 128, 140
atheism, 41
Athens, 81
authority, 92, 95, 152, 212

baptism, 149, 177
body, the, 71, 72, 86, 90, 127, 129, 130, 135, 136-138, 140
brotherly affection, 188

calling, 186
case of assent, 52
chastity, 190
choice and refusal, 52
church, 149, 152, 173
Christ, Jesus, 9, 156, 169, 175, 183, 184, 186, 192, 195, 198, 199, 209, 212, 216, 218, 222, 223, 224, 232; coming, 155, 161, 163, 179, 181, 228; crucifixion, 158; eternity, 186; excellence of, 184; death, 149, 156, 231; divinity of, 177, 178, 179, 219; glory, 179, 184, 185, 186, 219; God, as, 149, 230; judgement, 180, 186; knowledge of, 179, 186, 200; Lord, 178, 179, 195, 201, 207, 212, 219; majesty, 155, 161, 163, 178; Messiah, as, 147, 149, 153, 171, 211; power, 155, 161, 163, 185, 200; presence of, 185; rescuer, 186; resurrection, 149, 156, 173, 231; return, 202, 208, 210, 212; revealed, 229; righteousness of, 186; Saviour, 178, 184, 195, 201, 207, 219, 230; Shepherd, 208; Son, 177, 179, 180, 199, 218; sovereign, 186; teachings of, 200; transfiguration, 155-156, 177; union with, 186; worshipped, 177
community, 198, 200, 211, 212, 215-216, 220
confidence, 202, 231
consciousness, 71
contentment, 49, 61, 64, 70
cosmology, 45
courage, 72, 110, 128, 192
covenant, 109
creation, 163
Cynicism, 15

'day of the Lord, the', 206
death, 53, 58, 59, 68, 70-77, 134-144, 204-212, 224-227, 231
descent, 72
desire and aversion, 49, 61, 66
detachment, 29, 50, 62, 64
devil, the, 220
devotion, 60-64
Diaspora, the, 81
dignity, 73
duty, 42, 52, 54, 58, 65

Eclectic movement, the, 160
education, 23
election, 186
empathy, 64, 68
endurance, 190n.31, 202
Epicureans, 63, 157, 159, 160, 162, 213
Epicurean School, the, 1
eschatology, 173, 205, 206, 207
Essenes, the, 112, 118n.31, 119, 125, 128n.79, 132, 140, 158
ethics, 44, 46, 48, 54, 74, 95, 112

evil, 45, 54, 57, 107, 136
eyewitness, 155

faith, 122, 153, 153n.40, 166, 173, 181, 183, 184, 185, 186, 188-199, 200, 201, 202, 204, 207, 209, 211, 215, 216, 217, 219, 220, 222, 229, 230
false teachers, 5, 181, 182, 185, 194, 200, 201, 205, 215, 216, 217, 230
family, 29, 29n.117, 53
Fate, 51, 106
fear, 70, 73, 204, 231
flood, the, 208
forgiveness, 149, 186, 199, 201, 215, 223, 230
freedom, 23, 33, 47, 49, 50-51, 63, 64, 65, 70, 90, 109, 112, 116, 118, 121, 123, 126, 127-128, 138, 169, 214, 219, 221, 229, 231

gentleness, 192
Gnosticism, 158-159, 160
God (Christianity), acting agent, as, 179; active, 181; anger of, 179; authority, 156; coming of, 181, 181n.10, 205; communication, and, 179; Creator, as, 164, 232; excellence of, 192; Father, 177, 178, 179, 180, 212, 223; fellowship with, 203, 219; glorifying God, 204; glory, 179, 185, 220; goodness of, 185, 219, 220, 232; grace of, 41, 223; Guide, 232; holy, 201; judge, 156, 179; judgement of, 205, 206, 220, 229; King, 209; knowledge of, 179; majesty of, 179; mercy of, 223; moral perfection of, 179; patience of, 192; power of, 181, 183, 185, 189, 211, 216, 219, 220, 232; promises of, 181; providence, 158, redemption, 41; rescuer, 180; reward of, 186; righteousness of, 183, 185, 220; Sustainer, 232; Trinity, 177; wisdom, 214
God (Philo), benevolent, 104, 111, 123, 220; compassionate, 104; Creator (Maker), 88, 103, 107, 127, 128, 220, 232; Defender, the, 123; Deity, the, 103; deliverer, the, 122, 125; Father, 103, 107, 127, 128; fellowship with, 125; friend, as, 104, 114; goodness of, 219, 223, 232; grace of, 111, 122, 123, 143, 223; Guide, 232; immortal, 139; holy, 109, 110; judgement (judge), 90, 106, 129, 229; living, 105, 107, 109; Lord, 103; love of, 123; merciful, 104, 122, 123, 223; omniscient, 103; one; 105; order, and, 105; power of, 219, 220, 232; providence, 88, 109, 163, 164; revelation, and, 97; Ruler, 103; Saviour, 104, 123; self-sufficient, 104; sinless, 122; sovereignty of, 125, 142; study of, 103; Sustainer, 232; true, 105; uncreated, 139; wise, 104; word, his, 94
God (Stoicism), 38-46, all-knowing, 74; all-seeing, 74; benevolence, and, 42; commands of, 61; Creator, 218, 219, 232, Father, as, 42; friend, as 58; Fruit-giver, as, 42; goodness of, 219, 232; guide, as, 42, 232; limitations of, 45-46, 47, 219, 229; person, as, 43n.46; power of, 42, 219, 232; providence, and, 39, 41-42, 46, 51; Rain-bringer, as, 42; reason, and, 42; relational, 42; Saviour, as, 42; Sustainer,

219, 232; trustworthy, 42; weaknesses of, 45-46; will of, 50; wrath, 41n.24
godliness, 188, 195, 196, 215, 217
good, the, 85-86, 91, 110, 125
grace, 178, 184, 195, 207, 212, 215, 220, 224
gratitude, 201
greatness, 64-65
greed, 198
grief, 53, 61, 74
guilelessness, 190

Hades, 72, 136, 141n.53
happiness, 50, 55, 112n.103, 116, 128, 135, 137, 140, 219, 224, 229
heaven, 135, 135n.8, 137, 141n.53
hedonism, 128
hell, 204, 205
Hellenism, 4, 81, 82, 95, 98, 102, 144, 156, 196, 197, 231
heresy, 198
Holy Spirit, the, 115, 149, 150, 167, 177, 180, 194n.53, 201, 218
homosexuality, 82, 95
hope, 121, 141, 190, 190n.31, 199, 230, 231
human nature (humanity), 40, 106-108
humility, 58

indifference, 228
ignorance, 21, 57-58, 86, 105, 130, 168, 170
image (likeness), 201
imitation, 40
immortality, 134-135, 136, 141, 142, 231
infallibility, 52
intelligence, 190
isolation, 66-68

Jerusalem, 83
'Jew', 83, 83n.41
joy, 29, 30, 116, 137, 219
Judaism, 82, 98, 100, 101n.153, 102, 104n.24, 144
judgment, 137, 206, 207, 208
justice, 27, 89n.80, 110, 111, 117, 192
justification, 186

kingdom of heaven (of God, of Christ), 148, 180, 186, 201, 202, 207, 208, 210, 220, 231
knowledge, 48, 59n.77, 63, 115, 116, 130, 132, 144, 163, 167, 169, 172, 178, 181, 183, 184, 185, 188, 194, 195, 196, 205, 211, 214, 215, 216, 217, 218, 220, 228, 230

law (of Moses), 80, 83, 92, 94n.112, 95, 98, 98n.142, 100, 102, 108, 112, 117, 120, 122, 128, 129, 142, 143, 144, 198, 218, 221, 222, 229, 230
life, 47-69, 199
living well, 54-57, 74-75
logic, 15, 27, 47
love, 28, 29-30, 68, 110, 187, 189, 198, 199, 200, 215, 217

marriage, 28, 28n.108, 53, 95
maturity, 62
Messianic age, the, 140-141
miracles, 149, 220
modesty, 117, 123
monotheism, 105, 105n.29, 143

nature, 16n.29, 98-99, 109, 119, 126, 143
new heavens, new earth, 196, 209, 231

obedience, 117, 120, 191, 198, 222

parousia, the, 196, 205
patriarchs, the, 127, 132, 216, 223
pax Romana, 13
peace, 179, 184, 207
Pentateuch, the, 92, 93, 98, 121
Pentecost, 149
persecution, 153, 203
perseverance, 68-69, 195, 215, 217, 222
philosopher(s), 17-22, 36, 38-39, 55, 57, 58, 63, 66-67, 68-69, 70-71, 82; as deliverers, 21; as healers, 20, 59n.77, 66; praise of, 42-43
philosophy, 15n.21, 16, 30, 31, 47-49, 54, 61, 82
physics, 15
piety, 88, 89n.80, 110, 137, 143, 184, 196
Platonism, 4, 97, 97n.137, 229, 230, 231
poetry, 96
prayer, 124, 219
promises, 181
prophecy, 156
punishment, 129, 137n.27, 164

reason, 13n.11, 23, 30, 39, 42, 43, 46, 47, 47n.5, 48n.10, 49, 51, 63, 65, 90, 92, 98n.142, 100, 101, 106, 107, 118, 130, 131, 143, 213, 216, 218, 219, 222, 229, 230, 232
re-creation, 208
reincarnation, 141
repentance, 110, 119n.32, 121, 122, 122n.51, 125, 140, 149, 181, 192, 205, 206, 216, 220, 223, 230
resurrection, 135, 136, 205, 223
rewards, 112, 179
rhetoric, 33-34, 59, 85, 86, 89, 91, 170, 213, 228
righteousness, 194, 223, 231

sacrifice, 41, 61, 223
salvation, 181, 181n.10, 186, 192, 205, 212, 220, 223, 224n.11
Scripture, 181, 229
Second Sophistic, the, 1-2, 34, 84, 85n.56, 158, 161, 172, 174, 209, 228
self: self-concern, 65
self-control, 54, 59, 60, 110, 111, 111n.91, 116, 131, 173, 188, 192, 195, 215, 217
self-destruction, 65
self-examination, 19
self-interest, 27
self-preservation, 70
self-respect, 54
self-restraint, 190
Septuagint, the, 78, 83, 93n.112, 107n.50
servant, 151, 155, 172
Sheol, 142
simplicity, 190
sin, 121, 122, 125
society, 56-57
Sodom and Gomorrah, 180, 206
sophists, 33-37, 85, 101, 126, 139, 160, 161, 163, 165, 166, 167-168, 169, 170, 171, 173, 214, 228
sorites, 189-190, 190n.31, 199
soul, the, 86, 91, 91, 106, 107, 108, 111n.94, 114, 121, 129, 131, 135, 136-138, 139, 140, 141, 141n.53
spirit, the, 71
state, the, 56
steadfastness, 188
Stoicism, 1, 1n.1, 3, 11, 23, 29, 30, 33, 56, 58, 97n.137, 117, 129, 219, 220, 221; Stoic philosophy, 14-16, 77, 189, 208, 214; Stoics, 63, 92, 101, 116, 121, 141, 154, 157, 195, 215, 217, 229, 230
suffering, 13, 127, 140, 189n.31

Indexes

Tartarus, 135, 135n.8, 136, 141, 142
teaching, 156, 163, 171
theodicy, 106
theology, 39, 43, 44, 45, 46, 48
Therapeutae community, the, 115, 116, 123, 126, 128, 140, 223
Torah, the, 4, 92, 95, 100, 101, 118, 126, 128
tranquillity, 127
transformation, 199, 211
truth, 88, 91, 92, 96, 97, 98, 99, 109, 117, 132, 154, 155, 163, 165, 167, 170, 171, 172, 181, 182, 195, 198, 201, 205, 212, 214, 222, 232

vice(s), 54, 59-60, 61, 65, 96, 108, 123, 129
virtue(s), 22, 40, 54, 59, 59n.82, 60, 65, 74, 89, 90, 91, 92n.105, 95, 96, 108-112, 111n.94, 114, 115, 116, 117-122, 123, 125, 125n.66, 128, 130, 131, 132, 134, 139, 143, 188, 189, 190, 192, 193, 196, 200, 209, 214, 215, 217, 219, 220, 221, 224, 229, 230
volition, 28, 50, 52, 53, 60, 63, 65, 66, 68, 74, 120

war, 13
wealth, 53, 59, 126
wisdom, 64, 76, 90, 92, 96, 100, 110, 111, 116, 122, 127, 132, 139, 163, 172, 173, 182, 192, 214, 215, 221, 222
word, the, 192
worship, 80, 105, 107, 108, 109, 110, 149, 229

zeal, 188

www.ingramcontent.com/pod-product-compliance
Lightning Source LLC
Chambersburg PA
CBHW061433300426
44114CB00014B/1673